PICO'S *HEPTAPLUS* AND BIBLICAL HERMENEUTICS

STUDIES IN MEDIEVAL AND REFORMATION TRADITIONS

History, Culture, Religion, Ideas

FOUNDED BY HEIKO A. OBERMAN †

EDITED BY

ANDREW COLIN GOW, Edmonton, Alberta

VOLUME CXVI

CROFTON BLACK

PICO'S *HEPTAPLUS* AND BIBLICAL HERMENEUTICS

PICO'S
HEPTAPLUS AND BIBLICAL HERMENEUTICS

BY

CROFTON BLACK

BRILL
LEIDEN · BOSTON
2006

Cover illustration: The cover illustration, depicting the three worlds as Pico structured them in the *Heptaplus*, is taken from Nicolas Le Fèvre de la Boderie's "Le coeur Leb, ou les 32 sentiers de sapience", an essay on biblical interpretation published alongside his French translation of the *Heptaplus*. See *L'Heptaple ... translaté par N. Le Fèvre de la Boderie*, in F. Giorgio, *L'harmonie du monde*, tr. Guy Le Fèvre de la Boderie (Paris, 1578), sig. e 6ᵛ.

This book is printed on acid-free paper.

Library of Congress Cataloging-in-Publication Data

A C.I.P. record for this book is available from the Library of Congress.

ISSN   1573-4188
ISBN-13: 978-90-04-15315-8
ISBN-10: 90-04-15315-2

PRINTED IN THE NETHERLANDS

For my family
—Lesley, Glenn, Alicia and Imogen—
and for Amber

TABLE OF CONTENTS

ACKNOWLEDGEMENTS

This study started life as my doctoral thesis and as such was completed in 2004. My examiners, Stephen Clucas and Anthony Grafton, made several valuable suggestions, for which I am grateful, and which I have tried to incorporate. My initial research would have been impossible without the support of the University of London, which awarded me a Shelley studentship to enable me to undertake my first year of studies; and without funding from the Arts and Humanities Research Board, which provided for my second and third years. I am grateful to both these institutions for their generosity. Both the University of London Central Research Fund and the Warburg Institute awarded me grants for the purchase of copies of the manuscripts cited in this study and for a research trip to the Bibliothèque Nationale in Paris.

My thanks are due above all to Jill Kraye, who supported this project from its inception, for her advice, encouragement and good humour. I was also helped considerably by Charles Burnett, particularly with regard to manuscript transcriptions. Peter Adamson and Brian Copenhaver both gave generously of their time and knowledge. As for the small foray into Hebrew which this work has demanded, I must especially thank Peter Pormann and Joanna Weinberg. I am also grateful to Rafi Esterson, Stefan Reif and Ernest Nicholson, all of whom patiently listened to my questions and pointed me in the right direction. Staff and colleagues at the Warburg Institute have all assisted in various ways over the last few years; in particular, I cannot fail to thank my comrades in the MA class of 1999: Daniel Andersson, Stefan Bauer, Marta Cacho Casal and Susanne Meurer.

Needless to say, although the aforementioned may take considerable credit for the merits of this work, they are not responsible for its inaccuracies.

Parts of this study have been read at seminars at the Warburg Institute, at Senate House, University of London and at Lincoln College, Oxford; I am grateful to those who participated for their comments. Subsequently, further research and revision was undertaken in Paris in 2005; this was largely made possible by the generosity of Cassandra Purdy, Ludo Pélissier, Franck Pham-Van, James Tovey and Tom Bowring. I am also grateful to Andrew Gow, Boris van Gool and Ms Gera van Bedaf for their assistance in the publication process.

None of this would have taken place without the initial stimulus provided by a number of teachers over the years, so I should like to take this opportunity to thank Alan Butterworth, Stephen Sleigh, Martin Roberts, Lorne Denny, Tom Earnshaw, Richard Jenkyns and Tony Nuttall.

Finally, I should like to thank the inhabitants of Mirandola, where I spent a very enjoyable afternoon in the summer of 2004.

PREFACE

Except where noted, all translations are my own. In translating the *Heptaplus*, I have consulted the Italian version by Garin and the English one by Carmichael. The *Heptaplus* is much concerned with the concept of the proper end of human life, which Pico calls *felicitas*. As none of the usual English translations of this word has the equivalent scope, I have chosen to leave it untranslated.

In transcribing Latin manuscripts and printed books, I have expanded abbreviations and occasionally modified capitalization, but I have left -e in place of -ae and have not attempted to normalize spelling. Square brackets denote insertion or editorial intervention, angle brackets denote deletion. Page breaks in manuscripts are marked by a slash (/).

For transliteration of Hebrew I have followed the general system described in *Encyclopaedia Judaica*, ed. C. Roth, 16 vols (Jerusalem: Keter, 1972), I, 90 (except for bibliographical references to works adopting a different convention).

Bibliographical references are given in full on the first occasion a work is mentioned in the footnotes; subsequent references give only author and short title. Full references are also provided in the Bibliography. Citations of page numbers in modern editions are followed by standard references in brackets, where appropriate. In the case of patristic texts, these refer to Migne's *Patrologiae*.

ABBREVIATIONS

Conclusions	Pico, *900 conclusions philosophiques, cabalistiques et théologiques*, ed. B. Schefer (Paris: Allia, 1999)
Garin	Giovanni Pico della Mirandola, *De hominis dignitate, Heptaplus, De ente et uno e scritti vari*, ed. E. Garin (Florence: Vallecchi, 1942)
Opera omnia	Giovanni Pico della Mirandola, *Opera omnia*, I (Basel, 1557, repr. Hildesheim: Olm, 1969)
Vita	*Ioannis Pici Mirandulae viri omni disciplinarum genere consumatissimi vita per Ioannem Franciscum illustris principis Galeotti Pici filium conscripta*, ed. B. Andreolli (Modena: Aedes Muratoriana, 1994)

Quotations from the *Heptaplus* follow Garin's edition; I also indicate exposition and chapter, according to the following format:

H. P1	First proem
H. P2	Second proem
H. 1.1	First exposition, chapter one
H. 2.P	Second exposition, proem
H. 50	final (unnumbered) chapter

INTRODUCTION

This is a study in the history of allegory. It focuses on a particular theory of allegory, developed by the Italian philosopher Giovanni Pico della Mirandola in his *Heptaplus* (1489), a sevenfold commentary on the account of the six days of creation contained in Genesis 1. This theory, which differs in a number of ways from mainstream medieval and Renaissance thinking on biblical exegesis, is connected to a philosophical issue which was the subject of considerable debate at the time: the nature and action of the intellect.

A major aim of this study is to interpret the *Heptaplus* in relation to Pico's other works and known interests (among which I give prominent place to Neoplatonism, the problem of epistemology in scholastic Aristotelianism, and kabbalah). Aside from this, however, the *Heptaplus* offers a unique perspective on the field of allegorical biblical interpretation in general. The fifteenth century has been largely neglected in scholarly works on biblical hermeneutics, which tend to concentrate either on the earlier Middle Ages or on the Reformation. It is a fruitful period for study precisely because of its intermediate position between these two poles. The invention of print makes it possible to determine with a certain degree of accuracy which works were regarded as essential or popular at the time, since they were printed earlier and in greater numbers; there are enough of them to provide useful data and not so many that comparison becomes impossible.

Pico, certainly, was not particularly representative of the fifteenth century, just as he was not representative of any one school of philosophy; and although he carried the preconceptions of his era within him, his intellectual frame of reference extended out of the reach of most of his contemporaries. His reaction to contemporary exegetical norms nonetheless provides a standpoint from which to analyse those norms. As will be seen, he reacted not merely by developing a new allegorical theory but also by restating the fundamental case for allegorical reading, its purpose and its difference from literal reading. He did this in a manner opposed to the Christian consensus on this topic.

Like its subject, this study is divided into seven sections. Chapter 1 contains a brief biographical outline and an excursus on Pico's knowledge of Hebrew language and literature. Chapter 2 is a summary of the *Heptaplus* as a whole, not in any great depth, but enough, I hope, to orientate the reader throughout the rest of the discussion. Chapter 3 examines the general state of biblical hermeneutics during the second half of the fifteenth century. Its first purpose is to demonstrate that the medieval formulation of the four senses of Scripture remained the dominant model for interpretation, although the same period also saw the beginnings of the humanistic interest in philology which was to gather strength in the sixteenth century. Its second purpose is to show how Pico made use of these 'typical' approaches in his series of commentaries on the Psalms, which he was working on at the same time as writing the *Heptaplus*. Neither of these approaches features in the *Heptaplus*, however.

Chapters 4 and 5 deal with the two introductions or "proems" with which Pico prefaces his work. In the first proem he provides an overall justification for there being a hidden non-literal meaning in the Bible in general and the Genesis account in particular. His argument hinges on a semiotic and social distinction between esoteric and exoteric meaning. My aim in Chapter 4 is to contextualize this argument by tracing how the expression of this distinction evolved in the traditions which Pico drew on: Christian, Jewish and Neoplatonic. In the narrow focus my purpose is to show how Pico's argument derives from his previous works and to suggest source material for its various elements. In the broader focus I aim to show how his idea of the nature of non-literal reading differed from the mainstream medieval Christian commentary tradition.

In Chapter 5 I examine two major facets of the second proem: Pico's model of cosmic structure and his theory of allegory. Like his justification of esotericism in the first proem, his discussion of cosmic structure is developed from his previous works, although not without departing from them in some details. His theory of allegory is derived largely from the Neoplatonic tradition and particularly, I argue, from this tradition's Christian incarnation in the works attributed to Dionysius the Areopagite. The parallels between Pico and Pseudo-Dionysius lead to a consideration of epistemology, specifically in relation to the idea of intellectual ascent or 'anagogy' (to use Dionysius's term). In Chapter 6 I look further at this idea, both in medieval philosophy in general and in Pico's works in particular. I propose that the *Heptaplus* should be viewed as an expression of the role of the intellect in man's progress to *felicitas*. In the narrow focus this permits us to perceive more clearly the relationship between the *Heptaplus* and Pico's previous works, and thus to clarify certain ambiguities. In the broad focus it shows Pico engaging with the controversy (dating back to the thirteenth century, but still intense during his life and after) surrounding Aristotle, Averroes and competing interpretations of the nature and action of the intellect.

Pico's engagement with this matter was influenced by the Jewish tradition, not so much in the details of his epistemology as in his manner of applying it to hermeneutics. Levi ben Gershom, or Gersonides, whose commentary on the Song of Songs I discuss in Chapter 6, is one such source. In Chapter 7 I look more closely at the ways in which the Jewish tradition contributed to Pico's concept of exegesis. In so doing, I examine both the final chapter of the *Heptaplus*—containing Pico's interpretation of the opening word of the Bible, *bereshit*—and the structure of the work as a whole, which is based on the number seven (symbolizing the sabbath). In conclusion, I argue that this structure reflects the forty-nine gates of understanding through which, according to texts read by Pico, Moses ascended, and knowledge of which he concealed in the Genesis account.

CHAPTER ONE

PICO'S LIFE AND WORKS

1. *Giovanni Pico della Mirandola: Biographical Sketch*

The first biography of Pico was written by his nephew, Gianfrancesco Pico della Mirandola, and published in the *editio princeps* of Pico's *Opera omnia*, at Bologna, on 20 March 1496.[1] On the basis of this work, together with around 120 extant letters, as well as contemporary printed and archival material, we are fairly well informed about the outline of Pico's life. What follows is intended merely to be sufficient for preliminary orientation.[2]

Pico was born in 1463. His birth, Gianfrancesco tells us, was attended by prodigies.[3] Gianfrancesco also gives us a brief description of his uncle: he was of noble aspect, tall, with soft skin, a handsome face (white in colour, mingled with red), lively blue-grey eyes, blond hair, and white even teeth.[4] In 1477, aged 14, Pico went to Bologna to study canon law. He did not remain there long, however, moving

---

[1] Giovanni Pico della Mirandola, *De hominis dignitate, Heptaplus, De ente et uno e scritti vari*, ed. E. Garin (Florence: Vallecchi, 1942) (hereafter 'Garin'), 89, item 1. It was translated into English (in "a somewhat reduced and inaccurate version") by Sir Thomas More and printed in London in 1510: see Sir Thomas More, *Giovanni Pico della Mirandola: His Life by His Nephew Giovanni Francesco Pico, etc.*, ed. J.M. Rigg (London: D. Nutt, 1890), xxxix–xl; Garin, 98, item 87. The modern edition is *Ioannis Pici Mirandulae viri omni disciplinarum genere consumatissimi vita per Ioannem Franciscum illustris principis Galeotti Pici filium conscripta*, ed. B. Andreolli (Modena: Aedes Muratoriana, 1994) (hereafter *Vita*).

[2] It is not my intention in this study to try to revise the currently accepted facts concerning Pico's life. This section, therefore, is based on the standard works in the field. See, in general, Garin, 3–59; id., *Giovanni Pico della Mirandola: vita e dottrina* (Florence: F. Le Monier, 1937); D. Berti, "Intorno a Giovanni Pico della Mirandola: cenni e documenti inediti", *Rivista contemporanea*, 16 (1859), 7–56; F. Roulier, *Jean Pic de la Mirandole (1463–1494), humaniste, philosophe et théologien* (Geneva: Slatkine, 1989), 38–54; L. Valcke, *Pic de la Mirandole: un itinéraire philosophique* (Paris: Les Belles Lettres, 2005). Some useful references may also be found in W. Parr Greswell, *Memoirs of Angelus Politianus, Joannes Picus of Mirandula, etc.* (London: Cadell and Davies, 1805), 153–363.

[3] *Vita*, 32. Cf. G. Pico della Mirandola, *Opera omnia*, I (Basel, 1557; repr. Hildesheim: Olm, 1969) (hereafter *Opera omnia*), sig. * 3ʳ.

[4] *Vita*, 34 (cf. *Opera omnia*, sig. * 3ʳ): "Forma autem insigni fuit et liberali, procera et celsa statura, molli carne, venusta facie in universum, albenti colore decentique

first to the arts faculty at Ferrara, and some fifteen months later to Padua, where he studied Aristotelian philosophy. It was here that he met Elijah Delmedigo, whose literary contact with him will be described below. By 1482 he was pursuing literary and philosophical studies at Pavia. He then spent some time in Florence, making the acquaintance of several prominent humanists, writers and philosophers, including Angelo Poliziano, Girolamo Benivieni and Marsilio Ficino. It appears to be around this time that he became interested in what was to become a lifelong project: the reconciliation of Plato and Aristotle.[5]

Pico is often thought of as a humanist, and has been regarded as a prominent figure in Ficino's so-called Platonic Academy.[6] Some of these interests are apparent in his earliest major work, written around 1485–1486, the *Commento sopra una canzone d'amore*. This is a commentary, strongly influenced by Platonism and Neoplatonism, on a love poem by Benivieni, itself based on Ficino's commentary on Plato's *Symposium*.[7] Ficino's interpretation of Plato and Platonism was tendentious. He wished to establish it as the philosophy of choice for Christians, in comparison with scholastic Aristotelianism, which was (in his view) mired in the heresies of Alexander of Aphrodisias and Averroes regarding the soul and immortality.[8] Other of his contemporaries, too, criticized the philosophical productions of the Middle Ages for their "barbaric" Latin. Pico's own position was less partisan, as we can see from his response to one such attack, made by his friend Ermolao Barbaro in a letter to Pico of April 1485. In his reply, from Florence, dated 9 June 1485, Pico formulated a defence of scholasticism, arguing that the truth was the only thing of consequence, regardless of the manner in which it was expressed.[9] There seems little reason to doubt the sincerity of this

---

rubore interspersa, caesiis et vigilibus oculis, flavo et inaffectato capillitio, dentibus quoque candidis et aequalibus."

[5] This never saw written form as such, although a part of it is represented by *De ente et uno* (Garin, 386–441). Intimations of Pico's intended method also appear in the *Conclusiones*.

[6] J. Hankins, "Cosimo de' Medici and the 'Platonic Academy'", *Journal of the Warburg and Courtauld Institutes*, 53 (1990), 144–162; id., "The Myth of the Platonic Academy of Florence", *Renaissance Quarterly*, 44 (1991), 429–475.

[7] Garin, 443–581.

[8] On this, see below, Ch. 6, n. 42.

[9] E. Barbaro and G. Pico della Mirandola, *Filosofia o eloquenza?*, ed. F. Bausi (Naples: Liguori, 1998), 38: "Expertus sum ego cum semper alias tum hac proxima tua ad me epistola, in qua dum Barbaros hos philosophos inseris, quos dicis haberi vulgo sordidos, rudes, incultos, quos nec vixisse viventes, ne dum extincti vivant"; ibid.,

argument, even though it is put in the mouth of a "barbaric" medieval philosopher, since Pico followed this path in practice as well as in theory. He had previously spent time among the Averroists of Padua; and soon after writing this letter, he went to study in Paris, which retained its status as a foremost centre of scholastic theology and Aristotelianism.[10]

In March 1486 he returned to Florence. His next project, in line with his recent experience, was conceived after the style of "Parisian" disputation.[11] He proposed to hold a public debate in Rome on nine hundred 'conclusions' or 'theses', concise aphorisms which consisted of distillations of the works of previous thinkers and expressions of his own philosophical ideas. He appears to have compiled these in Florence over the summer of 1486. He then moved to Rome in the autumn of that year and published them on 7 November.[12] The *Conclusiones* are formally as far removed from the *Heptaplus* as can be imagined. While the later text exhibits a complete and perfected structure, the earlier one is a miscellaneous collection of bare bones, which do not, despite the best efforts of ingenious commentators, form a single skeleton, let alone a coherent body.[13]

40: "Atque in his quidem si quis nos arguat hebetudinis et tarditatis, age, amabo, quicumque is est, pedem conferat: experietur habuisse barbaros non in lingua sed in pectore Mercurium, non defuisse illis sapientiam, si defuit eloquentia, quam cum sapientia non coniunxisse tantum fortasse abest a culpa, ut coniunxisse sit nefas." Cf. *Opera omnia*, 351–352. See J.-C. Margolin, "Sur la conception humaniste du 'barbare': à propos de la controverse épistolaire entre Pic de la Mirandole et Ermolao Barbaro", in *Una famiglia veneziana nella storia: I Barbaro*, Atti del convegno di studi in occasione del quinto centenario della morte dell'umanista Ermolao, Venezia 4–6 novembre 1993, ed. M. Marangoni and M. Pastore Stocchi, 235–276 (Venice: Istituto Veneto di Scienze, 1996); L. Panizza, "Ermolao Barbaro e Pico della Mirandola tra retorica e dialettica: il *De genere dicendi philosophorum* del 1485", in *Una famiglia veneziana nella storia: I Barbaro*, ed. Marangoni and Pastore Stocchi, 277–330; id., "Pico della Mirandola's 1485 Parody of Scholastic 'Barbarians'", in *Italy in Crisis 1494*, ed. J. Everson and D. Zancani, 152–174 (Oxford: Legenda, 2000); M.L. McLaughlin, *Literary Imitation in the Italian Renaissance: The Theory and Practice of Literary Imitation in Italy from Dante to Bembo* (Oxford: Clarendon Press, 1995), 228–248.

[10] See L. Dorez and L. Thuasne, *Pic de la Mirandole en France (1485–1488)* (Paris: E. Leroux, 1897), 28–50.

[11] Pico, *900 conclusions philosophiques, cabalistiques et théologiques*, ed. B. Schefer (Paris: Allia, 1999), 18 (hereafter *Conclusions*) (cf. *Opera omnia*, 63): "in quibus recitandis, non Romanae linguae nitorem, sed celebratissimorum Parisiensium disputatorum dicendi genus est imitatus".

[12] Garin, 18–19.

[13] For a recent effort to interpret the *Conclusiones* as a whole, see S.A. Farmer, *Syncretism in the West: Pico's 900 Theses (1486): The Evolution of Traditional Religious and*

They were intended to be debated, following the scholastic method of *quaestiones*; but we do not know what position Pico would have taken on most of them, because the debate never took place. Instead there followed several months of scrutiny and disputation by a papal committee, which found fault first with seven, then thirteen of the nine hundred *Conclusiones*.[14]

Pico's response to this censure was the *Apologia*, which serves as both an explanatory preamble to his proposed debate, and a defence of the thirteen condemned propositions. The charge of heterodoxy, he complained, resulted from the failure of the examining committee to interpret the meanings of his words correctly.[15] The tactic was notably unsuccessful. The shadow of papal displeasure was now extended over all the *Conclusiones*, and Innocent VIII issued a bull, dated 8 August 1487, banning the book's dissemination. This was not actually promulgated until 15 December, however, and by this time Pico had fled to Paris; on the way he was captured and arrested.[16] His release was secured with the assistance of Lorenzo de' Medici, who offered him hospitality in Florence.[17] It was here that he was to remain, more or less, for the rest of his short life. One can see this as a pragmatic solution to a potentially embarrassing situation: Pico was kept out of Rome and his 'unsound' doctrines were confined to the rarefied atmosphere of Florentine libraries and the group of intellectuals who gathered around Lorenzo. He was an ornament to Lorenzo's circle without creating problems for the pope.

The Roman affair, then, produced a group of three works: the *Conclusiones* themselves, the *Apologia*, and the *Oratio*, now commonly subtitled "On the Dignity of Man". This last is essentially a version of the first part of the *Apologia*, presenting itself as an introductory speech to the proposed disputation.[18] In the period directly following his return to Florence, Pico turned his attention to biblical commentary. The pre-eminent result of this is the *Heptaplus*, published in the

---

Philosophical Systems (Tempe, Arizona: Medieval and Renaissance Texts and Studies, 1998).

[14] Roulier, *Pic de la Mirandole*, 41–42; Dorez and Thuasne, *Pic de la Mirandole en France*, 114–146.

[15] See my analysis of his defence of the ninth of the *Conclusiones magicae ... secundum opinionem propriam* in Ch. 4, section 5.

[16] Dorez and Thuasne, *Pic de la Mirandole en France*, 71–101.

[17] Roulier, *Pic de la Mirandole*, 43.

[18] Ibid., 50. B.P. Copenhaver, "The Secret of Pico's Oration: Cabala and Renaissance Philosophy", *Midwest Studies in Philosophy*, 26 (2002), 56–81, argues that the subtitle "On the Dignity of Man" is a misrepresentation of the work's content.

autumn of 1489.[19] Contemporary with it is an incomplete series of commentaries on the Psalms, begun in 1488 and continued over the next couple of years. A retranslation of and commentary on part of the Book of Job, probably dating from some time between 1486 and 1489, may also be considered part of this group.[20]

On 13 June 1489, Lorenzo de' Medici wrote to his ambassador in Rome, Giovanni Lanfredini, saying: Pico lives like a monk, he is constantly engaged in theological work—referring both to the Psalms and presumably the *Heptaplus*—and he leads a very simple and exemplary life.[21] The letter reads like an effort towards rehabilitation. It was unsuccessful, as a subsequent letter from Lanfredini attests: the pope finds Pico's continuing interest in theology intolerable and would prefer him to write poetry.[22]

As far as the pope was concerned, the *Heptaplus* was a continuation of the heretical tendencies Pico had displayed in the *Conclusiones*.[23] Lorenzo, however, once again defended Pico's work,[24] and it

---

[19] The *editio princeps* is catalogued in the Incunable Short Title Catalogue as *Heptaplus*, Florence c. 1490; see also J.V. Scholderer, *Catalogue of Books Printed in the XVth Century now in the British Museum*, VI (London, 1930), 662–663. Copies were in circulation by the autumn of 1489, however.

[20] Of the *Expositiones in Psalmos*, only the one on Psalm 15 made its way into early editions of Pico's works, starting with that of Bologna 1496; the others remained in manuscript. See Pico, *Expositiones in Psalmos*, ed. A. Raspanti (Florence: L.S. Olschki, 1997), 23–32. The Job translation and commentary, to be found in the Vatican library (Ottob. Lat. 607) is still unpublished: see C. Wirszubski, "Giovanni Pico's Book of Job", *Journal of the Warburg and Courtauld Institutes*, 32 (1969), 171–199.

[21] Garin, 29–30: "Il conte della Mirandola s'è fermo qui con noi dove vive molto santamenti e è come uno religioso, e ha fatto e fa continuamente degnissime opere in theologia: comenta e' psalmi, scrive alcune altre degne cose theologiche. Dice l'officio ordinario de' preti, osserva il digiuno e grandissima continentia; vive sanza molta famiglia e pompa; solamente si serve a necessità, e a me pare un exemplo degli altri uomini."

[22] Lanfredini to Lorenzo de' Medici, in Berti, "Intorno a Giovanni Pico della Mirandola", 29, quoted in O. Kristeller, "Giovanni Pico della Mirandola and his Sources", in *L'opera e il pensiero di Giovanni Pico della Mirandola nella storia dell'umanesimo: convegno internazionale, Mirandola*, 2 vols, I, 42–43 n. 18 (Florence: Nella Sede dell'Istituto, 1965): "Queste cose della fede sono troppo tenere et non posso tollerarle. Scrivete a Lorenzo se lui gli vuole bene, che lo facci scrivere opere di poesia et non cose teologiche, perchè saranno più da sua denti: perchè il conte non è bene fondato, et non ha visto tanto quanto bisogna ad chi scrive theologia".

[23] Lanfredini to Lorenzo de' Medici, in Berti, "Intorno a Giovanni Pico della Mirandola", 39: "essendosi trovata questa opera sopra il Genesi, et vista per questi docti di sacra scriptura, l'hanno dannata, perchè in molte parti entra nelle medesime heresie et quelle medesime cose che sono state detestate per indirecto lui le introduce in questa opera in molti luoghi."

[24] Ibid., 39–40: "Ho inteso con grandissima mia molestia il carico che si dà a

was enthusiastically received by a number of intellectuals and humanists. Several wrote to express their admiration: these included Matteo Vero, Gerolamo Donato, Cristoforo Landino, Bartolomeo Fontio and Ermolao Barbaro, among others.[25] When Gianfrancesco Pico edited the first *Opera omnia*, he placed the *Heptaplus* at its beginning, a position which it maintained throughout subsequent editions.[26] Less than a century after its first appearance it had been translated into both Italian (1555) and French (1578).[27]

The *Heptaplus* was Pico's last completed work. In 1490 he published a brief tract entitled *De ente et uno*, which is all he managed

---

quest'opera della Mirandola ... Qui è stata veduta da quanti religiosi dotti ci sono e uomini di buona fama e di santa vita, e da tutti è sommamente approvata; nè io sono però sì cattivo cristiano che quando ne credesi altro, me lo tacessi o sopportassilo. Sono certo se costui [i.e., Pico] dicesse il Credo, cotesti spiriti malvagi direbbero che è un'heresia ..."

[25] Vero, letter to Roberto Salviati, undated, *Opera omnia*, 393: "Visus est mihi Ioan. hic noster non modo philosophiam omnem et quicquid naturae legibus continetur callere ac bene sapere, sed super humana etiam sese attollere, pervolare sublimia, et arcana mysteria sacramentaque caelestia ad mysticos sensus allegoriasque flexisse, quae nostri temporis, qui sapientes habentur et eruditi, vix aut notant aut prorsus intentata praetereunt ..." Donato, letter to Salviati, 25 October 1489, ibid., 396: "Illius Heptaplum admirari magis quam iudicare convenit." Landino, letter to Salviati, 10 December [1489?], ibid., 397: "cum apud infinitos pene Hebraeos, plurimos Arabas, Graecosque ac Latinos non paucos docte, distincte, eloquenterque eam rem ita tractatam videamus, ut ne verbum quidem addi posse crederem, ipse tamen novo pene argumento, universam rem exordiens, atque insolita eodem via perveniens, quae tritissima iam et apud omnes vulgata viderentur, ita descripsit, ut etiam qui doctissimi sunt, veluti nova atque inaudita admirentur." Fontio, letter to Salviati, undated, ibid., 403: "Nam quid in Heptaplo commemorem, quae maxime operum authores commendant, nullam esse loquacitatem, nullum tumorem, et sine ulla livoris suspicione, modestiam in omnibus singularem." Barbaro, letter to Pico, 9 September 1489, in E. Barbaro, *Epistolae, orationes et carmina*, ed. V. Branca, 2 vols (Florence: Bibliopolis, 1943), II, 50–51: "Hexaemeron tuum nudiustertius ad nos Salviati opera delatum, ita avide legi, ut prima statim die, nec tota sine interspiratione totum hauserim. Tria me in eo mirifice delectant. Primum, quod oratio tua docet, et movet, id quod et in sacris litteris veteres theologos, et in philosophia etiam naturali Pythagoricos et Platonicos observasse constat, recentioribus in docendo tantum sudantibus." See also Berti, "Intorno a Giovanni Pico della Mirandola", 28: "I teologi romani erano i soli che non si lasciassero sedurre dalla congerie delle allegorie immaginose del Pico."

[26] This fact presumably accounts for the statement of Ernst Cassirer, *The Individual and the Cosmos in Renaissance Philosophy*, tr. M. Domandi (New York: Harper and Row, 1963), 61, that "Pico ... began his philosophical and literary activity with the *Heptaplus*".

[27] *Le sette sposizioni del S. Giovanni Pico della Mirandola intitolate Heptaplo, sopra i sei giorni del Genesi. Tradotte in lingua toscana da M. Antonio Buonagrazia Canonico di Pescia* ... (Pescia, 1555). *L'Heptaple ... translaté par N. Le Fèvre de la Boderie*, in F. Giorgio, *L'harmonie du monde*, tr. Guy Le Fèvre de la Boderie (Paris, 1578), 829–878.

to write of his proposed *Concordia Platonis et Aristotelis*.[28] He died on 17 November 1494, aged 31. His final and longest work, the *Disputationes adversus astrologiam divinicatricem* (of which he had composed twelve of a planned thirteen books) was published soon afterwards.[29]

Pico was famous and controversial within his own lifetime; and his nephew did not refrain from playing a role in these controversies after his death. Gianfrancesco's *Vita* emphasizes Pico's orthodoxy and holiness. The events of the Roman affair are dismissed as a youthful folly, equated with his early pursuit of women, from which he turned away to embrace a life of quiet sanctity and scholarship.[30] Likewise, Pico's interest in kabbalah—one of the factors in the *Conclusiones* scandal—is largely overlooked.[31]

Kabbalistic exegesis is one of the contexts of the *Heptaplus* which I shall discuss in this study, alongside the Greek and Latin traditions of biblical interpretation. The Hebrew literary tradition presented Pico with works of biblical exegesis and with works of philosophy; in the latter case, it represented one of his points of entry into the Arabic tradition as well, especially through several otherwise untranslated works of or on Averroes. There are specific problems regarding Pico's access to these texts, resting on the availability of translations and his own ability to read Hebrew. This is as much a question of biography as bibliography, and as such I shall give it some preliminary consideration here.

---

[28] Garin, 385–441.

[29] Ibid., 93.

[30] *Vita*, 40–42 (cf. *Opera omnia*, sig. * 3ᵛ–4ʳ): "Caeterum immensa Dei bonitate, quae ex malis etiam bona elicit, effectum esse (quemadmodum mihi retulit) iudicabat, ut calumnia illa falso a malevolis irrogata, veros errores corrigeret ... . Prius enim et gloriae cupidus, et amore vano succensus, muliebribusque illecebris commotus fuerat, feminarum quippe plurimae ... in eius amorem exarserunt, a quarum studio non abhorrens, parumper via vitae posthabita, in delicias defluxerat, verum simultate illa experrectus, diffluentem luxu animum retudit, et convertit ad Christum, atque feminea blandimenta, in supernae patriae gaudia commutavit, neglectaque aura gloriae, quam affectaverat, Dei gloriam et Ecclesiae utilitatem, tota cepit mente perquirere, adeoque mores componere, ut posthac vel inimico iudice, comprobari posset."

[31] There is a single reference in *Vita*, 36 (cf. *Opera omnia*, sig. * 3ᵛ). References to kabbalah were also removed from the printed edition of the *Commento*: see Garin, 17–18 and 535 n. 3. On the editing of the *Commento*, see Pico, *Commentary on a Canzone of Benivieni*, tr. S. Jayne (New York: Peter Lang, 1984), 7–20.

2. *Pico's Hebrew Studies*

Three scholars in particular played an important role in making works from the Jewish and Arabic traditions available to Pico, either orally or textually, and, if textually, either in Hebrew or in Latin translations. These are Elijah Delmedigo, Flavius Mithridates and Joḥanan Alemanno.

2.1. *Elijah Delmedigo*

Elijah Delmedigo (c. 1460–1497) was born and died in Crete; but the most productive period of his life, from 1480–1490, was spent in Italy, mainly in Venice, Padua and Florence.[32] He was primarily a philosopher of the Averroist persuasion.[33] He translated six of Averroes's commentaries on Aristotle into Latin: the *Quaestio* on the *Posterior Analytics*, the epitome and middle commentary on the *Meteorology*, the epitome and middle commentary on the *Metaphysics* and the proem to the twelfth book of the *Metaphysics*; he also translated Averroes's commentary on Plato's *Republic* and composed a number of supercommentaries on Averroes as well as several *quaestiones*.[34] Among these, we find his commentary on *De substantia orbis* (extant in both Hebrew and Latin); two treatises on the views of Averroes concerning the intellect (extant only in Hebrew); and a series of *quaestiones* on such subjects as *De primo motore*, *De mundi efficientia* and *De esse essentia et uno*. The only extant composition by Delmedigo which does not take the form of a commentary or translation is the *Beḥinat ha-dat* ("Examination of Religion"), written after his return to Crete, which discusses the relative roles of faith and reason, still within an Averroist framework.

---

[32] For biographical information, see M.D. Geffen, "Faith and Reason in Elijah del Medigo's *Beḥinat ha-Dat* and the Philosophic Backgrounds of the Work" (PhD Dissertation, Columbia University, 1970), 5–39, or the epitome of this dissertation published as "Insights into the Life and Thought of Elijah Medigo Based on his Published and Unpublished Works", *Proceedings of the American Academy for Jewish Research*, 41–42 (1973–1974), 69–86.

[33] For an account of Delmedigo's works, and his relationship with Pico, see Geffen, "Faith and Reason", 159–162; E.P. Mahoney, "Giovanni Pico della Mirandola and Elia Del Medigo, Nicoletto Vernia and Agostino Nifo", in *Giovanni Pico della Mirandola: convegno internazionale di studi nel cinquecentesimo anniversario della morte (1494–1994)*, ed. G.C. Garfagnini, 2 vols, I, 128–138 (Florence: L.S. Olschki, 1997).

[34] Autograph manuscripts of several of these, dedicated to Pico, are extant: see G. Mercati, *Codici Latini Pico Grimani Pio* (Vatican City: Biblioteca Apostolica Vaticana, 1938), 34–37.

Despite this apparently simple bibliography, Delmedigo's literary output has certain problematic features, which are connected to his contact with Pico. The two treatises on the intellect were initially composed in Latin at Pico's request; Delmedigo himself then translated them into Hebrew (between December 1481 and January 1482).[35] In an introductory passage to the Hebrew translation, he writes that he incorporated certain expansions on matters specific to a Jewish audience, which therefore (implicitly) he did not consider relevant to Pico.[36] The original Latin versions are not extant.[37] The Hebrew versions are contained in the same manuscript as the Hebrew version of the commentary on De substantia orbis.[38] The original Latin version of this latter work is extant in two manuscripts and comparison between the Latin and Hebrew versions shows that in this case, too, Delmedigo made additions to the text when rewriting it for a Jewish audience.[39] We cannot, therefore, use the Hebrew versions of the treatises on the intellect as a sure guide to what Delmedigo originally wrote for Pico.

We also possess a lengthy letter from Delmedigo to Pico, which is particularly interesting from our current perspective because it casts some light on Pico's literary research and includes three bibliographies.[40] According to Delmedigo, the bibliographies constitute a list of writers who will help to prove that the first principle is separate from matter; they support what Aristotle said, but they support this doctrine having received it "by revelation" and therefore must be believed.[41] The names on the first list are: "Abu al chagam filius

---

[35] Geffen, "Faith and Reason", 13.

[36] K.P. Bland, "Elijah del Medigo's Averroist Response to the Kabbalahs of Fifteenth-Century Jewry and Pico della Mirandola", The Journal of Jewish Thought and Philosophy, 1 (1991), 27.

[37] Ibid., 23 n. 2: Bland refers to certain Latin fragments of this original composition, or a paraphrase of it, but without giving details.

[38] Paris, Bibliothèque Nationale, Ebr. 968. These two treatises are discussed by K.P. Bland, "Elijah del Medigo, Unicity of the Intellect and Immortality", Proceedings of the American Academy for Jewish Research, 61 (1995), 1–22.

[39] Vatican City, Biblioteca Apostolica Vaticana, Lat. 4553; Paris, Bibliothèque Nationale, Lat. 6508. See Bland, "Elijah del Medigo's Averroist Response", 30–33.

[40] Paris, Bibliothèque Nationale, Lat. 6508, ff. 71ʳ–77ᵛ. Fragments of this letter were transcribed and discussed by J. Dukas, Recherches sur l'histoire littéraire du quinzième siècle (Paris: L. Techener, 1876), 48–65, and Garin, 67–72. The bibliographies are on f. 75ʳ, transcribed by Dukas, Recherches, 56–57.

[41] Dukas, Recherches, 55–56: "Vide ergo, domine mi, quomodo est necessaria doctrina Aristotelis et sui commentatoris in probando primum principium esse separatum a materia; et quod loquentes destruunt declarationem generis entis separati, tamen ipsi eam habuerunt per revelationem et eis est credendum."

Andris", "Abenthahar", "Abenalhacak filius Ptolamei" and "Abengaphar". The other two lists, underneath, are written in two columns of Hebrew, a fact which (together with the unusual spelling and peculiar combination of Italian and Latin throughout) suggests that this is an autograph letter. In the left-hand column, we find a series of Arabic authors. The right-hand column contains a list entitled "Kabbalah": Delmedigo notes the existence of the Zohar, the *Me'irat einayim* (probably referring to a commentary on Nahmanides by Isaac of Acre, late-thirteenth to mid-fourteenth centuries), the *Sha'arei orah* of Joseph Gikatilla (1248–c. 1325), Recanati, the *Ma'arekhet ha-elohut* (an anonymous treatise of the late thirteenth or early fourteenth century), a commentary on the *Sefer Yezirah* and, he adds, "many others, the names of which do not occur to me, because I am very busy".[42]

The letter is undated. It is, however, addressed to Pico in Rome, and must therefore have been written in late November 1486 at the earliest.[43] As Delmedigo himself observes in the letter, Pico's studies of kabbalah were already well underway.[44] As we shall soon see, several, though not all, of the books mentioned in the third list were translated for Pico by Flavius Mithridates at around this time.

This letter also sheds some light on Pico's book buying, as it shows two specific instances of Delmedigo acting—or more precisely, failing to act—as a procurer of books and translations for his patron. He regrets that he has not been able to translate "the opinion of Avempace" concerning the soul (or alternatively concerning Aristotle's *De anima*) as asked because he does not have a copy of the book to hand.[45] He intended to send Pico a copy of "Ricanato", but did not do so on account of the bad roads (a fact, incidentally, that supports Dukas's winter dating of the letter). He then discusses the price of this book, asking for a small present instead of money.[46]

---

[42] Ibid., 57: "et multa allia quorum nomina non ocurunt mihi quia multas habeo ocupationes" (spelling sic).

[43] Ibid., 45–48.

[44] Ibid., 62 (cf. Garin, 68): "Quia video dominationem tuum multum laborare in isto benedicto chabala ..."

[45] Garin, 70: "Quella parte dell'Anima che mi scriveste di tradurre de opinione Avempace non potei perchè non ho qui el libro et in verità mandai el famiglio di V.S. a Basciano per portarmi el libro et mio figlio non lo cognobbe et me ne mandò un altro; tamen, se Iddio vorrà, col nostro prete manderò quello et altre cose se la fortuna mi sarà prospera."

[46] Ibid.: "Voleva ancora mandarvi el Ricanato adesso, ma per cagione che le vie sono molto cattive et le poggie et è in carta buona dubitai non si guastassi. La Vostra S. mi scrive del pregio; sempre mai mi pare molto stranio come è possibile che tal parole se usa infra la S.V. et me. Io non sono huomo da denari, sed tantum quero

By "Ricanato" he means the kabbalist Menaḥem Recanati (late thirteenth-early fourteenth centuries), two of whose works were translated for Pico by Flavius Mithridates (see below): the commentary on the Pentateuch and the commentary on prayers. The latter translation is extant in Vat. Ebr. 190, ff. 275ʳ–336ʳ, under the title *Liber de secretis orationum et benedictionum cabale*, but there is nothing in the manuscript to connect it to Recanati; as with the majority of Mithridates's translations, no author is indicated. The former translation is no longer extant, although a summary of its contents by Cardinal Richlieu's librarian Jacques Gaffarel was published in 1651, and a fragment of it has recently been discovered in a manuscript in Genoa.[47] It has been demonstrated that this work was the single most influential source for Pico's interpretation of kabbalah in the *Conclusiones*.[48] Pico had therefore read it before these were completed in November 1486 and before Delmedigo wrote this letter. No volume of Recanati is identifiable in Pico's library inventory. We cannot, for this reason, be sure that Delmedigo ever sent this book or that, if he did, it was indeed the commentary on the Pentateuch.

Unlike Mithridates and Alemanno, Delmedigo was not involved with matters of biblical exegesis. His role in Pico's Hebrew studies, however, was by no means negligible; and he has further importance as a conduit for the thought of Averroes.

2.2. *Flavius Mithridates*

Flavius Mithridates was one of the names assumed by a converted Sicilian Jew; he also called himself Guilelmus Siculus, Willelmus Ramundus Monchates and variations on all of these.[49] His biographi-

---

necessaria; tamen per non credere che io non sono agresto quando la Vostra S. me manderà un piccol presente, non sì grande chome è usa, quello acceptarò sì contento chome se el gran Turcho mi donassi un chastello; et di questo non bisogna molto dilatare parole."

[47] Jacques Gaffarel, *Codicum cabbalisticorum manuscriptorum quibus est usus Joannes Picus Comes Mirandulus, index* (Paris, 1651), 11–20; see C. Wirszubski, *Pico's Encounter with Jewish Mysticism* (Cambridge, Massachusetts: Harvard University Press, 1989), 11. The extant fragment is in the Biblioteca Universitaria di Genova, A IX 29, ff. 117ʳ–124ʳ: see F. Bacchelli, *Giovanni Pico e Pier Leone da Spoleto: tra filosofia dell'amore e tradizione cabalistica* (Florence: L.S. Olschki, 2001), 89–94.

[48] Wirszubski, *Pico's Encounter*, 53–56.

[49] See Flavius Mithridates, *Sermo de passione Domini*, ed. C. Wirszubski (Jerusalem: Israel Academy of Sciences and Humanities, 1963), 48–49.

cal outline is somewhat less clear than that of Delmedigo.[50] On Good
Friday, 1481, he preached a sermon on Christ's Passion in the Vatican, in the presence of Pope Sixtus IV. An autograph manuscript of
this sermon exists;[51] the colophon reads "Fl. Guillelmus ramundus
mithridates artium medicine et sacre theologie professor et lin-
guarum hebraice, harabice, caldayce, grece et latine interpretes et
sacrosancte romane ecclesiae acolytus hanc orationem edidit."[52] He
was, then, a teacher and translator, and it is as such that he came into
contact with Pico some years later.

Documentation of their working relationship begins in 1486.
Around this time, as has already been mentioned, Mithridates translated a substantial corpus of Hebrew texts into Latin specifically
for Pico.[53] Some of these are no longer extant. What survives, in five
manuscripts held in the Vatican library, amounts to over 3,500 pages.
The surviving manuscripts are: Vat. Ebr. 189, Vat. Ebr. 190, Vat. Ebr.
191, Chigi A VI 190 and Vat. Lat. 4273. Mithridates attempted a
translation that was literal, yet capable of dealing with the subtleties
of kabbalistic wordplay. As will become clear from the passages I
quote, the result is in a highly idiosyncratic Latin, which presents
difficulties of translation into English.

Obviously such a large amount of work would have taken several months.[54] Links between these translated texts and Pico's own
Conclusiones demonstrate that a proportion of the translations, and
certainly those contained in Vat. Ebr. 190 as well as the lost Recanati manuscript mentioned above, had been completed (and read
by Pico) by November 1486.[55] On the other hand, evidence from
marginal notes made by Mithridates shows that Vat. Ebr. 189 post-
dates this.[56] This corpus is substantial and heterogeneous, although

[50] F. Secret, *Les kabbalistes chrétiens de la Renaissance* (Neuilly sur Seine: Arma Artis,
1985), 25–27, 41 n. 3, and Mithridates, *Sermo*, ed. Wirszubski, 12 n. 2.
[51] Vatican, Barb. Lat. 1775, ff. 90–216: see Mithridates, *Sermo*, ed. Wirszubski,
43–44.
[52] Mithridates, *Sermo*, 127.
[53] In a significant development in Pico studies, work is underway to edit this corpus,
in a series entitled The Kabbalistic Library of Giovanni Pico della Mirandola. The first
volume of this series has now been published: *The Great Parchment: Flavius Mithridates's
Latin Translation, the Hebrew Text, and an English Version*, ed. G. Busi, S.M. Bondoni
and S. Campanini (Turin: Nino Aragno, 2004).
[54] Wirszubski, *Pico's Encounter*, 61.
[55] Ibid., 60–61.
[56] Ibid., 16–19.

it omits two kabbalistic texts of central importance, the *Sefer Yezirah* and the Zohar. Pico was nonetheless aware of their existence.[57]

As recent research has emphasized, the history of kabbalah involves a complex and multi-faceted web of doctrines and schools of thought, and precise historical attention is required to unravel it.[58] The translated corpus includes more than one strand of kabbalah. We have no reason to believe that any such perspective was available or of interest to Pico.[59] His understanding was that the kabbalah had been handed down orally from Moses: the places and dates of composition of these texts were therefore of relative unimportance.

These manuscripts are the single most significant channel through which Hebrew thought, specifically kabbalah, was made available to Pico. The many instances of marginal markings (a vertical line surmounted by two dots) against sections of these manuscripts which were used, sometimes almost verbatim, in the *Conclusiones* provide evidence that Pico read these texts, marked passages of interest and then reused them in his own works. Several of these texts are concerned with matters of biblical exegesis, and they should therefore be considered as potentially important background material for the *Heptaplus*.

The other notable feature of these translations is that Mithridates introduced a number of interpolations of several different sorts. Some were evidently intended to make difficult passages (particularly those involving letters treated as numbers) more comprehensible to Pico; others lent a Christian veneer to the Jewish sources; and still others (identifiable, for example, in the translation of Gersonides's commentary on the Song of Songs, which I shall discuss in Chapter 6) added references to kabbalah and kabbalists where none was present in the original.[60]

Aside from these translations, there is one further significant document of the relationship between Pico and Mithridates, which also involves biblical exegesis. This is the retranslation, written jointly by Pico and Mithridates, of the Book of Job, which is now in the Vatican Library, Ottob. Lat. 607. I shall discuss this briefly below.

---

[57] See n. 42 above. The manuscript corpus does contain four commentaries on the *Sefer Yezirah*, however: Vat. Ebr. 191, ff. 1ʳ–43ᵛ.

[58] See, in general, M. Idel, *Kabbalah: New Perspectives* (New Haven: Yale University Press, 1988), xi–xx, 1–34.

[59] It appears that Mithridates's translations sometimes blur the distinctions between kabbalistic schools: see Wirszubski, *Pico's Encouter*, 77–83, 103–104.

[60] See Wirszubski, *Pico's Encounter*, 106–113.

2.3. *Joḥanan Alemanno*

Some time before March 1489, Pico's association with Mithridates apparently came to an end, for reasons that remain unclear.[61] Around 1488 Pico made the acquaintance of another Jewish scholar, Joḥanan Alemanno (c. 1434–after 1504).[62] Alemanno's interests, attested by his bibliography, have several points of contact with biblical interpretation in general and the *Heptaplus* in particular. He wrote a long commentary on the Song of Songs, apparently (he says in the introduction) after a request from Pico.[63] Furthermore, at around the same time that Pico was working on the *Heptaplus*, Alemanno was composing his own Genesis commentary, the *Einei ha-edah* ("Eyes of the Community").[64] But unlike Mithridates and Delmedigo, we have no record of Alemanno ever having provided Pico with anything in Latin. The point that Alemanno and Pico had a common interest in biblical exegesis and the idea of intellectual ascent is easily made. It is harder to demonstrate any concrete links between the texts of the two writers. Temporal coincidence notwithstanding, we have no evidence that Pico read (or had read to him) the *Einei ha-edah*.[65]

---

[61] Wirszubski, "Pico's Book of Job", 173 n. 7; two letters written by Pico in 1489 show that he was trying to use the influence of Lorenzo de' Medici and the pope to obtain certain books from Mithridates.

[62] On Alemanno's own testimony, he discussed the Song of Songs with Pico in 1488. It has been suggested that the "Johanan" mentioned by Pico in the *Commento* (Garin, 535) refers to Alemanno and that therefore Pico was already aware of his work in 1486; or that Pico revised the *Commento* after 1488 to include Alemanno's name. See A.M. Leslie, "The Song of Solomon's Ascents by Yohanan Alemanno: Love and Human Perfection according to a Jewish Colleague of Giovanni Pico della Mirandola" (MA Dissertation, University of California, Berkeley, 1966), 27–32; Wirszubski, *Pico's Encounter*, 256–257; B.C. Novak, "Giovanni Pico della Mirandola and Jochanan Alemanno", *Journal of the Warburg and Courtauld Institutes*, 45 (1982), 130–132; Alemanno, *Ḥay ha-'olamim: parte I: la retorica*, ed. F. Lelli (Florence: L.S. Olschki, 1995), 6–7, 15. It seems likely, however, that this name refers not to Alemanno, but to a "rabi Johanan" quoted in the *Bahir*: see *The Book of Bahir: Flavius Mithridates's Latin Translation, the Hebrew Text, and an English Version*, ed. S. Campanini (Turin: Nino Aragno, 2005), 94–98. Gianfranceso Pico writes in a letter to Pagnino Lucensi that he was tutored by the son of "Iochanae illius, quem Ioannes Picus patruus meus sibi magistrum ascivit": see Gianfrancesco Pico della Mirandola, *Opera omnia*, II (Basel, 1573, repr. Hildesheim: Olm, 1969), 1371. It is generally assumed that this refers to Alemanno (see, e.g., Wirszubski, *Pico's Encounter*, 256).

[63] Leslie, "Song of Solomon's Ascents", 27–29.

[64] The autograph of this text is to be found in Paris, Bibliothèque Nationale, Ebr. 270.

[65] Leslie, "Song of Solomon's Ascents", 49, writes: "There is no solid evidence for subsequent association between Pico and Yohanan, but the apparent parallelism of

Equally, given the rhetorical conventions of an introductory epistle, it might be unwise to put too much weight on Alemanno's attribution of his writing of the Song of Songs commentary to Pico; just as, in the introduction to the *Heptaplus*, we need not necessarily take literally Pico's attribution of his interest in Genesis to Lorenzo de' Medici.[66]

The recent advances made in the study of Alemanno's works still do not permit us to gain a clear idea of their relationship to Pico's works.[67] Apart from this, however, we must bear in mind the likelihood that information passed between Pico and Alemanno in conversation. We should therefore reckon with the possibility that Alemanno introduced other works to Pico and broadened his understanding of the textual bases of the doctrines to which Mithridates had already introduced him. Alemanno is undoubtedly a significant contemporary representative of a Jewish tradition in which Pico had a particular interest.

2.4. *Pico's Access to Untranslated Hebrew Sources*

These three scholars played a major part in making Jewish texts and ideas available to Pico. His knowledge of this tradition does not appear to have been based solely on translations and oral contact, however, since he accumulated a sizeable collection of Hebrew books and manuscripts which were not represented in the translated corpus.[68] He made use of some of these books in his biblical commentaries. Although this much is clear, the details recede into obscurity.

Not every question can be answered by an appeal to the inventories of his library. It is impossible to determine with complete accuracy how many books in Hebrew Pico possessed, let alone exactly what they were. Of the two library inventories, the second (made in

---

their writings after 1488 implies that they continued their relations for some time." For a discussion of one such apparent parallelism see below, Ch. 5, section 1.2.

[66] Garin, 168: "Movit aemulatio me studiorum tuorum, Laurenti Medices, ut arcana Moseos volumina recenserem".

[67] Much material remains unpublished, including the *Einei ha-edah* and most of the commentary on the Song of Songs.

[68] Two inventories of Pico's library have survived: see P. Kibre, *The Library of Pico della Mirandola* (New York: Columbia University Press, 1936), 3–22. The Hebrew and Aramaic books included in these inventories are discussed by G. Tamani, "I libri ebraici di Pico della Mirandola", in *Giovanni Pico della Mirandola: convegno internazionale*, ed. Garfagnini, II, 491–530.

1498, on the occasion of the sale of the library to Cardinal Domenico Grimani) is the more detailed. It explicitly identifies 58 books as being in Hebrew or Chaldean (i.e., Aramaic) and it is likely that several dozen further references, while not noting the language, refer to untranslated works in these languages.[69] Some works we must assume from their title and author were in Hebrew, as there is no evidence that they had ever been translated. Other works are simply designated by the word "Hebraeus", with no further indication of content.

It is probable that Pico (like many people) did not necessarily buy books because he needed (or was able) to read them. The presence of a small number of books in other languages with which he was certainly less well acquainted than Hebrew (some Arabic, some unidentified) suggests that likelihood of being read was not the sole criterion for purchase and storage in Pico's library.[70] He bought them because he was a book collector.[71] But there is no doubt that his interest in Hebrew literature was long-standing and serious. Aside from other considerations, it must have cost him a large sum of money both to obtain these volumes and to commission Mithridates to produce his translations.[72] The mere presence of the translations goes some way to arguing that, at least in 1486–1487, Pico was not able single-handedly to deal with the original texts.[73]

In a letter written in reply to one sent by Ficino on 8 September 1486, and probably not itself composed before 15 October of the same year, Pico wrote that he had spent the whole month studying Hebrew day and night, and that his command of it was now sufficient to compose a letter "not yet, indeed, worthy of praise, but without

---

[69] See the list of 123 Jewish works discussed by Tamani, "Libri ebraici", 497–523. Some of these are Latin translations.

[70] E.g. Kibre, *Library*, items 294, 297, 874?, 876, 877, 878.

[71] A. Grafton, "Giovanni Pico della Mirandola: Trials and Triumphs of an Omnivore", in his *Commerce with the Classics: Ancient Books and Renaissance Readers*, 100–108 (Ann Arbor, Michigan: University of Michigan Press, 1997).

[72] On the cost of Pico's book buying, see his comment in the *Oratio* (Garin, 160) referring specifically to the kabbalistic books he had procured: "Hos ego libros non mediocri impensa mihi cum comparassem, summa diligentia, indefessis laboribus cum perlegissem, vidi in illis—testis est Deus—religionem non tam Mosaicam quam Christianam." See also *Apologia, Opera omnia*, 123, 178.

[73] Note also the comment of Wirszubski, *Pico's Encounter*, 6: "Pico learned a great deal from the translations of Mithridates, infinitely more than he might or could have learned from the Hebrew originals, had he attempted to read them without translations."

fault".[74] But quite how much Hebrew this was is hard to say.[75] The real evidence of the direction of Pico's research lies in his writings, not in his library catalogue.

Mithridates's translations, as far as we can tell, are coterminous with the period of the *Conclusiones* and *Apologia*, although the Job manuscript may postdate this. Internal evidence from the second phase of Pico's works shows that his interest in Hebrew was still strong in 1489.[76] The *Expositiones in Psalmos* of 1488–1489 contain many citations of Jewish exegetes. The most frequently appearing are: Abraham ibn Ezra, whom Pico calls "Avenazra"; David Kimḥi, called "Chemoy" or "David"; Rashi, called "Rabi Salomon"; the Targum, referred to as "Chaldeus"; and a certain "Rabi Thobias".[77] It is noteworthy that these exegetes do not appear in the translated corpus, and a few remarks should be made about Pico's access to them. Kimḥi's commentary was included in two early editions of the Psalms (Bologna 1477 and Naples 1487). One of these is presumably the "Psalmi David cum expositione hebreus impressi" cited in the second library inventory.[78] Other incunables of the Psalms did not include commentaries, nor did the complete 'Soncino' Bible, printed in 1488. Pico's access to these sources was therefore limited to manuscripts. In the second library inventory we find a "Caldea expositio psalmorum liber parvus in hebreo manuscriptus in papiro" and an "Avenaza [sic] super esiam et duodecim prophetas et psalmos

---

[74] *Opera omnia*, 367: "Non poteras oportunius Maumethem tuum Latinum repetere, quam hoc tempore, quo me propediem Maumethem ipsum, patria lingua loquentem, auditurum spero: postquam enim Hebraicae linguae, perpetuum mensem, dies, noctesque invigilavi, ad Arabicae studium et Chaldaicae totus me contuli, nihil in eis veritus me profecturum minus, quam in Hebraica profecerim, in qua possum nondum quidem cum laude, sed citra culpam epistolam dictare." For the dating of this letter, see Wirszubski, *Pico's Encounter*, 3–4.

[75] See the comment of Wirszubski, "Pico's Book of Job", 173: "Precisely what this amounts to in terms of proficiency in Hebrew is hard to say: it is by no means negligible, but it need not be much." He also remarks that "such evidence as we have of his Hebrew studies does not suggest that his knowledge of Hebrew was as considerable before 1489 as it may have been some years later." But Pico died five years later and I am unaware of positive evidence of increasing proficiency in Hebrew during the last years of his life.

[76] See *Expositiones in Psalmos*, ed. Raspanti, 32.

[77] On the Targumim, or Aramaic translations of the Bible, see Ch. 3, section 4.4. The identity of "Rabi Thobias" is unclear; Raspanti in his edition of the *Expositiones in Psalmos* does not provide references for him.

[78] Tamani, "Libri ebraici", 505–506, item 31. See *Encyclopaedia Judaica*, ed. C. Roth, 16 vols (Jerusalem: Keter, 1972), IV, 835–836.

in hebreo manuscriptus in membrana".[79] As for the commentaries of Rashi and "Rabi Thobias", the inventories provide no information.

The *Expositiones in Psalmos* demonstrate that Pico had sufficient knowledge of Hebrew to draw material from these commentators, as well as to indicate instances in which the Latin or Greek text departed from the Hebrew. Commentaries arranged as glosses are easier to read than continuous prose. An examination of the citations of Hebrew writers in the *Expositiones in Psalmos* shows that they are contextually relatively simple. They occur in the initial philological section of each commentary, entitled "Defensio" or "Argumentum", and are confined to the exposition of individual words.[80] Given the absence of Hebrew from the university curriculum, such an ability was not widespread among Christian scholars; Pico's interest in the language was certainly above average.[81] This level of interest and knowledge does not necessarily imply the ability to read entire treatises by such writers as Recanati, Abulafia, Gikatilla and Alemanno, however.

If we turn to the Job manuscript, we again see Pico's knowledge of Hebrew at work, apparently impressively. The combination of retranslation (compared to the Vulgate) and marginalia found in this manuscript connect it decisively to the commentary on Job by Gersonides.[82] The translator was therefore not only able to read Job, linguistically the most difficult book of the Old Testament, but also Gersonides's commentary. We have no record that Pico possessed the commentary in translation. Nonetheless, it does not follow from the evidence of this manuscript that Pico himself necessarily read Gersonides's commentary in Hebrew, nor even that he himself translated the text of Job unassisted. The manuscript is in at least two hands: that of Pico and one or two others. The translation is in three sections: chapters 1–11.4, chapters 11–42.6, and chapter

---

[79] Tamani, "Libri ebraici", 500, items 6 and 7; ibid., 505, item 29. See also Kibre, *Library*, item 273.

[80] For examples, see Ch. 3, section 5.

[81] Poggio Bracciolini had studied the rudiments of Hebrew by 1416: see A. Botley, "Parallel Texts: Bruni, Manetti and Erasmus on the Art and Purpose of Translation" (PhD Dissertation, Cambridge University, 1999), 159. On Gianozzo Manetti's mid-15th-century translation of the Psalms, see Ch. 3, section 2. In the Middle Ages, too, a few scholars had shown a serious interest in Hebrew, among whom Nicholas of Lyra is especially worthy of note: see H. Hailperin, *Rashi and the Christian Scholars* (Pittsburgh, Pennsylvania: University of Pittsburgh Press, 1963), 137–246; B. Smalley, *The Study of the Bible in the Middle Ages* (Oxford: B. Blackwell, 1952, repr. 1984), 190.

[82] Wirszubski, "Pico's Book of Job".

42.7–16. The short first section is in Pico's hand and contains a copy of the Vulgate text, with the new translation appearing as an interlinear gloss. The second and third sections are written continuously, without the Vulgate text, in a different hand, annotated by Pico. The balance of probability, the name "Mitridate" as a colophon, and the presence in Pico's library inventory of a "Iob secundum translationem mitridatis" all suggest that the latter non-interlinear translation is that of Mithridates.[83] But what of the initial interlinear gloss?

Wirszubski proposed that "Pico, having reached the end of the tenth chapter, discontinued revising the Vulgate version and had a new translation, starting from chapter 11, made for him from Hebrew by Mithridates".[84] The strong influence of Gersonides in both translations, however—including the second, in which Pico was apparently not involved—suggests that it was Mithridates who read Job in this way, and therefore that Pico's initial 'Gersonidean' translation was also aided by Mithridates. In effect, my hypothesis is that Pico and Mithridates jointly embarked on the project of translating Job via Gersonides and that after they had reached the end of chapter 10, Mithridates continued in Pico's absence, subsequently giving the completed text to him, at which point Pico added further annotations throughout the second section.[85] We cannot, then, uncritically accept either the idea that Pico himself composed the translation in the first section unaided or that he read Gersonides's commentary. The manuscript appears very much to be the product of a teacher-pupil relationship.

Through such a relationship ideas can of course be propagated without reference to the texts in which they occurred. An example is Pico's discussion of Jewish exegetical terminology in the *Apologia*.[86] The terminology he uses is atypical of medieval Jewish exegesis and has a distinct source in the work of the biblical commentator Baḥya ben Asher (thirteenth century), whose commentary on the Pentateuch, in which this terminology is used, was published in Naples in 1492.[87] We have no record that Pico owned or read it.

[83] Ibid., 172–173; Kibre, *Library*, item 434.

[84] Wirszubski, "Pico's Book of Job", 172.

[85] Mithridates continued to translate for Pico after Pico had written the *Conclusiones* and gone to Rome; Mithridates's own whereabouts at this point are unclear. See Wirszubski, *Pico's Encounter*, 16–18.

[86] *Opera omnia*, 178. For a discussion of this passage see Ch. 3, n. 31.

[87] Baḥya ben Asher, *Perush ha-Torah* (Naples, 1492); see Wirszubski, *Pico's Encounter*, 262–263.

Instead, we find this unusual terminology written in Pico's hand in the margin of the manuscript of Gersonides's commentary on the Song of Songs, translated for him by Mithridates.[88] Since it does not derive from this work, it seems likely that this note reflects the oral transmission of information from Mithridates (or another Jewish associate) to Pico.

As I said with reference to Alemanno, we must not underestimate the importance of oral contact.[89] On the other hand, we cannot simply assume oral contact as a conduit for everything. We should remember that information would not necessarily have been shared fully or without ulterior motive. I have already mentioned the interpolations made by Mithridates, which in some cases distorted Hebrew texts in a Christianizing manner. We have to ask ourselves to what extent practicing Jews such as Alemanno or Delmedigo (as opposed to a convert such as Mithridates) would have been prepared to provide Pico with the key to what they would have regarded as the deepest mysteries of their faith.[90] In the case of Delmedigo, we have concrete evidence that he at certain points deliberately withheld information about kabbalah from works he produced for Pico.[91] Pico acted as patron to Delmedigo and Alemanno, as comments they make in their own compositions show; but there is no reason to believe that they would have helped him unreservedly in his endeavours. His own comments on Judaism in the *Heptaplus* are hardly complimentary.[92]

This survey of Pico's knowledge of Hebrew language and literature is more an outline of problems than a proposal of solutions. It is intended to demonstrate the limitations which the extant evidence imposes on our knowledge of Pico's linguistic command of Hebrew. On balance, given these limitations, we cannot assume that, even in 1489, he would have been able to read complete kabbalistic treatises unaided—particularly in manuscript and replete with abbreviations, or in a script unlike the simple non-cursive variety used in Mithri-

---

[88] Vat. Lat. 4273, f. 5^r.

[89] For a discussion of the contacts between Christian and Jewish scholars in Florence, with some observations on the importance of oral communication, see M. Idel, "Jewish Mystical Thought in the Florence of Lorenzo de' Medici", in *La cultura ebraica all'epoca di Lorenzo il Magnifico*, ed. D.L. Bemporad and I. Zatelli, 17–26 (Florence: L.S. Olschki, 1998).

[90] Pico noted in the *Apologia* that Hebrew texts were expensive because Jews were unwilling to circulate them to Christians. *Opera omnia*, 178: "Quos ego libros summa impensa mihi conquistos (neque enim eos Hebraei Latinis nostris communicare volunt)".

[91] See Bland, "Elijah Del Medigo's Averroist Response".

[92] See, e.g., H. 7.4; Garin, 346–360.

dates's translations. While I by no means wish to rob Pico of his status as a pioneer among Christian Hebraists, I believe that he is a pioneer in his particular area of interest—kabbalah—rather than in his linguistic ability; and this area of interest he approached first and foremost through the translated corpus and oral contact.[93]

This conclusion has provided the methodological basis for my analysis of the role of Jewish sources in Pico's works. I hope to demonstrate that Pico's interest in this material had an important influence on the *Heptaplus*; but I have generally sought to locate the origins of this influence in works which we know were available to him in Latin, whether through printed editions or Mithridates's corpus of translations.[94] I have, nonetheless, referred in several instances to Hebrew works by Alemanno and Delmedigo, as these provide evidence of contemporary Jewish thought in a circle to which we know Pico had a certain proximity.

---

[93] Pico was not the first Christian to take an interest in kabbalah: see Secret, *Les kabbalistes chrétiens*, 8–18. It is his initiative of commissioning the translations of these works which makes him historically so important.

[94] For a partial exception to this rule, see my comments on Nahmanides's commentary on the Pentateuch in Ch. 7, section 3.

CHAPTER TWO

THE *HEPTAPLUS* IN OUTLINE

In order to provide a basis for my discussion of the *Heptaplus*, I shall give here a skeleton outline of its contents. The full title is "*Heptaplus*: On the Sevenfold Narration of the Six Days of Genesis, for Lorenzo de' Medici".[1] In a brief dedicatory epistle, Roberto Salviati, the Florentine humanist who undertook the printing and distribution of the work, describes these "first fruits" of Pico as "most excellent, not just in my judgement, but in the judgement of everyone"; for this reason, he has printed an "accurate impression" at his own expense. The subject of the book, according to Salviati, is "physical and divine mysteries".[2]

Pico himself prefaces the work with two proems. As these will be discussed at length in Chapters 4 and 5, I shall largely pass over them here. Suffice it to say that most of the first proem consists of a justification, via ancient pagan and Christian examples, of an esoteric reading of the Bible: that is, of the distinction between literal and non-literal reading, or, as Pico calls it, the 'shell' and 'kernel'. His essential claim is that the "secrets of the whole of nature" are contained in the narrative of the six days of creation.[3] The second proem describes his theory of allegory. It is related to a cosmic model according to which the created universe is composed of three worlds: the sublunary, the celestial and the angelic or intellectual. Each of the seven expositions (with the exception of the last, which discusses

---

[1] Garin, 167: "Heptaplus: de septiformi sex dierum Geneseos enarratione ad Laurentium Medicem."

[2] Ibid., 168: "Is [i.e., Pico] cum nuper tibi [i.e., Lorenzo de' Medici] librum de septiformi sex dierum Geneseos enarratione, primitias studiorum suorum, dicaverit, opus, non meo modo, sed omnium iudicio excellentissimum, dare operam volui ut, mea impensa, emendata impressione publicaretur, nihil dubitans simul me et meo in illum amori et publicae studiosorum utilitati satisfacturum. Accessit quod non ingratam me tibi rem facturum speravi, si quae tibi illa physica et divina mysteria communicavit, per me denique omnibus fierent communia." The description of the *Heptaplus* as representing the "first fruits" of Pico's studies perhaps betrays a deliberate desire to overlook the recent scandal.

[3] H. P1; Garin, 170: "Accidit autem per hos dies ut in mundi fabrica et celebratis illis operibus sex dierum fuerim assiduus, quibus totius naturae secreta contineri ut credamus magnae se rationes offerunt."

man's *felicitas*) will address an aspect of these worlds: either separately
or in combination. Each of these expositions, in turn, is to have seven
chapters.

There follows a quotation of the opening of the first chapter of
Genesis, from verse 1 to verse 27, in the Latin of the Vulgate.[4] It is
this extract of the text that I shall refer to throughout this study as
the Genesis narrative. Note that it finishes with the creation of man
on the sixth day, and does not include the account of the seventh
day, which is to be found in Genesis 2.1.

The main part of the work now begins. At the start of each
exposition Pico defines a certain body of knowledge: Aristotelian
physics, for example, or the angelic metaphysics of Pseudo-Dionysius
the Areopagite. He then proceeds to derive information concerning
this body of knowledge from the Genesis narrative, by a process of
allegorical reading. In the interests of brevity, the following outline
concentrates largely on the ends of his allegorical readings rather
than the means. In some cases, however, I shall discuss the way he
constructs and justifies his interpretations, so as to give a flavour of
the text as a whole.

1. *First Exposition:* De mundo elementari

The frame of reference of the first exposition is natural philosophy
and the world of generation and corruption. It begins, not with a
discussion of the words "in principio creavit", nor even with the
Bible at all, but with a summary of the doctrines of "the natural
philosophers who discuss the nature of corruptible things". In other
words, it contains a brief dissertation on the most basic concept
of Aristotelian physics: the process by which any individual and
particular thing may come into being.

There are two *principii* of natural things: unformed matter and
privation.[5] Various causes act upon the unformed matter: the efficient cause, the final cause and the formal cause.[6] Form is identified

---

[4] H. P2; Garin, 198–202.

[5] H. 1.1; Garin, 204: "Naturales philosophi qui de natura rerum corruptibilium
disserunt, de principiis earum sic statuunt in universum: esse materiam rudem, formarum expertem, idoneam quidem omnibus formis suscipiendis, sua tamen natura
omnibus privatam, quare praeter materiam privationem etiam faciunt principium
rerum naturalium."

[6] Ibid.: "tum afferunt [i.e., natural philosophers] transmutantem causam, quam
vocant efficientem, cuius vi tractata materia, quod est potentia, actu fiat aliquando

as the third *principium*, but its reception by matter depends on the matter having previously been prepared with suitable qualities. When it has been prepared, and the necessary actions have taken place, the individual thing itself comes into being.[7]

Pico's reading of the events of the first day is therefore concerned with the fundamental process of becoming common to all sublunary entities. In the first phrase of the Genesis narrative, "in the beginning God created heaven and earth", heaven and earth are interpreted as the efficient and material cause respectively.[8] There are two justifications for this. The first is an appeal to ancient authority (*auctoritas*), namely the Stoics, according to Varro.[9] The second is an appeal to reason (*ratio*). Earth is the lowest of the four elements and the material cause is the lowest cause; the heavens are above the earth and the efficient cause is above the material cause.[10] The shadows which cover the face of the abyss (Gen. 1.2) are interpreted as the second *principium*, *privatio*, which is present in the unformed matter.[11] The waters, meanwhile, are interpreted as the qualities.[12] The Spirit of God hovers over the waters, and not directly over the earth, because the "force of the efficient cause" acting on matter

---

… . Quoniam autem nihil natura temere agit, sed boni alicuius consequendi gratia, finalis causa se statim infert et proximus quidem finis agentis causae forma est, quam de materiae gremio eruit."

[7] Ibid.: "unde et forma tertium principium ab Aristotele statutum [*Metaphysics* XII.2, 1069]. Haec autem de materiae sinu educi non potest, nisi affectae prius et preparatae congruis qualitatibus, circa quas totus opificis labor, tota actionis mora consumitur, ipsa scilicet specie individuo momento quasi praemio laboris statim effulgente."

[8] H. 1.2; Garin, 206: "Principio igitur duas statuit [i.e., Moses] causas: agentem et materiam, eam scilicet quae actu et eam quae est potentia; illam caelum hanc terram vocat …"

[9] Ibid.: "cui nostrae expositioni attestatur primum auctoritas Stoicorum, qui agentem causam caelum, materialem terram vocaverunt, ut scribit Varro [*De lingua latina*, V, 59], ne Graecos commemorem".

[10] Ibid: "Attestatur et ratio; nam et materia despicatissima omnium naturarum, uti est terra omnium elementorum, et simili omnino proportione respondent, ut probant Peripatetici, agens materiae et terrae caelum."

[11] Ibid., 208: "Abyssum vocat terram, idest materiam trino dimensu in altissimas profunditates extensam. Super hanc tenebrae, idest privatio est, principium apud Peripateticos in primis celebre, cui nulla magis appellatio quam tenebrarum congruerit."

[12] Ibid., 208–210: "Praeterea si subest terra aquis et irrigata inde parturit quae postremo et pariat, nonne aquae hoc loco accidentes materiae qualitates et affectiones significabunt? Quae vel suo fluxu tractabilique natura aquarum speciem gerunt, quibus, ut ita dixerim, humectata materia parturit formam, quam extremo temporis momento edit in lucem."

needs to be mediated by the qualities.[13] The coming of light removes the shadows and the imposition of form removes privation.[14]

In his first reading of day one, therefore, Pico sets out the context of Aristotelian physics and aligns its principal concepts with the events of the first day of the Genesis narrative. The result is an account of the relationship between matter and form and the interaction of the two to create an entity. His reading of day two moves from the general to the particular and begins to account for the classification of created entities.[15]

All bodies in the sublunary world fall into one of three groups: pure elements, totally impure elements, and imperfectly mixed elements which occupy the median position between these two extremes. Pico relates this fact to the division of the waters in Gen. 1.6–7. He takes the structure of the upper and lower waters, separated by the firmament, to represent two extremes and a mean. The higher waters represent pure and unmixed elements only, and the lower waters represent a totally impure mixture. Between these is the firmament, which represents an intermediate state of incomplete mixture.[16]

Following this basic classification, Pico moves on to more complex organisms, to complete the taxonomy of sublunary beings: plants, animals and man.[17] The sun, moon and stars created on the

---

[13] Ibid., 210: "Super has aquas Spiritus Domini, idest vis causae efficientis ... merito ferri dicitur, neque dicitur ferri super terram, quia non attingit agens subiectum aut permeat nisi mediis illis intercedentibus qualitatibus".

[14] Ibid., 210: "oritur lux, idest formae species et decor, tenebrarum quas diximus, idest privationis, expultrix et fugatrix."

[15] H. 1.3; Garin, 212: "Quoniam autem a communibus generalibusque ad specialia recto ordine descendimus, ut probat Aristoteles, facturus hoc idem Moses: postquam dixit de his, quae communia sunt rebus omnibus elementaribus, elementarem totam substantiam secunda die trifariam dividit."

[16] Ibid., 214: "Triplex enim partitio corporum sublunarium. Alia supra mediam regionem aeris sunt, suprema scilicet pars eiusdem elementi et purissimus ignis, quod totum aetheris nomine designatur; ibi pura, immixta et legitima elementa. Alia infra ipsum aeris meditullium, quae apud nos sunt, ubi elementum purum nullum (neque enim purum elementum sensibile) sed mixta omnia ex foeculenta crassioreque parte mundani corporis constant. Intercedens regio aeris, quae hic dicitur firmamentum, unde et aves sub firmamento caeli ab eo volantes introducuntur ... . Vide autem quam recte, non solum situ sed et naturae proprietate hoc firmamentum superiora elementa ab inferioribus quasi aquas ab aquis discriminat et distinguit. Supra eam pura sunt elementa; infra eam, perfecta mixtione, ab elementari simplicitate discedunt; inibi mixta sunt, sed imperfecta mediaque, ut dicatur verissime, inter mixtorum elementorumque naturam."

[17] H. 1.4; Garin, 216: "Si anima vegetalis mixtionis formam statim consequitur, quid aliud a nostro philosopho [i.e. Moses] expectabamus, quam ut post illam

fourth day (Gen. 1.14–19) are interpreted as the causes of weather and such transient phenomena as comets.[18] The final chapter discusses the status of Christ, who stands in the same relation to man as man does to the rest of creation.[19]

2. *Second Exposition:* De mundo caelesti

The transition from the first to the second exposition is an ascent from lower to higher.[20] The frame of reference of the second exposition is the nature and function of the ten heavenly spheres.[21] Pico begins with the empyrean:

> Why do I further delay the Prophet from proceeding, with his face unveiled, to tell us of these celestial mysteries? Before we hear him speaking, so that we may be more able to grasp his words, a few prefatory remarks on the tenth heaven will be useful.[22]

These prefatory remarks refer to the many authorities who confirm the existence of a tenth sphere, including Strabo, Bede, many Hebrew thinkers and certain other philosophers and "mathematici"

---

aquarum congregationem induceret statim terram, herbarum, fructicum, arborumque fecundam?"; H. 1.6; Garin, 218–220: "Post plantas enim ea sunt mixta quae sentiunt et moventur ... Haec autem animantia quae citra omnem controversiam motu sensuque participant, et hic a Mose et in Timaeo [40a], in volatilia et in aquis degentia distinguuntur. Supremus omnium et princeps homo, quo mundi corruptibilis natura progressa sistit pedem et receptui canit."

[18] H. 1.5; Garin, 216–218: "Sunt autem haec impressiones illae quae in sublimi, idest in media regione aeris, fiunt. ... has autem impressiones, secundarias stellas et sidera et astra a philosophis nuncupari notius est ... . Quoniam autem horum omnis diversitas ad duas primas causas refertur, caliditatem et frigiditatem, referemus convenienter quae a causa sunt calida ad solem, quae vero a frigida ad lunam." Aristotelian physics considered comets as sublunary because they were seen to change state and could not therefore be above the moon.

[19] H. 1.7; Garin, 220: "Quemadmodum autem inferiorum omnium absoluta consummatio est homo, ita omnium hominum absoluta est consummatio Christus".

[20] H. 2.P; Garin, 220: "Surgamus ab elementis ad caelum, a corruptibilibus ad incorrupta corpora ..."

[21] H. 2.1; Garin, 224: "Supra novem caelorum orbes, idest septem planetas et sphaeram octavam, quam vocant inerrantem, nonumque orbem, qui ratione non sensu deprehensus est primusque est inter corpora quae moventur, creditum esse decimum caelum, fixum, manens et quietum, quod motu nullo participet."

[22] H. 2.P; Garin, 224: "Sed quid Prophetam prodeuntem revelata facie moratur ultra, ut de caelestibus nos mysteriis alloquatur? Prius tamen quam loquentem ipsum audiamus, ut simus verborum illius capaciores, prefari paucula quaedam de caelo decimo utile fuerit."

(i.e., astronomers).[23] The empyrean is the source of all light. Pico passes by, without dwelling on, the question of whether its composition is corporeal or incorporeal, while implying that the former position is closer to the truth.[24] From the empyrean, light passes to the lower spheres.

In this context, applied to the Genesis account, 'heaven' is the empyrean, and the entire group of eight lower spheres (from the fixed stars down to, and including, the moon) are represented by the term 'earth'.[25] (The earth itself obviously does not figure because we are no longer occupied with the sublunary world.) Pico's justification

---

[23] H. 2.1; Garin, 224: "Neque hoc tantum creditum a nostris maxime iunioribus, Strabo et Beda, sed a pluribus etiam Hebraeorum, praetereaque a philosophis et mathematicis quibusdam." The reference to Strabo in all likelihood derives from the *Glossa ordinaria*: see *Biblia latina cum glossa ordinaria*, 4 vols (Strasbourg, 1480–1481; facsimile repr. Turnhout: Brepols, 1992), introd. K. Froehlich and M.T. Gibson, I, sig. a5ʳ. The reference to Bede is not to his *In Pentateuchum commentarii* (as proposed by Garin, 224) but rather to his *Libri quatuor in principium Genesis*, in *Opera*, II.1, Corpus Christianorum Series Latina 118A, ed. C.W. Jones (Turnhout: Brepols, 1967), 4 (13D–14A).

[24] H. 2.1; Garin, 226: "Dubitatum autem a quibusdam natura ne esset corporea an incorporea potius … . Sed quicquid de hac quaestione statuatur, remaneat inconcussum inibi esse thesauros lucis et inde, quicquid habetur luminis visiturque in corporibus, quasi a primo fonte in cetera derivari. Neque enim obstat si quis credere pertinacius quam verius velit, non esse illum natura vere corporea, quando in Phoenicum theologia est, ut scribit Iulianus Caesar in oratione De sole, emanare lucem corpoream ab incorporea natura." For the reference to Julian the Apostate, see his *De sole*, in *Oeuvres complètes*, II.2, ed. C. Lacombrade (Paris: Les Belles Lettres, 1964), 105 (134A–B).

[25] H. 2.2; Garin, 228: "Terram autem vocavit octo sphaeras postremas, neque id sine causa, sed ob id factum quoniam huius numeri extrema sibi terrae appellationem vendicant. Ea sunt luna et caelum stellatum, quorum utrumque terram vocare et veterum auctoritate et ratione praeterea cogimur. De sphaera enim octava frequentissimum fuit in Academia dare illi terrae appellationem. Lunam item Aristoteles terrae similem dixit, imitatus scilicet Pythagoricos, qui eam et terram caelestem et terrestre caelum appellant. Sed vide quae ratio ad utrumque nos ducat. Si enim in caelo quaerimus elementa, lunam terram statuimus, infimam ignobilissimamque omnium siderum, uti est terra omnium elementorum opacitate itidem substantiae et maculis illi persimilem; tum aquam Mercurium versipelle sidus et transformabile, ideoque apud Lucanum undae arbitrum appellatum [*Pharsalia*, X, 209]; Venerem aerem temperato calore vivificam, Solem ignem, ratione manifestissima. Tum, ordine inverso, Martem ignem, Iovem aerem cognatum Veneri natura, Saturnum aquam, senem scilicet damnatae frigiditatis; reliquum ut sphaeram octavam et non erraticam terram vocemus, vel sic ipso computationis ordine postulante." On the similarity of earth and moon in Aristotle and the Pythagoreans, see *Aristotelis qui ferebantur librorum fragmenta*, ed. V. Rose (Leipzig: B.G. Teubner, 1886), frag. 204; Averroes, *Commentaria magna in Aristotelem De celo et mundo*, ed. F.J. Carmody and R. Arnzen, 2 vols (Leuven: Peeters, 2003), I, 29, discussed in E. Grant, *Planets, Stars and Orbs: The Medieval Cosmos, 1200–1687* (Cambridge: CUP, 1994), 223 n. 17.

for this grouping is a good example of the way in which he interleaves arguments from *auctoritas* with arguments from *ratio*. Firstly, the two extremes of this group—the moon and the sphere of fixed stars—have both been correlated with the term *terra* by ancient example; the moon according to Aristotle and the Pythagoreans, and the fixed stars according to the Academy. Secondly, the moon is the lowest of the planets and therefore occupies the same space, analogically, in the celestial hierarchy as the element 'earth' does in the hierarchy of the four elements. Thirdly, the moon is similar to 'earth' because of its opaque substance and its markings.

Drawing on this analogy between moon and earth, Pico proceeds to correlate the entire series of heavenly spheres with the four elements. Mercury corresponds to water, on the authority of Lucan and because it is "fluctuating and transformable". Venus corresponds to air because it gives life through warmth. The sun, "for the most obvious of reasons", corresponds to fire. As the sequence of the four elements has now been exhausted, Pico reverses their order and continues. Mars corresponds to fire, Jupiter to air and Saturn—"an old man of doomed frigidity"—to water.[26] Pico concludes that "we call the eighth, non-moving sphere 'earth' because this is what the order of computation demands".[27] The identification of both extremes of the series of spheres with *terra* is justification for the use of this term to refer to the group as a whole.[28] The ninth sphere or *primum mobile* is represented by the undifferentiated mass of waters.[29]

---

[26] Several of these correspondences date back to antiquity. On the connection of Mars with fire, see J. Seznec, *La survivance des dieux antiques: essai sur le rôle de la tradition mythologique dans l'humanisme et dans l'art de la Renaissance* (London: Warburg Institute, 1940), 44. On the depiction of Saturn as an old man, see ibid., 152–153. The connection of Saturn with water, however, appears to have been less common, as he was often identified with dryness: see R. Klibansky, E. Panofsky and F. Saxl, *Saturn and Melancholy: Studies in the History of Natural Philosophy, Religion and Art* (London: Nelson, 1964), 128.

[27] For a possible source for this computation, unmentioned in the *Heptaplus*, see *Conclusions*, 74 (Conc. sec. Iamblichum, 4): "Elementa in octo caeli corporibus caelesti modo bis inveniuntur, quae quis inveniet si retrogrado ordine in illa bina numeratione processerit." I do not think that Farmer's understanding of "bina" as referring to the *sefirah Binah* is relevant here: see his *Syncretism in the West*, 310–311.

[28] H. 2.2; Garin, 228: "Recte igitur hoc totum, quod binis utrimque terris concluditur, supra quod nihil visibile nobis, terram vocavit."

[29] Ibid., 230: "Verum ne crederemus inter octavam sphaeram et sedes empyreas nihil medium esse, ut crediderunt multi, secuti inditia tantummodo sensuum, admonuit nos orbis intercedentis, quem per aquas ipse cum figuraverit consone a iunioribus crystallinum caelum est nuncupatum."

The interpretation of the first day, therefore, accounts for all ten spheres largely without differentiating between them. In the next chapter, Pico turns his attention to the second day and to a "more particular" discussion of the spheres.[30] The firmament, which he identifies with the eighth sphere (that of the fixed stars) separates the upper from the lower waters, which represent the ninth sphere and Saturn respectively.[31] The congregating of the lower waters, meanwhile, represents the way in which the power of all the planets is gathered together in the sun, and the earth, it is reiterated, represents the moon.[32] This leaves four planets (Mercury, Venus, Mars and Jupiter) so far unaccounted for. Pico had established a principle in the first proem that Moses should not be made to look as if he had left anything out.[33] This principle is invoked here.

> Why is [Moses] silent regarding the other [planets], when I promised in my introduction that he would treat of everything, sufficiently and learnedly?[34]

Two solutions propose themselves, both of which Pico refutes. The first suggestion, that Moses did not bother to discourse on the other planets because his uneducated listeners had no knowledge of them, contradicts Pico's principle of sufficiency and his belief that Moses wished to benefit the learned as much as the unlearned.[35] The second suggestion, that the assertions made regarding the sun and moon are sufficient to apply also to the other planets, which stand in relation to them as particular to general, is rejected as inconsistent because if Moses had followed this principle, he would not have included anything about Saturn either. Pico prefers a third solution:

> I believe that a deeper mystery of the ancient doctrine of the Jews lies hidden there. Among their beliefs about the heavens, this one is pre-

---

[30] H. 2.3; Garin, 230: "Iam vero de motis orbibus particularius pronuncians".

[31] Ibid., 230–232: "docet non erraticam sphaeram quam dicimus firmamentum mediam esse inter duas aquas, cuius dicti manifesta ratio ex his quae diximus, nam et nonus orbis et Saturni planetes, ut declaravimus, aquarum sibi appellationem vendicant."

[32] Ibid., 232: "Hae aquae congregatae in locum unum ideo sunt quia omnis planetarum virtus in uno sole collecta est ... . Terram autem quid aliud dicemus quam lunam".

[33] H. P1; Garin, 180.

[34] H. 2.3; Garin, 232: "Sed cur tacet de reliquis, quem tractaturum de omnibus sufficienter et docte in prooemiis nostris promittamus?"

[35] H. P1; Garin, 180: "Neque enim minus ille aut debuit aut potuit aut voluit iuvare doctos quam indoctos."

eminent: that Jupiter and Mars are included by the sun, and Venus and Mercury by the moon.[36]

These "ancient Hebrews" are not named: it is, after all, a "mystery", and as Pico remarked in the first proem things which are not hidden are not mysteries.[37] Although they themselves do not give reasons for their doctrine, *ratio* will shine a light on the obscurity which they have left behind them.[38] Pico considers the qualities of the planets and forms them into two groups. Jupiter, Mars and the sun all have the quality of 'heat'; its effect is beneficent in Jupiter, violent in Mars and mingled between these two extremes in the sun. The sun therefore unites the contraries and maintains the common properties of the other two. A similar procedure is followed for the moon, which includes the properties of both Mercury and Venus.[39] Pico concludes:

> Moses has so far spoken about the heavenly empyrean, the ninth sphere, the firmament [i.e., fixed stars], about the planet Saturn, and about the sun and the moon, which comprehend the others—reminding us sufficiently of this comprehension by his very silence.[40]

Following this discussion of the nature of the planets, he proceeds to examine their actions, which he describes as motion and illumination. Motion is twofold: the entire group of heavenly spheres (except obviously the empyrean) turns over a period of twenty-four hours, and the individual spheres follow their own particular motions. Principal among these motions is that of the sun, which circles the signs of the Zodiac in twelve months.[41] As for illumination, this is either

---

[36] H. 2.3; Garin, 234: "Altius credo latere mysterium veteris Hebraeorum disciplinae, inter cuius de caelo dogmata hoc est praecipuum: concludi a Sole, Iovem et Martem; a Luna vero Venerem et Mercurium."

[37] See Ch. 4, n. 10.

[38] H. 2.3; Garin, 234: "Nec si horum naturas siderum pensitemus, obscura est ratio opinionis quamquam ipsi rationem nullam sui dogmatis afferant."

[39] Ibid., 234–236: "Calet Iuppiter, calet Mars, calet et Sol, sed Martis calor acer et violentus, Iovis beneficus, in Sole et acre illud et violentum, Martis et Iovis beneficam proprietatem videmus ... . Veniamus ad Lunam, quae et aquis Mercurii manifeste participat, et quantam habeat cum Venere affinitatem praesertim hinc indicat quod ita in Tauro, Veneris domicilio sublimatur, ut nusquam felicior aut magis benefica iudicetur."

[40] Ibid., 236: "De caelo igitur empyreo, de nono orbe, de firmamento, de sidere Saturni, deque Sole ac Luna qui reliqua complectuntur, ipso silentio huius complexus nos admonens, sufficienter hactenus dixit."

[41] H. 2.4; Garin, 236: "Restabat ut postquam de natura siderum dixerat de operibus deque eorum officio dissereret, declarans in quem usum fundata et cui muneri delegata a Deo fuerint. ... Caelestium corporum duae in universum manifestae operationes: motus et illuminatio. Motus duplex statuitur: alter mundi totius ..."

limited to light alone, or to light and heat, or to "many and multiple other forces". Pico passes over doctrinal disputes on this matter; regardless of whether one follows the authority of Aristotle, Avicenna or Averroes, their words (correctly interpreted) are in accord with the words of Moses.[42]

The next section deals with the constellations. Following common contemporary practice, these are divided into two groups: the visible constellations, situated in the eighth sphere, and the "invisible, but much more powerful" constellations of the ninth sphere.[43] The final element of the heavens is their possession of a rational soul.[44] The exposition ends with a warning by Pico that we should not regard ourselves as lower than the heavenly bodies, for, on the authority of Plato and unnamed theologians, our souls were mixed in the same bowl as them; nor should we fear, love and honour them rather than Christ.[45]

---

alterum siderum proprius, multiplex et varius, inter quos principalis est motus solis … . Ille diem facit, unde et diurnus dicitur; hic autem annum; reliqui siderum motus variis temporum intervallis peraguntur."

[42] Ibid., 236–238: "Quamquam autem diversae sint sententiae veterum, quid caelestia influant inferioribus, in quamlibet tamen apte cadunt Moseos verba; nam, si nihil aliud influunt quam lucem, quod videtur Aristoteles voluisse, si religiose et non pro nostro arbitrio illius verba interpretemur, nihil poterit cogitari Mosaicis dictis convenientius; si praeter lucem calorem etiam influunt, nihilque praeterea aliud, ut Averrois Arabs et Abraam Iudaeus volunt, satis fuit dixisse de luce a qua idem auctores provenire calorem fatentur. Si item plures aliae virtutes atque multiplices isthuc caelitus demittuntur, ut Avicennae, ut Babyloniis visum, non temere de sola luce mentio facta, quando, ut ipse scribit Avicenna, sola est lux quae reliquas omnes virtutes de caelo vehit ad nos."

[43] H. 2.5; Garin, 238: "Reliquum erat ut et signorum quae spectabilia sunt in Zodiaco et eorum quae, quamquam invisa nobis, longe tamen efficaciora in caelo sunt crystallino, mentionem faceret." The visible sidereal zodiac, located in the eighth sphere, was commonly opposed to the invisible tropical zodiac of the ninth. Astrology concerned itself only with the latter, hence Pico's reference to the "more powerful" signs of the crystalline sphere, which, unlike some contemporary thinkers, he conflates with the *primum mobile* (see my comments in Ch. 5, section 1.1).

[44] H. 2.6; Garin, 240.

[45] H. 2.7; Garin, 242–244: "Nobilis haec creatura et nobis suspicienda et celebranda; sed, si vel platonicae sententiae, ut theologos taceam, cuius modo meminimus, non sumus obliti, temperatos animos nostros ab opifice Deo in eodem cratere ex iisdemque elementis cum caelestibus animis [Timaeus 41 d], videamus ne nos illorum servos velimus, quos nos fratres esse natura voluit. … Cavendum igitur ne, quod multi faciunt, plus caelo dantes, plus tribuentes quam sit necesse, et voluntati opificis et ordini universi repugnemus, simulque ipsi caelo, cui Dei consilia et mundi ordo maxime cordi sunt, dum studere placemus, displiceamus. Hoc admonent Chaldaei dicentes: 'Ne augeas fatum'. Hoc praedicat Hieremias: 'Ne timeatis, inquit, signa caeli, quae gentes timent' [Jeremiah 10.2]. Hoc praecipit alibi Propheta noster, admonens cavendum homini ne suspiciens solem lunam et stellas colat ea quae

3. *Third Exposition:* De mundo angelico et invisibili

From consideration of the celestial spheres Pico ascends to contemplation of the intellectual world above them.[46] He had initially intended to provide two expositions of the angelic world, one based on the teachings of the Jews, the other on Pseudo-Dionysius, but for reasons of space and time has decided to concentrate on the latter alone. He plans to devote another book to the Jewish doctrine, in which he will sift those elements of their teaching which are in accordance with the Catholic faith from those which are not.[47] The third exposition will therefore concentrate on Dionysius.[48]

The exposition begins with an analysis of the relationship between *unitas* and *numerus*. The latter is dependent on the former; the former depends only on itself.[49] This philosophy of number is then applied to the relationship between God and creation, which, Pico says, is a Pythagorean technique.[50] For unity—"which is from nothing, from which all things are"—he substitutes God.[51] Just as *numerus* depends on *unitas*, angels depend on God.[52] How does

---

Deus creavit in ministerium cunctis gentibus [Deuteronomy 17.3] ... . Illum igitur timeamus, amemus et veneremur in quo, ut inquit Paulus [Coloss. 1.16], creata sunt omnia, sive visibilia sive invisibilia; quod est principium in quo fecit Deus caelum et terram: hoc autem est Christus." For the citation of the Chaldeans, see *Oracles chaldaiques avec un choix de commentaires anciens*, ed. E. des Places (Paris: Les Belles Lettres, 1971), 90–91 (frag. 103).

[46] H. 3.P; Garin, 246: "Nunc autem quis dabit mihi pennas sicut columbae, pennas deargentatas et rutilas pallore auri? Et volabo insuper caelestem regionem, ubi vera est quies, vera pax, vera tranquillitas, pax utique quam hic visibilis et corporeus dare non potest. Revelate vos oculos meos, ultramundani spiritus, et contemplabor miracula vestrae civitatis ..."

[47] Ibid., 246–248.

[48] Ibid., 248: "Interea, Dionysii vestigiis insistentes, aut Pauli potius et Hierothei, quos ille est sequutus, conabimur tenebris legis, quas auctor legis Spiritus Dei posuit suum latibulum, pro nostra imbecillitate, lucem invehere." Pseudo-Dionysius refers to his 'teacher', Hierotheus, on several occasions, although the existence of this person has been doubted. See Pseudo-Dionysius, *Complete Works*, tr. C. Luibheid (New York: Paulist Press, 1987), 69 n. 128.

[49] H. 3.1; Garin, 248: "Quicquid est post unitatem numerus, unitate perfectus et consummatus est. Sola unitas, omnino simplex, a se perfecta, non egreditur se, sed individua simplicitate et solitaria sibi cohaeret quia superest sibi, nullius indiga, plena suis divitiis."

[50] Ibid.: "Transferamus haec ad divina, more pythagorico."

[51] Ibid.: "Solus Deus, qui a nullo, a quo sunt omnia, simplicissima essentia et individua est; quicquid habet, a se habet; eadem re qua est, eadem sapit, eadem vult, eadem bonus, eadem iustus."

[52] Ibid., 248–250: "Igitur angelus non est ipsa unitas, alioquin Deus esset, aut plures essent Dei, quod concipi ne potest quidem. Quid enim erit unum sin ipsa

this identification of angels and numbers help to define the nature of the former? "Every number," he says, "is imperfect insofar as it is a multiplicity, but perfect insofar as it is unity."[53] This interplay between perfection (through participation in unity) and imperfection (through multiplicity) is used as the definition of the nature of angels in general.[54] An angel is imperfect in two aspects. Regarding "essence", it is not "being itself", but only "an essence to which being comes by participation, so that *it may be*". Regarding cognition, it is not, in itself, *intellectio*, but "it happens to it that it understands".[55]

Pico's reading of the first day, spread over chapters one and two, concerns the drama of the angel overcoming this double imperfection.[56] Chapter one deals with the question of its essence. Earth refers to the angel's "rough and unformed essence, deprived of life and being".[57] Heaven is the "acting of its essence and the participation of unity in multiplicity", in other words, its connection to *ipsum esse*.[58] Chapter two turns to its cognition. The angel has an intellectual capacity but needs to be given intelligible forms to fulfil its function of contemplation.[59] The absence of such forms is expressed by the shadows on the face of the abyss—the abyss being the angel's

---

quidem unitas una? Reliquum ut angelus numerus sit." Another discussion of the dependency of all creation on God is found in Pseudo-Dionysius, *Corpus Dionysiacum*, II, ed. G. Heil and A.M. Ritter (Berlin: De Gruyter, 1991), 20 (*De caelesti hierarchia*, 177B), immediately preceding the discussion of the hierarchies of angels.

[53] H. 3.1; Garin, 250: "Est autem omnis numerus eatenus imperfectus quatenus multitudo, perfectus autem quatenus unus." On the idea that every number "participates unity", see Proclus, *Elements of Theology*, ed. and tr. E.R. Dodds (Oxford: Clarendon Press, 1933, repr. 1964), 2–3 (Proposition 1).

[54] H. 3.1; Garin, 250: "Quare quicquid in angelo imperfectum est, angelicae multitudini quam inde habet unde est numerus, idest creatura, et quicquid perfectum est, accedenti unitati, quam inde habet unde Deo coniungitur, adscribamus."

[55] Ibid.: "Imperfectionem in angelo duplicem invenimus: alteram, quia non est ipsum esse, sed essentia tantum cui participatu esse accidit ut sit; alteram, quia non est ipsa intellectio, sed advenit ei ut intelligat, cum ipse sua natura intellectus sit intelligentiae capax."

[56] Ibid.: "Quemadmodum autem duplex est imperfectio, quasi duplex multitudo, ita duplicem intelligamus unitatis accessum ut utraque perficiatur."

[57] Ibid.: "Prima ea est, qua est essentia rudis ac informis expers vitae et esse, haec est terra inanis et vacua".

[58] Ibid.: "simul cum terra creavit et caelum, idest actum illius essentiae participatamque unitatem in multitudine, hoc est ipsum esse".

[59] H. 3.2; Garin, 252: "Est angelus, per ea quae diximus, iam suam naturam perfecte adeptus intellectualemque proprietatem; verumtamen nondum habet unde sua munera impleat, intelligendi scilicet et contemplandi, nisi a Deo prius formis intellegibilibus vestiatur."

intellect.[60] These intelligible forms are represented by light; they are accidents of the angel's intellect and do not pertain to its essence.[61] Nonetheless, the bond which links these forms to the angelic intellect is stronger than the equivalent bond between forms and the human intellect. This is made clear in the exegesis of the conjunction of morning and evening which makes "one day" (Genesis 1.5):

> There was from evening and morning one day, because, as Averroes proved, from the intellect and the intelligible is made a greater 'one' than from matter and form; because, as he himself affirms and as Maimonides also writes, the truth is perceived far more in angels than in men. Leaving aside these writers, let this reason be enough for us: that the forms are united to the angelic mind with an indivisible bond—not, as happens in the human intellect, with a vague and ordinary one—and with unbroken entwinings.[62]

Once these matters have been dealt with, the simpler question of the division of the angels into ranks is approached.[63] Pico follows Pseudo-Dionysius by dividing the angelic hierarchy into three groups; he represents these by the two groups of waters and the firmament.[64] The lowest of these groups of angels have one goal, which is to assist man.[65] With their help, the dry land—which Pico here takes to refer

---

[60] Ibid.: "Propterea adhuc sunt tenebrae super faciem abyssi. Abyssus intellectualis proprietas est, profunda quaeque penetrans et perscrutans."

[61] Ibid.: "Super hanc tenebrae sunt, donec spiritalium notionum, quibus omnia videt et intuetur, radiis non illustratur. ... Lux autem, idest species intelligibiles faciem tenent, idest extrema angelici intellectus, quia accidentes ei sunt qualitates, non ad ipsius essentiam spectant."

[62] Ibid., 254: "fuit ex vespere et mane dies unus, quia, ut probavit Averrois, ex intellectu et intelligibili fit magis unus quam ex materia et forma, quod, ut idem affirmat et scribit etiam Moses Aegyptius [i.e. Maimonides], longe magis in angelis quam in homine verum deprehenditur. Cuius ut illos omittamus, haec nobis satis sit ratio, quod species angelicae menti individua copula, non ut humano intellectui accidit vaga et translatitia, perpetuis nexibus uniuntur."

[63] H. 3.3; Garin, 254: "Videamus nunc quo inter se ordine angelici exercitus distinguuntur."

[64] Ibid.: "Legimus autem positum firmamentum in medio aquarum, ubi tres nobis angelicae hierarchiae (sic enim eas semper usitato vocabulo appellabimus) indicantur. ... Quae omnia, si naturam trium hierarchiarum et officia pensitemus, consonare Dionysii doctrinae magis nequeant." See Pseudo-Dionysius, *Corpus Dionysiacum*, II, ed. Heil and Ritter, 26 (*De caelesti hierarchia*, 200D).

[65] H. 3.4; Garin, 256: "Unde possumus intelligere subcaelestes has aquas, idest angelicos exercitus, ad unum locum, ad unius scilicet hominis bonum salutemque procurandam congregatos, pro qua et mittuntur ad nos et nunc secundum quietem, nunc etiam vigilantibus nobis aliis atque aliis et formis et locis et temporibus apparent."

to man's soul—will bear fruit.[66] The middle group are charged with
the administration of the celestial spheres, while the highest group
are engaged only in contemplation.[67] The final chapter addresses
the question of the relationship of angels to humans, and states that
Christ, though a man, was superior to the angels.[68]

4. *Fourth Exposition:* De mundo humano idest de hominis natura

The fourth exposition begins with the assertion that all the details
in the creation narrative which Pico has so far related to the three
worlds can also be interpreted as referring to man himself.[69] To
do this requires a philosophical framework for understanding what
man is.[70] Chapter one identifies three fundamental parts of man: the
body, the rational soul, and the *spiritus*, a fine corporeal substance
which links these two extremes and provides a conduit for the soul's
virtues to pass into the body. These are represented by earth, heaven
and light respectively.[71] In chapter two, further intermediate parts

---

[66] Ibid., 258–260: "Quare et quid sibi velit illa aquarum collectio, statim Moses
intulit ut terra det fructum, herbas, plantas et arbores. Quae autem haec terra
est praeter eam de qua scriptum in Evangelio quod alia quidem affert fructum
centesimum, alia sexagesimum, alia trigesimum? Terra utique animi nostri ..." The
citation of the Gospel is Matt. 13.8. Pico notes that, like many previous commentators,
he does not treat *caelum* as synonymous with *firmamentum*, nor *terra* with *arida*.
H 3.4; Garin 260: "Nec miretur quispiam aliud caelum nobis et terram primo die
significare, aliud nunc firmamentum et aridam, id quod etiam in superioribus libris
observavimus, quando et Basilius et Origenes et plerique alii volunt aliud esse apud
Mosem caelum et terram primo die, aliud aridam et firmamentum die secundo."

[67] H. 3.5; Garin, 260–262: "Diximus de ultima hierarchia delegata curandis
rebus quae sunt sub luna, idest humanis. Nunc de media agitur, cui caelestium
administratio demandata. Neque erit de tertia similiter expectandum ut dicat, de qua
discendum nihil praeter ea quae dicta sunt, esse scilicet eam super caelos, idest super
omnem actionis motum, supraque rerum omnium mundanarum administrationem,
contemplationi tantum addita."

[68] H. 3.6–7; Garin, 264–266.

[69] H. 4.P; Garin, 266–268: "hoc re ipsa comprobaturi: nullam esse in universo
hoc opere orationem, quae uti de tribus mundis, de quibus actum superius, ita de
hominis etiam natura reconditos sensus et veritates altissimas non complectatur."

[70] H. 4.1; Garin, 270: "Priusquam iuxta verba ordinemque Prophetae expositionem accuratius digeramus, oportet praefari aliqua de hominis natura obiterque
dictiones aliquas exponere".

[71] Ibid., 270–272: "Constat homo ex corpore et anima rationali. Rationalis animus
caelum dicitur ... . Corpus dicitur terra, quoniam terrosa et gravis substantia est.
... Verum inter terrenum corpus et caelestem animi substantiam opus fuit medio
vinculo, quod tam distantes naturas invicem copularet; huic muneri delegatum illud

of man are introduced, corresponding to the two groups of waters. Below the rational soul there is a "sensual part", which is shared with animals; above the rational soul, there is "intelligence", which is shared with angels.[72] The Spirit of God, which moves over the upper waters, is identified with "a greater and more divine intellect" which illuminates the human intellect.[73]

The third chapter looks at the "sensual powers", represented by the lower group of waters and previously identified as lying between the rational soul and the body. They are identified as the five senses, which flow towards the single "common sense" located by Aristotle in the heart, and their function is to give life and nourishment to the body.[74]

In the fourth chapter Pico discusses "rational nature" in more detail. Referring obscurely to a "great controversy" between himself and certain unnamed "recent philosophers", he denies the possibility that the sun represents the "intellect which is in actuality", and the moon, the "potential intellect". Rather, he takes the two appellations to refer to a double aspect of the one human intellect: it can either turn upwards, towards the "greater intellect" (previously identified

---

tenue et spiritale corpusculum, quod et medici et philosophi spiritum vocant ... ; hic lux nuncupatur ... . Accedit quod, quemadmodum omnis caelorum virtus (ut scribit Avicenna) vehiculo lucis ad terram transfertur, ita omnis animi virtus quem caelum vocavimus, omnis potestas, vita scilicet, motus et sensus, lucido spiritu intercedente, ad hoc corpus terrenum, quod terram vocavimus, comeat et transfunditur."

[72] H. 4.2; Garin, 274: "Nam inter partem rationalem, qua homines sumus, et omne illud quod corporeum est in nobis, sive sit crassum sive sit tenue et spiritale, media est pars sensualis, qua brutis communicamus, et quoniam non minor nobis cum angelis quam cum brutis communicatio, quemadmodum infra rationem est sensus unde commercium cum animalibus, ita supra rationem intelligentia est, per quam dicere illud Ioannis possumus 'societas nostra cum angelis est'." The citation of John appears to be an imprecise reference to 1 John 1.3, "societas nostra sit cum Patre, et cum Filio eius Jesu Christo".

[73] H. 4.2; Garin, 274–276: "Intellectum enim, qui est in nobis, illustrat maior atque adeo divinus intellectus sive sit Deus (ut quidam volunt), sive proxima homini et cognata mens, ut fere omnes Graeci, ut Arabes, ut Hebraeorum plurimi volunt." See Ch. 6, section 2.

[74] H. 4.3; Garin, 276: "Restat ut exponamus quid sit quod ait aquas quae sunt sub caelo, idest sensuales vires quae sub parte sunt rationali, congregari ad locum unum. ... Nam sensitivae omnes virtutes ad sensum quem ex re ipsa vocamus communem (hic autem si Aristotelem sequimur est in corde), uti flumina ad mare confluunt. Nec absurde dixerimus ab eo mari quinque corporis sensus quos videmus: auditum, visum, gustum, tactum, olfactum ... et quoniam ex perfectione sensitivarum virium, quam ex hac ad suum fontem collectione intelligimus, corpori quod vocamus terram et vita et nutrimentum provenit". For the reference to Aristotle, see, e.g., *Parva naturalia*, 469a.

with the "Spiritus Domini"), or downwards, towards the "sensual powers".[75] This latter occurence, which Pico identifies with the moon, dominates man's earthly life. The moon's coexistence with the stars illustrates the limits of the human intellect as it tries to know through "combining and dividing, reasoning and defining". The sun, on the other hand, represents the clearer knowledge that will be available to man after death.[76]

Chapters five and six turn from the cognitive aspects of the soul to the sensual ones. Pico identifies two sorts of sensual desire: one stemming from the body, the other from "the inner sense which philosophers call *phantasia*". The former covers the impulses for food and sex, the latter, for "fame, anger, revenge" and so on, which are necessary in moderation but to which humans tend in excess.[77] The curbing of these necessary but dangerous appetites is

---

[75] H. 4.4; Garin, 278: "Hoc est quod scribit posita in firmamento lunam solem et stellas; et quidem philosophi iuniores solem intellectum qui actu est, lunam eum qui est potentia forte interpretarentur; sed quoniam nobis magna de hac re cum illis controversia, nos interim sic exponamus ut qua parte ad aquas superiores, ad Domini Spiritum animus vergit, propterea quod totus lucet, sol nuncupetur; qua vero aquas inferiores, idest sensuales potentias respicit, unde infectionis aliquam contrahit maculam, lunae habeat appellationem." See Ch. 6, section 2.

[76] Ibid., 278–280: "Quoniam autem, dum a patria peregrinamur et in hac vitae praesentis nocte et tenebris vivimus, ea parte plurimum utimur quae ad sensus deflectitur, unde et plura opinamur quam scimus, cum vero dies futurae vitae illuxerit, alieni a sensibus ad divina conversi, superiori alia parte intelligemus, recte est dictum hunc nostrum solem praeesse diei, lunam autem praeesse nocti. Itidem quia exuti nos moribundam hanc vestem, unico solis lumine id contuebimur quod in hac corporis miserrima nocte plurimis viribus atque potentiis videre potius conamur quam videamur, idcirco unico sole dies lucescit; nox contra plurimas stellas, componendi scilicet vim et dividendi, ratiocinandi item definiendi, et quae sunt reliquae, lunae, quasi minus potenti, auxiliares corrogat et counit."

[77] H. 4.5; Garin, 280–284: "Hactenus de viribus animi cognoscentibus. Nunc ad eas se transfert, quorum opus appetere, irae videlicet et libidinis, idest concupiscentiae, sedes. Has per bestias designat et irrationale genus viventium ... . Alia ab aquis, quae sunt sub caelo, alia a terra producuntur. ... Consideremus igitur an, ex affectibus quibus movemur, alii ad corpus, alii ad sensum interiorem, quem phantasiam vocant philosophi, magis attineant. Ad corpus spectare mihi videntur qui vel ad cibum vel ad venerem impellunt ... . Ad aquas autem, idest sensum imaginationis, affectiones illas referamus, quae spiritales magis et nostrae potius cogitationis quam carnis soboles dici possunt; quod genus sunt quae ad honores, ad iram, ad ultionem, et cognatas his reliquas affectiones nos vocant; necessaria haec et utilia modice utentibus ... . Bona igitur illa omnia et homini necessaria, sed nos inde ad ambitionem, furorem, excandescentiam superbiamque excedentes, mala facimus nostra culpa quae Ille optimus optima instituerat."

the work of the rational soul.[78] In the final chapter, Pico portrays the intercession of Christ as a reversal of the action of the first man, Adam.[79]

5. Fifth Exposition: De omnibus mundis divisim ordine consequenti

At the outset of the fifth exposition, Pico writes that he will now dedicate the first "particula" (in other words, the section concerned with the account of the first day) to the first world (that is, the angelic) and the other parts to the other worlds, in succession.[80] The first four expositions presented self-contained bodies of knowledge drawn from the three worlds and man and including physics, astronomy, metaphysics and psychology. In the fifth exposition Pico promises to observe, in Moses's words, "that golden chain of Homer, the rings of Plato hanging from the living power of the fabricator, as if from the true stone of the unconquered Hercules".[81] In other words, he will now focus on the vertical hierarchy of the cosmos as a whole.

The fifth exposition opens with an account of angelic cognition. The comparison of the eye and the mind serves as an example of the correspondences inherent in the cosmos: "To talk about the angelic nature, which is pure intellect, let us first consider that minds are somehow like eyes; the eye, in corporeal things, is the same as the mind in spiritual things."[82] As light entering the eye makes it possible to see colours, so "forms and ideas of things" must enter the intellect for it to be able to perceive intelligible truth.[83] Pico notes that the

---

[78] H. 4.6; Garin, 284: "Sic etenim a natura institutus homo, ut ratio sensibus dominaretur, frenareturque illius lege omnis tum irae tum libidinis furor et appetentia".

[79] H. 4.7; Garin, 286: "Verum sicut omnes in primo Adam, qui oboedivit Sathanae magis quam Deo cuius filii secundum carnem, deformati ab homine degeneramus ad brutum, ita in Adam novissimo Iesu Christo ... reformati per gratiam regeneramur ab homine in adoptione filiorum Dei".

[80] H. 5.P; Garin, 286–288: "Quod ostensuri incipiemus primam particulam de primo mundo, idest angelico, interpretari, tum deinceps reliquas de reliquis ..."

[81] Ibid., 288: "auream illam homericam catenam et platonicos anulos a viva opificis virtute, quasi a vero lapide indomiti Herculis appensos, in Moseos verbis sagaciter speculantes". The image of the golden chain ultimately derives from Iliad, VII, 19–20. It was used by Plato in Theaetetus, 153C–D; see Garin, 288 for other references. See Ch. 5, n. 85.

[82] H. 5.1; Garin, 288: "Dicturi autem de natura angelica, quae purus est intellectus, id primum animo concipiamus, mentes esse quasi oculos quosdam; quod enim est oculus in rebus corporeis, id ipsum est mens in genere spiritali."

[83] Ibid.: "Oculus, etsi mixtura suae substantiae intimae aliquid lucis possideat,

precise details of angelic cognition are not entirely agreed on, but that it somehow involves a combination of actuality and potentiality.[84] These two aspects are represented in the Genesis narrative by heaven and earth respectively.[85]

In the second chapter, he turns to the celestial world and its role as mediator between the angelic world and the sublunary world.[86] In the third chapter, looking at the sublunary world, he discusses the laws which hold the elements in their place, preventing (for example) the seas from overwhelming the earth. This is attributed not to any intrinsic force of the elements themselves but strictly to their adherence to their final cause, that is, to God.[87] This emphasis on the *dependence* of the universe on its creator reiterates the initial description of the chain of Homer.

Two brief sections follow, on the stars (criticizing astrology) and on the generation of the animals, before Pico turns to the matter which will occupy the remainder of this exposition, and set the tone for the next two: the dignity of man. The entirety of the sixth chapter is reminiscent of the *Oratio*.[88] Pico begins by reminding us that man

ut visionis tamen munere fungatur externa indiget luce, in qua rerum colores et differentias speculatur. ... Intellectus oculi sunt, intelligibilis veritas lumen est, et intellectus ipse intelligibilis cum sit intimae aliquid lucis habet, qua se ipsum potest videre, sed non potest et reliqua. Verum indiget formis ideisque rerum quibus, uti radiis quibusdam invisibilis lucis, intelligibilis veritas indubie cernitur."

[84] Ibid., 290: "Oculus, idest substantia intellectualis, non omnino est simplex, alioquin adventantis lucis compositionem non pateretur. Hinc commune proloquium, constare angelos ex actu et potentia, quamquam anxia est disputatio quid ille actus quid illa potentia et quae ratio compositionis, quid idem Averrois Arabs voluerit cum utrumque intellectum, et eum qui actu et eum qui potentia est, in omnibus citra Deum intellectibus esse dixerit; sed sufficit nobis, quantum attinet ad locum, communis sententia utcumque accipiatur."

[85] Ibid.: "Partitur enim substantiam angeli in caelum et terram, naturam scilicet actus et naturam potentiae."

[86] H. 5.2; Garin, 292: "Huic mundo proximus est caelestis, cuius illa prima proprietas quod interstitium est utriusque mundi, intelligibilis scilicet, de quo nunc diximus, et sensibilis huius, quem nos incolimus."

[87] H. 5.3; Garin, 294: "Nihil est enim quod magis indicet esse in elementis, praeter corporeae brutaeque naturae inclinationem, inditas leges ab intelligente causa, a qua et reguntur et suis in sedibus detinentur, quam haec aquarum repagula, quibus coercitus Oceanus, cuius ad totum se terrae ambitum impetus ferret, quemadmodum ignis totus toti aeri incubat, quasi tamen virga admonitus pedagogi pedem refert, nec se ulterius profert quam nostra salus et vita omnium animantium postulat. Hoc neque ad materiae necessitatem, quae ad globi figuram omnia potius elementa pariter inclinat; nec ad fortuitum atomorum concursum ... nec ad vim seminariam naturae mutae ... sed ad solam finalem causam, ad quam dirigere solius est mentis et providentiae intellectualis."

[88] Among verbal and thematic echoes, note especially the placing of man in the

was created in God's image; the question he addresses in this chapter
is what this means and how the unique godliness of man is to be
comprehended.[89] Firstly, he rejects the notion that God and man
share physical form; secondly, he argues that their similarity cannot
be predicated on the action of mind, since in this sense there is a
closer affinity between angels and God than between man and God.[90]
Instead, he concludes that the unique affinity between man and God
derives from the way in which man's "substance" has bound up within
it, *in itself* ("re ipsa") "the substances of all natures and the fullness
of the entire universe".[91] By "in itself" he means to distinguish this
essential quality of man from the accidental way in which angels and
other intelligent creatures can be said to "contain" things when they
manage to "know" them.[92] Man and God, then, share an analogous
action which belongs to no other creature: in their own way, each
unites the different parts of the universe.[93] The difference in how they
do this is that God contains all things through being their *principium*,
man through being their *medium*; God contains all things but of
better quality than they are in themselves, whereas man contains

---

midpoint of the world (H. 5.6; Garin, 300–302. *Oratio*; Garin, 104) and the Hermetic
citation (H. 5.6; Garin, 304: "Magnum, o Asclepi, miraculum est homo". *Oratio*;
Garin, 102).

[89] H. 5.6; Garin, 302: "Sed ardua est quaestio cur hoc privilegium sit hominis,
imaginem habere Dei."

[90] Ibid.: "Nam si Melitonis explosa insania, qui humana effigie Deum figuravit, ad
rationis mentisque naturam recurramus, quae uti Deus intelligens est invisibilis item
et incorporea, inde utique comprobabimus esse hominem similem Deo, praesertim
qua parte in animo Trinitatis imago representatur. Verum agnoscemus haec eadem,
quanto in angelis sunt quam in nobis et potiora et contrariae minus naturae admixta,
tanto cum divina natura plus similitudinis et cognationis habentia." Melito of Sardis
(2nd century) was believed through some sources to have maintained a doctrine of
divine corporeality; see, e.g., the exegetical fragment on Genesis 1.26, attributed
to Origen, in F. Petit, *Catenae graecae in Genesim et in Exodum, II. Collectio Coisliniana
in Genesim* (Turnhout: Brepols, 1986), item 73; cf. Origen, *Selecta in Genesim*, in
Patrologiae graecae cursus completus, ed. Migne, XII, 93A.

[91] H. 5.6; Garin, 302: "Id quid esse aliud potest quam quod hominis substantia
(ut Graeci etiam aliqui interpretes innuunt) omnium in se naturarum substantias et
totius universitatis plenitudinem re ipsa complectitur?"

[92] Ibid.: "Dico autem re ipsa, quia et angeli et quaecumque creatura intelligens
in se quodammodo continet omnia, dum plena formis et rationibus omnium rerum
omnia cognoscit."

[93] Ibid.: "At vero quemadmodum Deus non solum ob id quod omnia intelligit,
sed quia in seipso verae rerum substantiae perfectionem totam unit et colligit, ita et
homo (quamquam aliter, ut ostendemus, alioquin non Dei imago, sed Deus esset) ad
integritatem suae substantiae omnes totius mundi naturas corrogat et counit. Quod
de nulla alia creatura, sive angelica, sive caelesti, sive sensibili, dicere possumus."

things that are higher on the chain of being than himself in an inferior quality, and things that are lower on it than he is, in a superior one.[94]

This discussion of man's dignity is complemented in the seventh chapter by an account of his duties: a moral perspective, introducing here a new dimension which will continue throughout the remainder of the work.

> Terrestrial things are subject to man, celestial things are well-disposed to man, because he is the bond and the link of both the celestial and the terrestrial things; both cannot but be in peace with him, provided he himself, who sanctions their peace and their pacts in himself, is at peace with himself.[95]

The moral behaviour of man, therefore, has an effect on the cosmos as a whole, and the cosmos, together with God, will revenge itself upon him if he does not fulfil his obligations.[96]

6. *Sixth Exposition:* De mundorum
inter se rerum omnium cognatione

The sixth exposition comprises two separate readings of the Genesis narrative: the first running from chapters one to four, and the second from chapters five to seven. It also suggests another way of looking at the structure of the *Heptaplus*, which is to divide it into three sections: the first five expositions, the sixth exposition and the seventh exposition. This structural division of the text takes its cue from Pico's understanding of the Trinity, the definition of which

---

[94] Ibid., 302–304: "Est autem haec diversitas inter Deum et hominem, quod Deus in se omnia continet uti omnium principium, homo autem in se omnia continet uti omnium medium; quo fit ut in Deo sint omnia meliore nota quam in seipsis, in homine inferiora nobiliore sint conditione, superiora autem degenerent."

[95] H. 5.7; Garin, 304: "Homini mancipantur terrestria, homini favent caelestia, quia et caelestium et terrestrium vinculus et nodus est, nec possunt utraque haec non habere cum eo pacem, si modo ipse secum pacem habuerit, qui illorum in se ipso pacem et foedera sancit."

[96] Ibid., 304–306: "At caveamus, quaeso, ne in tanta dignitate constitui non intelligamus, verum illud ante oculos semper animi habeamus, uti et certam, exploratam et indubiam veritatem, sicuti favent omnia nobis eam legem servantibus quae nobis est data, ita si per peccatum, per legis praevaricationem deorbita defecerimus, omnia adversa infesta inimicaque habituros. Rationabile enim ut quemadmodum non modo nobis, sed universo quod in nobis complectimur, sed auctori ipsius mundi omnipotenti Deo iniuriam facimus, experiamur etiam omnia quae in mundo sunt, et Deum in primis, potentissimos vindices et acceptae iniuriae gravissimos ultores."

constitutes the opening sentence of the sixth exposition: "God is unity, divided into three in such a way that he does not depart from the simplicity of unity."[97] There are, says Pico, many traces of the Trinity in creation, but he intends to concentrate on just one, which has not previously been discussed by anyone. This is the fact that each created thing has *three* different aspects of unity:

1. Each thing is united with itself.[98]
2. Each thing is united with another thing; hence, eventually, all parts of the world are one world.[99]
3. Most importantly, the whole universe is united with its maker as an army is with its leader.[100]

These three aspects of unity are reflected in the structure of the *Heptaplus*, insofar as the first five expositions present the first aspect, the sixth presents the second aspect and the seventh presents the third aspect. The subject matter of the sixth exposition, then, is simply summarized as the unity "in which the different parts are joined together by a mutual alliance".[101] This theme is developed at the beginning of the second chapter. The first four expositions have shown "the distinct natures of things and their dispositions in separate positions". Having argued in the second proem that "each thing is contained by each thing according to the condition of its nature", Pico now wishes to demonstrate the way in which "the Prophet wanted to indicate, in his own context, what and how many ways there are by which the natures of things are mutually bonded among themselves". When we understand this, we should let ourselves be instructed by it in the "way and manner by which we may join ourselves to those things that are better than us".[102]

---

[97] H. 6.P; Garin, 308: "Deus unitas est ita ternario distincta ut ab unitatis simplicitate non discedat."

[98] Ibid., 310: "Est enim primum ea in rebus unitas, qua unumquodque sibi est unum sibique constat atque cohaeret."

[99] Ibid.: "Est ea secundo, per quam altera alteri creatura unitur et per quam demum omnes mundi partes unus sunt mundus."

[100] Ibid.: "Tertia atque omnium principalissima est, qua totum universum cum suo opifice quasi exercitus cum suo duce est unum."

[101] Ibid.: "Reliqua ea est qua diversae partes mutuo foedere invicem copulantur, de qua in praesentia a nobis agendum est."

[102] H. 6.1; Garin, 312: "Postquam igitur distinctas rerum naturas vidimus et separatis (ut ita dixerim) stationibus dispositas, ne crederemus idcirco tantum ex his omnibus unum fieri universum quia singula a singulis, ut supra ostendimus, pro suae naturae conditione contineantur, indicare in suo etiam contextu Propheta voluit, qui et quot modi essent, quibus naturae rerum inter se invicem copular-

The last sentence explains the rationale underlying the double nature of this exposition. The two interpretations each revolve around the notion of "copulare". The former aspect concerns knowledge; the latter, morality. I shall have more to say concerning the connection of the two in Chapter 6.

The first of these two parts of the exposition presents a universal taxonomy of logical and formal relationships between entities. According to "all the teachings of the philosophers", there are no more than fifteen such relationships.[103] The majority of these fifteen forms of "affinity" comprise subdivisions of three basic groups.

[A] "Five ways by which something can be joined to something else":

> What is joined to something, is either its essence, or a property of its essence, or is in it as a form is in a subject, or is connected to it either by changing that which is changed, or as an art is connected to the material subject to it.[104]

This subdivision corresponds to a reading of the narrative of day one, which exhibits five 'connections' or 'couplings': heaven and earth, earth and the void, darkness and the abyss, the spirit of God and the waters, and light and bodies.[105] The correspondence is worked out as follows:

1. A as essence of B: equivalent to relationship of the void and the earth, because matter (identified with the earth) is by nature void unless it is filled by a form coming from elsewhere.[106]
2. A as property of essence of B: equivalent to relationship of darkness and the abyss, because the abyss is not by nature

---

entur, *non solum ad curiosam hanc intelligentiam nos vocans, sed per hoc instruens et demonstrans, qua nos via et ratione his quae nobis sunt meliora copulari possimus.*" (My italics.)

[103] Ibid.: "Cogitanti autem mihi priusquam accederem ad verborum enarrationem, quot modi aut essent aut cogitari possent quibus res aliquae invicem vel affinitatem vel copulam nanciscerentur, et discurrenti per omnia dogmata philosophorum, quibus a puero insudavi, haud ultra quam quindecim occurrerunt."

[104] H. 6.2; Garin, 312: "Quod enim alteri coniunctum est, aut eius essentia est, aut est essentiae proprietas, aut inest ei ut forma subiecto, aut eum attingit vel sicut transmutans id quod transmutatur, vel sicut ars subiectam sibi materiam."

[105] There is no mention of "corpora" in the Genesis narrative, at this point or any other. Pico is stretching the text to enable his allegorical reading.

[106] H. 6.2; Garin, 314: "Primum igitur coniunctionis modum designat nobis terra inanis et vacua, quoniam terra, idest materia, sua natura inanis est, nisi aliunde formis adimpleatur."

either dark or light but is accompanied by darkness unless light intervenes.[107]

3. A as form to subject B: equivalent to relationship of light and bodies.[108]

4. A as efficient cause of B: equivalent to relationship of heaven and earth, because the heavens are not a form or an accident of earth but rather its efficient cause or "cause of change".[109]

5. A as art operating on material B: equivalent to the relationship of spirit and waters. The spirit is the wisdom of God, which has no connection to matter and therefore can only be joined to it in the way that the architect's mind is joined to stone and wood.[110]

[B] Parts and wholes

6. A part is inseparable from the whole, like the heavenly bodies in the firmament.

7. A part is separable from the whole, like the various parts of water from the whole into which they flow.[111]

[C] Causes and Effects

8. The effect has an intrinsic cause: equivalent to plants sprouting from the earth.[112]

9. The effect is the result of a mixture of its principles: equivalent to the composition of bodies of animals from water and earth.[113]

---

[107] Ibid.: "Secundum indicant tenebrae super faciem abyssi; nam abyssus sua quidem natura nec lucidus nec tenebrosus, sed illius tamen naturam tenebrae consequuntur nisi accedens lumen illas fugaverit, quemadmodum et materiae informitatem inanitatemque privationis tenebrae consequuntur, donec adveniens eas species expulerit."

[108] Ibid.: "Tertium ostendit lux oborta corporibus. Est enim in eis lux uti forma in subiecto."

[109] Ibid.: "Quartum, caelum et terra, quoniam non inhaeret terrae caelum uti forma vel accidens inest rei quam perficit, sed coniungitur ei uti efficiens patienti et transmutans causa corpori quod transmutatur."

[110] Ibid.: "Postremi exemplum est Spiritus Domini qui fertur super aquas. Artifiex enim Domini sapientia et spiritalis natura omnino abiuncta a commertio corporis, haud aliud iungi corporibus intelligitur quam ars, quae in mente est architecti, caemento lignis et lapidibus iungatur."

[111] H. 6.3; Garin, 316: "si est pars, aut pars individua est a suo toto, quo pacto et sol et luna et stellae in firmamento sunt, aut separabilis quemadmodum aquae partes ab integritate sui elementi ad quod confluxerunt."

[112] Ibid.: "... aut a seminaria ratione intrinseca pullulat, sicut plantae e terra pullulant, ipsi tamen suae parenti affixae et naturalibus vinculis ligamentisque connexae ..."

[113] Ibid.: "... aut ex suis principiis constat et conflatur, ut mixtum ex elementis, quo pacto ex aquis et terra animalium corpora fiunt ..."

10. The effect has an efficient, extrinsic cause: this is the manner in which God creates man.
11. The effect has an exemplary, extrinsic cause: this is the manner in which man is created in God's image.
12. The effect has a final, extrinsic cause: this is the manner in which animals are under man and are made on account of man as their end and purpose.[114]
13. The effect is operated on by a secondary or proximate cause, working under a more powerful primary cause. This is how it may be said that the waters produce fish, although they are really produced by God who is the primary cause.[115] Equally, it accounts for the double action of the stars, which is to shine (primarily) in the heavens and to illuminate (proximately) the earth.[116]

Two miscellaneous types of conjunction, which are in contradistinction to each other, complete the total of fifteen:

14. Species. Two men or two lions are related ("cognatus"), but not as part to whole or as effect to cause, unless specifically related by birth. This is exemplified in the Genesis narrative by the uniting of the birds and beasts.[117]
15. The mean. It does not share the same essence as the extremes from which it is composed but is some sort of compound from them. This is exemplified by the firmament, which is placed between the waters.[118]

---

[114] Ibid.: "... aut causam habet extrinsecam, quae trifariam dividi potest, in efficientem, exemplar et finem. Quorum trium exempla habemus a Mose, dum et hominem Deus creat, et efficit et creat ad suam imaginem tamquam ad exemplar, et bestiae homini subsunt fiuntque propter hominem ut propter finem."

[115] H. 6.4; Garin, 316–318: "Nam et de causa ea est reliqua species affinitatis, qua causa secundaria primariae oboedit et adiungitur, sicut cum Deus producit aquae producunt, et hae quidem primo quia proxima sunt causa, sed non aliter quam Deo praecipiente, quia causa primaria magis influit quam secunda."

[116] Ibid., 318: "Similiter est finis secundarius principali appendens et annexus, quod sapienter significat dicens posita sidera ut lucerent in caelo et illuminarent terram. Neque enim bonum inferiorum primarius finis est caelestium. Sed id primum intendunt, ut sibi luceant, tum postremo ut et nos illuminent."

[117] Ibid.: "Est item praeter haec omnia et homo homini et leo leoni cognatus, et tamen leo neque pars neque effectus leonis est, si ab illo genitus non sit. Hoc Propheta significat cum simul pisces, simul aves, simul bestias terrae colligit et adunat."

[118] Ibid.: "Nam convenit homo homini, animal animali, quia eamdem participant essentiae rationem, vel specialem vel generalem. At medium non eadem est essentia quam et extrema, sed temperatum quoquo modo ex illis ita ab utroque dissentit, ut cum utroque communicet. Quod indicatum nobis a Mose cum ponit firmamentum aquarum medium".

This taxonomy of relationships gives way, in the fifth chapter, to the second interpretation, concerned with the second notion of "copulare" mentioned above. Pico's subject here is how "we may unite with better things", leading to "total and highest power of our *felicitas*".[119] The necessary beginning of this journey is purification, as examples from all cultures—Christian, Greek, Indian, Persian—demonstrate. Man must turn to higher things through "holy religion, mysteries, vows, hymns, prayers and supplications".[120] The advice is directed particularly towards philosophers. If it is necessary for people in general to indulge in the aforesaid "mysteries, vows and hymns", how much more so it must be for those who "have devoted themselves to the study of letters and to the life of contemplation"; "for them, nothing is more necessary than that they repeatedly direct the eyes of their mind constantly towards the divine and purify them by integrity of life". The chief spur to this end is prayer.[121]

Having dealt with this matter, Pico warns the would-be philosopher, if his activity is to bear fruit, to avoid "the whirlpools and torrents of pleasure" which will otherwise distract him from his task.[122] He then alludes to a "deeper mystery": the eventual ("aliquando")

---

[119] H. 6.5; Garin, 318: "Admonemur autem et hinc quid facto opus sit nobis, ut naturis melioribus uniamur, in quo vis tota et summa posita est nostrae felicitatis."

[120] Ibid., 320: "profecto omne studium nostrum in eo esse debet ut conversi ad supera, quod sit per sacram religionem, per mysteria, per vota, per hymnos, preces et supplicationes, inde nostrae infirmitatis vires quaeramus. Hinc platonicae et pythagoricae disputationes a sacris precibus exorsae desinunt in easdem, quibus et Porphyrius et Theodorus et omnes Academici nihil utile magis, immo necessarium homini esse uno ore confirmant. Indorum Brachmanae et Magi Persarum nihil aggressi umquam leguntur, nisi oratione praemissa." Porphyry discusses the necessity of prayer in his *Letter to Marcella*: see *Lettre à Marcella*, ed. and tr. E. des Places (Paris: Les Belles Lettres, 1982). The philosopher Theodorus of Asine (4th century) is quoted on this matter in Proclus's *Commentary on the Timaeus*; see *In Platonis Timaeum commentaria*, ed. E. Diehl, 3 vols (Leipzig: B.G. Teubner, 1903–1906), I, 213.

[121] H. 6.5; Garin, 320: "neque ridendam neque inutilem neque indignam rem esse philosopho, operam sumere et quidem magnam atque assiduam in sacris precationibus, in mysteriis, in votis, in hymnis Deo iugiter decantandis. Quae res si quod hominum genus et iuvat maxime et decet, illis praesertim utilis et decora qui studiis literarum et contemplandi ocio se dederunt. Quibus nihil necessarium magis quam ut, quos in divina identidem mentis oculos intendunt, et vitae integritate depurent et petita per ferulam orationis desuper luce largius illuminent admonitique propriae semper imbecillitatis cum Apostolo dicant: 'sufficientia nostra ex Deo est' [2 Corinthians 3.5]."

[122] H. 6.6; Garin, 322: "Discamus a terra non edituros nos frugem quam parturimus nisi invadentis nos fluxae materiae atque caducae impetum represserimus depulerimusque, et e sedibus nostris exturbaverimus irruentium in nos, quasi aquarum, voluptatum gurgites et torrentes."

union of "that part of intellectual light which is in us" with "the first mind, where there is the plenitude and totality of all understanding".[123] Finally, in the seventh chapter, he turns to union with God himself, which is only to be accomplished through the intercession of Christ.[124] This last point serves to bind the two halves of the sixth exposition together. Christ is identified as the last of the "modi coniunctionis" enumerated in the first half: the mean. The mean, as described in chapter four, is something different from the two extremes, but it unites them both.[125] That description is reinforced here: it is

> the coupling of extremes, which cannot be achieved, except by that nature which, since it is in the middle of the extremes, including each of them in itself, unites them to each other appropriately, because in itself it united them previously through the property of its nature.[126]

It is Christ alone who combines man and God; therefore he alone can unite them.

This account serves as a preliminary to the main discussion of *felicitas* in the seventh exposition.

7. *Seventh Exposition:* De felicitate, quae est vita aeterna

The seventh exposition is concerned with *felicitas*. The proem starts by distinguishing two sorts, "natural" and "supernatural".[127] It goes on to discuss the relationship between them. Natural *felicitas* is when something attains God in *itself*; supernatural, when it attains God in *Himself*.[128] Natural *felicitas* is therefore limited by the nature of

---

[123] Ibid.: "Continetur autem et hic altius mysterium: quemadmodum scilicet guttis aquae ea est felicitas ut ad oceanum, ubi aquarum plenitudo, accedant, ita esse nostram felicitatem ut, quae in nobis intellectualis luminis portio est, ipsi primo omnium intellectui primaeque menti, ubi plenitudo, ubi universitas omnis intelligentiae, aliquando coniungatur."

[124] H. 6.7; Garin, 322–324.

[125] See n. 118 above.

[126] H. 6.7; Garin, 322: "Ita nos animo proponamus extremorum copulam non nisi per eam naturam fieri posse quae, media extremorum cum sit, utrumque in se complexa ideo illa, idest extrema, inter se commode unit, quia in se ipsa illa per proprietatem suae naturae prius univit."

[127] H. 7.P; Garin, 324–326: "Est autem felicitas (ut theologi praedicant) alia quam per naturam, alia quam per gratiam consequi possumus. Illam naturalem, hanc supernaturalem appellant."

[128] Ibid., 328: "Bonum hoc adipisci dupliciter possunt res creatae, aut in se ipsis, aut in ipso. Nam et in se ipso hoc bonum est super omnia exaltatum, suae

the thing in question.[129] This, in turn, has an adverse effect on the dignity of man, as "philosophers" have conceived of it. Although most schools of philosophy allow man some form of attainment of truth, none of them grants him a complete return "to his beginning or end", which only theology can offer.[130] Pico therefore asks us to "listen to the holy theologians, reminding us of our dignity".[131] What, then, is "supernatural" *felicitas*?

> The true and consummate *felicitas* carries us back and draws us to the perfect union with that beginning from which we emanated—for the purpose of gazing on the face of God, which is the whole good, as He Himself says.[132]

This capacity is limited to man and the angels;[133] neither man nor angel can progress to this level without the help of Christ.[134]

Within the remainder of the seventh exposition, however, the progression to supernatural *felicitas* is presented not in terms of a single individual's attainment but in terms of the whole of humanity. It is articulated as a journey through sacred history. The journey

---

inhabitans divinitatis abyssos et per omnia diffusum in omnibus invenitur, hic quidem perfectius, illic imperfectius, pro rerum conditione a quibus participatur." See also the reiteration, 332: "Diximus supra summam felicitatis in Dei esse adeptione, quod est summum bonum et principium omnium; dupliciter autem illam posse contingere, quoniam vel in creaturis, quibus se Deus participat, vel in ipso Deo Deum assequimur."

[129] Ibid., 330: "Qua propter et pro naturarum capacitate gradatim felicitatis ratio variatur."

[130] Ibid.: "De homine autem, etsi diversi diversa senserint, omnes tamen intra humanae facultatis angustias se tenuerunt, vel in ipsa tantum veri vestigatione, quod Academici, vel in adeptione potius per studia philosophiae, quod Alpharabius dixit, felicitatem hominis determinantes. Dare aliquid plus visi Avicenna, Averrois, Abubacher, Alexander et Platonici, nostram rationem in intellectu, qui actu est, aut aliquo superiore, nobis tamen cognato, quasi in suo fine firmantes, sed neque hi hominem ad suum principium nec ad suum finem adducunt." I discuss this passage in Ch. 6.

[131] H. 7.P; Garin, 332: "Audiamus igitur sacros theologos dignitatis nostrae nos admonentes".

[132] Ibid.: "Vera autem et consummata felicitas ad Dei faciem contuendam, quae est omne bonum, ut ipse dixit, et ad perfectam cum eo principio a quo emanavimus unionem nos revehit et adducit."

[133] Ibid., 334: "Ideoque solus homo et angelus ad eam sunt facti felicitatem, quae est vera felicitas."

[134] Ibid., 332–334: "Ad hanc angeli attolli quidem possunt, sed non possunt ascendere. ... Ad hanc ire homo non potest, trahi potest; unde Christus de se, qui est ipsa felicitas, dixit: 'Nemo venit ad me nisi Pater meus traxerit illum'." The quotation is from John 6.44. See also the role of Christ as mean, nn. 118 and 126 above, and H. 6.7 (Garin, 322–324).

starts with the Fall, from which man slowly returns via the imposition of the law by Moses, the coming of Christ and the continuing progress towards the heavenly Jerusalem. The central chapter of this exposition, the fourth, is taken up with the demonstration that Christ is the Messiah, based on a polemical reading of Jewish sources. The exposition ends with a vision of Christians taking possession of their inheritance as sons of God:

> Those who live in the Spirit, they are sons of God, they are brothers of Christ, they are destined for eternal inheritance, a reward for faith and for a life lived well which they will possess *feliciter* in the heavenly Jerusalem.[135]

8. *"Expositio primae dictionis, idest in principio"*

At this point the main body of the *Heptaplus* is complete. There follows, however, a final section in which Pico returns to the first word of the Bible—*bereshit* in Hebrew—which he has until now neglected. He also turns away from the allegorical method which he has applied to the preceding seven expositions to "another method of interpretation".[136] I shall discuss this in Chapter 7. For now, it must suffice to say that he adopts a technique of letter combination, derived from his reading of kabbalistic exegetical works, and uses it to construct a series of words from the single term *bereshit*. These words, put in order, produce a sentence which summarizes the *Heptaplus* as a whole. It is therefore further confirmation of his initial claim that everything can be discovered in Moses's text.

9. *Conclusion*

As we have seen throughout this chapter, the *Heptaplus* consists of an array of allegorical identifications between things mentioned in the Genesis account and things or concepts in a variety of philosophical disciplines. The selection of disciplines is broadly determined by Pico's cosmic model of three interlinked worlds, which will be dis-

---

[135] H. 7.7; Garin, 372: "Qui igitur Spiritu vivunt, ii sunt filii Dei, ii Christi fratres, ii destinati aeternae hereditati, quam mercedem et fidei et bene actae vitae in caelesti Hierusalem feliciter possidebunt."

[136] H. 50; Garin, 374: "Sed cogitamus, per aliam interpretandi rationem, gustum dare lectoribus mosaicae profunditatis."

cussed in Chapter 5. The allegorical identifications are constructed generally from previous example (*auctoritas*) or from *ratio*. By *ratio* Pico refers to patterns of similarity or analogy between the structure of the entities intrinsic to the Genesis account (heaven, earth, waters, etc.) and the structure of the entities or concepts extrinsic to it (causes, celestial spheres, relationship between body and soul etc.).

Distinct from this practice of allegorical reading, however, the *Heptaplus* also contains a *theory* of allegory. This theory, the way in which it relates to the work's form and content, and the way in which it relates to other theories of biblical allegory, is my subject of study.

CHAPTER THREE

EXEGETICAL CONTEXTS

Pico tells his audience that his work is unprecedented and that he has not derived his interpretations from previous commentators. In other words, he frames the *Heptaplus* in opposition to the various commentary traditions which preceded it. The purpose of this chapter is to determine what he was reacting against. This involves consideration of several contexts.

In the first section I outline the general state of the Latin commentary tradition in the fifteenth century. My intention here is to try to delineate the perspective of the 'average' reader of these works during this period. I therefore discuss hermeneutic methods and the ways in which these methods circulated. I also indicate the principal focal points of biblical commentary, as determined from publishing records: which commentaries had the widest reception and which books of the Bible were most commonly commented on.

In the second section I discuss Pico's own perspective on biblical interpretation. I examine his roll-call of significant exegetes and compare it to the 'typical' perspective outlined in the first section.

Finally, I compare his engagement with standard interpretative methods in the *Expositiones in Psalmos* with the lack of these methods in the *Heptaplus*.

1. *Biblical Interpretation in the Fifteenth Century*

Although the interpretative attitudes of the Middle Ages and the Reformation have been copiously documented, the fifteenth century, lying as it does between these two periods, has been less well served. To my knowledge, there is no comprehensive account of how the Bible was read at this time. My first task, therefore, is to give a brief outline of the state of exegetical theory, or, to put it another way, of the expectations (insofar as we can determine them) that an educated contemporary reader would have brought to an encounter with the *Heptaplus*.

In this respect I discuss two different attitudes to the biblical text. One is the medieval tradition of the four senses of Scripture, which, I argue, maintained its place as the dominant hermeneutic model during this period. A second approach can be seen in the humanistic interest in Greek and Hebrew philology. In the latter half of the fifteenth century it becomes possible to gauge which works were considered popular or important by seeing how soon and how often they were printed. Incunable catalogues, for this reason, offer us a snapshot of trends at the time Pico was writing.

1.1. *The Fourfold Method and its Reception*

Medieval readers of the Bible generally felt that its text contained more than one level of meaning. This impulse towards plurality, after many vicissitudes which need not be recounted here, eventually coalesced into a codification of four senses: the literal or historical, the allegorical, the moral or tropological and the anagogical.[1] Pico himself, in the *Apologia*, recognized that this was the normal Christian way of interpreting the Bible.[2] Two texts in particular contributed to the reception of the fourfold method: the *Glossa ordinaria* and the *Postilla* of Nicholas of Lyra.

The *Glossa* is a compilation of Latin patristic exegetical material, combining short interlinear and longer marginal notes, which was put in its standard form in the twelfth century.[3] The Franciscan Nicholas of Lyra completed his *Postilla super totam Bibliam* in 1331, and its sequel, the *Moralia*, in 1339. Broadly speaking, the *Postilla* is dedicated to literal explication and the *Moralia* to non-literal, although the prologues to the *Postilla* contain a general discussion of biblical hermeneutics and are not confined to the literal sense. Between the periods of the *Glossa* and the *Postilla*, the reception of the fourfold model, both conceptually and terminologically, was already pervasive enough for it to have been encapsulated in a pedagogically orientated couplet: "littera gesta docet, quid credas allegoria, moralis

---

[1] On the history of the fourfold interpretation of Scripture, see generally C. Spicq, *Esquisse d'une histoire de l'exégèse latine au Moyen Age* (Paris: J. Vrin, 1944); H. De Lubac, *Exégèse médiévale: les quatres sens de l'Ecriture*, 4 vols (Paris: Aubier, 1959); Smalley, *Study of the Bible*; *The Cambridge History of the Bible*, II; *The West from the Fathers to the Reformation*, ed. G.W.H. Lampe (Cambridge: CUP, 1969, repr. 1980), 155–279.

[2] *Opera omnia*, 178: "apud nos est quadruplex modus exponendi Bibliam, literalis, mysticus sive allegoricus, tropologicus et anagogicus".

[3] On the *Glossa*, see Smalley, *Study of the Bible*, 56–62 and J. Swanson, "The *Glossa ordinaria*", in *The Medieval Theologians*, ed. G.R. Evans, 156–167 (Oxford: B. Blackwell, 2001). On glossed reading of the Bible in general during the 12th and 13th centuries, see also J. van Engen, "Studying Scripture in the Early University", in *Neue Richtungen in der hoch- und spätmittelalterlichen Bibelexegese*, ed. R.E. Lerner and E. Müller-Luckner, 17–38 (Munich: Oldenbourg, 1996).

quid agas, quo tendas anagogia".[4] This contains merely the residue of centuries of debate. For a more detailed description of how the four senses work, we must look to the prologues of the *Glossa* and the *Postilla*. According to the *Glossa*, Scripture has four "measures" (*regulae*):

> History speaks of events; allegory is when something stands for something else; tropology, that is, moral instruction treats of the ordering of behaviour; anagogy, that is, spiritual understanding, by treating of the highest heavenly things, leads us to higher things.[5]

Scripture as a whole revolves around these four "measures" as if they were "wheels". To illustrate the point, the reader is given the example of the word "Jerusalem", which:

> according to the historical sense, is a city; according to the allegorical, it signifies the Church; according to the tropological—that is, the moral— sense, it is the soul of every faithful person that pants for eternal peace; according to the anagogical, it is the life of all heavenly things, which behold God with his face revealed.[6]

The formulation of Nicholas of Lyra is more complex. It begins with a semiotic discussion. Generally, words signify things; this is a normal feature of all human communication. The Bible, however, has a second layer of meaning, in which those things initially signified by the words are able to signify, in turn, other things. The first layer constitutes the literal or historical sense; the second layer, the "mystical" or "spiritual", which, Nicholas writes, is usually divided into three categories:

> because if the things signified by the words are referred to for the purpose of signifying things which are to be believed in the new law, this is understood as the allegorical sense; but if they are referred to for

---

[4] The couplet is quoted by Nicholas of Lyra in his first prologue: *Postilla super totam Bibliam*, 4 vols (Strasbourg, 1492; repr. Frankfurt am Main: Minerva, 1971), I, sig. a2ᵛ.

[5] *Biblia latina cum glossa*, I, sig. a3ᵛ: "Notandum quia haec scriptura ita allegoricis verbis texitur ut allegoricum sensum contineat: et hystoricam fidem rerum gestarum non amittat. ... Quattuor sunt regulae sacrae scripturae idest hystoria: quae res gestas loquitur. Allegoria in qua aliud ex alio intelligitur. Tropologia idest moralis locutio: in qua de moribus ordinandis tractatur. Anagoge idest spiritualis intellectus: per quem de summis et caelestibus tractaturi ad superiora ducimur."

[6] Ibid.: "His quattuor quasi quibusdam rotis: tota divina scriptura volvitur. Verbi gratia: Hierusalem secundum hystoriam est civitas. Allegoria ecclesiam significat. Secundum tropologiam idest moralitatem animam cuiuslibet fidelis: quae ad pacem aeternam anhelat. Secundum anagogen caelestium omnium vitam: qui revelata facie vident Deum."

the purpose of signifying things which should be done by us, this is the moral or tropological sense; and if they are referred to for the purpose of signifying things which should be expected in the future beatitude to come, this is the anagogical sense.[7]

The reader is again given the example of how to interpret "Jerusalem":

according to the literal sense, it signifies a certain city, which at one time was a metropolis in the kingdom of Judea ... ; according to the moral sense, it signifies the faithful soul ... ; according to the allegorical sense, it signifies the Church Militant ... ; according to the anagogical sense, it signifies the Church Triumphant ... . And just as this example is posited in relation to one word, so it could be posited in relation to a passage; and as in one, so in others.[8]

There are certainly differences between these two discussions, written approximately two centuries apart.[9] But what is important for our purposes here is that, despite these differences, they confirmed a clear and common terminology. This terminology did not originate in the *Glossa*.[10] Nor did the stricter definition given in the *Postilla* originate from the pen of Nicholas of Lyra: he copied, almost

---

[7] Nicholas of Lyra, *Postilla*, I, first prologue, sig. a2ᵛ: "Habet tamen iste liber hoc speciale quod una littera continet plures sensus. Cuius ratio est quia principalis huius libri auctor est ipse Deus: in cuius potestate est non solum uti vocibus ad aliquid significandum (quod etiam homines facere possunt et faciunt), sed etiam rebus significatis per voces utitur ad significandum alias res: et ideo commune est omnibus libris, quod voces aliquid significent, sed speciale et huic libro quod res significatae per voces aliud significent. Secundum igitur primam significationem, quae est per voces, accipitur sensus litteralis seu historicus: secundum vero aliam significationem, quae est per ipsas res, accipitur sensus mysticus, seu spiritualis, qui est triplex in generali; quia si res significatae per voces referantur ad significandum ea quae sunt in nova lege credenda, sic accipitur sensus allegoricus; si autem referantur ad significandum ea quae per nos sunt agenda, sic est sensus moralis vel tropologicus; si autem referantur ad significandum ea quae sunt speranda in beatitudine futura, sic est sensus anagogicus."

[8] Ibid.: "Et istorum quatuor sensuum potest poni exemplum in hac dictione Hierusalem quae secundum sensum litteralem significat quamdam civitatem, quae fuit quondam metropolis in regno Judeae ... Secundum sensum vero moralem significat fidelem animam ... Secundum vero sensum allegoricum significat Ecclesiam militantem ... Secundum vero sensum anagogicum significat Ecclesiam triumphantem ... Et sicut positum est exemplum in una dictione, ita posset poni in una oratione: et sicut in una, ita et in aliis."

[9] I shall make some remarks on these differences in my discussion of hermeneutics and esotericism in the Middle Ages: see Ch. 4, section 4.

[10] The first to use this terminology was, it appears, John Cassian (c. 360–435): see A.J. Minnis and A.B. Scott, with D. Wallace, *Medieval Literary Theory and Criticism c. 1100 – c. 1375* (Oxford: OUP, 1988), 203.

verbatim, the discussion of the same matter given by Thomas Aquinas at the beginning of the *Summa theologiae*.[11] It is in terms of circulation, rather than originality, that the importance of the *Glossa* and the *Postilla* is to be measured.

Both the *Glossa* and the *Postilla* circulated very widely in manuscript.[12] The *Postilla* was first printed in 1471 and the *Glossa* in 1480–1481; the two appeared in print together in a 1495 Venice edition; and there were numerous other reprints in between and after.[13] Owing to their vast diffusion, these two works inevitably conditioned the reception of patristic and medieval controversy over the interpretation of the Bible; and the *Postilla*, especially, served to clarify and codify the previous arguments.[14]

---

[11] Thomas Aquinas, *Summa theologiae*, I.1.10: "Auctor sacrae scripturae est Deus, in cuius potestate est ut non solum voces ad significandum accommodet (quod etiam homo facere potest) sed etiam res ipsas. Et ideo, cum in omnibus scientiis voces significent, hoc habet proprium ista scientia, quod ipsae res significatae per voces, etiam significant aliquid. Illa ergo prima significatio, qua voces significant res pertinet ad primum sensum, qui est sensus historicus vel litteralis. Illa vero significatio qua res significatae per voces, iterum res alias significant, dicitur sensus spiritualis; qui super litteralem fundatur, et eum supponit. Hic autem sensus spiritualis trifariam dividitur. Sicut enim dicit Apostolus, ad. Heb. 7[.19], lex vetus figura est novae legis: et ipsa nova lex, ut dicit Dionysius in Ecclesiastica Hierarchia, est figura futurae gloriae [501 C–D]: in nova etiam lege, ea quae in capite sunt gesta, sunt signa eorum quae nos agere debemus. Secundum ergo quod ea quae sunt veteris legis, significant ea quae sunt novae legis, est sensus allegoricus; secundum vero quod ea quae in Christo sunt facta, vel in his quae Christum significant, sunt signa eorum quae nos agere debemus, est sensus moralis; prout vero significant ea quae sunt in aeterna gloria, est sensus anagogicus." Cf. Nicholas of Lyra, *Postilla*, quoted in nn. 7–8 above. Note also the similarity between the passage quoted here and the relevant sections of Hugh of St Victor, *Didascalion: De studio legendi*, ed. C.H. Buttimer (Washington DC: Catholic University of America Press, 1939), 5.3 (96–97) and 6.4 (117–122). It is clear from this that these ideas did not originate with Thomas Aquinas either. See G.R. Evans, *The Language and Logic of the Bible: The Road to Reformation* (Cambridge: CUP, 1985), 4.

[12] Over 800 manuscripts of the *Postilla* are extant: see *Nicholas of Lyra: The Senses of Scripture*, ed. P.D.W. Krey and L. Smith (Leiden: Brill, 2000), 8–9. For manuscript circulation of the *Glossa*, see *Biblia latina cum glossa*, I, vii–viii.

[13] On the printing history of the *Glossa* and the *Postilla*, see *Biblia latina cum glossa*, I, xii–xxvi; K. Froehlich, "The Fate of the *Glossa Ordinaria* in the Sixteenth Century", in *Die Patristik in der Bibelexegese des 16. Jahrhunderts*, ed. D.C. Steinmetz, 20–24 (Wiesbaden: Harrassowitz, 1999); *Nicholas of Lyra*, ed. Krey and Smith, 11–12; K. Jensen, "Printing the Bible in the Fifteenth Century", in *Incunabula and their Readers: Printing, Selling and Using Books in the Fifteenth Century*, ed. K. Jensen, 123–125 (London: British Library, 2003).

[14] See A. Scafi, "The Notion of the Earthly Paradise from the Patristic Era to the Fifteenth Century" (PhD Dissertation, Warburg Institute, University of London, 1999), 167: "Nicholas of Lyre was not, of course, the first exegete to explain the literal sense of the Bible; but he is considered by modern scholars to be the link between

The very pervasiveness of these texts is enough to suggest that the fourfold method was deeply rooted in general consciousness. Evidence from printed copies of the *Glossa* confirms this. Although the prologues to the *Glossa* promulgated the terminology of the fourfold method, it was applied inconsistently throughout the text. The interlinear glosses are not categorized according to sense; they are merely placed one after another and related to the relevant biblical word by a system of signs. The marginal gloss, meanwhile, on the relatively rare occasions when it does classify the senses, tends to note simply "historice" or "mystice".[15] In the Venice 1495 combined edition of the *Glossa* and *Postilla* an attempt was made to include more precise marginal lemmata, such as "lit.", "allegor." or "anagogice".[16] The publisher clearly felt that readers would welcome this increased visibility of the fourfold framework.

Relatively few other biblical commentaries were printed in the fifteenth century; and fewer were printed in northern Italy, it seems, than north of the Alps. None comes close to the *Glossa* and *Postilla* in terms of number of surviving copies. Nevertheless there is some evidence which further attests to the widespread continued acceptance of the terminology of the four senses. A Psalms commentary printed in Venice in 1496 and attributed either to Hugh of St Cher or Alexander of Hales has the relevant sense noted in the margin, as "ad litteram", "allegorice", "moraliter" and sometimes "mistice".[17] Also printed (Rome, 1480) was the commentary on Job by Gregory the Great, which presents a variant of the fourfold schema, lacking the anagogical sense but using the other three. Outside Italy, a wider variety of commentaries was printed; among those using the fourfold method, we find the commentary on the Song of Songs of Honorius of Autun (early twelfth century).[18] The continuing influence of Nicholas of Lyra, meanwhile, is further seen from the example of an incunable edition of the *Expositio in Psalterium* of Ludolph of Saxony (c. 1300–1378): the entire text of Nicholas's discussion of the four

---

the Middle Ages and modern times, the commentator who freed medieval exegesis from its prolixity. Yet, in doing so, he also deprived it of much of its complexity and richness."

[15] See the comment of Smalley, in *Cambridge History of the Bible*, II, ed. Lampe, 214.

[16] See *Biblia latina cum glossa*, I, xvii.

[17] Hugh of St Cher, *Postilla super Psalterium* (Venice, 1496).

[18] Honorius Augustodunensis, *Expositio in librum Salomonis qui dicitur Cantica Canticorum* (Cologne, c. 1490), sig. a2ᵛ: "Hic liber agit de nuptiis que fiunt quatuor modis scilicet hystorice allegorice tropologice anagogice."

senses finds its way, unattributed, into Ludolph's introduction.[19] For a final indication of the dominance of this terminology, we can turn to the *Tractatus de investigatione Sacrae Scripturae*, written in 1486 by Johannes Trithemius, Abbot of the Benedictine Abbey of St Martin at Sponheim.[20] Although his chief source, the *Didascalion* of Hugh of St Victor (d. 1141), recognizes only three senses, Trithemius felt compelled always to insert the fourth.[21]

In the early sixteenth century, the four senses (and the books which promulgated them) remained a common point of reference. Erasmus made ambivalent use of the *Glossa*, sometimes criticizing it, sometimes appropriating it for his own ends.[22] Likewise, he sometimes used the framework of the four senses, but criticized the idea that it should be applied everywhere, rather than only where appropriate.[23] Jacques Lefèvre d'Etaples also refers to the fourfold method: without explicitly criticizing it, he prefers not to use it himself.[24] His colleague, Josse Clichtove, maintained a more conventional stance and in 1517 published a work attributed to Hugh of St Victor, the *Allegoriae in Vetus et Novum Testamentum*, which he prefaced with a standard account of the four senses.[25] In the introduction to the Com-

---

[19] Ludolphus de Saxonia, *Expositio in Psalterium* (Speyer, 1491), sig. a4^r.

[20] See K. Froehlich, "Johannes Trithemius on the Fourfold Sense of Scripture: The *Tractatus de investigatione Sacrae Scripturae* (1486)", in *Biblical Interpretation in the Era of the Reformation: Essays Presented to David C. Steinmetz in Honor of His Sixtieth Birthday*, ed. R.A. Muller and J.L. Thompson, 23–60 (Grand Rapids, Michigan: W.B. Eerdmans, 1996).

[21] Ibid., 51.

[22] Froehlich, "The Fate of the *Glossa*", 31.

[23] The *Enarratio primi Psalmi*, 1515, for example, is explicitly concerned with expounding the tropological sense; Erasmus mentions allegory and anagogy in passing. For his mockery of inappropriate application of the fourfold framework, see *Moriae encomium*, in his *Opera omnia*, IV.3, ed. C.H. Miller (Amsterdam and Oxford: North-Holland, 1979), 166 (477a). Discussions of Erasmus's attitude to biblical exegesis are in his *Collected Works*, LXIII, ed. D. Baker-Smith (Toronto: University of Toronto Press, 1997), xxiv–xxx; M.J. Heath, "Allegory, Rhetoric and Spirituality: Erasmus's Early Psalm Commentaries", in *Acta Conventus Neo-Latini Torontonensis: Proceedings of the Seventh International Congress of Neo-Latin Studies*, ed. A. Dalzell, C. Fantazzi and R.J. Schoeck, 363–370 (Binghamton, New York: Medieval and Renaissance Texts and Studies, 1991).

[24] J. Lefèvre d'Etaples, *Quincuplex Psalterium* (Paris, 1509), prefatory epistle; in *The Prefatory Epistles of Jacques Lefèvre d'Etaples and Related Texts*, ed. E.F. Rice (New York: Columbia University Press, 1972), 193–194: "Videor mihi alium videre sensum, qui scilicet est intentionis prophetae et spiritus sancti in eo loquentis, et hunc litteralem appello, sed qui cum spiritu coincidit; neque prophetis neque videntibus alium littera praetendit (non quod alios sensus, allegoricum, tropologicum et anagogicum, praesertim ubi res exposcit negare velim)."

[25] Ibid., 388–391.

plutensian Polyglot (completed in 1514, but not circulated before 1520), one of the most important sixteenth-century tools for the philological analysis of the Bible, we find the same traditional formulation of the fourfold method which Nicholas of Lyra had adopted and popularized.[26]

Equally, we can note that when Reformers denigrated the scriptural interpretations of their predecessors, it was often the fourfold method that they attacked. Explicit criticism is found in the works of Melanchthon, Luther, Calvin and Tyndale.[27] Finally, as late as 1576, the Counter-Reformation polemicist Robert Bellarmine reasserted the four senses, following Thomas Aquinas's formulation.[28] Throughout the sixteenth century, the *Glossa* and the *Postilla* continued to be published, but they no longer dominated the market as they had in the second half of the fifteenth century.[29]

This, then, was what Pico was referring to when he mentioned the interpretative method "apud nos".[30] The context in which he makes this comment is his defence of kabbalah in the *Apologia*. One of the elements of this defence was to point out that the Jews, too, had a fourfold scheme of reading parallel to that of the Christians and that kabbalah fitted into the Jewish scheme in the same way that anagogy fitted into the Christian one. The Jewish scheme, Pico says, is "Pesat" for the literal meaning, "Midras" for the allegorical, "Sechel" for the tropological and "Cabala" for the anagogical.[31] This alignment of the

---

[26] *Vetus testamentum multiplici lingua nunc primo impressum. Et imprimis Pentateuchus Hebraico Greco atque Chaldaico idiomate. Adiuncta unicuique sua latina interpretatione*, 6 vols (Alcalá de Henares, 1514–1517), I, sig. + 6ʳ.

[27] See, e.g., Philipp Melanchthon, *Elementa rhetorices*, in his *Opera omnia*, ed. C. Bretschneider, XIII (Berlin: C.A. Schwetschke et Filium, 1846), col. 466; Jean Calvin, *Commentarii in secundam Pauli epistolam ad Corinthios*, 3.6–7, in his *Opera exegetica*, XV, ed. H. Feld (Geneva: Droz, 1994), 53–58; William Tyndale, *The Obedience of a Christian Man* (Marlborough 1528, repr. Menston: Scolar Press, 1970), ff. 129ʳ–135ʳ; Martin Luther, *Werke*, Abt. 2, *Tischreden*, 6 vols (Weimar: H. Böhlau, 1912–1920), V, item 5285, 45.

[28] Robert Bellarmine, *De verbis Dei*, III.3, in his *Opera omnia: editio nova iuxta Venetam anni 1721*, 8 vols (Naples, 1872), I, 101.

[29] Sixteenth-century editions include Basel 1502 and 1508; Lyon 1520, 1528–1529 and 1545; Venice 1588; Paris 1590. For details, see *Biblia latina cum glossa*, I, xix–xxiv.

[30] See n. 2 above.

[31] *Opera omnia*, 178: "Est autem ulterius sciendum, quod ista expositio Bibliae proportionatur modo exponendi Bibliam, qui apud nos dicitur Anagogicus: sicut enim apud nos est quadruplex modus exponendi Bibliam, literalis, mysticus sive allegoricus, tropologicus et anagogicus. Ita est et apud Hebraeos. Literalis apud eos dicitur Pesat, quemadmodum tenent apud eos Rabi Salomon [i.e. Rashi], Chemoy [i.e. Kimḥi] et similes. Allegoricus Midras [i.e. Midrash], unde saepe apud eos

two traditions was intended to make kabbalah appear less alien to Christian readers by inserting it into a recognizable framework; as such, Pico's argument depends on the reader perceiving the fourfold method as the norm.

1.2. *Humanist Philology*

It should be pointed out that the idea of 'literal' interpretation expressed in the fourfold model of exegesis does not imply any use of philology. The medieval interest in what is commonly (and perhaps confusingly) referred to as the literal sense was more specifically an interest in the historical: that is, in the events narrated in the Bible on the plane of history as it occurred *at the time*. Literal interpretations of Genesis concerned themselves which such questions as whether a day of creation lasted twenty-four hours, and whether Eden existed

---

audies Midras ruth, Midrastillym, Midras coeleth, id est, expositio per Midras, id est mystica super Ruth, super psalmos, super ecclesiasten: et sic de aliis. Et istum modum sequuntur maxime doctores Talmutici. Tropologicus dicitur Sechel, quem sequuntur Abraham Abnazara [i.e. Ibn Ezra], ubi literaliter non exponit, et Levi Bengerson [i.e. Gersonides] et multi alii, et ante omnes Rabi Moses Aegyptius [i.e. Maimonides]. Anagogicus dicitur Cabala, et hoc quia illa expositio quae dicitur ore Dei tradita Moysi, et accepta per successionem, modo praedicto, quasi semper sensum sequitur Anagogicum, qui etiam inter omnes est sublimior et divinior, sursum nos ducens a terrenis ad coelestia, a sensibilibus ad intelligibilia, a temporalibus ad aeterna, ab infimis ad suprema, ab humanis ad divina, a corporalibus ad spiritualia: et hinc est, quod validissima inde argumenta habentur contra Iudaeos, quia discordia quae est inter eos et nos, ut maxime patet ex epistolis Pauli, hinc tota praecipue dependet, quod ipsi sequuntur literam occidentem, nos autem spiritum vivificantem". There seems to be a mistake in Pico's attributions here. 'Sechel' (שכל) as practised by Gersonides, Maimonides and Abraham ibn Ezra he equates with the tropological method whereas it would more accurately be the allegorical; and 'midras', which he equates with the allegorical, should rather be the tropological. The parallel between the Jewish and Christian fourfold methods is noted on the manuscript containing Mithridates's translation of Gersonides's commentary on the Song of Songs. Here, however, 'sechel' is rendered as 'intellectus' (Vat. Lat. 4273, f. 5ʳ). This is a more accurate translation of the term. The mistake here may merely be due to Pico's haste in writing the *Apologia*. See G. Scholem, *On the Kabbalah and its Symbolism*, tr. R. Manheim (London: Routledge and Kegan Paul, 1965), 62 n. 1; Wirszubski, *Pico's Encounter*, 262–263. On Jewish exegesis in general, see A. van der Heide, "Midrash and Exegesis", in *The Book of Genesis in Jewish and Oriental Christian Interpretation: A Collection of Essays*, ed. J. Frishman and L. van Rompay, 43–56 (Leuven: Peeters, 1997); D.W. Halivni, *Peshat and Derash: Plain and Applied Meaning in Rabbinic Exegesis* (Oxford: OUP, 1991); S. Klein-Braslavy, "The Philosophical Exegesis", in *Hebrew Bible, Old Testament: the History of its Interpretation, I: From the Beginnings to the Middle Ages (until 1300). Part 2: The Middle Ages*, ed. C. Brekelmans, M. Haran, M. Saebo, 302–320 (Göttingen: Vandenhoeck and Ruprecht, 2000).

in time and space. Philology strictly speaking—that is, an interest in such languages as Greek and Hebrew for the purpose of undoing corruption introduced into the biblical text by previous translations and centuries of copying—had a much less distinguished role to play in the development of medieval biblical studies, although this was not always for want of trying.

Essentially, the activity of philology, as defined above, meant taking up a position regarding the Vulgate, the Latin translation which had become standard through custom, although not yet by decree.[32] Regarding the Old Testament, the Vulgate had initially vied for authority with the Septuagint, the Greek translation from the Hebrew made, according to popular account, by seventy (or seventy-two) learned Jews for Ptolemy II Philadelphus (285–246 BC).[33] An early expression of this debate can be found in the disagreement between Augustine (who argued in *De civitate Dei* that the Septuagint was divinely inspired) and Jerome (who stated in the prologue to his version of the Pentateuch that "it is one thing to be inspired, another thing to be a translator").[34] Throughout the Latin Middle Ages, up to and including the fifteenth century, the Septuagint was very much sidelined by the Vulgate. Initially this was obviously due to the general ignorance of Greek. In the fifteenth century, however, when knowledge of Greek was somewhat more common, there was still comparatively little interest in it as an expression of Scripture.[35] The earliest Greek printed books were produced in Italy; but of over sixty incunables, we find no Septuagint (except for three Psalters) and no Greek New Testament.[36]

The study of Hebrew was likewise of relatively minor importance, although throughout the Middle Ages there was some gen-

---

[32] The Vulgate was authorized by decree at the Council of Trent, 8 April 1546: see *Canones et decreta Concilii Tridentini*, ed. F. Schulte and A.L. Richter (Leipzig: Typis et sumptibus Bernhardi Tauchnitii, 1853), 12. For a general overview of the contents of the Vulgate, see *Biblia sacra iuxta vulgatam versionem*, ed. R. Weber, 2 vols (Stuttgart: Württembergische Bibelanstalt, 1969), I, xx–xxi.

[33] W. Schwarz, *Principles and Problems of Biblical Translation: Some Reformation Controversies and their Background* (Cambridge: CUP, 1970), 17–44.

[34] Augustine, *De civitate Dei*, XVIII.43; Jerome, Prologue to the Pentateuch, in *Biblia latina cum glossa*, I, sig. a3ʳ; cf. *Biblia sacra iuxta vulgatam versionem*, ed. Weber, I, 3: "Aliud est enim esse vatem, aliud est esse interpretem: ibi spiritus ventura praedicit, hic eruditio et verborum copia ea quae intellegit transfert."

[35] On the development of Greek studies in Italy in the 15ᵗʰ and early 16ᵗʰ centuries, see Botley, "Parallel Texts", 9–52, 224–247.

[36] Schwarz, *Principles and Problems*, 92–93. Psalters were printed in Milan (1481) and Venice (1486 and 1496–1498).

eral knowledge of and interest in it among Christian scholars and theologians.[37] In the twelfth century, Hugh of St Victor compared the Vulgate with a different translation of the Hebrew; he discussed exegetical matters with Jewish scholars and learnt a small amount of Hebrew himself.[38] In the thirteenth century, knowledge of Hebrew became more widely diffused, if not more accurate.[39] Several figures campaigned to increase the study of oriental philology, notably Raymond Martin, Robert Grosseteste and Roger Bacon.[40] Nonetheless, a figure as important as Thomas Aquinas could carry out his work in ignorance of both Hebrew and Greek.[41] The organized teaching of semitic languages was officially declared a *desideratum* when the Council of Vienne, in 1311, decreed that chairs of Hebrew, Aramaic and Arabic should be founded at major European universities;[42] the effect of this decree was far from immediate, however.[43]

Regarding both Greek and Hebrew, in the fifteenth century, the necessary tools for philological analysis of Scripture were absent. The Greek text of the Bible was not widely available. Several editions of parts of the Hebrew Bible were printed in Italy and Spain, but none north of the Alps, and there was no comprehensive grammar of Hebrew in a European language until that of Johannes Reuchlin, *De rudimentis Hebraicis* (1506).[44]

Generally it appears that prior to the sixteenth century, the intense activity of the commentary tradition was not matched by

---

[37] See, generally, De Lubac, *Exégèse médiévale*, III, 238–262.

[38] See Smalley, *Study of the Bible*, 102–103.

[39] Ibid., 338–345.

[40] D.C. Klepper, "Nicholas of Lyra and Franciscan Interest in Hebrew Scholarship", in *Nicholas of Lyra*, ed. Krey and Smith, 289–311.

[41] See Spicq, *Exégèse latine au Moyen Age*, 192.

[42] Council of Vienne, Decree 24: *Conciliorum oecumenicorum decreta*, ed. J. Alberigo et al. (Basel: Herder, 1962), 355–356.

[43] Spicq, *Exégèse latine au Moyen Age*, 187–188. See the comment of C. Roth, *The Jews in the Renaissance* (Philadelphia, Pennsylvania: Jewish Publication Society of America, 1959), 145: "The ill-fated Ludovico il Moro, Duke of Milan (1481–1499) founded a chair of Hebrew at the University of Pavia for one Benedetto Ispano, presumably a Spanish refugee, but it was abolished in 1491 as it did not seem to serve any useful purpose. In 1521, however, it was reestablished, the first incumbent being that erudite apostate, Paolus Riccius." Hebrew teaching was also established at the *Collegium trilingue* in Leuven in 1517.

[44] Three grammatical works predated this: a six-page introduction found in Peter Schwartz's *Stella Meschiah* (Eszling, 1477); the eight-page *Introductio utilissima Hebraice discere cupientibus* (first printed c. 1501) and the *De modo legendi et intelligendi Hebraeum* of Conrad Pellican (1503–1504). See Schwarz, *Principles and Problems*, 66. The *Introductio utilissima Hebraice discere cupientibus* was quickly reprinted, which suggests a certain significant interest prior to Reuchlin's work.

philological advances; and the invention of printing, which sealed the dominance (at least up to the Reformation) of certain central texts in the commentary tradition, had little positive effect on biblical philology.[45]

A few scholars of the fifteenth century were exceptions to this general trend; the limited reception of their work proves the rule. Two among them deserve mention here. Gianozzo Manetti, a Florentine who was taught Greek by Ambrogio Traversari, translated the New Testament from Greek into Latin (starting after 1453) and the Psalms from Hebrew into Latin (1454–1455). The former was the first new translation of the New Testament since Jerome's. It does not seem to have circulated widely, however, and only two manuscripts survive, both of which remained in private collections throughout the rest of the fifteenth century.[46] As for the translation of the Psalms, it clearly circulated to some extent, because it encountered a sufficiently hostile reception for Manetti, about a year later, to compose an *Apologeticus* directed against those men, "some slothful, some learned, but not very erudite in Holy and Divine Scripture" who had criticized him for his new translation which was made "de hebraica veritate".[47] Among his humanist contemporaries Manetti's enthusiasm for Hebrew philology was not universally shared. Leonardo Bruni, for example, compared it to drinking wine from the press rather than from the cask.[48]

---

[45] Nicholas of Lyra, however, whom we have already identified as the high point of scholastic commentary, was also notable for his knowledge of Hebrew. It is this, and specifically his careful reading of the 11th-century exegete Solomon ben Isaac, known as Rashi, that underpins much of the *Postilla*: See Hailperin, *Rashi and the Christian Scholars*, 137–264. Rashi was known and cited before Nicholas: see Smalley, *Study of the Bible*, 190. With this in mind, the opposition I draw here between philology and commentary should be regarded more as a principle of organization than as a historical fact: see D.C. Steinmetz and R. Kolb, "Introduction", in *Die Patristik in der Bibelexegese*, 8.

[46] Botley, "Parallel Texts", 138: "Today only two manuscripts survive: the copy which [Gianozzo Manetti's son] Agnolo brought back from Naples after his father's death, and which remained in the private library of the Manettis until 1529, and a beautifully-produced apograph of it which entered the library of the Dukes of Urbino, probably in the 1470s. Neither of these libraries was easily accessible during the fifteenth century."

[47] G. Manetti, *Apologeticus*, ed. A. de Petris (Rome: Edizioni di storia e letteratura, 1981), 3: "Cum novam quandam totius Psalterii de hebraica veritate in latinam linguam traductionem, anno iam propemodum elapso, absolvissem ... a non nullis partim ignavis, partim doctis hominibus, sed in sacris ac divinis Litteris parum eruditis, me in eo opere quodam arrogantie crimine insimulatum ac reprehensum et obiurgatum fuisse audivi."

[48] Leonardo Bruni, letter to Giovanni Cirignani, 1442: "Dare igitur te operam

Lorenzo Valla, at around the same time, produced two works on the New Testament, the *Collatio Novi Testamenti* and a revised series of notes entitled *Adnotationes in Novum Testamentum*. The *Adnotationes* were composed in 1453–1457; their circulation, however, remained minimal until they were discovered (near Leuven) and published by Erasmus in 1505.[49] Valla's interest was in pointing out errors in the Vulgate, with reference to the Greek text. He did not edit the Greek text itself; but his success in solving a number of instances of textual corruption demonstrated that Greek was a necessity for the correct interpretation of Scripture.[50]

These attempts to improve the Vulgate, however, were the vanguard of a movement which only gained momentum in the sixteenth century. During Pico's lifetime, the Vulgate remained the principal medium of expression for the Bible; the examples of Manetti and Valla show that contemporary attempts to challenge its authority were either ignored or met with hostility.[51] The first two decades of the sixteenth century, by contrast, saw the publication of a series of tools for philological analysis which attest to a growing interest in scriptural texts in languages other than Latin and a growing scrutiny of the issue of translation. These include, with reference to Greek studies, Erasmus's New Testament (1516) and the *editio princeps* of the Septuagint (1519); with reference to Hebrew, Reuchlin's *De rudimentis Hebraicis* (1506) and a four-volume Hebrew Bible replete with commentaries and Targum, the *Biblia Hebraica rabbinica cum utraque Masora et Targum cum commentariis rabinorum* (1517); and combining Greek and Hebrew, several polyglot psalters and finally the Complutensian Polyglot in six volumes.[52]

---

hebraicis litteris, voluptatem fortassis animi afferre tibi aliquam potest: utilitatem vero nullam. Ceu si quis vinum ex praelo haurire malit, quam ex dolio, quoniam praelo ante, quam in dolio fuit." (Quoted in Botley, "Parallel Texts", 158).

[49] L. Valla, *Collatio Novi Testamenti*, ed. A. Perosa (Florence: Sansoni, 1970); id., *Adnotationes in Novum Testamentum*, ed. D. Erasmus (Paris, 1505). See S.I. Camporeale, *Lorenzo Valla: umanesimo e teologia* (Florence: Istituto nazionale di studi sul Rinascimento, 1972), 277–403; P.R. Hardie, "Humanist Exegesis of Poetry in Fifteenth-Century Italy and the Medieval Tradition of Commentary" (M.Phil Dissertation, Warburg Institute, University of London, 1976), 70–71; J.H. Bentley, *Humanists and Holy Writ: New Testament Scholarship in the Renaissance* (Princeton, New Jersey: Princeton University Press, 1983), 32–69.

[50] Bentley, *Humanists and Holy Writ*, 39–41.

[51] See the comment of Botley, "Parallel Texts", 167: "Discussions about translation had a very limited audience: most fifteenth-century readers did not need to make their own translations themselves, and were not equipped to assess those of others."

[52] On Erasmus's New Testament, see ibid., 112–193; *Le temps des Réformes et la Bible,*

1.3. *Early Printed Commentaries: A Brief Survey*

We have seen that, in the fifteenth century, the use of the fourfold method of interpretation was marked by a lack of innovation, coupled with increasing circulation in print. In the case of philology, this picture is reversed: there was innovation, but little circulation. So, of the two main currents of biblical exegesis, one was somewhat stagnant, the other still in its early stages. A general indication of contemporary interest in biblical interpretation can be gleaned from printing records. As a representative sample, a list of eighty-seven incunables containing biblical commentary, taken from the *Incunable Short Title Catalogue* (ISTC), reveals the following trends. Among commentaries not devoted to individual books of the Bible, the most popular is the *Postilla super totam Bibliam* of Nicholas of Lyra, of which five editions are listed. Nicholas's companion volume to the *Postilla*, the *Moralia super totam Bibliam*, exists in two editions.[53] There are four editions of Jerome's *Prologi in Bibliam*, and one of Petrus Aureoli's *Compendium litteralis sensus totius bibliae* (early fourteenth century). When we turn to works devoted to particular books of the Bible, the following facts emerge. There are six different Psalms commentaries—Peter Lombard (c. 1100–1160), Hugh of St Cher (c. 1200–1263), Ludolph of Saxony, Petrus de Harentals (late fourteenth century), Theodoricus Engelhusen (1365–1434) and Strabo;[54] six different editions of Gregory the Great's *Expositio in Job*; and three different works on the Song of Songs—Gregory the

---

ed. G. Bedouelle and B. Roussel (Paris: Beauchesne, 1989), 74–77. On Reuchlin, see Evans, *Road to Reformation*, 77. On the *Biblia hebraica rabbinica*, printed by Daniel Bomberg, see *Le temps des Réformes et la Bible*, ed. Bedouelle and Roussel, 78–79. On the Complutensian Polyglot, see Bentley, *Humanists and Holy Writ*, 70–111; *Le temps des Réformes et la Bible*, ed. Bedouelle and Roussel, 81–83. On the polyglot psalters, see ibid., 81. I have described these as tools for philological analysis, in that the availability of such texts, preferably in a form allowing easy comparison of languages, was indispensable for such analysis; but it should be noted that the production of these texts in itself does not imply that the authority of the Vulgate was being challenged. The Complutensian Polyglot, for example, printed the Vulgate text in between the Hebrew and the Septuagint, "tanquam duos hinc et inde latrones, medium autem Jesum, hoc est Romanam sive latinam Ecclesiam" (*Vetus testamentum multiplici lingua*, I, sig. + 3ᵛ). Also of interest in this context is the work of Elijah Levita: see *Encyclopaedia Judaica*, ed. Roth, XI, cols 132–135.

[53] On the reception and printing of Nicholas of Lyra's *Postilla* and *Moralia*, see *Le temps des Réformes et la Bible*, ed. Bedouelle and Roussel, 47–52.

[54] The *Scriptus compendiosum Psalterii intentionem declarans* (Basel, 1472–1474) attributed to Strabo does not match the commentary on the Psalms in the *Glossa ordinaria*.

Great, Honorius of Autun and Pierre d'Ailly (late fourteenth–early fifteenth centuries). The New Testament, meanwhile, is represented by three works on Paul's letters and three on the Gospels—Ambrose on Luke, Augustine on John, and three editions of the *Expositio super totum corpus Evangeliorum* by Simon de Cassia (d. 1348), two of which are Italian adaptations. The remainder of the list is composed largely of reference works for preachers and readers of the Bible. Notably, there are five editions of the *Mammotrectus super Bibliam* of Johannes Marchesinus, a glossary and theological manual for priests compiled around 1300. There are also various works of Antonius Rampegollis (c. 1360–c. 1423), including two editions of his *Aurea Biblia*, two of the *Figurae Bibliae*, and one of the *Compendium morale*; and the *Distinctiones dictionum theologicalium* of Alan of Lille (c. 1114–c. 1203). There appear to be no printed commentaries solely and specifically on Genesis.

This is not to assert, of course, that other general works, and works specifically on Genesis, were not available in manuscript: the Vatican, to give but one example, was well endowed with such texts.[55] If, however, it is legitimate to draw some conclusions from the appearance of printed editions, then the following suggestions may be made. A significant corpus of the familiar names of patristic and scholastic theology soon got into print; this includes Jerome, Augustine, Gregory the Great, the *Glossa*, Nicholas of Lyra, and several more minor and derivative medieval commentators such as Ludolph and Honorius. The most popular portions of the Bible for commentaries, meanwhile, were Job, the Psalms and the New Testament. This statistic finds a parallel in the broader context of fifteenth- and early sixteenth-century biblical activity and orientation, as we have seen—the Psalms and the New Testament were retranslated by Manetti, the New Testament scrutinized and edited by Valla and Erasmus.

This survey of texts and methods presents the norms for biblical interpretation in the late fifteenth century. A largely antithetical perspective is to be found in Pico's own comment regarding which authors he considered to be of relevance to an analysis of the Genesis narrative.

---

[55] See E. Müntz and P. Fabre, *La bibliothèque du Vatican au XVe siècle d'après des documents inédits* (Paris: E. Thorin, 1887); R. Devreesse, *Le fonds grec da la bibliothèque vaticane des origines à Paul V* (Vatican City: Biblioteca Apostolica Vaticana, 1965).

2. *The Authorities Pico Rejected*

Before telling his readers what the *Heptaplus* is, Pico informs them of
what it is not. He claims that his method of interpretation is new. To
substantiate this claim, he gives a list of authorities—"robust minds"
in the field of biblical commentary—whose work he will not imitate
and whose methods he will not follow. This list should be considered
as another context for the *Heptaplus*, since it represents Pico's own
perspective on the field of biblical commentary: the authors whom
he knew or regarded as significant.

> The things that were written about this book [i.e., Genesis] by those holi-
> est of men, Ambrose and Augustine, and by Strabo too, and Bede and
> Remigius, and (among the more recent authors) Aegidius and Alber-
> tus; likewise, among the Greeks, by Philo, Origen, Basil, Theodoretus,
> Apollinarius, Didymus, Diodorus, Severus, Eusebius, Iosephus, Genna-
> dius, Chrysostomus—will be left completely untouched by us. It would
> be both rash and superfluous for a weak man to venture into that part of
> the field where the most robust minds have toiled before him. Likewise,
> we shall make no mention at this time of the things which the Chaldeans
> Ionethes, Anchelos and ancient Simeon handed down, or of what was
> written by the Hebrews, whether the ancients—Eleazarus, Aba, Ioannes,
> Neonias, Isaac and Ioseph—or the more recent authors—Gersonides,
> Sadias, Abraham, both of those named Moses, Salomon and Manaem.
> Let us rather, beyond all these, contribute seven other expositions, the
> product of our own invention and reflection.[56]

The *Heptaplus*, then, is explicitly defined by its author *against* a
background of exegesis drawn from four languages and two faiths.
This background extends from several of the fundamental and well-
known Latin exegetes mentioned above into a vague and uncertain
twilight of Greek and Hebrew figures who were certainly not representative of Christian biblical commentary in the fifteenth century.
How well acquainted could Pico have been with these writers? In

---

[56] H. P1; Garin, 178–180: "Quae igitur super hoc libro viri sanctissimi, Ambro-
sius et Augustinus, Strabus item et Beda et Remigius et, ex iunioribus, Aegidius et
Albertus; quae item apud Graecos Philon, Origenes, Basilius, Theodoretus, Apollinarius, Didymus, Diodorus, Severus, Eusebius, Iosephus, Gennadius, Chrisostomus,
scripserunt, intacta penitus a nobis relinquentur, cum et temerarium et superfluum
sit in ea se agri parte infirmum hominem exercere, ubi se pridem robustissimae
mentes exercuerint. De his item quae vel Ionethes vel Anchelos vel Simeon antiquus
chaldaice tradiderunt vel, ex Hebraeis, aut veteres: Eleazarus, Aba, Ioannes, Neonias,
Isaac, Ioseph; aut iuniores: Gersonides, Sadias, Abraam, uterque Moses, Salomon et
Manaem conscripserunt, nullam nos in praesentia mentionem habebimus. Affer-
emus autem, praeter haec omnia, septem alias expositiones, nostra inventa et
meditata ..."

answering this it is necessary to identify those who are referred to ambiguously. I have generally been guided in this attempt by Pico's own comment, that these are the authors who have previously produced significant work "super hoc libro", that is, specifically on Genesis. It is also necessary to consider to what extent the works of these authors were available to Pico. In this respect we have the good fortune to possess his library inventories and my analysis is largely based on these. I have on occasion noted instances where works were available in other collections, notably the Vatican Library. This is intended as an indication of general circulation; Pico's own access to the Vatican appears to have ended in March 1487, however.[57]

2.1. *Latin exegetes*

Several mainstream Latin exegetes, patristic and scholastic, are represented in the list. They are Ambrose, Bishop of Milan (c. 339–397); Augustine of Hippo (354–430); the Venerable Bede (c. 673–735); Remigius of Auxerre (c. 841–c. 948); Albertus Magnus (late twelfth century–1280) and Aegidius Romanus (c. 1243–1316).

Augustine produced three works devoted exclusively to the analysis of the Genesis narrative: *De Genesi contra Manichaeos, De Genesi ad litteram inperfectus liber* and *De Genesi ad litteram*. One or more of these was in Pico's library.[58] Despite the 'literalness' espoused in the titles of the last two, Augustine indulged in a great deal of non-literal interpretation. The last three books of *De civitate Dei* also comprise a hexaemeral commentary, while *De doctrina Christiana* is a more general treatise on semiotics and the interpretation of Scripture.[59] Augustine's reception in the Middle Ages and Renaissance was wide. Apart from the direct circulation of his writings, he was cited frequently by name in the *Glossa*—in the Genesis gloss, he appears several times per page. Pico also made frequent use of his work in the *Expositiones in Psalmos*.[60]

Ambrose, the Venerable Bede, Albertus Magnus and Aegidius Romanus were all widely diffused authors whose books were present in Pico's library in large numbers. Both Bede and Ambrose produced

---

[57] Dorez and Thuasne, *Pic de la Mirandole en France*, 66; Grafton, "Giovanni Pico della Mirandola", 93.

[58] Kibre, *Library*, item 547: "Augustinus super genesim et cetera".

[59] See T. Todorov, *Théories du symbole* (Paris: Editions du Seuil, 1977), 13–58.

[60] *Expositiones in Psalmos*, ed. Raspanti, 64, 66, 96, 102, 106, 110, 112, 114, 188, 206, 244.

detailed exegetical works on Genesis.[61] Bede, like Augustine, was
frequently cited in the Genesis gloss. Albertus Magnus wrote a treatise
entitled *De causis et procreatione universi*, possibly owned by Pico.[62]
Aegidius wrote commentaries on the *Liber de causis*, Aristotle's *Physics*
and the *Sententia* of Peter Lombard (the second book of which is
partially concerned with creation). His biblical exegesis is less well
known; a *Hexameron sive mundo sex diebus condito* exists but was not
printed until 1544. Pico owned all of these works by Aegidius, except,
as far as we know, the last. Altogether seventeen books by Aegidius
were listed in the Vatican catalogue at the time of Sixtus IV.[63] Both
Albertus and Aegidius figure in Pico's *Conclusiones*, Aegidius with
eleven conclusions and Albertus with sixteen.[64] This leaves, among
the Latins, only Remigius of Auxerre. No copy of his *Expositio super
Genesim* is listed in Pico's inventories but it was present in the Vatican
library.[65]

The "Strabo" mentioned by Pico is Walafrid Strabo (c. 808–849).
His works do not survive in direct transmission but he is one of the few
exegetes cited by name on the first page of the *Glossa*. It is probable,
therefore, that it is to that work that Pico is referring here.[66]

2.2. *Greek exegetes (transmitted directly)*

This second group comprises Philo Judaeus (c. 20 BC–c. 50 AD), Origen (c. 185–254), Basil (c. 330–379) and John Chrysostom (c. 347–
407). It comes as little surprise to find Philo Judaeus here rather
than among the "Hebraei". His work in general circulated widely
in the Middle Ages and Renaissance, although a look at the Vatican library catalogues of the fifteenth century points to a certain
ambiguity of status: he is not included among the theologians but

---

[61] Bede, *Libri quatuor in principium Genesis*, ed. Jones. Ambrose, *Exameron*, in
Opera, I, Corpus Scriptorum Ecclesiasticorum Latinorum 32, ed. C. Schenkl (Vienna:
F. Tempsky, 1897).

[62] Kibre, *Library*, items 2 and 679.

[63] Müntz and Fabre, *La bibliothèque du Vaticane*, 190.

[64] *Conclusions*, 20–22 and 38–39.

[65] Vat. Lat. 646. See Remigius of Auxerre, *Expositio super Genesim*, ed. B. v-N. Edwards (Turnhout: Brepols, 1999), xxi; Müntz and Fabre, *La bibliothèque du Vaticane*,
163.

[66] After Pico's time it became standard practice to attribute the entire *Glossa* to
Strabo. The first occurrence of this seems to have been Trithemius's *De scriptoribus
ecclesiasticis* (1494). Subsequently the 'fact' of Strabo's authorship was cemented by
the editors of the Paris 1590 edition of the *Glossa*, who put Strabo's name on the
title-page. See *Biblia latina cum glossa*, I, xxiii–iv.

among the philosophers (alongside the pagans).[67] Philo devoted two exegetical works to Genesis, the *Quaestiones in Genesim* and *De opificio mundi*. The former is to be found in Pico's library inventory.[68] It also appears in the Greek *catena* tradition—a compilation of scriptural glosses roughly equivalent to the *Glossa*, but less widely circulated. The *Quaestiones* neglect the opening chapter of Genesis altogether, however, making it more likely that Pico regarded Philo as significant in this context on account of the *De opificio mundi*. Philo is notable as an early exponent of the sort of allegorical interpretation which later became especially linked to the city of Alexandria.[69] For this reason he can be paired with Origen. Pico was particularly interested in Origen;[70] he owned copies of his *Contra Celsum*, his *Letters* and his *In Iosue*. The bulk of Origen's extant writings, in the original Greek, are contained in the *Philocalia*, which was compiled by Gregory of Nazianzus and Basil of Caesarea in the fourth century. Manuscripts of this work were present in the Vatican library in large numbers. The *Philocalia* did not, however, include Origen's *Homilies on Genesis*, which were therefore only extant, aside from a few excerpts in the *catena* tradition, in the Latin translation of Rufinus, made around 400 AD.[71] The manuscript circulation of this work was wide and it was presumably the main source of Pico's knowledge of Origen's Genesis exegesis.[72]

Broadly speaking, the form of exegesis practised by Philo and Origen is opposed to that of Basil and John Chrysostom—at risk of over-simplification, it reflects the opposition between the Alexandrian and Antiochene schools of thought.[73] Of Basil's anti-allegorical

---

[67] Devreesse, *Le fonds grec*, 54 (item 217), 58 (items 304 and 307), 92 (item 225).

[68] Kibre, *Library*, item 471; F. Petit, *L'ancienne version latine des Questions sur la Genèse de Philon d'Alexandrie* (Berlin: Akademie-Verlag, 1973), 1–39; id., *Catenae graecae in Genesim et in Exodum, I. Catena Sinaitica* (Turnhout: Brepols, 1977), xv–xvi.

[69] For Philo, see generally J. Pépin, *La tradition de l'allégorie de Philon d'Alexandrie à Dante* (Paris: Etudes Augustiniennes, 1987), 7–40; F. Ó Fearghail, "Philo and the Fathers: The Letter and the Spirit", in *Scriptural Interpretation in the Fathers*, ed. T. Finan and V. Twomey, 39–59 (Dublin: Four Courts Press, 1995).

[70] See his defence of Origen's orthodoxy in the *Apologia*, in *Opera omnia*, 199–224; H. Crouzel, *Une controverse sur Origène à la Renaissance: Jean Pic de la Mirandole et Pierre Garcia* (Paris: J. Vrin, 1977). On the medieval reception of Origen, see De Lubac, *Exégèse médiévale*, I, 221–304.

[71] Origen, *Homélies sur la Genèse*, ed. L. Doutreleau (Paris: Editions du Cerf, 1976), 13.

[72] Doutreleau notes the existence of 75 manuscripts: ibid., 14.

[73] See L. van Rompay, "Antiochene Biblical Interpretation: Greek and Syriac", in *Genesis in Jewish and Oriental Christian Interpretation*, ed. Frishman and van Rompay, 103–123; J.L. Kugel and R.A. Greer, *Early Biblical Interpretation* (Philadelphia, Pennsylvania: Westminster Press, 1986), 178–199.

stance, I shall give an example later.[74] Chrysostom is the central
representative of the form of exegesis practised in Antioch; he
was a pupil of Theodore of Mopsuestia and Diodorus of Tarsus,
whom Pico also mentions in this list. The *hexaemera* of Basil and
John Chrysostom were, by the standards of Greek patristic works
in the fifteenth century, widely available in Italy.[75] The success of
Basil's work is attested in numerous ways: it was used by Ambrose
and Augustine (via the Latin translation of Eustathius), and traces
of it can be found in the work of Isidore of Seville, Bede and
Thomas Aquinas.[76] A copy of his *Hexaemeron* was to be found in
Pico's library.[77]

These are four of the most influential and (with the partial exceptions of Philo and Origen) widely circulated of the Greek patristic
authors. Given the split here between representatives of the Alexandrian and Antiochene persuasions, it is fair to say that Pico provides
a representative and balanced list of important commentators within
the Greek tradition.

2.3. *Greek exegetes (transmitted indirectly)*

This second group of Greek Church Fathers includes those whose
writings were no longer extant, except in fragmentary form: Apollinarius of Laodicea (c. 310–c. 390); Diodorus of Tarsus (d. c. 390);
Didymus the Blind (c. 313–398); Gennadius of Constantinople (d.
471); Theodoretus; Eusebius; Severus; Josephus. Most of these names
do not appear in Pico's library inventories, nor in the Vatican inventories of the fifteenth century. We can safely assume that Didymus
refers to Didymus the Blind, an Alexandrian exegete in the tradition of Origen. We should note, however, that although his *De Spiritu
Sancto* (as translated by Jerome) was well known, the text of his commentary on Genesis was lost until 1941, when it was rediscovered on

---

[74] See Ch. 4, nn. 67–69.

[75] Devreesse, *Le fonds grec*, 62–71 (items 412, 420, 424, 432, 484, 487, 489,
500, 520, 534, 560, 572, 582, 598, among others). For Chrysostom, note also the
presence in the Medici library of a manuscript containing 67 homilies on Genesis:
Ms. Laur. 8.7, in E.B. Fryde, *Greek Manuscripts in the Private Library of the Medici*, 2 vols
(Aberystwyth: National Library of Wales, 1996), I, 120–121. See also J. Gribomont,
"Les succès littéraires des Pères grecs et les problèmes d'histoire des textes", *Sacris
Erudiri*, 22.1 (1974–1975), 23–49.

[76] Basil, *Homélies sur l'Hexaéméron*, ed. S. Giet (Paris: Editions du Cerf, 1949), 70–
71.

[77] Kibre, *Library*, item 661: "Examero S. Basilii".

papyrus at Toura in Egypt.[78] Pico's only access to this material must therefore have been through the *catena*, several manuscripts of which were to be found in the Vatican.[79] A glance at the modern edition of the *catena* on Genesis by Françoise Petit shows numerous citations of Apollinarius of Laodicea, Didymus of Alexandria and Diodorus of Tarsus, and sparser references to Gennadius of Constantinople.[80] It also prominently features excerpts from those exegetes who were directly transmitted, including the ones mentioned above: Basil, John Chrysostom and Origen.[81] If we accept that the key to Pico's knowledge of many of these Greek figures is to be found in the *catena*, we may try to clarify some other points.

The existence in Pico's library of several different books by Eusebius of Caeserea could imply that he is the "Eusebius" mentioned in the list.[82] Of these works, much of the first two books of the *Preparatio evangelica* is devoted to accounts of the creation of the world according to various philosophies. None of these is an interpretation of Genesis, however, which leads me to propose that "Eusebius" in fact refers to Eusebius of Emesa (c. 300–c. 359) whose commentary on the Octateuch, although not extant in direct transmission, was one of the most widely cited works in the Genesis *catena*.[83] Eusebius of Emesa was an early representative of the Antiochene school and an important influence upon Diodorus of Tarsus.[84] As in the case of Didymus, Pico's mention of an author does not imply that his works were directly available to him. We shall encounter further examples of this.

The name "Theodoretus" has previously been assumed to refer to the Bishop of Cyrrhus (c. 386–457).[85] Pico did indeed possess two

---

[78] Didymus the Blind, *Sur la Genèse*, ed. P. Nautin, 2 vols (Paris: Editions du Cerf, 1976).

[79] These are Vat. Gr. 747, Vat. Gr. 746 and Vat. Gr. 383, among others. The first two are attributed by Devreesse to the "Genesis cum expositione et pictura" in the inventories: see *Le fonds grec*, 74, 82, 122. They represent not the primary but a secondary textual tradition of the *catena*: see F. Petit, *La chaîne sur la Genèse*, 4 vols (Leuven: Peeters, 1992), I, xxi–xxv.

[80] Petit, *La chaîne sur la Genèse*, I, 334–337.

[81] Basil, in particular, is emphasized in the *catena*, as fragments from other authors were often attributed to him: see, e.g., Petit, *La chaîne sur la Genèse*, I, items 62, 67, 68, 70, 103, 112, 129, 131.

[82] Kibre, *Library*, items 120, 682, 719, 736, 1088.

[83] Petit, *La chaîne sur la Genèse*, I, includes 35 attributions to this text.

[84] R.B. ter Harr Romeny, "Eusebius of Emesa's Commentary on Genesis and the Origins of the Antiochene School", in *Genesis in Jewish and Oriental Christian Interpretation*, ed. Frishman and van Rompay, 125–142.

[85] See Giovanni Pico della Mirandola, *On the Dignity of Man, On Being and the One,*

biblical commentaries by this author, but these are on the Psalms and the Song of Songs. The Genesis *catena* cites another work by him, the *Quaestiones in Octateuchem*, several times. These citations are far outnumbered, however, by the very large number of references it contains to the *Commentarii in Genesim* of Theodore of Mopsuestia (c. 350–428), tutor of John Chrysostom. In any case, excerpts from this "Theodorus" are sometimes labelled in the *catena* as coming from "Theodoretus" or simply the abbreviated "Theod.".[86] Which of these two authors this name refers to, then, must remain an open question; both were a part of the Antiochene school.

Two copies of the *catena*, dating from around the eleventh and tenth centuries respectively and now in the Biblioteca Mediceo-Laurenziana, confirm its importance as a source for these names. The first is catalogued as containing "Sanctorum Patrum excerpta", among whom we find both "Theodorus" and "Theodoretus".[87] The description of the second is more expansive:

> In the middle of the page, there is the Sacred Text, in quite large letters, yellowish in colour, set down very carefully without any abbreviating signs. The very copious *catena*, or rather, perpetual commentary, of the Greek Fathers goes everywhere around the very broad margins, in very tiny but clear letters, written in full and of the same age, of which the following are the principal names: **Theodoretus, Basilius, Joannes Chrysostomus**, Severianus, Accacius Caesariensis, **Diodorus, Gennadius**, Gregorius Nazianzanus, Hippolytus, **Apollinaris, Didymus, Eusebius**, Cyrillus, **Origenes**, Ephraem, Theophilus, Gregorius Nyssenus, Serapio, Philo Episcopus, Eustathius Antiochensis, **Philo Hebraeus, Joseph**, Isidorus, Meletius, Aquila, Symmachus, **Severus,** etc.[88] (My emphasis.)

Heptaplus, tr. C.G. Wallis, J.W. Miller and D. Carmichael (Indianapolis: Bobbs-Merrill, 1965), 72.

[86] See, e.g., Petit, *La chaîne sur la Genèse*, I, items 104, 177, 183, 206 etc. On the ambiguity of some of the lemmata in the *catena* manuscripts, see Petit, *Catena Sinaitica*, ciii.

[87] Plut. VI, cod. 35; A.M. Bandini, *Dei princìpi e progressi della Real Biblioteca Mediceo Laurenziana*, ed. R. Pintaudi, M. Tesi and A.R. Fantoni (Florence: Gonnelli, 1990), 274.

[88] Plut. VI, cod. 44; see Bandini, *Dei princìpi e progressi della Real Biblioteca Mediceo Laurenziana*, ed. Pintaudi et al., 278: "Adest in medio paginae Sacer Textus, grandiori Littera, subflava, absque ullis compendiariis notis diligentissime exaratus. Amplissimos autem margines undequaque ambit uberrima Graecorum Patrum Catena, seu potius perpetuus Commentarius minutissimis sed perspicuis litteris, eiusdem aetatis perscriptus, quorum nomina haec praecipue sunt: Theodoretus, Basilius, Joannes Chrysostomus, Severianus, Acacius Caesariensis, Diodorus, Gennadius, Gregorius Nazianzenus, Hippolytus, Apollinaris, Didymus, Eusebius, Cyrillus, Origenes, Ephraem, Theophilus, Gregorius Nyssenus, Serapio, Philo Episcopus, Eustathius

We can see in the context of the *catena* the appearance of the names "Severus" and "Joseph" as well as many of those authors already discussed.[89] "Severus" presents us with a similar problem to "Theodorus/Theodoretus": the *catena* includes many citations of "Severianus" and "Severus", but it is the former whose work appears more relevant to Genesis, since it goes under the title *De mundi creatione homiliae*. As for "Josephus", the occurrence of "Joseph" in the Laurenziana manuscript cited above is our only clue. It is possible that this is a reference to Flavius Josephus, but his relevance to Genesis is not obvious. These questions must remain unanswered; it is not my intention to pursue a holy grail of positive attribution when the evidence suggests that many of these authors could have come down to Pico only as names and fragments. What this analysis does show is that the *catena* played a decisive role in the formation of his list, whether or not it played any role in his actual exegesis.

2.4. *The Targumim and the Zohar*

"Chaldean" to Pico and his contemporaries meant Aramaic; the "Chaldeans", "Anchelos" and "Ionethes", are the two names traditionally connected to two of the Targumim or Aramaic biblical translations.[90] The Targum Onkelos, to which the first of these names refers, was committed to writing around the third century AD and represents the Babylonian tradition of Judaism. Jonathan ben Uzziel, the "Ionethes" listed by Pico, was the supposed author of the Palestinian Pentateuch Targum properly known as the Targum Yerushalmi, the final compilation of which dates to around the seventh or eighth century AD. This attribution is thought to have been the work of Menaḥem Recanati, of whom more later.[91] The main exegetical innovation of the Targumim was the systematic avoidance of anthropomorphisms relating to God. Pico possessed an edition of the Pentateuch, published in 1482, which included the Targum Onkelos, as well as the commentary of Rashi.[92] The earlier of

---

Antiochensis, Philo Hebraeus, Joseph, Isidorus, Meletius, Aquila, Symmachus, Severus, etc."

[89] It is unlikely that Pico read these actual manuscripts, as the group to which they belong appears to have been acquired by the library at the end of the 18th century.

[90] See *Encyclopaedia Judaica*, ed. Roth, IV, cols 842–851: "Bible: Translations: Ancient Versions".

[91] Ibid., col. 845. The abbreviation ת״י was taken to refer to Targum Jonathan instead of Targum Yerushalmi.

[92] I. Zatelli, F. Lelli and M.V. Avanzinelli, "Pico: la cultura biblica e la tradizione

Pico's library inventories includes a manuscript of "Ionathan in Bibliam": this could refer to the pseudo-Jonathan Targum Yerushalmi
on the Pentateuch, but could equally be the Targum Jonathan on
the Prophets.[93]

Given that "Simeon", too, is a "Chaldean", it is likely that Pico was
referring to the Palestinian Simeon bar Yoḥai (mid-second century
AD); but, in fact, what lies behind this reference is the Zohar, written
in Aramaic in the thirteenth century and attributed to Simeon bar
Yoḥai.[94] Pico knew of the Zohar, but he refers to it by name only once
and we have no evidence that the work itself was available to him.[95]
His knowledge of it appears to have been gained from intermediary
sources, notably the commentary on the Pentateuch of Menaḥem
Recanati, which quotes the Zohar (in Aramaic) extensively.[96]

2.5. The "more recent" Hebrew exegetes

This next group comprises Rashi (1040–1105); Moses ben Maimon (1135–1204); Moses ben Naḥman (1194–1270); Menaḥem
Recanati (late thirteenth–early fourteenth centuries); Levi ben Gershom (1288–1344); Sadias; and Abraam. By "both of those named
Moses" Pico means Moses ben Maimon (Maimonides) and Moses
ben Naḥman (Nahmanides), otherwise known as Moses of Gerona
or Gerundensis. Maimonides was known to the Latin Middle Ages
for his *Guide of the Perplexed*, which was originally composed in Arabic (c. 1190), translated into Hebrew by Samuel ibn Tibbon in the
thirteenth century, and circulated in Latin as the *Dux neutrorum*.[97]

---

rabbinica", in *Pico, Poliziano e l'umanesimo di fine quattrocento*, ed. P. Viti, 163–165
(Florence: L.S. Olschki, 1994); Tamani, "Libri ebraici", 500.

[93] Kibre, *Library*, item 290, equates this with the "Caldeus super prophetas" of the
second inventory; see Tamani, "Libri ebraici", 499.

[94] G. Scholem, *Major Trends in Jewish Mysticism* (New York: Schocken, 1954), 156–
204; *The Wisdom of the Zohar: An Anthology of Texts*, ed. I. Tishby and F. Lachower, tr.
D. Goldstein, 3 vols (Oxford: OUP, 1989, repr. 1994), I, 13–17.

[95] *Conclusions*, 212 (Conc. cabalisticae ... sec. opinionem propriam, 24). Elijah
Delmedigo mentions the Zohar in his kabbalistic bibliography written for Pico: see
BN Lat. 6508, f. 75ʳ, and my comments above, Ch. 1, section 2.1. Delmedigo, in
his *Beḥinat ha-dat*, summarized the argument between kabbalists and non-kabbalists
over the attribution of the Zohar to Simeon bar Yoḥai: Geffen, "Faith and Reason",
431–433; but there is no evidence that Pico was aware of this argument. See also
F. Lelli, "Pico tra filosofia ebraica e 'qabbala'", in *Pico, Poliziano e l'umanesimo di fine
quattrocento*, ed. Viti, 211–212.

[96] Wirszubski, *Pico's Encounter*, 55.

[97] The *Guide* was translated into Latin several times in the Middle Ages but not
printed until 1520. According to W. Kluxen, "Literargeschichtliches zum lateinischen

Two manuscript copies of the Latin text are listed in the earlier of Pico's two library inventories.[98] Although the *Guide* is known as a philosophical text, it was written, so Maimonides says in the introduction, as a work of biblical exegesis.[99] It includes a detailed section on the opening of Genesis,[100] and it is worth noting that one of Pico's copies of the *Guide* was originally bound with Philo's *Quaestiones in Genesim.*[101]

Pico regarded Maimonides as a kabbalist.[102] He was particularly influenced in this regard by the commentary on the *Guide* of Abraham Abulafia (1240–after 1291), entitled *Sitrei Torah* ("Secrets of the Torah"), which was translated for Pico by Mithridates under the title *De secretis legis.*[103] This latter work played a formative role in Pico's conception of kabbalah.[104] Its chapter headings include "de principio et causa", "de actu et potentia", "de opere geneseos", "de caelo et terra", "de aquis superioribus" and "de materia et forma", among others, which suggests that Pico would have considered it as a source of relevant information on the Genesis narrative. It is conceivable, then, that the "Abraam" in the list refers to Abulafia.

Nahmanides wrote a well-known commentary on the Pentateuch, a printed edition of which was in Pico's library.[105] There were three incunable editions: one printed in Rome (1469–1472), one

---

Moses Maimonides", *Recherches de théologie ancienne et médiévale*, 21 (1954), 24, this edition substantially reflects the common manuscript tradition as used by the scholastics. My citations of the *Guide* will therefore follow the 1520 edition: Maimonides, *Dux seu Director dubitantium aut perplexorum ...* (Paris, 1520). I shall also provide bracketed cross-references to the English translation, *The Guide of the Perplexed*, tr. S. Pines (Chicago, Illinois: University of Chicago Press, 1963).

[98] Kibre, *Library*, items 235 and 694.

[99] Maimonides, *Dux*, ff. 2^{r-v} (*Guide*, tr. Pines, 5–6): "Istius libri prima intentio est explanare diversitates nominum quae inveniuntur in libris prophetarum, quorum quaedam sunt aequivoca ... . Commentatur etiam in hoc libro modum secundum: qui est ad exponendum similitudines nimis occultas, quae sunt in libris prophetarum, et non dicitur manifeste quod sunt similitudines".

[100] Maimonides, *Dux*, ff. 56^{r}–61^{v} (*Guide*, tr. Pines, 327–360).

[101] See Mercati, *Codici latini e graeci*, 21–22.

[102] *Conclusions*, 224 (Conc. cabalisticae ... sec. opinionem propriam, 63): "Sicut Aristoteles diviniorem philosophiam, quam philosophi antiqui sub fabulis et apologis velarunt, ipse sub philosophicae speculationis facie dissimulavit, et verborum brevitate obscuravit, ita Rabi Moyses Aegyptius in libro, qui a latinis dicitur Dux neutrorum, dum per superficialem verborum corticem videtur cum philosophia ambulare, per latentes profundi sensus intelligentias mysteria complectitur Cabalae."

[103] Vat. Ebr. 190, ff. 336–end; Chigi A VI 190, ff. 232–262.

[104] See Wirszubski, *Pico's Encounter*, especially 84–100 and 121–132.

[105] Kibre, *Library*, item 306, "Gerona in bibliam / Rabi moyses super pentateucham".

in Lisbon (1489) and one in Naples (1490).[106] Pico also owned the shorter redaction of this work, described as "Commentum breve super pentateucum rabi moises et alia quaedam in cabala".[107] The commentary on the Pentateuch does not figure in the translated corpus, however, although Mithridates did translate another of Nahmanides's works, to which he gave the title *Liber de secretis legis manifestatis*.[108] Pico mentions Nahmanides once in the *Apologia* and once in the *Expositiones in Psalmos*.[109] He also cites him in the *Heptaplus*.[110] Here, however, the reference could equally have come from Recanati's quotation of Nahmanides in his commentary on the Pentateuch.[111] Pending further analysis, it is not yet clear to what extent Pico actually read Nahmanides.

Levi ben Gershom (otherwise known as Gersonides), on the other hand, exercised an undeniable influence on Pico's concept of exegesis. In the first place, this is evident from Pico's Job manuscript, which bears the imprint of Gersonides's own commentary on Job.[112] In the second place, Pico owned and annotated a translation made for him by Mithridates of Gersonides's commentary on the Song of Songs.[113] Pico refers to Gersonides in the *Apologia*, where he cites him, along with Maimonides and Abraham ibn Ezra, as one of the Jewish exegetes who engage in *sechel* (שכל).[114] As with Nahmanides, however, it is not clear that Pico actually read Gersonides's commentary on the Pentateuch, although he did own a printed copy of it.[115]

"Manaem" refers to Menaḥem Recanati, whose commentary on the Pentateuch, as noted above, was Pico's principal point of entry to the Zohar. As we saw in Chapter 1, it was translated for him by

---

[106] Tamani, "Libri ebraici", 501, item 12.

[107] Ibid., item 13.

[108] Vat. Ebr. 190, ff. 207–222; see, for the original text, Tamani, "Libri ebraici", 501–502, item 14.

[109] *Opera omnia*, 175; commentary on Psalm 10: *Expositiones in Psalmos*, ed. Raspanti, 84.

[110] H. 7.4; Garin, 350.

[111] See Bacchelli, *Giovanni Pico e Pier Leone da Spoleto*, 92–93.

[112] Discussed above, Ch. 1, section 2.4. Although it is not possible to prove that Pico owned Gersonides's commentary, it may have been in the volume entitled (in the first inventory) "Levii super cantica et alia multa": Kibre, *Library*, item 865; Tamani, "Libri ebraici", 505, item 30. Another item in the inventory represents a Hebrew commentary on Job, but no author is given: Kibre, *Library*, item 891; Tamani, "Libri ebraici", 506, item 32.

[113] Vat. Lat. 4273, ff. 5ʳ–54ʳ; see Zatelli et al., "Pico: la cultura biblica", 170–172, item 57.

[114] On Pico's mistranslation of this term, see above, n. 31.

[115] Kibre, *Library*, item 276; Tamani, "Libri ebraici", 502, item 15.

Mithridates at some point in 1486, but this version is largely no longer extant. Recanati's commentary on the Pentateuch was an influential source for Pico's interpretation of kabbalah in the *900 Conclusiones*.[116]

"Salomon" we can safely assume is Solomon ben Isaac, otherwise known as Rashi. He is regularly cited under this name in the *Expositiones in Psalmos*.[117] As we have seen, Pico owned a copy of the Pentateuch which included Rashi's commentary.[118] He also owned Rashi's commentary on the Talmud.[119]

If "Abraam" does not refer to Abulafia, it is plausible that he is Abraham ibn Ezra (1089–1164), although in the *Expositiones in Psalmos* (where he is one of the most frequently cited exegetes), Pico calls him "Avenazra", and in the *Apologia*, "Abnazara".[120] Pico possessed a 1488 printed edition of Ibn Ezra's commentary on the Pentateuch and a manuscript copy of a group of commentaries on Isaiah, the Prophets and the Psalms.[121] It appears that Mithridates may have translated portions of Ibn Ezra's Genesis commentary into Latin.[122]

It is possible that "Sadias" refers to Saadiah Gaon (882–942), two of whose books were probably in Pico's library.[123] Neither of them appears to relate specifically to Genesis, however, and he does not figure in the translated corpus, so this attribution should remain tentative.[124]

---

[116] Wirszubski, *Pico's Encounter*, 53–56.

[117] *Expositiones in Psalmos*, ed. Raspanti, 62, 80, 82, 88, 98, 100, 102, 104, 106, 144, 202.

[118] See above, n. 92.

[119] Kibre, *Library*, item 868.

[120] *Expositiones in Psalmos*, ed. Raspanti, 62, 66, 96, 102, 104, 146, 158, 178; *Opera omnia*, 178.

[121] Commentary on the Pentateuch: Kibre, *Library*, item 864 ("Auenazra in pentateucon"); Zatelli et al., "Pico: la cultura biblica", 168–169, item 56; Tamani, "Libri ebraici", 501, item 11. For the other works, see Kibre, *Library*, item 273 ("Aduenasra in bibliam") and Tamani, "Libri ebraici", 505, item 29.

[122] F. Secret, "Nouvelles precisions sur Flavius Mithridates maître de Pic de la Mirandole et traducteur de commentaires de kabbale", in *L'opera e il pensiero di Giovanni Pico della Mirandola nella storia dell'Umanesimo: convegno internazionale*, II, 169 n. 2, signals a manuscript found by M. Berlin at the Proprietary and Cottonian Library of Plymouth, catalogued as "Abrahamus Abenazra super Genesim et Exodum, latine per Methrydatem. Gaonis commentum super ultimam prophetiam Danelis ... cum additionibus ben Caspi. 180 fol." See M. Berlin, "A Curious Ibn Ezra Manuscript", *Jewish Quarterly Review*, 8 (1896), 711–714.

[123] Kibre, *Library*, items 284 ("Commentum Gaon super proverbia") and 790 ("Liber Saadias Gaon de credibilibus").

[124] Saadiah Gaon's *Sefer ha-emunot ve ha-de'ot* starts with a discussion of creation.

This group, in sum, represents an accurate cross-section of the most well-known and influential medieval Jewish exegetes. It is clear that Pico had access to their works, but in many cases he was limited to Hebrew texts. The citations in the *Expositiones in Psalmos*, discussed below, show that he was able to draw on some of these untranslated works, such as Ibn Ezra and Rashi.

2.6. *The ancient Hebrew commentators*

It is harder to say what context lies behind the names of the "ancient" commentators, Eleazarus, Aba, Ioannes, Neonias, Isaac and Ioseph. "Neonias" probably refers to Neḥunya ben Ha-Kanah, to whom the *Sefer Bahir* was sometimes attributed.[125] The *Bahir* starts with a quotation from him, spelt (in Mithridates's translation) "Nehonias".[126] Pico read the *Bahir* in this version and used it in the *Conclusiones*.[127] The *Bahir* is essentially an exegetical work, and a fair proportion of its sections relate to the Genesis narrative. It is structured as a series of brief citations of ancient rabbis. Among these, we find a Rabbi Joḥanan, who comments on certain verses from Genesis 1, but it is not clear whether Pico would have changed Mithridates's spelling of "Iohanan" to "Ioannes".[128] Rabbis by the name of Eleazar, Abba and Isaac are all cited regularly in the Zohar and hence in Recanati's commentary on the Pentateuch. These names, as well as Joḥanan, are also to be found in the Midrash on Genesis, *Bereshit Rabbah*, of which Pico owned an untranslated copy.[129] There may well have been other such sources.[130] These ancient figures are not referred to in the *Expositiones in Psalmos*.

---

[125] G. Scholem, *Origins of the Kabbalah*, ed. R.J. Werblowsky, tr. A. Arkush (Princeton, New Jersey: Princeton University Press, 1987), 52–53. For another instance of pseudonymous attribution to Rabbi Neḥunya, in this case the *Epistula de secretis* published around 1487 by Paulus de Heredia, see F. Secret, "Pico della Mirandola e gli inizi della cabala cristiana", *Convivium*, 25 (1957), 32; id., "L'*Ensis Pauli* de Paulus de Heredia", *Sefarad*, 26 (1966), 91. Neḥunya is also mentioned in Alemanno's *Ḥay ha-'olamim*, ed. Lelli, 109.

[126] Vat. Ebr. 191, f. 288ʳ: "Incipiunt fragmenta libri bahir: dixit rabi nehonias filius accana ..."

[127] Wirszubski, *Pico's Encounter*, 58–59.

[128] *Bahir*, sections 21 and 147; *Le Bahir: le livre de la clarté*, ed. and tr. J. Gottfarstein (Lagrasse: Verdier, 1983), 28, 106; see, e.g., Vat. Ebr. 191, ff. 290ʳ⁻ᵛ.

[129] See Tamani, "Libri ebraici", 506, item 36; cf. *Midrach Rabba: tome I: Genèse Rabba*, tr. B. Maruani and A. Cohen-Arazi, introd. and notes B. Maruani (Lagrasse: Verdier, 1987).

[130] Many rabbis going under the names of Joḥanan, Eleazar or Eliezar, Joseph, Isaac and Abba can be found in early Jewish literature: see E.E. Urbach, *The Sages: Their*

What can we conclude from this analysis? Clearly, one essential function of the list is to impress the reader. While not neglecting a representative sample of canonical works, it serves to emphasize Pico's acquaintance with a remarkably wide range of commentaries. Many of them would have been unfamiliar to an educated Christian reader and several were only available in Hebrew. As Pico himself noted, access to such texts was both difficult and expensive.[131] By formulating this list negatively, as comprising those authors whom he will *not* use, Pico doubles its rhetorical impact. The implication is that he was sufficiently learned not only to read these authors but also to proffer interpretations that they had missed. It is not the only instance in which he began a book with obscure references.[132]

Beyond this rhetorical level, however, the question of exactly what the list represents is not entirely clear-cut. Although, as we have seen, almost all the names can be connected either to works available to Pico or to figures mentioned in works available to him, knowledge of the name does not necessarily imply knowledge of the text. Of the Hebrew and Aramaic works, several of the most notable were only available in their original languages. We shall see in the next section that Pico was able to make some use of untranslated Hebrew glosses. Many of the "ancient Hebrews", meanwhile, were known to him through citations in intermediary works such as the *Bahir* and Recanati's commentary on the Pentateuch. The same is true of a substantial proportion of the early Greek exegetes, who were not passed down in direct transmission but had survived only as fragments in the *catena*. We shall see in the next chapter that the question of transmission is of great importance regarding these early Greek commentators.

Despite the questions raised by this list, it shows that Pico's frame of reference was broad in comparison to contemporary norms and that his exegetical toolkit was better stocked than most. The *Expositiones in Psalmos* demonstrate the use he was able to make of some of these less well known writers.

Concepts and Beliefs, tr. I. Abrahams (Cambridge, Massachusetts and London: Harvard University Press, 1975, repr. 2001).

[131] See Ch. 1, nn. 72, 90.

[132] See the opening sentence of the *Oratio*: "Legi, Patres colendissimi, in Arabum monumentis, interrogatum Abdalam Sarracenum ..." (Garin, 102).

3. *Pico's Other Commentaries*

In section 1.3 of this chapter we saw that in commenting on Job and the Psalms Pico was in step with his contemporaries, whereas Genesis was less popular at the time as a subject of commentary. Further examination will confirm that the attention which Pico pays to Genesis in the *Heptaplus* is of a fundamentally different nature from that of his other exegetical works.

The *Heptaplus* relies on the Vulgate, the relevant section of which (Genesis 1.1–27) is included at the end of the second proem.[133] Slight differences between Pico's text and the Vulgate as now received are attributable to variant textual traditions, as the Vulgate, prior to 1590, was still unstandardized. These differences do not amount to a different translation. By contrast, both Pico's Job manuscript and his Psalms commentaries display a marked scrutiny of scriptural translation.

The Job manuscript has already been mentioned in connection with Pico's knowledge of Hebrew.[134] As we saw then, it combines a retranslation of, and marginal commentary on, Job, and was the joint work of Pico and Mithridates. In the shorter opening section written by Pico, the new translation is written between the lines of the Vulgate. Pico's focus was not on removing faults from the Vulgate Job; the retranslation was made for the purpose of interpretation, not for the sake of removing problems caused by transmission.[135] It cannot therefore be treated as an example of the sort of humanistic philology noted above. Nonetheless, in its revision of the Vulgate, it differs from the *Heptaplus*.

More illuminating is the comparison between the *Heptaplus* and the *Expositiones in Psalmos*. In the *Expositiones*, parts of which are contemporary with the *Heptaplus*, Pico engages with both of the currents of exegesis which I outlined above: philology and the four senses. This twofold intention is clear from his letter of 1489 to Andrea Corneo, in which he writes that he has in hand "a new work, with the encouragement of Lorenzo de' Medici". Firstly, he will "illuminate, with a longish interpretation, the Psalms of David". Secondly, he will defend the Septuagint version, which the Jews falsely claim departs from the Hebrew in over six hundred places.[136] This

---

[133] H. P2; Garin, 198–202.

[134] See Ch. 1, section 2.4.

[135] Wirszubski, "Pico's Book of Job", 187.

[136] *Opera omnia*, 383: "Differt autem emendationem instans ratio, et urgens novi

summary of the double nature of the *Expositiones in Psalmos* was repeated at the beginning of the *Heptaplus*, revealing the practice and purpose of philology as Pico and his contemporaries saw it:[137] philological analysis works by confronting different versions, and its purpose is polemical, not simply scholarly. In this purpose, Pico is in step with Manetti, who (with regard to his own version of the Psalms) argued that the purpose of learning Hebrew was to refute the interpretations of the Jews in order to convert them.[138]

All but two of the eight *Expositiones in Psalmos* have linguistic discussions at the beginning. These take the form of glosses of individual words, comparing the Septuagint, the Hebrew text, the Gallician Psalter, the *Psalterium iuxta Hebraeos* and the expositions of various commentators.[139] The method is best illustrated by a series of brief examples.

Psalm 6: "Defensio translationis":

> The difference in this Psalm between the Hebrew text and the translation of the Septuagint translators is not worthy of note. I touch only on this, that [the word] for "inveteravi" among the Hebrews is עתקה, which according to Ibn Ezra is expressed as "urgere", according to Kimḥi, "evellere" and according to Jerome "consumptum esse". The Targum, however, and the ancient scholars, and all the Midrashim on the Psalms, whom Rashi follows, express it as "inveterascere".[140]

---

operis quod habeo in manibus hortatu Laurentii Medicis, in quo Davidicos hymnos non solum illumino longiori interpretamento, sed quoniam quos ecclesia decantat, hi a septuaginta versi sunt interpretibus, eamque translationem plus quam sexcentis locis, uti parum fidelem Hebraei coarguunt, ego proprietati innixus Hebraicae et Chaldaicae literaturae, cum et sensuum integritati illos ab omni Iudaeorum calumnia assero et defendo."

[137] H. P1; Garin, 170: "operi alteri meo, tuo quidem auspicio iam pridem sed et in tuum nomen crescenti, quo davidicos hymnos a LXX versos interpretibus et in ecclesia iugiter personantes, non modo a suspitione omni calumniaque asserere, sed interpretamenti quoque facibus illuminare tentavi".

[138] See Botley, "Parallel Texts", 159–165. On the use of Hebrew scholarship to refute Jewish scriptural interpretation, cf. H. 7.4; Garin, 346–360.

[139] The Gallician Psalter was translated by Jerome from the Septuagint text in c. 392. The version *iuxta Hebraeos* was made c. 400. Pico, however, only refers to the second one as the work of Jerome.

[140] *Expositiones in Psalmos*, ed. Raspanti, 62: "Inter Hebreum contextum et translationem Septuaginta interpretum super hoc psalmo differentia non est annotatione digna. Illud solum tangimus quod pro inveteravi apud Hebreos est hatcha [עתקה], quod secundum Avenazra exponitur 'urgere', secundum Chemoy 'evellere', secundum Hieronymum 'consumptum esse'. Chaldei tamen et veteres doctores et omnes Midrastillistae, quos sequitur Rabi Solomon, 'inveterascere' exponunt." For references to these writers, see Raspanti's notes.

The comment refers to verse 8, which in the different versions reads as follows:

Hebrew: עששה מכעס עיני עתקה בכל-צוררי

Septuagint: ἐταράχθη ἀπὸ θυμοῦ ὁ ὀφθαλμός μου, ἐπαλαιώθην ἐν πᾶσιν τοῖς ἐχθροῖς μου.

Gallician Psalter: "Turbatus est a furore oculus meus; inveteravi inter omnes inimicos meos."

Psalterium iuxta Hebraeos: "Caligavit prae amaritudine oculus meus; consumptus sum ab universis hostibus meis."

As Pico points out, the verb עתק can mean to advance either in position (i.e., "urgere") or in age (i.e., "inveterascere"). The Septuagint translators chose the latter when rendering this verse into Greek with the verb παλαιόω. Some influential medieval Jewish exegetes disagree with this interpretation, but Pico defends it with reference to earlier Jewish sources.

Psalm 10.2, "in pharetra":[141]

The Hebrew word is *iether*, from [the letters] י ת ר, and David [Kimḥi] expresses this as "the string of a bow". Jerome followed this and translated it as "above the bowstring". But to signify "string" properly we say *iethed*, from [the letters] י ת ד; thus, the ר is changed into ד, from which comes *iethed*. *Iether* properly signifies "quiver", as Rashi expresses it.[142]

Again, to make sense of this note, it helps to juxtapose the different versions:

Hebrew: כי הנה הרשעים ידרכון קשת כוננו חצם על-יתר לירות במו-אפל לישרי-לב

Septuagint: ὅτι ἰδοὺ οἱ ἁμαρτωλοὶ ἐνέτειναν τόξον, ἡτοίμασαν βέλη εἰς φαρέτραν τοῦ κατατοξεῦσθαι ἐν σκοτομήνῃ τοὺς εὐθεῖς τῇ καρδίᾳ.

Gallician Psalter: "Quoniam ecce peccatores intenderunt arcum paraverunt sagittas suas in faretra ut sagittent in obscuro rectos corde".

Psalterium iuxta Hebraeos: "Quia ecce impii tetenderunt arcum posuerunt sagittam suam super nervum ut sagittent in abscondito rectos corde".

Pico's point is that in this instance the Septuagint and the Gallician Psalter are correct in regard to their translation of the word יתר from

---

[141] In the Hebrew text this Psalm is numbered 11.

[142] *Expositiones in Psalmos*, ed. Raspanti, 80: "Dictio Hebraica est iether, ex iod tau et res, et David exponit 'cordam arcus'. Quod sequutus Hieronymus transtulit 'super nervum'. Verum proprie significantes 'cordam' dicimus scilicet iethed, ex iod tau et daled: ecce res mutatur in daled, unde iethed; et iether proprie significat 'pharetram', ut exponit Rabi Salomon."

Hebrew; the reading in the *Psalterium iuxta Hebraeos* is based on a confusion—also attributed by Pico to Kimḥi—of two similar-looking consonants, ר and ד.[143]

Psalm 47.14, "et distribuite domos eius":[144]

Jerome [puts] "separate his palaces". "Pasagu" (פסגו) is a verb which signifies something high and elevated, on account of which some [put] "elevate his palaces". Kimḥi explains it as "fortify" or "strengthen", but in his commentary on the psalm he explains it as "seeing" and "contemplating", because things placed up on high are visible. The word is ambiguous among the Hebrews, in which case the Septuagint should especially be believed. The word "pasach" (פסק) signifies "divide and distribute a part", but the ק is often changed into a ג.[145]

Hebrew: שיתו לבכם לחילה פסגו ארמנותיה למען תספרו לדור אחרון

Septuagint: θέσθε τὰς καρδίας ὑμῶν εἰς τὴν δύναμιν αὐτῆς καὶ καταδιέλεσθε τὰς βάρεις αὐτῆς, ὅπως ἂν διηγήσησθε εἰς γενεὰν ἑτέραν.

Gallician Psalter: "Ponite corda vestra in virtute eius et distribuite domus eius ut enarretis in progeniam alteram".

Psalterium iuxta Hebraeos: "Ponite cor vestrum in moenibus separate palatia eius ut enarretis in generatione novissima".

The sense of this appears to be as follows. The word that occurs in the Psalm is פסגו, which according to Pico means "something high".[146] The Latin translations, however, both have the idea of 'separating':

---

[143] Modern dictionaries note that יתר means 'cord or bow-string' and יתד 'tent-peg'. Pico's interpretation is hard to account for. Rashi does not seem to support Pico here, as he glosses the phrase כוננו חצם על-יתר simply with the word הקשת, i.e. 'string [of the bow]', and does not mention the quiver: *Rashi's Commentary on Psalms 1–89 (Books I–III) with English Translation and Notes*, ed. M.I. Gruber (Atlanta, Georgia: Scholars Press, 1998), 88 (English section), 6 (Hebrew section). Pico's implication that Jerome "followed" Kimḥi is anachronistic.

[144] In the Hebrew text this Psalm is numbered 48.

[145] *Expositiones in Psalmos*, ed. Raspanti, 204–206: "Hieronymus 'separate palatia eius'. Pasagu est verbum, significat rem altam et elevatam; unde aliqui 'elevate palatia eius'. Chemoi exponit 'fortificate' sive 'munite', sed in expositionem psalmi exponit spectationem et visionem, quia res in altum positae sunt spectabiles. Verbum est ambiguum apud Hebreos, in quo maxime sit credendum LXX. Sed pasach significat partem partimini et distribuite; mutatur autem saepe coph in gimel."

[146] R. Alcalay, *The Complete Hebrew-English Dictionary* (Jerusalem: Massadah, 1963), col. 2065: פסגה translated as 'summit'. Of Kimḥi's two expositions given here, the first is found in his dictionary, *Sefer ha-shorashim* (Naples, 1490): חזקו ובצרו. A previous edition exists (Rome, 1469–1472) and a manuscript copy of this work is listed in Pico's library inventory, although containing only the first half, stopping at the letter *lamed*: see Tamani, "Libri ebraici", 521. For the second gloss, see *The Commentary of Rabbi David Kimḥi on the Psalms (42–72)*, ed. S.I. Esterson (Cincinnati, Ohio, 1935), 34.

"distribuite" or "separate". This idea is also found in the Septuagint: καταδιέλεσθε from καταδιαιρέω, 'I divide' The word for 'divide' in Hebrew, he continues, is פסק, but this can become פסג since the *koph* (ק) is often changed into a *gimel* (ג). Therefore, following the Septuagint, he chooses 'divide' as his translation.[147]

These are no more than soundings, but they are enough to illustrate Pico's method. The philological sections of his Psalm commentaries proceed by comparing the four versions of the text; in fact, without the different versions arrayed in front of one, Pico's notes are hardly comprehensible. Beyond this initial textual stratum are considered the glosses of the Targum, Midrash and various exegetes. When the texts disagree, the Septuagint, in the examples above at least, is given precedence. The Hebrew exegetes are 'corrected' on this basis, with reference to common mistakes of textual transmission. Although Pico's interest in the Septuagint is more marked than that of most of his contemporaries, we should note that in defending the Septuagint version of the Psalms, he is also defending the Gallician Psalter, which was translated from it. It was this, rather than the *Psalterium iuxta Hebraeos*, which was commonly accepted as the standard text.[148] His defence of established Christian versions of the Bible makes Pico a more conservative philologist than Valla or Manetti.

Aside from this philological content, each of the *Expositiones in Psalmos*, as Pico himself explains, has "a longish interpretation" or commentary section, which operates broadly (although not exclusively) within the standard fourfold framework.[149] All the salient vocabulary—"litteralis", "moralis", "allegorica" and "anagogica"— is used. But there is little consistency, and this cannot merely be attributed to the fact that the *Expositiones* are fragmentary. A brief description will show that Pico sometimes links the senses in over-

---

[147] In fact, according to M. Jastrow, *Dictionary of the Targumim, Talmud Babli and Yerushalmi, and the Midrashic Literature* (New York: Judaica Press, 1996), and likewise, Alcalay, *Hebrew-English Dictionary*, both פסק and פסג can mean 'to divide'. Raspanti, in his edition of *Expositiones in Psalmos*, 206, interprets this passage differently, seeing Pico's 'pasach' as refering to the word פסח, which means 'to pass over' or 'to limp'. The sense is better served by פסק, which makes Pico correct in his translation and in calling ק 'koph'. On Pico's ideas of consonantal change in Hebrew, see further, Ch. 7, n. 11.

[148] This is what is implied by Pico's comment in the *Heptaplus* that the text of the Psalms which he defends is "in ecclesia iugiter personantes" (Garin, 170); the comment is reiterated in the letter to Corneo mentioned in n. 136 above ("quos ecclesia decantat", *Opera omnia*, 383).

[149] See, in general, Hardie, "Humanist Exegesis of Poetry", 72–80.

lapping ways, and sometimes turns away from the canonical four to a non-canonical "physical" sense.

An "expositio litteralis" is allotted to Psalms 6, 10, 11 and 47.[150] In 6 and 10 it is paired with an "expositio moralis", subtitled, in the former, "in modum theologicae meditationis".[151] A typical example of the division between the two is the first verse of Psalm 6 ("Domine ne in furor tuo arguas me, neque in ira tu corripias me") in which the literal exposition explains the apparent hendiadys by commenting: "*Furor* signifies a swift and hasty desire for vengeance, *ira* a slow and weighty one."[152] The moral exposition, taking the form of a meditation on the relationship of God and the sinner, concludes that, although such anger is justified, "God's goodness is greater than our evil".[153] A similar, but rather less precise, division of sense is to be observed in the expositions of Psalm 17. The first exposition is untitled, the second is entitled "moralis". The first, however, combines two senses, beginning with a literal exposition up to verse 16, then starting back at verse 8 with a more tropological exposition. Verse 8 ("et commota est et contremuit terra et fundamenta montium conturbata sunt") is therefore interpreted twice in the first exposition; firstly as describing "the miracles which God showed to Israel" and secondly as referring to the action of divine anger on the bodies and thoughts of enemies.[154] Since these enemies are those of the speaker, in other words, of David, this "tropological" exposition does not really depart from the literal, insofar as it remains projected into the historical time of the text. We might call the first meaning the

---

[150] *Expositiones in Psalmos*, ed. Raspanti, 66–72, 88–92, 106–110, 208–212.

[151] Ibid., 72–78; 92–96.

[152] Ibid., 66: "Furor subitarium et velocem vindictae appetitum denotat, ira tardum et gravem. Tunc Dominus neque in furore neque in ira castigat cum punit corporaliter in bonum animae, et ita castigat ut non consummat nos, neque peccati morte auferens gratiam neque morte Gehennae privans gloria." See Hardie, "Humanist Exegesis of Poetry", 76: "Characteristic of the philosophising exegete ... is the extraction of over-specific senses from literary texts, where language is deliberately left vague and considerations of form and style are as important as the distinct presentation of thought. This is Pico's procedure in the literal exposition of the sixth psalm. From the first two lines ... he derives a distinction between *furor* (which results in the figurative death of mortal sin) and *ira* (which results in literal death in Hell)."

[153] *Expositiones in Psalmos*, ed. Raspanti, 72: "Maior tamen, Domine, tua bonitas quam nostra malitia, maior misericordia tua quam mea miseria."

[154] Ibid., 144: "volunt Chaldei interpretes et aliqui ex consuetis enarratoribus intelligi de miraculis quae Deus Israeli monstravit"; ibid., 146: "*Commota igitur et tremefacta est terra* humani corporis hostium meorum et eorum fundamenta superbae et altae nimis cogitationis loco sunt mota ex manifesta divinae irae significatione." (Glossed phrase in italics.)

'literal-historical' and the second the 'literal-moral'. The difference between these and a properly tropological sense is illustrated by the exegesis of the same verse in the second exposition, which directs the verse away from the temporal frame of the speaker towards that of the reader. The "earth" is sensual desire, the "mountains" are the "angry height of ambition"; they are the rebels who wage war within man and whom the Lord's anger shakes.[155]

Psalm 11 is allotted literal and moral expositions, and an additional "expositio allegorica".[156] Of these, pride of place is given to the allegorical interpretation:

> The literal commentaries on this Psalm are able to take many things from the ancient commentators, Augustine, Jerome and others, which we also touched on above in our explanation of the title and argument. I think, however, that it is more rewarding to deal with the allegorical sense, both in this Psalm and in the following ones, as indeed we promised in the introduction.[157]

On reaching Psalm 47, the model broadens again. The title is "Expositiones quattuor, prima scilicet litteralis, secunda allegorica et anagogica, tertia physica, quarta allegorica et moralis."[158] The "expositio allegorica et anagogica" discusses the "true rest and true sabbath, when, after the resurrection, the Church which was militant on earth will be triumphant in heaven".[159] The "expositio allegorica et moralis", meanwhile, takes as its theme the movement "not only from the life of the flesh to the life of the mind, but also from the active life to the contemplative":[160] the moral passage from Babylon

---

[155] Ibid., 168: "Primum autem id est necessarium ut et libidinis et ambitionis impetus coerceantur, immo eradicentur vires omnes; neque enim vitia bona fide mansuescant. Per 'terram' igitur libidinem significat, per 'montes' irascibilem arcem ambitionis. Haec turbavit et excussit iratus Deus utili utique et salutari nobis ira dum ulturus interiorem hominem, in quem illae rebelles insurgunt, compescit acri castigatione, exurens quicquid in eis terrenum est et foeculentem et veluti Hydrae capita sic purgatorio igne perimens ut non sit amplius unde repullulent."

[156] Ibid., 98–120.

[157] Ibid., 114: "Litterales psalmi huius expositiones accipi plures possunt ex antiquis expositoribus, Augustino, Hieronymo, aliis, quod et supra in argumento et tituli expositione tetigimus. Allegoricum autem sensum tractare magis opere pretium duco cum in hoc psalmo tum in sequentibus psalmis, quemadmodum et in introductorio polliciti sumus ..." The "introduction", if it was ever written, has not come down to us.

[158] Ibid., 202.

[159] Ibid., 212: "vera requies et verum sabbatum, cum scilicet post resurrectionem triumphabit in coelo Ecclesia quae militavit in terris".

[160] Ibid., 224: "non solum de carnali vita ad rationalem, sed de ipsa activa ad contemplativam".

to Jerusalem. The application of the anagogical and moral senses is therefore traditional. Pico's treatment of the allegorical, however, is unusual. The strict way in which it was defined in opposition to the other two non-literal senses by the the *Glossa*, Thomas Aquinas and Nicholas of Lyra breaks down. There, 'allegory' lay in the relationship between the Old Testament and the New.[161] Here, it becomes a vague category, capable of including both the moral and the anagogical, and not contrasted with them.

The other unusual aspect of Pico's work on Psalm 47 is the inclusion of an *expositio physica*: "Departing from theological mysteries, let us also contemplate many physical truths in this Psalm."[162] He considers the nature of *mens*, its ability to descend *ad sensum* or rise *ad intelligentiam*. By basing his interpretation on this motion, he can write that:

> The "city of God" will be understood as the spiritual world; the "kings of the earth" as corporeal spheres separated from corruption, with jurisdiction over only the earth and earthly things. They come together in one through the movement of the universe, and they see in the spiritual world things which they admire, and from that admiration follows movement, and from there the nature of things conceives; and what it conceives with reasons, it unfolds in matter; because it does not give birth without the effort of time and the work of movement and change, these are therefore called "labour pains".[163]

We find a similar sense discussed in Pico's only extant exposition on Psalm 18, entitled *naturalis*. The mention of the sun in verses 4–5 leads to a long digression based on Julian the Apostate's oration *De sole*, in which it is posited that there are two suns, one invisible, the other visible.[164] Pico therefore interprets the Psalm in a Neoplatonic framework: not only in his citations of Julian, but also by mention of Plato, Plotinus, and the Platonic doctrines inherited by Augustine.

---

[161] Thomas Aquinas, *Summa theologiae*, I.1.10: "Secundum ergo quod ea quae sunt veteris legis, significant ea quae sunt novae legis, est sensus allegoricus"; Nicolas of Lyra, *Postilla*, I, sig. a2ᵛ: "si res significatae per voces referantur ad significandum ea quae sunt in nova lege credenda, sic accipitur sensus allegoricus".

[162] *Expositiones in Psalmos*, ed. Raspanti, 218: "Possimus autem a theologicis mysteriis discedentes et multas in hoc psalmo veritates physicas contemplari."

[163] Ibid., 222: "Capienda erit et civitas Dei mundus spiritualis; erunt reges terrae corporei globi seiuncti a corruptione, qui non imperant nisi terrae et terrenis, ii conveniunt in unum per motum universi, et vident in mundo spirituali quae admirantur et ex illa admiratione sequitur motus et inde concipit natura rerum et quae concipit rationibus explicat in materia, quae, quia non parit nisi conatu temporis et motus et transmutationis opere, ideo dicuntur dolores parturientis."

[164] Ibid., 178–188.

4. *Conclusion*

In the *Expositiones in Psalmos* Pico produced a series of commentaries which, although fragmentary and not entirely consistent with
each other, are nonetheless fairly representative of fifteenth-century
exegetical norms. These norms, we have established, are reflected
in their subject matter (the Psalms being at that time among the
most popular sections of the Bible for explication), their philological aspect and their basis on the accepted four senses of Scripture.
Pico's philological frame of reference is wider than that of the majority of his contemporaries, partly through the prominence he gives
to the Septuagint—which, as we have seen, was still at the end of
the fifteenth century not a very widely available tool for biblical
analysis—and partly through his use of Hebrew exegetical material.

The survey of commonly circulating texts carried out earlier in
this chapter showed that the four senses of Scripture retained their
canonical status at the end of the fifteenth century; the introduction
of printing, and the wide dissemination of a limited number of
texts which resulted from it, appears in the first instance to have
reinforced their dominance. In the *Apologia* Pico takes them as given.
He compares them to a similar fourfold method existing in the Jewish
tradition and uses the alignment to justify the use of kabbalah as an
interpretative technique. In the *Expositiones in Psalmos* he engages
with exegesis as commonly practised at the time and experiments
with the parameters of the typical model without abandoning it.
Although he adheres most of the time to the terminological compass
points of literal, allegorical, tropological and anagogical, in some
instances he redefines allegory so that it includes the other two non-
literal senses rather than excluding them. He does not explicitly
theorize this shift in definition. Its difference from the prevailing
ethos of strict comparmentalization transmitted by Nicholas of Lyra
and his followers is clear, however. His occasional inclusion of an
expositio physica or *naturalis* is further evidence of a desire to expand
or reshape the confines of the traditional four senses of Scripture.

The *Heptaplus*, on the other hand, represents a decisive break
from this tradition. Here, Pico refers to his method as 'allegory', but
he frees the word from the structure of the four senses. They, along
with their concomitant terminology, are abandoned, and in their
place is established a new concept of allegory, explicitly theorized
and, so he claims, unique to his work. It is probably fair to say that
one of the most striking features of the *Heptaplus* to a contemporary
reader would have been its neglect of the fourfold structure.

The other striking way in which the *Heptaplus* differs from the *Expositiones in Psalmos* is the lack of interest in philology, as defined above. Questions of textual transmission are never posed. On the rare occasions when he glosses words with reference to the Hebrew or the Septuagint, Pico's intention remains interpretative rather than textual. As an example, we can consider his exegesis of "inanis et vacua" in the first exposition of the *Heptaplus*:

> This earth, that is, matter, is "inanis et vacua" as Jerome translated it or, according to the Septuagint, "invisibilis et incomposita". ... But the Hebrew words *tohu* and *bohu* which are read in this place are explained in another way by many Jewish scholars. *Tohu* they interpret as something insensible, senseless, thunder-struck, which they relate to the shadowy and formless aspect of matter ... . *Bohu*, from the force of the word, many explain as the beginning and initial stage of form; for if we translate it verbatim, *bohu* is as if to say, "it is in it" or "something is in it".[165]

Here he compares the Vulgate, Septuagint and Hebrew texts; but his aim is not to eliminate an instance of corruption introduced by transmission. He uses a traditional Jewish interpretation, probably drawn from the *Sefer Bahir*, to contribute to an allegorical identification of a phrase in the Genesis account ("inanis et vacua") with a philosophical doctrine concerning the reception of form by matter.[166] The same is true of the other instance in which he draws on the Hebrew text, when in the second proem he demonstrates the median position of the heavens by deriving the word "asciamaim" (in his transcription) from "es", meaning "fire" and symbolizing the highest world, and "maim", meaning "water" and symbolizing the lowest world.[167]

---

[165] H. 1.2; Garin, 206–208: "Terra autem haec, idest materia inanis et vacua, ut transtulit Hieronymus, vel, ut Septuaginta, invisibilis et incomposita, et haec quidem omnia rudi materiae informique conveniunt, quae et expers formarum omnium merito inanis et vacua dicitur, et omnino incomposita et invisibilis est. Verum hebraicae dictiones *tou* et *bou* quae hoc loco leguntur a pluribus Hebraeis aliter exponuntur. *Tou* quidem rem brutam interpretantur, stupentem, attonitam, quod ad materiae etiam tenebricosam deformemque faciem ab illis refertur ... *Bou* autem ex vi dictionis inchoationem et rudimentum formae multi exponunt; idem enim, si verbum verbo reddamus, est *bou* ac si dicamus 'in eo est' sive 'eo aliquid est'."

[166] *Bahir*, ed. and tr. Gottfarstein, 18 (section 2); Vat. Ebr. 191, f. 288^r. On the dating of this manuscript, see Wirszubski, *Pico's Encounter*, 5, 12–21.

[167] H. P2; Garin, 184: "caelum natura media idcirco ab Hebraeis *asciamaim*, quasi ex *es* et *maim*, idest ex igne et aqua quam diximus, compositum nuncupatur." Pico used the same exegesis in the *Conclusiones*: see *Conclusions*, 204 (Conc. cabalisticae ... sec. opinionem propriam, 67), as discussed in Wirszubski, *Pico's Encounter*, 180. The

The *Heptaplus*, therefore, differs not only from contemporary norms but also from Pico's other exegetical work. He uses neither philological analysis nor the four senses of Scripture. Furthermore, he does not merely maintain the broad frame of reference characteristic of his Psalms commentaries; he surpasses it by claiming that he will not follow the works of any previous exegetes. Despite his protestations to the contrary, however, I hope to show in the remainder of this study that it is possible to establish clear links between the theory of allegory developed in the *Heptaplus* and ideas contained in other texts which he read and wrote.

---

exegesis is commonplace: see, e.g., *Bahir*, ed. and tr. Gottfarstein, 52 (section 59); Menaḥem Recanati, *Commentary on the Torah* (Venice, 1545), f. 3ᵛ; Joḥanan Alemanno, *Ḥay ha-'olamim*, ed. Lelli, 113.

CHAPTER FOUR

THE FIRST PROEM: TRADITIONS OF ESOTERICISM

At the heart of the first proem of the *Heptaplus* is a complex justification, not of Pico's allegorical theory as such, but of his general attitude to Moses's text. In outline, it has two central arguments. The first is to align Moses with ancient philosophy. Once this is accepted, it is used to justify a second, but related, argument according to which the Bible, and especially Genesis, has a concealed layer of meaning. In short, Pico argues for the existence of an esoteric philosophical dimension to the biblical text before going on (in the second proem) to discuss how to access it. The *Heptaplus* was not the first work in which Pico proposed this programme of esoteric hermeneutics: it is expressed in very similar terms in the *Commento* and the *Apologia*.

This chapter asks how Pico's esoteric stance relates to the two general contexts outlined in the previous chapter—the mainstream tradition of Christian exegesis and the broader range of approaches known to Pico. I shall argue that although such a stance was characteristic of an early phase of Christian biblical interpretation (lasting roughly until the sixth century), later developments, particularly in the Middle Ages, moved away from it. On the other hand, the same esoteric attitude is discernible in two non-Christian traditions: the Neoplatonic and the kabbalistic. The former had a significant Christian manifestation in the writings of Pseudo-Dionysius the Areopagite, which were highly esteemed by Pico and widely circulated in the fifteenth century. The latter was known to him through the translations made for him by Mithridates, and was also a contemporary subject of discussion in the Italian Jewish community, with which he had personal links.

Nonetheless, when in the *Heptaplus* he reformulated the esoteric stance which he had proposed in his previous works, Pico deliberately removed references to the word 'kabbalah'. This expurgation was, I shall argue, more apparent than substantial, although it is notable that several typical kabbalistic approaches to the biblical text are absent from the *Heptaplus*.

1. Moses and the Philosophers

Pico's project is predicated on the idea that "the secrets of all nature" are contained in the Genesis narrative.[1] His first justification for this is that Moses was inspired by the Holy Spirit; this in itself needs no argument, nor is one offered. His second justification, for which he provides a certain amount of documentation, is that among Christians, Jews and gentiles alike, Moses is renowned as a master of knowledge, specifically "of the wisdom of all doctrines and of all literature".[2] This claim he supports by reference to the following evidence:

a) the existence of a mysterious book, written in a secret language, entitled *Sapientia* and attributed to Solomon. The author of this book is thought to be an "interpreter of the universe", but he himself admits that he got his learning from the Pentateuch.[3]

b) Luke and Philo attest that Moses was very learned in all the doctrines of the Egyptians.[4]

c) the Egyptians were the teachers of the more divine Greek philosophers: Pythagoras, Plato, Empedocles and Democritus.[5]

d) Numenius called Plato an "Attic Moses": that is, he recognized that their doctrines were the same, although expressed in different languages.[6]

e) Hermippus attested that Pythagoras transferred very many things from Mosaic law into his own philosophy.[7]

---

[1] H. P1; Garin, 170: "Accidit autem per hos dies ut in mundi fabrica et celebratis illis operibus sex dierum fuerim assiduus, quibus totius naturae secreta contineri ut credamus magnae se rationes offerunt."

[2] Ibid.: "... nonne eumdem nobis cum nostrorum, tum suorum, tum gentium denique testimonia prorsus humanae sapientiae doctrinarumque omnium et litterarum consultissimum prodiderunt?"

[3] Ibid.: "Extat apud Hebraeos, Salomonis illius cognomento sapientissimi, liber cui Sapientia titulus, non qui nunc in manibus est, Philonis opus, sed alter, hierosolyma quam vocant secretiore lingua compositus, in quo vir, naturae rerum sicuti putatur interpres, omnem se illiusmodi disciplinam fatetur de Mosaicae legis penetralibus accepisse." For suggestions for the sources of this and the following points, see the end of this chapter.

[4] Ibid.: "Sunt item, quantum attinet ad nostros, et Lucas et Philon auctores gravissimi illum in universa Aegyptiorum doctrina fuisse eruditissimum."

[5] Ibid.: "Aegyptiis autem usi sunt praeceptoribus Graeci omnes qui habiti fuere diviniores: Pythagoras, Plato, Empedocles et Democritus."

[6] Ibid., 170–172: "Notum illud Numenii philosophi, non aliud esse Platonem quam Atticum Mosem."

[7] Ibid., 172: "Sed et Hermippus pythagoricus attestatur Pythagoram de mosaica lege plurima in suam philosophiam transtulisse."

The argument of this part of the proem is directed against a group of unidentified opponents. These people assume a distinction between Moses's text (that is, the Pentateuch) and the writings of the philosophers. Moses, they say, appears "rough and popular" in comparison to the philosophers.[8] Pico wishes to break down this distinction and bring Moses into line with these philosophers. The five points listed above (a. to e.) contribute to this on a historical level, by inserting Moses into one of the central traditions of Western philosophy. But for his argument to be convincing, Pico must also explain the disparity between the apparent simplicity of Moses's book and the complexity regarded as proper to a great work of philosophy. To do this, he invokes the idea of esotericism: that "it was a celebrated custom of ancient wise men that they either did not write about divine things at all, or that they wrote about them in a concealed fashion."[9]

2. Three Redactions of an Argument for
Esotericism: Commento, Apologia, Heptaplus

Pico's argument, in the first proem, develops as follows:

f) These "divine things" are called "mysteries". They would not have this name if they were not secret.[10]

g) Indians, Ethiopians and Egyptians practised this secrecy; the Egyptians symbolized it by placing Sphinxes in front of their temples.[11]

h) Pythagoras, who learnt from the Egyptians, became "a master of silence" and did not commit his doctrines to writing, with the exception of "a very little which, when dying, he entrusted to his daughter Dama". Hence, he was not the actual author of the *Aurea carmina*; Philolaus was.[12]

---

[8] Ibid.: "Quod si rudis in suis libris et popularis interim Moses potius quam aut philosophus, aut theologus, aut magnae alicuius sapientiae artifex apparet ..."

[9] Ibid.: "revocemus eo mentem, fuisse veterum sapientum celebre institutum res divinas ut, aut plane non scriberent, aut scriberent dissimulanter".

[10] Ibid.: "Hinc appellata mysteria (nec mysteria quae non occulta)".

[11] Ibid.: "hoc ab Indis; hoc ab Aethiopibus, quibus de nuditate cognomen; hoc ab Aegyptiis observatum, quod et Sphinges illae pro templis insinuabant".

[12] Ibid.: "ab eis edoctus Pythagoras silentii factus est magister, nec ipse quicquam litteris mandavit praeter omnino paucula quae Damae filiae moriens commendavit. Non enim quae circumferuntur aurea carmina Pythagorae sunt, ut vulgo etiam doctioribus persuasum est, sed Philolai."

i) The Pythagoreans effectively turned the anti-literary stance of their founder into a practical injunction, as can be seen from the complaint of Lysis that Hipparchus had violated it.[13]

j) The same injunction was sworn to by the three disciples of Ammonius, who were Herennius, Origen and Plotinus.[14]

k) Plato concealed his doctrines "wrapped in enigmas, veiled by myth, with mathematical images and with obscured indications of withdrawn senses"; and he himself wrote in his *Letters* that no one could clearly understand his views about divine things from what he had written.[15]

l) Jesus "did not write, but preached". He preached to the masses in parables and to a few disciples "openly and without figures"; and even then he did not teach everything to all of his disciples, as there were many things which "they could not bear". Given that "so few disciples, chosen from among so many, were unable to bear so much", it is hardly surprising that the common people would not have been able to bear it. This is why Moses, on Mount Sinai, spoke to the people with his face veiled.[16]

m) Likewise, the Apostles generally tried to maintain their secrets. Matthew, the first, limited his account solely to Jesus's actions. John, many years later, revealed more secrets, but only to combat heresy, and even then his pronouncements were obscure.[17]

---

[13] Ibid.: "Legem deinceps eam Pythagorici religiosissime tutati sunt. Eam Lysis ab Hypparco violatam quaeritur."

[14] Ibid.: "In eam denique iuratos Ammonii discipulos, Origenem Plotinum et Herennium, Porphyrius est auctor."

[15] Ibid.: "Plato noster ita, involucris aenigmatum, fabularum velamine, mathematicis imaginibus et subobscuris recedentium sensuum indiciis, sua dogmata occultavit, ut et ipse dixerit in Epistulis neminem ex his quae scripserit suam sententiam de divinis aperte intellecturum, et re minus credentibus comprobaverit."

[16] Ibid., 174: "Iesus Christus, imago substantiae Dei, Evangelium non scripsit sed praedicavit; praedicavit autem turbis quidem in parabolis, seorsum autem, paucis discipulis quibus datum erat nosse mysteria regni caelorum, palam citraque figuras; neque omnia paucis illis, quia non omnium capaces, et multa erant quae portare non poterant, donec adveniens Spiritus docuit omnem veritatem. Discipuli Domini tam pauci, electi de tot milibus, tam multa ferre non poterant; turba omnis israelitica, sartores, coci, macellarii, opiliones, servi, ancillae, quibus omnibus legenda lex tradebatur, totius mosaicae vel divinae potius sapientiae ferre onus potuissent? Ille quidem in montis sublimitate, montis utique illius in quo et Dominus saepe discipulos alloquebatur, divini solis lumine collustratus tota facie mirum in modum splendescebat; sed quia lucem ferre non poterat populus oculis caecutientibus et noctuinis, velata facie illis verba faciebat."

[17] Ibid., 174–176: "Scripsit Matthaeus primus Evangelium et, ut inquit Propheta, abscondens in corde suo Dei eloquia ne peccaret [Psalms, 118.11], ita solum quae ad Christi humanitatem attinebant historia prosequutus est, ne intercideret

n) Paul, writing to the Corinthians, distinguished the "laws of the flesh" from the "laws of the spirit"; he would only discuss wisdom among "the perfect".[18]

o) Dionysius the Areopagite wrote that it was a holy institution in the Church not to transmit secret doctrines in writing, but only orally.[19]

Comparison with Pico's previous works shows that a substantial proportion of this passage is composed from the same historical and thematic references as corresponding passages in the *Commento*, the *Apologia* and the *Oratio*. The following table presents these common elements in juxtaposition: on the left, the *Heptaplus* passage, and on the right, corresponding quotations from the *Commento* and the *Apologia*. The *Oratio*, at this point, is essentially a verbatim transcript of the *Apologia*.[20] I have, for reasons of space, omitted two sections of the *Heptaplus* passage which have no direct verbal correspondence with the other works, although they develop the same themes: one from the middle,[21] and one at the end.[22] The list of direct thematic and verbal borrowings includes: the role of the Sphinxes; Pythagoras's transmission of his doctrines to his daughter; the letter from Lysis to Hipparchus; the "veils of enigmas" of Plato; and the remarks of Pseudo-Dionysius on the importance of oral

---

oblivione memoria rerum gestarum, ut propterea in mystico Ezechielis spectaculo per hominem figuratum illum intelligamus [Ezek., 8.2]. Ioannes, qui prae omnibus maxime divinitatis secreta revelavit, tribus pridem vulgatis Evangeliis et a Domini cruce multis exactis annis, coactus loqui quae diu tacuerat ad abolendam haeresim Ebionitarum, quae Christum hominem non etiam Deum asseverabat, de aeterna Filii generatione, sed paucis, sed obscure pronunciavit, inde exorsus: in principio erat Verbum [John, 1.1]."

[18] Ibid., 176: "Paulus Corinthiis negat solidum cibum, propterea quod adhuc carnis legibus vivant, non autem spiritus, et sapientiam loquitur ante perfectos [Cor. I, 5.11]."

[19] Ibid.: "Discipulus Pauli Dionysius Areopagita sanctum et ratum institutum fuisse scribit ecclesiis ne dogmata secretiora per litteras, sed voce tantum, iis qui rite essent initiati communicarentur." On the identity and reception of Pseudo-Dionysius the Areopagite, see section 5 below.

[20] For the passage as it appears in the *Apologia*, see *Opera omnia*, 122; cf. Garin, 154–156 for the *Oratio*. For the *Commento*, see Garin, 580–581.

[21] Ibid., 174–176: "Discipuli Domini tam pauci ... et sapientiam loquitur ante perfectos" as quoted in nn. 16 to 18 above.

[22] Ibid., 176: "Quod si satis est confutatum, iam illud creditu facile, sicubi de natura, de totius opificio mundi tractatum ab eo, idest, si qua in parte operis sui velut agri cuiuspiam sint ab eo thesauri defossi omnis verae philosophiae, factum in primis hoc in hac parte, ubi vel ex professo de rerum omnium emanatione a Deo, de gradu, de numero, de ordine partium mundanarum altissime philosophatur."

transmission. Less direct correspondences, which are nonetheless present in the argument as a whole, are: the initial remarks on secrets and mysteries; the distinction of sense between "shell" and "kernel"; Jesus's double standard of teaching; and the reference to Plato's Second Letter.

Heptaplus (Garin 172–176)	*Commento* (= C) / *Apologia* (= A)
1 Quod si rudis in suis libris et popularis interim Moses potius quam aut philosophus, aut theologus, aut magnae alicuius sapientiae artifex apparet, revocemus eo mentem, fuisse veterum sapientum celebre institutum res divinas ut, aut plane non scriberent, aut scriberent dissimulanter. Hinc appellata mysteria (nec mysteria quae non occulta);	[C, Garin 580:] Fu opinione degli antiqui teologi non si dovere temeramente publicare le cose divine e e' secreti misterii, se non quanto di sopra n'era permesso; però finge el Poeta sè, come quasi apparecchiato a ragionare più oltre, essere da Amore ritratto e da lui essergli comandato che al vulgo de' misterii amorosi solo la corteccia monstri riservando le midolle del vero senso agli intelletti più elevati e più perfetti, regula osservata da chiunque delle cose divine appresso gli antiqui ha scritto.
	[A, *Opera omnia* 122:] at mysteria secretiora, et sub cortice legis rudique verborum praetextu latitantia, altissimae divinitatis arcana, plebi palam facere, quid erat aliud, quam dare sanctum canibus, et inter porcos spargere margaritas?
2 hoc ab Indis; hoc ab Aethiopibus, quibus de nuditate cognomen;	
3 hoc ab Aegyptiis observatum, quod et Sphinges illae pro templis insinuabant;	[C, Garin 581:] nè per altra ragione gli Egizii in tutti e' loro templi aveano sculpte le Sfinge ...
	[A, *Opera omnia* 122:] Aegyptiorum templis insculptae sphinges, hoc admonebant, ut mystica dogmata, per aenigmatum nodos, a prophana multitudine inviolata custodirentur ...
4 ab eis edoctus Pythagoras silentii factus est magister, nec ipse quicquam litteris mandavit praeter omnino paucula quae Damae filiae moriens commendavit. Non enim quae circumferuntur aurea carmina Pythagorae sunt, ut vulgo etiam doctoribus persuasum est, sed Philolai.	[A, ibid.:] Pythagoras nihil scripsit, nisi paucula quaedam, quae Damae filiae moriens commendavit.

5 Legem deinceps eam Pythagorici religiosissime tutati sunt. Eam Lysis ab Hypparco violatam quaeritur.

[C, Garin 581:] Quanto fussi el medesimo stilo da' Pitagorici osservato si vede per la epistola di Liside ad Ipparco ...

6 In eam denique iuratos Ammonii discipulos, Origenem Plotinum et Herennium, Porphyrius est auctor.

7 Plato noster ita, involucris aenigmatum, fabularum velamine, mathematicis imaginibus et subobscuris recedentium sensuum indiciis, sua dogmata occultavit, ut et ipse dixerit in Epistulis neminem ex his quae scripserit suam sententiam de divinis aperte intellecturum, et re minus credentibus comprobaverit.

[C, ibid.:] se non per dichiarare doversi le cose divine, quando pure si scrivano, sotto enigmatici velamenti e poetica dissimulazione coprire ...

[A, *Opera omnia* 122:] Plato, Dioni quaedam de supremis scribens substantiis, Per aenigmata, inquit, dicendum est, ne si epistola forte ad aliorum pervenerit manus, quae tibi scribimus, ab aliis intelligantur.

8 Quare, si ob id Moseos lectionem velut exculcatam putamus, quod nihil habeat in primori fronte non vulgare, non rude, damnemus eodem exemplo antiquos omnes philosophos ruditatis et ignorantiae, quos totius sapientiae magistros veneramur.

9 Iesus Christus, imago substantiae Dei, Evangelium non scripsit sed praedicavit; praedicavit autem turbis quidem in parabolis, seorsum autem, paucis discipulis quibus datum erat nosse mysteria regni caelorum, palam citraque figuras;

[C, Garin 580:] Scrive Origene avere Iesu Cristo revelato molti misterii a' discepoli, e' quali loro non volsono scrivere, ma solo a bocca, a chi loro ne parea degno, gli comunicarono ...

[A, *Opera omnia* 122:] Iesum Christum vitae magistrum, asserit Origenes multa revelasse discipulis, quae illi, ne vulgo fierent communia, scribere noluerunt ...

10 neque omnia paucis illis, quia non omnium capaces, et multa erant quae portare non poterant, donec adveniens Spiritus docuit omnem veritatem.

11 [see n. 21]

12 Discipulus Pauli Dionysius Areopagita sanctum et ratum institutum fuisse scribit ecclesiis ne dogmata secretiora per litteras, sed voce tantum, iis qui rite essent initiati communicarentur.

[C, Garin 580:] e questo Dionisio Areopagita conferma avere osservato di poi e' sacerdoti nostri, che per suscessione l'uno dall'altro ricevessi la intelligenzia de' secreti che non era lecito a scrivere ...

[A, *Opera omnia* 122:] quod maxime confirmat Dionysius Areopagita, qui secretiora mysteria, a nostrae religionis authoribus ἐκ νοὸς εἰς νοῦν διὰ μέσου λόγου σωματικοῦ μὲν ἀϋλοτέρου δὲ ὅμως γραφῆς ἐκτὸς, id est, ex animo in animum, sine literis, medio intercedente verbo, ait, fuisse transfusa.

13 Haec pluribus sum prosequutus, quod sunt multi qui Moseos librum, ducto argumento de rudi cortice verborum, tamquam aliquid de medio et triviale contemnant et aspernentur, nihilque apud eos minus credibile quam habere illum in recessu divinius aliquid quam quod fronte promittat.

[see above, item 1.]

14 [see n. 22]

We are dealing, then, with a hermeneutic stance already for the most part developed by Pico by 1486; there are additions of details, but no substantial deviations. The version in the *Heptaplus* is an expansion of the previous versions. The Indians and the Ethiopians, absent from previous accounts, are introduced, but these are simply passing references which do not add any new dimension or idea. Other references are given in greater detail. The common denominator of all these historical examples is the idea of a demarcation between the uninitiated and the initiated, between the masses and the elite, which in turn leads to a division of biblical interpretation between exoteric or literal and esoteric or non-literal. There is, in other words, a sharp dichotomy of reading, along both social and semiotic lines. Pico argues, through historical example, that this dichotomy is fundamental to the reception of the revelations contained in the Bible. Furthermore, he equates the two aspects of this dichotomy: the literal reading corresponds to the multitude, and the non-literal to the elite—or, as he sometimes refers to them, in the terminology of Paul and the early Christians, "the perfect".[23]

---

[23] See n. 18 above. 'Perfectus' translates τέλειος: see, e.g., Matt. 5.48; 1 Cor. 2.6; Philipp. 3.15; Coloss. 1.28; etc.

Perhaps it is not surprising that Pico the aristocrat should have expressed disdain for cooks, butchers and the like. But the resonances of this attitude as a literary trope or theoretical position require more investigation. This approach was by no means typical of Christianity throughout its history. On the contrary, it developed at a particular time, for particular reasons, and was then superseded, as the following discussion will, I hope, make clear.

We shall need to revisit here the distinctions drawn by medieval Christian theologians between the senses of Scripture, initially discussed in Chapter 3. But before this it will be helpful to look back at earlier proponents of non-literal reading. An outline will emerge of how Christian attitudes to non-literal reading changed over time, enabling us more accurately to contextualize the *Heptaplus*.

3. *In Favour of Esotericism: Early Christian Hermeneutics*

Pico argues that the discriminatory function of allegory is historically sanctioned by Christian and pagan tradition alike. The evidence for the Christian tradition is drawn from the Gospels and the letters of Paul. It is here that Christian allegory begins, and already at this stage the Christian tradition has echoes of the Greeks, in its use of terms such as *gnosis* and *mysteria*.[24] The evidence for the pagan tradition, meanwhile, is centred on Pythagoras and his followers and on Plato. In terms of named points of reference, Pico's account emphasizes the most ancient figures of each tradition. The references to the Egyptians are further evidence of this trend;[25] and Pseudo-Dionysius, it must be recalled, he regarded as a convert of Paul, and therefore as having lived in the first century AD. It is likely, however, that the direct sources for Pico's idea of esotericism were of a later date, as the following discussion will show.

The essential elements of his account, as listed above, were current in the development of Christian biblical exegesis in the late

---

[24] See J. Pépin, *Mythe et allégorie: les origines grecques et les contestations judéo-chrétiennes* (Paris: Etudes Augustiniennes, 1976), 251, who argues that we perceive "une inconsciente communauté de culture, plutôt que d'emprunts délibérés", and further, 257, that the resemblance between New Testament and Greek philosophical allegory "s'explique, mieux que par un influence grecque, par la structure propre à cette démarche, dans quelque contexte culturel qu'elle s'exprime".

[25] On the Egyptians as a source of the knowledge of the *prisci theologi*, see D.P. Walker, *The Ancient Theology: Studies in Christian Platonism from the Fifteenth to the Eighteenth Century* (London: Duckworth, 1972), 19–21.

second and early third centuries, and found their fullest expression in the *Stromata* of Clement of Alexandria. Much of the subsequent history of Christian hermeneutics can be regarded as a withdrawal— sometimes stealthy, sometimes radical—from the position developed by Clement. The scattered arrangement of the *Stromata*—the title means "Miscellanies"—precludes a simple account of its structure. It is nonetheless marked by the persistent reappearance of a limited number of themes. Prominent among these is the distinction between two classes of audience, one worthy to receive secret teachings, the other not.[26] This division requires an analogous division of interpretation. The *Stromata*, it is announced at the beginning of the first book, conceal truth, like a nut in a shell:

> The *Stromateis* will encompass truth mixed up with the opinions of philosophy, but veiled and concealed, exactly like the edible portion of the nut in the shell; for it is most suitable, I think, that the seeds of truth should be kept solely for the cultivators of belief.[27]

Essentially, Clement distinguishes between two forms of 'understanding' which can be applied to Scripture: 'belief' (πίστις) and 'knowledge' (γνῶσις).[28] The dichotomy is clear from the following extract:

> Those who only taste the Scriptures are 'believers' (πιστοί), whereas those who have gone further and become precise examiners of truth are possessed of *gnosis* (γνωστικοί); similarly, in life, the skilled are better than the unskilled and model what is beyond common conceptions.[29]

---

[26] See E.L. Fortin, "Clement of Alexandria and the Esoteric Tradition", in *Studia Patristica IX: Papers presented to the Fourth International Conference on Patristic Studies held at Christ Church, Oxford, 1963, Part III*, ed. F.L. Cross, 41–56 (Berlin: Akademie-Verlag, 1966).

[27] Clement of Alexandria, *Stromata I–VI*, ed. O. Stählin, L. Früchtel and U. Treu (Berlin: Akademie-Verlag, 1985), 13 (708A–B): "περιέξουσι δὲ οἱ Στρωματεῖς ἀναμεμιγ-μένην τὴν ἀλήθειαν τοῖς φιλοσοφίας δόγμασι, μᾶλλον δὲ ἐγκεκαλυμμένην καὶ ἐπικεκρυμ-μένην, καθάπερ τῷ λεπύρῳ τὸ ἐδώδιμον τοῦ καρύου· ἁρμόζει γάρ, οἶμαι, τῆς ἀληθείας τὰ σπέρματα μόνοις φυλάσσεσθαι τοῖς τῆς πίστεως γεωργοῖς."

[28] The distinction has further ramifications. Clement uses πίστις in several senses, two of which are concerned with logical and scientific demonstration, and one of which is concerned with scriptural reading. In general, he uses the former two in his polemics against philosophers, and the last in his polemics against gnostics. The idea in each case is to demonstrate that Christianity is not inferior to either philosophy or gnosticism. It is the last type of πίστις which is opposed to γνῶσις. See, for a full discussion, S.R.C. Lilla, *Clement of Alexandria: A Study in Christian Platonism and Gnosticism* (Oxford: OUP, 1971), 118–226; and the briefer comments of E.A. Clark, *Clement's Use of Aristotle: The Aristotelian Contribution to Clement of Alexandria's Refutation of Gnosticism* (New York: E. Mellen Press, 1977), 16–26.

[29] Clement, *Les stromates*, VII, ed. A. Le Boulluec (Paris: Editions du Cerf, 1997), 290 (533A): "οἱ μὲν ἀπογευσάμενοι μόνον τῶν γραφῶν πιστοί, οἱ δὲ καὶ προσωτέρω

The idea that an intellectually superior group of believers could extract a higher level of knowledge from Scripture was already current in the exegetical work of Philo.[30] The word *gnosis* was commonplace in the Septuagint and the New Testament.[31] Clement's use of the word, however, is also rooted in the contemporary controversy with the gnostics. They had appropriated it for their own cult, and Clement's response can be seen as a Christian attempt to reappropriate this originally biblical term. Early Christian polemics against the gnostics attacked their belief that they had attained an independent and higher sphere of knowledge, or revelation, which was inaccessible to others (such as Christians).[32] But Clement's attack on the gnostics was not intended to invalidate the social dichotomy which they proposed. On the contrary, he, and to a lesser extent other related figures, took this dichotomy as a given.[33] What was unacceptable was the lines along which the dichotomy was drawn. Clement's form of *gnosis* is attainable in its initial stages by study and contemplation, and in its final stages through the intervention of Christ.[34] In this matter he opposes the gnostics, who believed that *gnosis* could only be attained by those who participated in secret ceremonies.[35]

χωρήσαντες ἀκριβεῖς γνώμονες τῆς ἀληθείας ὑπάρχουσιν, οἱ γνωστικοί, ἐπεὶ κἂν τοῖς κατὰ τὸν βίον ἔχουσί τι πλέον οἱ τεχνῖται τῶν ἰδιωτῶν καὶ παρὰ τὰς κοινὰς ἐννοίας ἐκτυποῦσι τὸ βέλτιον."

[30] E.g. Philo, *De vita contemplativa*, in *Oeuvres*, XXIX, ed. F. Daumas (Paris: Editions du Cerf, 1963), 96–98 (28), where he discusses the interpretative methods of the higher believers, whom he calls θεραπευταί. They read Scripture by allegorizing ancient philosophy: "ἐντυγχάνοντες γὰρ τοῖς ἱεροῖς γράμμασι φιλοσοφοῦσι τὴν πάτριον φιλοσοφίαν ἀλληγοροῦντες, ἐπειδὴ σύμβολα τὰ τῆς ῥητῆς ἑρμηνείας νομίζουσιν ἀποκεκρυμμένης φύσεως ἐν ὑπονοίας δηλουμένης. ἔστι δὲ αὐτοῖς καὶ συγγράμματα παλαιῶν ἀνδρῶν, οἳ τῆς αἱρέσεως ἀρχηγέται γενόμενοι πολλὰ μνημεῖα τῆς ἐν τοῖς ἀλληγορουμένοις ἰδέας ἀπέλιπον, οἷς καθάπερ τισὶν ἀρχετύποις χρώμενοι μιμοῦνται τῆς προαιρέσεως τὸν τρόπον." On Philo's influence on Clement, see *Cambridge History of the Bible*, II, ed. Lampe, 159–163; A. van den Hoek, *Clement of Alexandria and his Use of Philo in the Stromateis: An Early Christian Reshaping of a Jewish Model* (Leiden and New York: E.J. Brill, 1988).

[31] There are numerous occurrences of this word in the Septuagint and more than two dozen in the New Testament.

[32] See, e.g., the account of Irenaeus, *Adversus haereses*, I.1.6.2, quoted in W. Foerster, *Gnosis: A Selection of Gnostic Texts*, 2 vols (Oxford: Clarendon Press, 1972), I, 138–139.

[33] See the comment of H.G. Marsh, quoted by Lilla, *Clement of Alexandria*, 146 n. 3: "We must not forget that there are two Clements, the Alexandrine philosoper and the Christian evangelist. The former defended the restriction of esoteric truth, the latter knew that the gospel for the salvation of mankind must be proclaimed to all."

[34] Lilla, *Clement of Alexandria*, 163–173.

[35] See, e.g., the account of the 'love-feast' of the Carpocratians: Clement, *Stromata I–VI*, ed. Stählin et al., 200 (1112A).

Otherwise, regarding the general idea that *gnosis* was an esoteric accomplishment open to very few, Clement is in agreement with his adversaries; they merely differed as to what the qualifications of these few should be.[36] In Clement's view, the attainment of *gnosis* by a Christian is facilitated by two factors: non-literal reading of Scripture and oral transmission of secret doctrine:[37]

> If we say Christ himself is wisdom and his activity showed itself in the prophets, through which it is possible to learn the transmission of *gnosis*, as he himself taught the holy Apostles at his appearance, *gnosis*, then, should be wisdom, which is a knowledge and apprehension of things which are, which will be and which have passed, and which, insofar as it was transmitted and revealed by the Son of God, is firm and reliable. Therefore, if contemplation is the goal of the wise man, then the contemplation of those who are still philosophers seeks, to be sure, divine wisdom, which it does not attain unless through learning it receives the prophetic voice revealed to it, by which it comprehends what is, will be and was before—how these things are, were and will be. *Gnosis* itself is what has descended by transmission to a few, imparted by the Apostles without writing.[38]

As part of his argument in favour of this esoteric hermeneutics, Clement puts together a list of historical examples, showing how different philosophical schools were united in concealing the truth from the unworthy.[39] The general lines are as follows. Anything which appears through a veil seems "better and holier".[40] The words of Scripture act as this sort of covering. The ignorant err, but "the

---

[36] On the formulations of the gnostics, see Lilla, *Clement of Alexandria*, 155–163.

[37] Ibid., 144–146.

[38] Clement, *Les stromates*, VI, ed. P. Descourtieux (Paris: Editions du Cerf, 1999), 184–186 (281C–284A): "εἰ τοίνυν αὐτόν τε τὸν Χριστὸν σοφίαν φαμὲν καὶ τὴν ἐνέργειαν αὐτοῦ τὴν διὰ τῶν προφητῶν, δι' ἧς ἔστι τὴν γνωστικὴν παράδοσιν ἐκμανθάνειν, ὡς αὐτὸς κατὰ τὴν παρουσίαν τοὺς ἁγίους ἐδίδαξεν ἀποστόλους, σοφία εἴη ἂν ἡ γνῶσις, ἐπιστήμη οὖσα καὶ κατάληψις τῶν ὄντων τε καὶ ἐσομένων καὶ παρῳχηκότων βεβαία καὶ ἀσφαλής, ὡς ἂν παρὰ τοῦ υἱοῦ τοῦ θεοῦ παραδοθεῖσα καὶ ἀποκαλυφθεῖσα. καὶ δὴ καὶ εἰ ἔστι τέλος τοῦ σοφοῦ ἡ θεωρία, ὀρέγεται μὲν ὁ ἔτι φιλοσοφῶν τῆς θείας ἐπιστήμης, οὐδέπω δὲ τυγχάνει, ἢν μὴ μαθήσει παραλάβῃ σαφηνισθεῖσαν αὐτῷ τὴν προφητικὴν φωνήν, δι' ἧς τά τ' ἐόντα τά τ' ἐσόμενα πρό τ' ἐόντα, ὅπως ἔχει τε καὶ ἔσχεν καὶ ἕξει, παραλαμβάνει. ἡ γνῶσις δὲ αὕτη κατὰ διαδοχὰς εἰς ὀλίγους ἐκ τῶν ἀποστόλων ἀγράφως παραδοθεῖσα κατελήλυθεν." On the oral tradition among the Apostles, see also *Stromata* I.11 and the article of J. Daniélou, "Les traditions secrètes des Apôtres", *Eranos Jahrbuch*, 31 (1962), 199–214; this quotation is discussed at 200–201.

[39] Clement, *Les stromates*, V, ed. A. Le Boulluec, 2 vols (Paris: Editions du Cerf, 1981), I, 114–134 (88B–101A).

[40] Ibid., 116 (88B): "ὅσα διά τινος παρακαλύμματος ὑποφαίνεται, μείζονά τε καὶ σεμνοτέραν δείκνυσι τὴν ἀλήθειαν."

one possessed of knowledge" (ὁ γνωστικός) understands.[41] Clement quotes the letter of Lysis to Hipparchus, in which it is argued that among the Pythagoreans "the mysteries of the *logos*" were not to be revealed to the uninitiated.[42] Likewise, the Epicureans, Stoics, Aristotelians and the "founders of the mysteries" all maintained a form of secrecy, either by expressing themselves in a covert fashion or by preventing certain texts from circulating.[43] The Pythagorean school distinguished between two types of pupil, and thus between an open and a hidden part of philosophy.[44] Clement posits a similar notion among the Peripatetics, who distinguished between the reason which was 'opinion' and that which was 'knowledge': the former fits into his scheme as exoteric, the latter as esoteric.[45] Moving away from the pagans, Clement turns to Paul. When Paul, in the Letter to the Colossians 1.28, writes that "we admonish every man, and teach every man, in all wisdom, so that we should render every man perfect in Christ", Clement interprets this esoterically: "he does not say simply 'every man' (since that would mean that there was no unbeliever) but 'all man', that is to say, 'the whole man', that is, the one purified in body and soul".[46] Nor is this an isolated instance: Clement tends to capitalize, in his interpretations, on the Apostles' use of such words as μυστήριον and σοφία.[47]

Slightly later in *Stromata* V, Clement returns to Plato, quoting the Second Letter: "I must state it to you in enigmas, so that if something happens to the letter 'in the folds of land or sea', the reader will not understand it".[48] In *Stromata* VI, meanwhile, he comments on the esotericism of Christ: "Neither prophecy nor the saviour himself

---

[41] Ibid, 116 (88C).

[42] Ibid.: "οὐ γὰρ θέμις … βεβήλοις τὰ τοῦ λόγου μυστήρια διηγεῖσθαι". The reference to *logos* is an alteration; the letter itself refers to the mysteries of Eleusis (ibid, II, 209).

[43] Ibid., I, 118 (89A–92A).

[44] Ibid., 122 (92A).

[45] Ibid., 122 (92B): "τὸ ἐν τοῖς λόγοις ἔνδοξόν τε καὶ ἐπιστημονικὸν καλούμενον". See Aristotle, *Topics*, I.1.100b for this distinction.

[46] Clement, *Les stromates*, V, ed. Le Boulluec, I, 126 (93C–96A): "οὐ 'πάντα' ἁπλῶς 'ἄνθρωπον', ἐπεὶ οὐδεὶς ἂν ἦν ἄπιστος … ἀλλὰ 'πάντα ἄνθρωπον' λέγει, ὡς εἰπεῖν ὅλον τὸν ἄνθρωπον, οἷον σώματι καὶ ψυχῇ ἡγνισμένον". Cf. Coloss. 1.28: "ὃν ἡμεῖς καταγγέλλομεν νουθετοῦντες πάντα ἄνθρωπον καὶ διδάσκοντες πάντα ἄνθρωπον ἐν πάσῃ σοφίᾳ, ἵνα παραστήσωμεν πάντα ἄνθρωπον τέλειον ἐν Χριστῷ."

[47] See Lilla, *Clement of Alexandria*, 146–148.

[48] Clement, *Les stromates*, V, ed. Le Boulluec, I, 132 (100A–B): "εἰκότως τοίνυν καὶ Πλάτων ἐν ταῖς Ἐπιστολαῖς περὶ θεοῦ διαλαμβάνων· φραστέον δή σοι, φησί, δι' αἰνιγμάτων, ἵν' ἤν τι δέλτος ἢ πόντου ἢ γῆς ἐν πτυχαῖς πάθῃ, ὁ ἀναγνοὺς μὴ γνῷ." See Plato, *Letter* II, 312D.6–8.

announced the holy mysteries simply so as to be easily understood
by passing strangers; but rather he expressed them in parables."[49]
The argument recurs elsewhere. For now, it is sufficient to note the
following passage from *Stromata* I:

> Christ ... allowed us to impart the holy mysteries and his holy light "to
> those able to make progress". Further, he did not reveal to the many
> the things which did not belong to the many, but to the few, to whom
> he knew they belonged, and who were able to receive them and to be
> modelled on them; but secrets are entrusted to speech, not to writing,
> as with God.[50]

From Clement, these ideas passed to Origen. Eusebius of Caesarea
says that Origen was taught by Clement at Alexandria; this is not
necessarily so.[51] Porphyry, on the other hand, says that Origen was
taught by Ammonius and was his pupil at the same time as Plotinus;
although these two, along with Herennius, made a pact not to reveal
in writing the doctrines of their teacher, both Herennius and Origen
broke their promise.[52] Regardless of the veracity of this anecdote, it
places Origen within the same esoteric tradition as Clement;[53] and,
in broad outline, his own writing supports this.

Origen distinguishes sharply between the literal and the non-
literal senses, and argues that reliance on the former causes theological error.[54] He, too, adopts the terminology of "mysteries". He

---

[49] Clement, *Les stromates*, VI, ed. Descourtieux, 308 (348C): "οὔτε γὰρ ἡ προφητεία
οὔτε ὁ σωτὴρ αὐτὸς ἁπλῶς οὕτως, ὡς τοῖς ἐπιτυχοῦσιν εὐάλωτα εἶναι, τὰ θεῖα μυστήρια
ἀπεφθέγξατο, ἀλλ᾽ ἐν παραβολαῖς διελέξατο."

[50] Clement, *Stromata I–VI*, ed. Stählin et al., 9–10 (701B): "ἧ καὶ οὐ κεκώλυκεν ὁ
κύριος ἀπὸ ἀγαθοῦ σαββατίζειν, μεταδιδόναι δὲ τῶν θείων μυστηρίων καὶ τοῦ φωτὸς
ἐκείνου τοῦ ἁγίου ᾽τοῖς χωρεῖν δυναμένοις᾽ [Matt. 19.12] συγκεχώρηκεν. αὐτίκα οὐ
πολλοῖς ἀπεκάλυψεν ἃ μὴ πολλῶν ἦν, ὀλίγοις δέ, οἷς προσήκειν ἠπίστατο, τοῖς οἵοις τε
ἐκδέξασθαι καὶ τυπωθῆναι πρὸς αὐτά· τὰ δὲ ἀπόρρητα, καθάπερ ὁ θεός, λόγῳ πιστεύεται,
οὐ γράμματι." A recently published fragment of a letter, attributed to Clement,
shows this dualism recurring in a discussion of the Gospel of Mark. See M. Smith,
Clement of Alexandria and a Secret Gospel of Mark (Cambridge, Massachusetts: Harvard
University Press, 1973), 446–450. This double gospel is discussed by Eusebius, *Histoire
ecclésiastique*, ed. G. Bardy, 4 vols (Paris: Editions du Cerf, 1952–1960), II, 107 (552A–
B).

[51] Eusebius, *Histoire ecclésiastique*, ed. Bardy, II, 94 (536A). See Origen, *Contra Celsum*, tr. H. Chadwick (Cambridge: CUP, 1965), ix; H. Crouzel, *Origen*, tr. A.S. Worrall
(Edinburgh: T. and T. Clark, 1989), 7.

[52] See below, n. 210.

[53] See Porphyry, *La vie de Plotin*, ed. L. Brisson et al., 2 vols (Paris: J. Vrin, 1982–
1992), II, 385–418.

[54] Origen, *Traité des principes*, ed. H. Crouzel and M. Simonetti, 3 vols (Paris:
Editions du Cerf, 1978–1980), II, 300 (360B): "αἰτία δὲ πᾶσι τοῖς προειρημένοις [i.e.,
Jews and heretics] ψευδοδοξιῶν καὶ ἀσεβειῶν ἢ ἰδιωτικῶν περὶ θεοῦ λόγων οὐκ ἄλλη τις

notes that even the simplest believer knows that there are mysteries in the Scriptures;[55] but that these mysteries are hidden under a veil of "visible" things from those who are unable to bear them.[56] The literal meaning is like a garment for the non-literal, and its purpose is to "improve the many".[57] Like Clement, Origen uses the word *gnosis* to designate the understanding of the non-literal sense.[58] Notably, it appears in the often-cited verse from Proverbs (22.20) which he takes as the foundation of his exegetical theory.[59] He mocks, however, the idea (of the gnostics themselves) that it is not available in Scripture, but is instead to be found in certain other books which "contain the secret and perfect mysteries of *gnosis*".[60] To this extent he follows the polemical reappropriation of the term *gnosis* into the Christian sphere initiated by Clement. At the same time, however, he responds to the criticism directed against Christianity—in the mouth of the Greek philosopher Celsus—that it is "secret" (κρύφιος). His response is ambiguous, designed to demonstrate the incoherence of Celsus's position. He refutes him, firstly, by denying the charge: the doctrines of Christianity are known almost everywhere, so it is absurd to call them secret; and secondly, by admitting the charge but also incriminating philosophers: "the existence of something beyond the exoteric, inaccessible to the masses, is not peculiar to Christianity alone, but is also true of philosophers, some of whose teachings are exoteric, and some esoteric".[61]

εἶναι δοκεῖ ἢ ἡ γραφὴ κατὰ τὰ πνευματικὰ μὴ νενοημένη, ἀλλ᾿ ὡς πρὸς τὸ ψιλὸν γράμμα ἐξειλημμένη." The original Greek version of this passage was in fact transmitted in the *Philocalia*: see ibid., I, 22–26.

[55] Ibid., II, 302 (360B): "καὶ ὅτι μὲν οἰκονομίαι τινές εἰσι μυστικαί, δηλούμενοι διὰ τῶν θείων γραφῶν, πάντες καὶ οἱ ἀκεραιότατοι τῶν τῷ λόγῳ προσιόντων πεπιστεύκασι". For examples of mysteries in the New Testament, see ibid., 304–308 (361B–364A).

[56] Ibid., 332 (373A): "διὰ τοὺς μὴ δυναμένους τὸν κάματον ἐνεγχεῖν ὑπὲρ τοῦ τὰ τηλικαῦτα εὑρεῖν, κρῦψαι τὸν περὶ τῶν προειρημένων λόγον ἐν λέξεσιν ἐμφαινούσαις διήγησιν περιεχούσαν ἀπαγγελίαν τὴν περὶ τῶν αἰσθητῶν δημιουργημάτων".

[57] Ibid., 334 (373A): "προέκειτο γὰρ καὶ τὸ ἔνδυμα τῶν πνευματικῶν, λέγω δὲ τὸ σωματικὸν τῶν γραφῶν, ἐν πολλοῖς ποιῆσαι οὐκ ἀνωφελὲς δυνάμενόν τε τοὺς πολλοὺς, ὡς χωροῦσι, βελτιοῦν."

[58] Ibid., 280–284 (352B–353B) and 382–384 (393C–396A).

[59] Ibid., 310 (364B): "καὶ σὺ δὲ ἀπόγραψαι αὐτὰ τρισσῶς ἐν βουλῇ καὶ γνώσει, τοῦ ἀποκρίνασθαι λόγους ἀληθείας τοῖς προβαλλομένοις σοι".

[60] Ibid., 308 (364A): "καὶ ἀπαγγελλέτωσαν οἱ μὴ βουλόμενοι παρ᾿ αὐτοῖς πρὸ τῆς ἐπιδημίας τοῦ Χριστοῦ τὴν ἀλήθειαν τυγχάνειν, πῶς ἡ τῆς γνώσεως κλεὶς ὑπὸ τοῦ κυρίου ἡμῶν Ἰησοῦ Χριστοῦ λέγεται παρ᾿ ἐκείνοις τυγχάνειν, τοῖς, ὥς φασιν αὐτοί, μὴ ἔχουσι βίβλους περιεχούσας τὰ ἀπόρρητα τῆς γνώσεως καὶ παντελῆ μυστήρια." On this point, see the argument of Crouzel, *Origen*, 104, 114.

[61] Origen, *Contre Celse*, ed. M. Borret, 5 vols (Paris: Editions du Cerf, 1967–1976),

Nonetheless, as his large output of sermons, expounding non-literal meanings in simple language, shows, Origen did not regard the non-literal sense as necessarily fit solely for a select audience.[62] More than Clement, he made use of the evangelical potential of non-literal readings. The dichotomy between those capable of understanding the mysteries, and those to whom they must not be revealed, is correspondingly less emphatic. It is essentially a quantitative rather than a qualitative difference, so that Origen appears to be a watered-down version of Clement.[63]

There is, then, a tension inherent in the hermeneutics of the early Christian exegetes, who maintain a high degree of esoteric exclusivity in relation to a portion of their knowledge, while simultaneously criticizing the heretical esotericism of the gnostics. The difference between the masses and elite as discrete groups, and the masses and elite as the opposite ends of a continuum, is necessarily somewhat blurred. In this context it is not necessary to try to impose a clarity that neither Clement nor Origen brought to the matter. What is clear is the rhetorical distinction that these writers enforce between the two groups, and it is this distinction which we shall observe to be fading in the examples which follow. Eventually, in the Middle Ages, hermeneutic theory, too, bridged the gap.

4. The Christian Reaction against Esotericism: Late Antiquity and the Middle Ages

Two factors served drastically to limit the proportion of early Greek Christian writing which was passed on to later ages through direct transmission. These are the doctrinal orthodoxy of Byzantine theologians, as established from the sixth century onwards, and the

---

I, 92–94 (668A–B): "εἶτ' ἐπεὶ πολλάκις ὀνομάζει κρύφιον τὸ δόγμα, καὶ ἐν τούτῳ αὐτὸν ἐλεγκτέον, σχεδὸν παντὸς τοῦ κόσμου ἐγνωκότος τὸ κήρυγμα Χριστιανῶν μᾶλλον ἢ τὰ τοῖς φιλοσόφοις ἀρέσκοντα. ... ἐπὶ τούτοις οὖν λέγειν κρύφιον εἶναι τὸ δόγμα πάνυ ἐστὶν ἄτοπον· τὸ δ' εἶναι τινα οἷον μετὰ τὰ ἐξωτερικά, μὴ εἰς τοὺς πολλοὺς φθάνοντα, οὐ μόνου ἴδιον τοῦ Χριστιανῶν λόγου ἀλλὰ γὰρ καὶ τοῦ φιλοσόφων, παρ' οἷς τινες μὲν ἦσαν ἐξωτερικοὶ λόγοι ἕτεροι δὲ ἐσωτερικοί". See also Pépin, La tradition de l'allégorie, 109.

[62] See Crouzel, Origen, 43–44.

[63] Ibid., 99, 114, where Crouzel makes an eloquent attempt to disassociate Origen from Clement, in particular regarding his attitude to gnosis. But Origen, as the examples above show, did not exclusively use the word gnosis in a pejorative sense in relation to gnostic heretics; and the "accusation of elitism" which Crouzel finds levelled at him is not entirely undeserved, even though Origen moved away from the more extreme position of Clement.

obsolescence of the uncial script, around the ninth century, which rendered many old manuscripts effectively unreadable unless they had been transcribed into minuscule.[64] For much of this older material, medieval and Renaissance scholars were dependent on Latin translations, florilegia and the *catena* tradition.

The compilation of the *catena* began with Procopius of Gaza (460–526).[65] By the sixth century there was already a broad division between those commentators who were considered orthodox and those who were regarded as heterodox. We find Basil, Cyril, Gregory Nazianzus and John Chrysostom, among others, in the former camp; Origen, Didymus, Apollinarius, Theodoretus and Severus in the latter.[66] Both camps were included in the compilation, but the focus was on literal exegesis, of the sort which was characteristic of the orthodox group.

The attitude of this group may be summed up by the curt comment regarding philosophers and theologians who allegorize which Basil was moved to make in his exegesis of the separation of the waters in his third homily on Genesis. The philosophers, who in their "meddlesomeness" speculate upon the heavens, refute themselves through their lack of agreement with each other and therefore can be automatically discounted.[67] The opinion of the theologians, however, who "under the pretext of the anagogical sense and of higher thoughts, take refuge in allegories" and say that the waters signify spiritual and incorporeal powers, is a pernicious compound of dreams and old wives' tales: "let us think of water as water".[68] This anti-allegorical stance is visible elsewhere in Basil's work.[69]

---

[64] See, in general, M. Richard, "La transmission des textes des Pères grecs", *Sacris Erudiri*, 22.1 (1974–1975), 51–60. On the effect of the change from uncial to minuscule, see Fryde, *Greek Manuscripts*, I, 36–39.

[65] G. Dorival, "Des commentaires de l'Ecriture aux chaînes", in *Le monde grec ancien et la Bible*, ed. C. Mondésert, 363–368 (Paris: Beauchesne, 1984).

[66] Ibid., 364–365. Origen's writings were finally condemned in 553.

[67] Basil, ed. Giet, 232–234 (73B): "καὶ μηδεὶς τῇ περιεργίᾳ τῶν περὶ οὐρανοῦ φιλοσοφησάντων τὸ ἁπλοῦν καὶ ἀκατάσκευον τῶν πνευματικῶν λόγων παραβαλλέτω. ... καὶ τί δεῖ πράγματα ἔχειν ἡμᾶς τὸ ψευδὲς αὐτῶν διελέγχοντας, οἷς ἐξαρκεῖ τὰς αὐτῶν ἐκείνων βίβλους ἀλλήλαις ἀντιπαραθέντας ἐν ἡσυχίᾳ πολλῇ θεατὰς αὐτῶν τοῦ πολέμου καθῆσθαι."

[68] Ibid., 234–236 (73C–76A): "ἡμῖν δὲ καὶ πρὸς τοὺς ἀπὸ τῆς Ἐκκλησίας ἐστί τις λόγος περὶ τῶν διακριθέντων ὑδάτων, οἳ προφάσει ἀναγωγῆς, καὶ νοημάτων ὑψηλοτέρον, εἰς ἀλληγορίας κατέφυγον, δυνάμεις λέγοντες πνευματικὰς καὶ ἀσωμάτους τροπικῶς ἐκ τῶν ὑδάτων σημαίνεσθαι· ... τοὺς δὴ τοιούτους λόγους ὡς ὀνειράτων συγκρίσεις καὶ γραώδεις μύθους ἀποπεμψάμενοι, τὸ ὕδωρ, ὕδωρ νοήσωμεν ..."

[69] See, e.g., ibid., 478–480 (188B–C).

By the time of the compilation of the *catena,* many of the hetero-dox exegetes were already extant only via citations in intermediary texts.[70] The compilers did not change the words of their sources.[71] In some cases, however, they cut them; and, more importantly, in their selection they, too, tended to exercise an anti-allegorical stance by concentrating on the literal sense. Looking through the *catena* on Genesis, we find that the sort of questions addressed are: how deep is the abyss?[72] what is the nature of God's speech?[73] and how many hours of day and of night were there?[74] Similarly, when extracting from an author such as Didymus who expounded both the literal and the allegorical sense, it appears that the compilers confined them-selves mainly to the former; and, in more than one instance, they attributed these extracts to Basil.[75] To take a single example of an early allegorical interpretation, the exegesis of Gen. 1.10–12 that the "earth", having been given the name "dry land", represents the soul which was to give fruit "a hundred-, sixty- or thirtyfold", is found in both Origen and Didymus.[76] It also finds its way into the *Heptaplus,* presumably via Origen.[77] It is missing, however, from the exegesis of those verses in the *catena.*[78]

The case of the influence of Clement of Alexandria is relevant here. I argued above that Clement is an important early represen-tative of esotericism in the Christian tradition. Evidently there are similarities between his approach to non-literal reading and that of Pico. Despite these similarities, however, it is highly unlikely that Clement was Pico's direct source. The only surviving manuscript of the *Stromata* was indeed to be found in the Medici library; it was con-sulted by Poliziano and subsequently used as the basis for the 1550 Greek *editio princeps.*[79] A record of purchase, however, shows that

---

[70] Petit, *Catena Sinaitica,* xvi–xix.

[71] R. Devreesse, *Les anciens commentateurs grecs de l'octateuque et des rois (fragments tirés des chaînes)* (Vatican City, 1959), viii.

[72] Petit, *La chaîne sur la Genèse,* I, item 25.

[73] Ibid., item 38.

[74] Ibid., item 43.

[75] See Ch. 3, n. 81.

[76] Origen, *Homélies sur la Genèse,* ed. Doutreleau, 36 (149D–150A); Didymus, *Sur la Genèse,* ed. Nautin, I, 82.

[77] H. 3.4; Garin, 260: "Quae autem haec terra est praeter eam de qua scriptum in Evangelio [Matt. 13.8] quod alia quidem affert fructum centesimum, alia sexagesi-mum, alia trigesimum? Terra utique animi nostri …"

[78] Petit, *La chaîne sur la Genèse,* I, item 62.

[79] Ms. Laur. 5.3, edited by Pietro Vettori: Clement of Alexandria, τα εὑρισκομενα ἅπαντα (Florence, 1550). See Fryde, *Greek Manuscripts,* I, 102–103.

this manuscript did not arrive in the library until 1492.[80] Poliziano referred to it in his *Miscellanea II* (unfinished at his death in 1494) but not in his *Miscellanea I* (which appeared at the same time as the *Heptaplus*, in September 1489). We know that, in the early 1490s, Lorenzo de' Medici was making a concerted effort to procure rare texts from early Greek Christianity; so, for example, we find him commissioning a copy of the *Philocalia* (a compilation of Origen's writings made by Gregory of Nazianzus and Basil), and another of the Latin translations of Origen by Rufinus, including *De principiis*.[81] Pico accompanied Poliziano on various research and buying missions to this end, notably in the summer of 1491.[82] If the otherwise unattributed manuscript listed in the earlier of Pico's library inventories as *stromata graeca* refers to Clement's work, it was presumably obtained by Pico after this date.[83]

Clement was an important source for Eusebius of Caesarea. Excerpts from the *Stromata*, many of them lengthy, are among the fundamental building blocks of his *Preparatio evangelica*. Clement (and Origen) are also important presences in Book VI of Eusebius's *Historia ecclesiastica*.[84] But otherwise, Clement's later direct reception was minimal. Pico makes no mention of him in the *Heptaplus*. There are several general references to Clement in the *Apologia*, one in the discussion of kabbalah summarized below, and a number in the defence of Origen.[85] The only specific citation of the *Stromata* comes in the *Disputationes*.[86] This lends further weight to the information

---

[80] This manuscript, the only extant copy of the *Stromata*, was purchased by Giovanni Lascaris, acting on behalf of Lorenzo de' Medici, during a mission to Greece in 1491–1492: see E. Piccolomini, "Due documenti relevati ad acquisti di codici greci, fatti da Giovanni Lascaris per conto di Lorenzo de' Medici", *Rivista di filologia e d'istruzione classica*, 2 (1874), 409–410; Fryde, *Greek Manuscripts*, I, 102, 159 n. 88; II, 730.

[81] Ms. Laur. 4.15 (*Philocalia* in Greek) and Ms. Laur. 22.9 (Rufinus's Latin translations of other works). See Fryde, *Greek Manuscripts*, II, 479, 684–685, who suggests on the basis of the illumination that the latter manuscript was not produced until 1489–1492.

[82] Ibid., 686–687.

[83] Kibre, *Library*, item 42.

[84] See R.M. Grant, *Eusebius as Church Historian* (Oxford: Clarendon Press, 1980), 63–83.

[85] *Opera omnia*, 180: "Talmuticos allegari ab antiquis doctoribus nostris, non est credendum, tum quia Clemens et multi alii, qui Hebraeos allegant, fuerint ante compositionem ipsius Talmut, quae fuit post Christi mortem, plus quam per 150 annos, tum quia doctrina Talmutica est totaliter contra nos"; see also 204, 214, 215.

[86] Pico, *Disputationes adversus astrologiam divinicatricem*, 4.4, in *Opera omnia*, 527.

given above, that no copy of the *Stromata* was available before Lorenzo's purchase of 1492.

The remains of the early Greek tradition, therefore, tended not to reflect the esoteric approach to hermeneutics. What this implies is that Greek *allegorical* exegesis of Genesis, particularly of the Alexandrian school, was actually available to Pico only in a limited number of texts—more limited than his roll-call of authors, discussed in the previous chapter, would suggest. We may, in fact, reduce it to a core of Origen (in the translation of Rufinus) and Philo.[87] The Christian reception of Philo's *De opificio mundi* appears to have largely died away after the fourth century, when considerable use was made of it by Ambrose.[88] It is not clear whether this work was included in the Philo manuscripts of the Medici library.[89] On the other hand, it is attested in two manuscripts in the Vatican, which were included in the inventories of 1475, 1481 and 1484.[90] Origen on Genesis, in the Latin of Rufinus, is likewise listed in Vatican inventories made under Eugenius IV and Sixtus IV.[91] Other than through these sources, early Greek allegorical exegesis had little direct transmission. We must now address the question of indirect transmission: the adaptation and development of early Christian ideas by later exegetes writing in Latin.

Origen exerted an important early influence on Jerome, who later renounced his Origenist position on non-literal reading.[92] Jerome lent weight to the idea of the availability of Scripture, not only through his translations, but also through his exegetical theory. We should consider, in this respect, this comment taken from his interpretation of Psalm 86.6:

> "The Lord will set forth in the writing of the people", in holy writings. This writing is read by all the people, that is, so that everyone understands it. This is what it says. The Apostles wrote like this, and the Lord himself spoke like this in his Gospel: not so that the few should understand, but so that everyone should. Plato wrote [things down]

---

[87] We must bear in mind, however, that to a certain extent this allegorical tradition was also received into Latin, notably by Augustine.

[88] Philo, *On the Creation of the Cosmos according to Moses*, tr. D.T. Runia (Leiden and Boston, Massachusetts: Brill, 2001), 36–38.

[89] See Fryde, *Greek Manuscripts*, I, 290–291. These are Laur. 10.20, Laur. 11.13, Laur. 10.23 and Laur. 85.10.

[90] Vat. Gr. 380 and 382; see Devreesse, *Le fonds grec*, 54, 58, 92, 97, 129, 134.

[91] Müntz and Fabre, *La bibliothèque du Vaticane*, 12, 187, 264.

[92] *Cambridge History of Bible*, II, ed. Lampe, 91.

in writing; he did not, however, write for the people, but for the few. Scarcely three men understand [what he wrote]. These people, on the other hand, that is, the leaders of the Church and the leaders of Christ, did not write for the few, but for all people.[93]

It is not my intention to take this brief remark out of context and turn a single gloss into a programmatic statement. Nevertheless, Jerome's use of Plato as a contrast to Christian authors, rather than as an *a fortiori* exemplum, is indicative of a change in paradigm that was to become increasingly marked. Christian biblical interpretation, from late antiquity to the late Middle Ages, attempted to define more and more strictly what was 'literal' and what 'non-literal'. This was not undertaken in order to separate the two sorts of reading; on the contrary, it aimed to unite them more closely than they previously had been.

Augustine addressed his *De doctrina Christiana* (written 396–427) to all those who were "willing and able to learn".[94] In its first three sections he advises his readers on the correct understanding of the signs which compose the Bible. In the last section, he turns to the dissemination of the knowledge which they have acquired. There are, he says, some things which simply cannot be understood, no matter how plainly one tries to express them, and when preaching there is a case for avoiding such things. This does not, however, apply to books: he draws a distinction between hearing and reading, and argues that what is inappropriate in the former context is not so in the latter. In books the writer has a duty to make himself understood regardless of subject matter. There are stipulations on both sides: desire for learning and mental capacity on the part of those being taught are to be matched by an interest in 'clarity' over 'eloquence'

---

[93] Jerome, *Tractatus de Psalmo LXXXVI*, in his *Opera pars II*, Corpus Christianorum Series Latina 78, ed. G. Morin (Turnhout: Brepols, 1958), 115–116 (1148B–1149A): "*Dominus narrabit in scriptura populorum*, in scripturis sanctis: quae scriptura populis omnibus legitur, hoc est, ut omnes intellegant. Quod dicit, hoc est. Sic scripserunt apostoli, sic et ipse Dominus in evangelia sua locutus est, non ut pauci intellegerent, sed ut omnes. Plato scripsit in scriptura: sed non scripsit in populis, sed paucis. Vix enim intellegunt tres homines. Isti vero, hoc est principes ecclesiae et principes Xpisti, non scripserunt paucis, sed universo populo." The italics designate the phrase of the Psalm that is glossed. Compare Jerome's contention that the Church Fathers wrote "universo populo" with Clement's esoteric interpretation of the same idea, quoted in n. 46 above.

[94] Augustine, *De doctrina Christiana*, ed. R.P.H. Green (Oxford: Clarendon Press, 1995), 2 (15): "Haec tradere institui volentibus et valentibus discere."

on the part of the teacher.[95] The ultimate goal of the teacher is to reveal what was previously hidden.[96]

Augustine's account works by the pairing of *docere* and *discere*. The linking of the two is a part of the mechanism by which the purpose of all knowledge, that of scriptural interpretation included, is to promote unity among believers and between believers and God: "the twin *caritas* of God and neighbour", as he calls it.[97] His view of scriptural interpretation was that it should promote the Christian community through the comprehension of shared signs. A secret system of language, comprehensible only to a few and thus subverting the community, was, for Augustine, the defining feature of magic.[98]

If we turn to Gregory the Great, we find a different approach to the technique of allegory.[99] But a similar model of knowledge and its use is visible. In the preface to his commentary on Kings I, Gregory distinguishes, certainly, between the "level ground of the historical sense" and the "secrets of the spiritual senses". But this distinction presents them not in sharp opposition but as two ends of a continuum. The one leads to the other: Scripture in general and the historical sense in particular are "steps" (though difficult ones).[100] Scripture has an outer and an inner meaning; the purpose

---

[95] Ibid., 222–224 (99): "Sunt enim quaedam quae vi sua non intelleguntur aut vix intelleguntur, quantolibet et quantumlibet quamvis planissime dicentis versentur eloquio. Quae in populi audientiam vel raro, si aliquid urget, vel numquam omnino mittenda sunt. In libris autem, qui ita scribuntur ut ipsi sibi quodam modo lectorem teneant cum intelleguntur, cum autem non intelleguntur molesti non sint volentibus legere, et in aliquorum collocutionibus non est hoc officium deserendum, ut vera quamvis ad intellegendum difficillima, quae ipsi iam percepimus, cum quantocumque labore disputationis ad aliorum intellegentiam perducamus, si tenet auditorem vel collocutorem discendi cupiditas nec mentis capacitas deficit, quae quoquo modo intimata possit accipere, non curante illo qui docet quanta eloquentia doceat sed quanta evidentia."

[96] Ibid., 226–228 (100): "Prorsus haec est in docendo eloquentia, qua fit dicendo non ut libeat quod horrebat aut ut fiat quod pigebat sed ut appareat quod latebat."

[97] Ibid., 48 (34): "Quisquis igitur scripturas divinas vel quamlibet earum partem intellexisse sibi videtur, ita ut eo intellectu non aedificet istam geminam caritatem dei et proximi, nondum intellexit." See, for a discussion of this, T. Williams, "Biblical Interpretation", in *The Cambridge Companion to Augustine*, ed. E. Stump and N. Kretzmann, 66–68 (Cambridge: CUP, 2001).

[98] See R.A. Markus, *Signs and Meanings: World and Text in Ancient Christianity* (Liverpool: Liverpool University Press, 1996), ch. 1, esp. 32–43; and for Augustine's semiotics of magic, ibid., ch. 4, esp. 133–146.

[99] Ibid., 60–61.

[100] Gregory the Great, *Commentaire sur le premier livre des Rois*, ed. A. de Vogüé, 5 vols (Paris: Éditions du Cerf, 1989–2003), I, 158 (22A–B): "Verum nec planitiem historiae quis hac aestimatione consideret, quia plerumque tanto difficilius ad

of this dichotomy is to provoke the reader to search for the inner meaning.[101] In the preface to his homilies on Job, Gregory remarks that Scripture is suited to both simple and advanced minds; it satisfies both in different ways and hence is "like a river, deep and wide, in which the lamb paddles and the elephant swims".[102] In the tenth homily on Ezekiel, he reminds the reader that half of the purpose of understanding Scripture is to hand on this understanding to others: "receive and disseminate" ("accipe et sparge").[103] This is not to say that Gregory did not envisage a hierarchy within the community of believers; but the purpose of the hierarchy was pedagogic not elitist. Gregory's sermons were addressed to those who would, in turn, go and teach others; and his purpose was to facilitate and structure learning, which was to be open to all—even, famously, the illiterate.[104]

Moving on to consider the central documents of later medieval exegesis, we find that the same position is maintained but with greater emphasis. The *Glossa ordinaria,* even without its framework of prefaces and introductions, encompasses all senses equally by presenting them non-hierarchically: all senses and interpretations coexist on the page. In the case of the interlinear gloss, a brief example from the opening of Genesis 1 will serve to show the extent to which all the senses are indiscriminately jumbled. I have put the interlinear gloss inside square brackets:

---

spiritalium sensuum secreta pertingimus, quanto in littera planiori secretorum aditum situm longius videmus, et eo eius tangere summa non possumus, quo gradus est inferior unde tangere summa cogitamus. Quid enim est intellectus divinitatis, nisi ineffabilis quaedam summa celsitudinis? Et quia omnipotens Deus per scripturas agnoscitur, quid est eadem sacra scriptura nisi gradus quidam qui conscenditur, ut illa sublimitas contingatur? Quotiens ergo historia planior est sed altior intellectus, quid est aliud, nisi quia talem gradum illa sublimitas habet, a quo facile contingi non potest?"

[101] *Cambridge History of the Bible,* II, ed. Lampe, 14.

[102] Gregory the Great, *Morales sur Job: Livres 1 + 2,* ed. R. Gillet and A. de Gaudemaris (Paris: Editions du Cerf, 1950), 120 (515A): "Divinus etenim sermo sicut mysteriis prudentes exercet, sic plerumque superficie simplices refovet. Habet in publico, unde parvulos nutriat, servat in secreto, unde mentes sublimium in admiratione suspendat. Quasi quidem quippe est fluvius, ut ita dixerim, planus et altus, in quo et agnus ambulet et elephas natet."

[103] Gregory the Great, *Homélies sur Ezéchiel,* ed. C. Morel, 2 vols (Paris: Editions du Cerf, 1986–1990), I, 384 (887B): "Ad hoc enim intellegenda sunt, ut et nobis prosint, et intentione spiritali aliis conferantur. Unde bene nunc dicitur: Comede volumen istud, et vade, loquere ad filios Israel. Ac si ei de sacro cibo diceretur: Comede et pasce, saturare et eructa, accipe et sparge, confortare et labora." See also Markus, *Signs and Meanings,* 51–53.

[104] See R.A. Markus, *Gregory the Great and his World* (Cambridge: CUP, 1997), 175–177.

In the beginning [of time, or before other things, or in his son] God
created the heaven [that is, spiritual beings who reflect on celestial
things] and the earth [carnal beings, namely, those who have not yet
put aside earthly man / that is, the spiritual and the corporeal creation
/ that is, all corporeal creation above and below].

But the earth [the corporeal substance of our flesh] was void [before it
received the form of doctrine / unformed and imperfect] and empty
[of those things which were to be formed from it].

And shadows [of sins / signifies the spiritual nature of blind ignorance,
which after being turned to the creator is formed and illuminated /
because there was not light which would overcome and overflow] were
over the face of the abyss [of the human heart].[105]

Not only do the different literal and non-literal senses all happily
cohabit in the interlinear gloss, there is no attempt made to distinguish one from the other, nor to force the terminology of the
fourfold method on them. This is equally the case in the marginal
glosses. These are often not introduced at all, or, if they are, it is by
the name of the writer from whose work they are taken, or merely
by the word *mystice*. This apparent confusion can only have contributed to the scholastic desire to circumscribe the spheres of operation of each sense.[106] The redefinition of the distinction between
literal and non-literal senses, as we saw in passing in Chapter 2, was
established by Thomas Aquinas in the *Summa theologiae* and confirmed by Nicholas of Lyra's adoption of it in the *Postilla*. The literal sense became the original meaning of the words—the things to
which they referred. This therefore included the (previously non-
literal) meanings of metaphors, prophecies, proverbs and parables.

---

[105] *Biblia latina cum glossa*, I, sig. a5^r: "In principio [temporis, vel ante cetera, vel
in filio suo] creavit Deus caelum [i.e. spirituales qui celestia meditantur] et terram
[carnales scilicet qui terrenum hominem necdum deposuerunt / i.e. spiritualem
et corporalem creaturam / omnem scilicet creaturam corporalem superiorem et
inferiorem]. Terra [nostre carnis corporalis substantia] autem erat inanis [priusquam
doctrine formam acciperet / informis imperfecta] et vacua [his que de ipsa erant
formanda]. Et tenebrae [peccatorum / ignorantie cecitatis spiritualem naturam
significat, que conversa ad creatorem formatur et illuminatur / quia non erat lux
que superesset et superfunderetur] erant super faciem abyssi [humani cordis]."

[106] See the comment of Smalley in *Cambridge History of the Bible*, II, ed. Lampe, 214:
"[The Doctor of Theology] was obliged to tell [his class] which of the senses he
was treating at a given moment; they would want to know. What hardly mattered to
monks imposed itself as essential in schools. Worse still, his Bible was glossed. The
glossators, unconcerned with his present problem, had not labelled their glosses as
treating of this sense or that. He had to decide which gloss should be attached to
which sense."

The non-literal was derived from the things initially represented by the literal meaning.[107] But again, we are misled if we interpret this apparent demarcation of literal and non-literal sense as an expression of social and semantic separateness. When Nicholas of Lyra added prologues to the *Glossa*, it was the exaggerated *division* made by some exegetes between the literal and non-literal senses that he condemned:

> As was explained in the preceding prologue, this book is the holy Scripture, which is said to have been written externally with respect to the literal sense and internally with respect to the mystical and spiritual sense. In general, this last may be divided into three, as was stated above. In particular, the multiplication of mystical expositions may be made according to any division. Nonetheless, all of the senses are predicated on the literal as their basis. Just as a building, sliding away from its foundation, is disposed to ruin, so a mystical sense which is not in agreement with the literal sense should be regarded as inappropriate and inept. ... You should also know that the literal sense is largely clouded over, on account of the mode of exposition commonly handed down by others, who, although they have said many good things, have nonetheless hardly touched the literal sense, and have multiplied the mystical senses so greatly that the literal sense, cut off amid so many mystical expositions, is sometimes stifled.[108]

Nicholas is often thought to have emphasized the literal at the expense of the non-literal sense. The *Postilla* was intended as a literal commentary, and the *Moralia* as a non-literal commentary; so the difference between them is partially accounted for by their different aims. But from his prologues it appears that what Nicholas actually viewed as damaging was the *division* made by previous exegetes between the literal and non-literal senses. He wished to realign the

---

[107] For one influential discussion of this distinction, see Smalley, *Study of the Bible*, 292–300.

[108] Nicholas of Lyra, *Prologus secundus* to *Glossa ordinaria*, in *Patrologiae latinae cursus completus*, ed. Migne, CXIII, 29B–30C: "Sicut dictum est in prologo praecedenti, liber iste est sacra Scriptura, qui dicitur scriptus exterius, quantum ad sensum litteralem, et interius, quantum ad sensum mysticum et spiritualem. Qui licet trifarium dividatur in generali, ut praedictum est; et licet sub quolibet membro possit fieri expositionum mysticarum multiplicatio in speciali; omnes tamen praesupponunt sensum litteralem tanquam fundamentum. Unde sicut aedificium declinans a fundamento, disponitur ad ruinam: ita expositio mystica discrepans a sensu litterali, reputanda est indecens et inepta ... . Sciendum etiam quod sensus litteralis est multum obumbratus, propter modum exponendi communiter traditum ab aliis: qui, licet multa bona dixerint, tamen parum tetigerunt litteralem sensum, et sensus mysticos in tantum multiplicaverunt, quod sensus litteralis inter tot expositiones mysticas interceptus, partim suffocatur."

two sides, not to dispose of one or the other. The distinction that
he maintained between the two types of sense was pragmatic and
pedagogical; his exegesis was designed for "readers and preachers"
alike, for both sides of the *docere / discere* dichotomy which we first
noted in Augustine's writings:

> But now that I have expounded the holy Scripture (with God's help)
> according to the literal sense, and God has granted me the length of life,
> relying on God's aid, I am setting forth again to expound it according
> to the mystical sense, where it should be expounded mystically, insofar
> as God will grant [this] me; but I do not strive to write all the mystical
> senses, nor to range over each and every word but rather to arrange
> some things briefly and in an ordered fashion, so that readers of the
> Bible and preachers of God's word alike will be able to resort to it, as
> and when it seems necessary to them.[109]

As the last sentence makes clear, although there is a distinction
between the literal and non-literal senses of the Bible, they are not
aimed at different audiences.

That medieval Christians did not, in general, regard allegory as
something destined only for an elite group of initiates is evident from
the content of sermons. Medieval sermons, like those of Augustine,
included allegories.[110] In a Church service, the reading from the Old
Testament was generally interpreted non-literally, as a preliminary
to the reading from the New Testament; the Old Testament was
less heavily 'literalized' than the New, and less emphasis was laid
on its status as a historical account.[111] Evidence from preaching
manuals shows that the multiplication of senses was an integral part
of the sermon, as does the invention in the thirteenth century of
Distinctiones, that is, word lists which gave different senses for the
same word from different parts of the Bible.[112] In short, sermons
were fertile ground for non-literal exegesis, which cannot, therefore,
be considered as 'elitist' in practice, any more than it can in theory.
Non-literal reading, throughout the Middle Ages, was directed at

---

[109] Nicholas of Lyra, *Prologus in Moralitates Bibliorum*, in ibid., cols 35–36: "Postquam
autem sacram Scripturam cum Dei adiutorio exposui secundum litteralem sensum, et
Deus dedit mihi spatium vitae: confisus de Dei auxilio propono eam iterum exponere
secundum sensum mysticum, ubi est mystice exponenda, prout mihi Dominus dabit;
non tamen intendo omnes sensus mysticos scribere, nec per singula verba discurrere;
sed aliqua breviter ordinare, ad quae lectores Bibliorum, ac praedicatores verbi Dei
recurrere poterunt, prout et quando eis videbitur expedire."

[110] *Cambridge History of the Bible*, II, ed. Lampe, 166–168, 182, 216.

[111] Ibid., 221.

[112] Evans, *Road to Reformation*, 144.

a mass audience.[113] This remained true even in the most rigorous attempts to limit the scope of the non-literal senses.

The non-literal senses were to become, in the sixteenth century, the object of attack by Reformers, and part of the rhetoric of this attack was that they distracted attention unnecessarily, and indeed dangerously, away from the literal sense.[114] But this reading of the fourfold model was essentially polemical. Calvin, Luther, Melanchthon, Tyndale and others ignored the hermeneutic arguments of the Catholic theologians and exegetes, seeing them as merely another manifestation of the issues of authority which preoccupied them. They wished to avoid the intermediary status of commentaries and glosses, just as they wished to avoid the intermediary status of the popes.[115] Given that commentaries and glosses were concerned, sometimes at considerable length, with the non-literal senses, it was clearly a useful strategy to attack these senses. The logical extension of this attitude was the final denial of complexity and the removal of all senses other than the literal. We can see this approach in Zwingli's reading of Genesis 1, in his *Farrago annotationum in Genesim* (1527): those who think that Moses wrote about obscure and difficult things are simply wrong; he wrote so that even idiots could understand him.[116]

Such a stance makes for effective polemic. But when we look at the theories of the central figures in the pre-Reformation exegetical tradition—the *veteres* who are the object of Zwingli's attack—we find that they did not, as a rule, envisage different audiences for the different senses, nor did they regard the literal and non-literal senses as mutually exclusive. On the contrary, they devoted considerable effort to combatting, in their theories, the kind of mutual exclusivity which tended to arise in practice.[117]

---

[113] See Spicq, *Exégèse latine au Moyen Age*, 362.

[114] See the references given in Ch. 3, n. 27.

[115] See Evans, *Road to Reformation*, 101.

[116] H. Zwingli, *Farrago annotationum in Genesim* (Zurich, 1527), sig. a2ʳ: "Quod se hic torserunt veterum plerique, in causa fuit, quod ad simplicitatem sermonis Mosaici non respexerunt, qua rem maximam, verbis simplicissimis, ac maxime cognitis enunciare voluit. Nam hoc est clare dicere, dum quis res arduas simplicissime ac clarissime ita ob oculos ponit, ut etiam idiotae ac rudes intelligant. Sunt qui hoc magnifice dictum esse putant, si quis ita dicat, ut a nemine intelligatur. Hi quidem existimant Mosen in tam ardua re voluisse aliquid obscurissimum dicere: at falluntur. Voluit Moses magnum illud opificium clarissime omnibus proponere: atque ideo utitur clarissimis et notissimis verbis, terra, aqua, aer etc."

[117] For another reading of the Christian reaction against esotericism, describing

5. *Esotericism Maintained: Later*
Neoplatonism, Pseudo-Dionysius, Kabbalah

The Latin Christian tradition struggled lengthily and eventually successfully to overcome the dichotomies of audience and text which it had initially inherited and developed. Nonetheless, the opposition of initiate and uninitiate, as a basis for allegorical interpretation, was preserved throughout later antiquity and the Middle Ages in two traditions. One of these circulated widely in the Latin West; the other was more or less entirely unknown there.

The first of these is the Neoplatonic tradition, in both its pagan and Christian manifestations. An esoteric attitude is to be found, for example, in the works of Julian the Apostate and Simplicius.[118] But from the perspective of the Latin Middle Ages, two authors in particular stand out: Macrobius (late fourth to early fifth centuries) and Pseudo-Dionysius the Areopagite (late fifth to early sixth centuries).

The allegorical exposition of Macrobius's *Commentary on the Dream of Scipio* is introduced by a discussion of why and when philosophers should frame their expositions in a *narratio fabulosa*.[119] Macrobius concludes that since nature hides herself from the gaze of the multitude, so the discussion of her secrets should be veiled from the common view.[120] As an example he relates the story of Numenius, who interpreted the Eleusinian mysteries in a manner accessible to the masses and for this reason was visited in a dream by the irate goddesses of Eleusis dressed as prostitutes.[121]

---

it in somewhat different terms and concentrating on the later Middle Ages, see C. Ocker, *Biblical Poetics before Humanism and Reformation* (Cambridge: CUP, 2002).

[118] Pépin, *La tradition de l'allégorie*, 117–127.

[119] Macrobius, *Commentarii in Somnium Scipionis*, ed. L. Scarpa (Padua: Liviana, 1981), 76–80 (I, 2.4–18). On the diffusion of this work, see Ch. 5, n. 19. Pico owned a printed edition: see Kibre, *Library*, item 244.

[120] Macrobius, *Commentarii in Somnium Scipionis*, ed. Scarpa, 80 (I, 2.17–18): "De dis autem, ut dixi, ceteris et de anima non frustra se nec ut oblectent ad fabulosa convertunt, sed quia sciunt inimicam esse naturae apertam nudamque expositionem sui quae, sicut vulgaribus hominum sensibus intellectum sui vario rerum tegmine operimentoque subtraxit, ita a prudentibus arcana sua voluit per fabulosa tractari. Sic ipsa mysteria figurarum cuniculis operiuntur ne vel haec adeptis nudam rerum talium natura se praebeat sed summatibus tantum viris, sapientia interprete veri arcani consciis, contenti sint reliqui ad venerationem, figuris defendentibus a vilitate secretum."

[121] Ibid., 80 (I, 2.19–20): "Numenio denique, inter philosophos occultorum curiosiori, offensam numinum, quod Eleusinia sacra interpretando vulgaverit, somnia prodiderunt, viso sibi ipsas Eleusinias deas habitu meretricio ante apertum lupanar videre prostantes, admirantique et causas non convenientis numinibus turpitudinis

The Pseudo-Dionysian corpus, a group of religious works written in Greek by an unknown author in the late fifth or early sixth century and heavily influenced by the later Neoplatonists, was attributed (at its first recorded appearance in 532) to one Dionysius the Areopagite, a figure passingly referred to in the New Testament as having been converted to Christianity by Paul (Acts 17.34).[122] Concerning the author of these works, Bertrand Russell remarked that "nothing more is known about this man, but in the Middle Ages a great deal more was known."[123] The corpus was believed to date from the second half of the first century. It comprises four treatises (*On the Divine Names*, the *Mystical Theology*, the *Celestial Hierarchy* and the *Ecclesiastical Hierarchy*) and ten letters. Its reception throughout the Middle Ages and Renaissance was extremely wide. At least six different Latin translations of the corpus (or parts of it) were made between the ninth and fifteenth centuries;[124] the 1990 critical edition lists over 120 manuscripts containing works of Pseudo-Dionysius copied during or before the fifteenth century; and there were nine different printed editions before 1500. Aside from their direct circulation in Latin, these works were received into scholastic theology and philosophy by, among others, Albertus Magnus and his student Thomas Aquinas.

The Dionysian corpus is thoroughly infused with that same form of esotericism which we initially found in Clement, as the following quotations show:

> See that you do not betray the holy of holies, but rather honour the things of the hidden God by intellectual and unseen *gnoses*, preserving them from the participation and pollution of the uninitiated, and reverently, by a holy enlightenment, sharing holy things solely with the holy.[125]

---

consulenti respondisse iratas ab ipso se de adyto pudicitiae suae vi abstractas et passim adeuntibus prostitutas."

[122] See the comment of E.R. Dodds, in his edition of *Elements of Theology*, xxvi–xxvii: "The influence which Proclus exercised upon early medieval thought may be called accidental, in the sense that it would scarcely have been felt but for the activity of the unknown eccentric who within a generation of Proclus's death conceived the idea of dressing his philosophy in Christian draperies and passing it off as the work of a convert of St. Paul."

[123] B. Russell, *History of Western Philosophy, and its connection with political and social circumstances from the earliest times to the present day* (London: George Allen and Unwin, 1946), 424.

[124] See Pseudo-Dionysius, *Dionysiaca*, ed. P. Chevallier, 2 vols (Paris: Desclée, de Brower et Cie., 1937–1950), I, civ.

[125] Pseudo-Dionysius, *Corpus Dionysiacum*, II, ed. Heil and Ritter, 63 (*De ecclesiastica*

It is not right to interpret in writing the invocations which belong to
the mysteries, nor to bring from secrecy into public knowledge their
mysterious meaning or the powers of God working in them.[126]

It is necessary for you to guard these things, my dear Timothy, according
to the very holy guidance, and to make the holy things neither be spoken
commonly nor divulged to the uninitiated.[127]

Let us not think that the outward appearances of the compositions
have been modelled for their own sake, but that they have been made
to shield the secret and invisible knowledge from the multitude, since
all-holy things should not be accessible to the multitude.[128]

You, my son, according to the divine decree of the hierarchy handed
down by us, listen in a manner befitting a sacred place to the inspired
holy sayings, becoming inspired yourself through initiation into inspired things; and having enfolded the holy things in the most secret
part of your mind, guard them as a unity from the unholy multitude. It
is not licit, as the Scriptures say, to cast before swine the pure, luminous,
beauty-producing comeliness of intelligible pearls.[129]

In 1457, Lorenzo Valla observed that it was unknown whether the
Dionysius mentioned in the Acts had ever written anything and that
fifteenth-century Greek scholars attributed the corpus to Apollinaris
(of Laodicea).[130] As mentioned in Chapter 3, the *Adnotationes* (in

---

hierarchia, 372A): "ἀλλ' ὅρα, ὅπως οὐκ ἐξορχήσῃ τὰ ἄγια τῶν ἀγίων, εὐλαβηθήσῃ δὲ
καὶ τὰ τοῦ κρυφίου θεοῦ ταῖς νοεραῖς καὶ ἀοράτοις γνώσεσι τιμήσεις ἀμέθεκτα μὲν αὐτὰ
καὶ ἄχραντα τοῖς ἀτελέστοις διατηρῶν, ἱεροῖς δὲ μόνοις τῶν ἱερῶν μεθ' ἱερᾶς ἐλλάμψεως
ἱεροπρεπῶς κοινωνῶν."

[126] Ibid., 130 (565C): "τὰς δὲ τελεστικὰς ἐπικλήσεις οὐ θεμιτὸν ἐν γραφαῖς ἀφερμηνεύ-
ειν οὐδὲ τὸ μυστικὸν αὐτῶν ἢ τὰς ἐπ' αὐταῖς ἐνεργουμένας ἐκ θεοῦ δυνάμεις ἐκ τοῦ κρυφίου
πρὸς τὸ κοινὸν ἐξάγειν ..."

[127] Pseudo-Dionysius, *Corpus Dionysiacum*, I, ed. B.R. Suchla (Berlin: De Gruyter,
1990), 121 (*De divinis nominibus*, 597C): "σοὶ μὲν οὖν ταῦτα φυλάξαι χρέων, ὦ καλὲ
Τιμόθεε, κατὰ τὴν ἱερωτάτην ὑφήγησιν καὶ μήτε ῥητὰ μήτε ἔκφορα τὰ θεῖα ποιεῖν εἰς τοὺς
ἀμυήτους."

[128] Pseudo-Dionysius, *Corpus Dionysiacum*, II, ed. Heil and Ritter, 197 (*Epistola IX*,
1105C): "μὴ γὰρ οἰώμεθα τὰ φαινόμενα τῶν συνθημάτων ὑπὲρ ἑαυτῶν ἀναπεπλάσθαι,
προβεβλῆσθαι δὲ τῆς ἀπορρήτου καὶ ἀθεάτου τοῖς πολλοῖς ἐπιστήμης, ὡς μὴ τοῖς βεβήλοις
εὐχείρωτα εἶναι τὰ πανίερα· μόνοις δὲ ἀνακαλύπτεσθαι τοῖς τῆς θεότητος γνησίοις ἐρα-
σταῖς ..."

[129] Pseudo-Dionysius, *Corpus Dionysiacum*, II, ed. Heil and Ritter, 16–17 (*De caelesti
hierarchia*, 145C): "σὺ δέ, ὦ παῖ, κατὰ τὴν ὁσίαν τῆς καθ' ἡμᾶς ἱεραρχικῆς παραδόσεως
θεσμοθεσίαν αὐτός τε ἱεροπρεπῶς ἄκουε τῶν ἱερῶς λεγομένων ἔνθεος ἐνθέων ἐν μυήσει
γινόμενος καὶ τῇ κατὰ νοῦν κρυφιότητι τὰ ἄγια περιστείλας ἐκ τῆς ἀνιέρου πληθύος ὡς
ἑνοειδῆ διαφύλαξον. οὐ γὰρ θεμιτόν, ὡς τὰ λόγιά φησιν [Matt. 7.6], εἰς ὗας ἀπορρίψαι
τὴν τῶν νοητῶν μαργαριτῶν ἀμιγῆ καὶ φωτοειδῆ καὶ καλλοποιὸν εὐκοσμίαν."

[130] L. Valla, *Annotationes in Acta Apostolorum*, 17, in his *Opera omnia*, 2 vols (Basel
1540, repr. Turin: Bottega d'Erasmo, 1962), I, 852: "Denique hic Dionysius an aliquid

which this comment appeared) did not achieve any significant circulation in the fifteenth century and it is unclear whether Pico came
across them. Valla's work was finally published in 1505 by Erasmus,
and Erasmus himself repeated Valla's doubts about Dionysius in his
subsequent works.[131] But reports of the death of Dionysius the Areopagite were exaggerated. A new translation of the complete works
was produced in 1536; nor was this the last. The redating of the
corpus did not remove it from the canon of Christian theology. In
any case, in 1489 Dionysius was still, by and large, the Areopagite;
the criticism of Valla had yet to take effect; and Marsilio Ficino was
about to produce his own translations of part of the corpus—the second translation produced in Florence in the fifteenth century. Pico's
admiration for Pseudo-Dionysius is clear in the *Commento*.[132] On the
role of Dionysius as a model for Pico's actual interpretative theory, I
shall have more to say in Chapter 5. It is sufficient to note, for the
moment, that this widely disseminated corpus of texts strongly pro-
moted the esoteric stance of the early Christians after their original
writings had become inaccessible.

The second tradition which maintained this stance is missing
from Pico's account of esotericism in the first proem, despite the
fact that only a couple of years previously he had made it central to
his corresponding accounts in the *Commento* and the *Apologia*. This
is the kabbalistic tradition.

In the *Commento*, Pico introduces kabbalah as just one among
many examples of the esoteric transmission of doctrines. The purpose of the argument is to justify his interpretation of Girolamo

---

scripserit, incertum est, cuius neque Latini, neque Graeci meminerunt. At ne ipse
quidem Gregorius indicat fuisse illum areopagitam, qui hos libros qui in manibus
versantur, scripserit, quorum autorem quidam nostrae aetatis eruditissimi Graeci
colligunt fuisse Apollinarem." See also Valla's *Encomium Sancti Thomae Aquinatis*, in his
Opera omnia, II, 351: "comparaverim ... Gregorium cum Dionysio, quem Areopagitam
vocant, quod eius ipse primus Latinorum quantum invenio facit mentionem: nam
superioribus, quos nominavi, non modo Latinis, verum etiam Graecis, opera Dionysii
fuere ignota." Valla's remarks are discussed by J. Monfasani, "Pseudo-Dionysius
the Areopagite in Mid-Quattrocento Rome", in *Supplementum Festivum: Studies in
Honor of Paul Oskar Kristeller*, ed. J. Hankins, J. Monfasani and F. Purnell, 189–219
(Binghamton, New York: Medieval and Renaissance Texts and Studies, 1987).

[131] Erasmus, *Annotationes in Novum Testamentum* (Basel, 1535), 312–317; facsimile
reproduction in *Erasmus's Annotations on the New Testament: Acts, Romans, I and II
Corinthians*, ed. A. Reeve and M.A. Screech (Leiden: Brill, 1990). See also J.B. Trapp,
"Erasmus on William Grocyn and Ps-Dionysius: A Re-examination", *Journal of the
Warburg and Courtauld Institutes*, 59 (1996), 299–300.

[132] Garin, 462: "Dyonisio Areopagita, principe de' teologi cristiani".

Benivieni's *canzone* as presenting metaphysical truths in a veiled manner. The sense is as follows: Dionysius commanded his disciple Timothy to communicate his teachings to only a few, and only if they were worthy. The Jews, too, followed this rule; this is why their exposition of the hidden mysteries of Scripture is called "kabbalah", a word which means "reception" and signifies that these expositions are not written but rather passed on orally. The same rule was observed by the Pythagoreans, as the letter from Lysis to Hipparchus demonstrates.[133]

In the *Apologia*, the emphasis is different. Kabbalah is now the overall subject of the argument. The goal is to align it more closely with less alien traditions so as to make it comprehensible and acceptable to a Christian audience. To accomplish this, Pico draws on much the same information as in the *Commento* passage. He begins with Christian testimonies to the existence of a secret tradition handed down to Moses on Mount Sinai.[134] This leads to a general consideration of esotericism, with the familiar examples: Paul, Pythagoras, the Egyptians, Plato, Dionysius and Jesus. Once this background is set out, we return to the initial subject: kabbalah itself, says Pico, is nothing other than this same esoteric tradition, well known to Christians.[135]

---

[133] Garin, 580–581 (*Commento particulare*, stanza ultima): "e Dionisio a Timoteo, esponendo de' nomi di Dio e della gerarchia angelica e ecclesiastica molti profundi sensi, gli comanda che tenga el libro nascoso e non lo comunichi se non a pochi, che di tale cognizione siano degni. Questo ordine appresso gli antiqui ebrei fu santissimamente osservato e per questo la loro scienzia, nella quale la esposizione delli astrusi e asconditi misterii della legge si contiene, Cabala si chiama, che significa recezione, perchè non per scritti ma per successione a bocca l'uno dall' altro la ricevono. Scienzia per certo divina e degna di non participare se non con pochi, grandissimo fundamento della fede nostra, el desiderio solo del quale mi mosse all'assiduo studio della ebraica e caldaica lingua, sanza le quali alla cognizione di quella pervenire è al tutto impossibile. Quanto fussi el medesimo stilo da' Pitagorici osservato si vede per la epistola di Liside ad Ipparco ..." The sentence "Scienza per certo ... al tutto impossibile", although it does cast light on Pico's view of kabbalah, is effectively a parenthesis and does not contribute to the argument, which is why I have not taken it into account in the summary above.

[134] *Opera omnia*, 122: "Scribunt non modo celebres Hebraeorum doctores, sed ex nostris quoque Esdras, Hilarius, et Origenes, Mosem non legem modo, quam quinque exaratam libris posteris reliquit, sed secretiorem quoque, et veram legis enarrationem, in monte divinitus accepisse. Praeceptum autem ei a Deo, ut legem quidem populo publicaret, legis interpretationem nec traderet literis nec invulgaret, sed ipsi Iesu Naue tantum, tum ille, aliis deinceps succedentibus sacerdotum primoribus, magna silentii religione revelaret."

[135] Ibid., 122–123: "Hoc eodem penitus modo, cum ex Dei praecepto, vera illa legis interpretatio Mosi deitus tradita, revelaretur dicta est Cabala, quod idem est apud Hebraeos, quod apud nos receptio."

Rhetorically, this passage acts as a preamble to his rather more complex defence of his definition of kabbalah, which occurs in the section where he defends the ninth of the *Conclusiones magicae numero xxvi secundum opinionem propriam*, which was the fifth of the condemned conclusions: "Nulla est scientia, quae nos magis certificet de divinitate Christi, quam Magia et Cabala."[136]

It is necessary to summarize this defence in order to understand precisely what Pico thought kabbalah was. He begins by noting that Jewish and Christian *doctores* attest that two traditions were handed down to Moses on Mount Sinai: one is the written law, that is, the Pentateuch, and the other is the "true exposition" of the Pentateuch, that is, an explanation of the mysteries which lie hidden underneath the surface of its words.[137] There was a double law: one part literal and written down, the other spiritual and communicated by word of mouth.[138] It was merely because it was transmitted orally that the science of the hidden exposition of the law was given the name "kabbalah".[139] These mysteries were subsequently transcribed in the so-called "books of kabbalah" and were not afterwards corrupted. For this reason almost everything in them confirms the truth of Christianity.[140] As evidence that God "revealed the mysteries contained in the law", Pico cites five credible witnesses: Esdras, Paul, Origen, Hilary and Matthew.[141] After reconstructing the history of the transmission of these "books of kabbalah", drawing on passages from these five

---

[136] *Conclusions*, 194. Incorrectly called the fourth in the *Apologia* (*Opera omnia*, 166).

[137] *Opera omnia*, 175: "Est ergo sciendum opinionem esse ... ut infra ostendam, praeter legem, quam Deus dedit Moysi in monte, et quam ille quinque libris contentam, scriptam reliquit, revelatam quoque fuisse eidem Moysi, ab ipso Deo, veram legis expositionem, cum manifestatione omnium mysteriorum et secretorum, quae sub cortice et rudi facie verborum legis continerentur." On Pico's source for this, see Wirszubski, *Pico's Encounter*, 123–132.

[138] *Opera omnia*, 175: "Denique duplicem accepisse legem Moysen, in monte, literalem et spiritalem, illam scripsisse, et ex praecepto Dei populo communicasse, de hac vero mandatum ei a Deo, ne ipsam scriberet, sed sapientibus solum qui erant septuaginta communicaret".

[139] Ibid., 176: "Ex quo modo tradendi istam scientiam per successivam, scilicet receptionem, unius ab altero dicta est ipsa scientia, scientia Cabalae, quod idem est, quod scientia receptionis, quia idem significat Cabala apud Hebraeos, quod apud nos receptio."

[140] Ibid.: "Fuerunt autem postea haec mysteria literis mandata ... et illi libri dicti sunt libri Cabalae, in quibus libris, multa imo pene omnia inveniuntur consona fidei nostrae. Fuerunt enim et ab ore Dei traditi, et a Iudaeis ante Christum scripti, quo tempore nulla passione moveri poterant, ad viciandam vel corrumpendam ipsam veritatem."

[141] Ibid.: "Quod autem ita sit, ut supra diximus, quod Deus Moysi praeter literalem legem, quam ipse scripsit, dederit etiam et revelaverit mysteria in lege contenta,

sources, Pico reiterates that the books can be used as an arsenal against the Jews, who hold them in such respect that they cannot deny what is written in them.[142]

He then notes that something else must be known: that the method of interpreting the law set down in these books is equivalent to the Christian method of anagogy.[143] It is, he says, precisely because the Jews fail to use this form of exegesis that they refuse to convert to Christianity—they have misunderstood the statements of the prophets regarding the coming of the Messiah because they have interpreted them literally.[144] Christians, on the other hand, because their reading of the law is according to the spirit, not the flesh, should be considered "spiritual, not fleshly, Israelites".[145] To the objection that the Church Fathers never mention this doctrine, Pico replies that they do, but not explicitly, as he has already shown in relation to his five sources; they simply remark, "this is what the Jews say" or some equivalent phrase.[146] Among the patristic authors, the reference to a doctrine as Jewish implies approval.[147] Since there are three Jewish sects (kabbalists, Talmudists and philosophers), and the latter two postdate these patristic writers, the Christians, when they cite a Jewish doctrine with approval, can *only* be referring to the kabbalists, that is, to the true revelation of God to Moses, which confirms Christianity.

---

habeo ex nostris quinque testes, Esdram, Paulum, Origenem, Hilarium, et Evangelium." The citation given from "evangelium", ibid., 177, is Matt. 23.2.

[142] *Opera omnia*, 178: "Quos ego libros ... cum diligenter perlegerim, inveniens ibi multa, imo pene omnia consona fidei nostrae, visum est mihi habere posse Christianos, unde Iudaeos suis telis confodiant, cum ab eis authoritas Cabalistarum quos habent in magno honore et reverentia negari non possit."

[143] Ibid.: "Est autem ulterius sciendum, quod ista expositio Bibliae proportionatur modo exponendi Bibliam, qui apud nos dicitur Anagogicus".

[144] Ibid., 178–179: "Nam cum eis in eis prophetiis promittitur, quod Messias eos liberabit de captivitate ... ipsi haec literaliter intelligentes ... non possunt credere illum fuisse Messiam, per quem eiecti sunt de illa terra".

[145] Ibid., 179: "Sunt autem maxime digni Christiani hac scientia, quia sicut ipsa est lex spiritualis non carnalis, ita nos spirituales sumus Israelitae, non carnales."

[146] Ibid.: "Quod autem dicant se mirari doctores Ecclesiae de ista doctrina nunquam fecisse mentionem, satis nos supra ostendimus, et Hilarium et Origenem, et Esdram, et iuxta hos Paulum et Evangelium huius scientiae meminisse. Est autem et advertendum, quod nunquam invenies aut rarissime doctorem aliquem, ex nostris, loquor de antiquis, aliquem ex Hebraeis nominatim allegantem, sed in universali tantum videbis dicentes: Sic dicunt Hebraei, Haec est sententia Hebraeorum."

[147] Ibid., 180: "Cum volunt approbare quod dicunt, Eusebius maxime, Origenes et Clemens, et quamplures alii ad Hebraeos se semper referunt dicentes: Referebat mihi Hebraeus, Audivi ab Hebraeo, Hebraeorum ista sententia est. Et ipse Hieronymus etiam eos Magistros vocet dicens, Haec est sententia Magistrorum."

Kabbalah, in sum, is this tradition, which the Church Fathers refer to with the phrase "so says the ancient tradition".[148]

Now that the true kabbalah has been sufficiently sanitized to make it acceptable to the sensibilities of his audience, Pico goes on to discuss how it gained its subsequent disrepute. He does this in an entirely scholastic manner, by dividing the word "kabbalah" into its different senses:

1. The "primary and proper" sense.[149] This is the "first and true kabbalah", as defined above.
2. The "usurped" sense. Because the mode of oral transmission deployed in the dissemination of the proper sense seems suitable "for any secret and mystical thing", the Jews also use this name to refer to any science or body of knowledge transmitted in this manner.[150]
3. Two "transumptive" senses:[151]
    a) An *ars combinandi* which is in certain respects similar to the *ars Raymundi*, though the procedure is very different,

---

[148] Ibid.: "Nihil dubitandum est de doctoribus Cabalae, eos intelligere, quod evidenti ratione potest demonstrari, est enim omnis schola Hebraeorum in tres sectas divisa: in philosophos, in Cabalistas et in Talmuticos. ... Relinquitur ergo, ut haec Hebraeorum doctrina, cui doctores Catholici ex Hieronymi testimonio tantum deferunt, et quam adeo approbant, sit illa, quam ipsimet nostri doctores fatentur, et credunt a Deo Moysi, et a Moyse per successionem aliis sapientibus fuisse revelatum, et est illa quae ex hoc modo tradendi, dicitur Cabala, quam saepe etiam video a nostris authoribus, hoc modo designari, dicendo: Ut dicit antiqua traditio. Haec est prima et vera Cabala, de qua credo me primum apud Latinos explicitam fecisse mentionem, et est illa, qua ego utor in meis conclusionibus, quas cum expresse ponam contra Hebraeos, ad confirmationem fidei nostrae, nescio quomodo isti Magistri habere potuerunt pro suspectis in fide."

[149] Ibid., 181: "ex primaria et propria impositione".

[150] Ibid., 180: "Verum quia iste modus tradendi per successionem, qui dicitur Cabalisticus, videtur convenire unicuique rei secretae et mysticae, hinc est quod usurparunt Hebraei, ut unamquanque scientiam, quae apud eos habeatur pro secreta et abscondita, Cabalam vocent, et unumquodque scibile, quod per viam occultam alicunde habeatur, dicatur haberi per viam Cabalae."

[151] Ibid., 180–181: "In universali autem duas scientias, hoc etiam nomine honorificarunt, unam quae dicitur ars combinandi, et est modus quidam procedendi in scientiis, et est simile quid, sicut apud nostros dicitur ars Raymundi, licet forte diverso modo procedant. Aliam quae est de virtutibus rerum superiorum, quae sunt supra lunam, et est pars Magiae naturalis suprema. Utraque istarum apud Hebraeos etiam dicitur Cabala, propter rationem iam dictam, et de utraque istarum etiam aliquando fecimus mentionem in conclusionibus nostris: illa enim ars combinandi, est quam ego in conclusionibus meis voco, Alphabetariam revolutionem, est ista quae de virtutibus rerum superiorum, quae uno modo potest capi, ut pars Magiae naturalis, alio modo, ut res distincta ab ea: est illa de qua loquor in praesenti conclusione, dicens:

and which Pico in his *Conclusiones* refers to as *alphabetaria revolutio.*[152]

   b) a science concerning the powers of superlunary things. This can itself be understood in two ways:

     i. "as part of natural magic";

     ii. "as something distinct from this"—apparently a perversion by necromancers, who also assert that Christ's miracles were accomplished by means of kabbalah, which, says Pico, he explicitly denied in his *Conclusiones.*[153]

It would take an entire book, he claims, to discuss all the different senses of this one word; a publication that the commitee which scrutinized his *Conclusiones* would hardly have welcomed.[154]

    The effect of this argument is to divert the blame from the actual *phenomenon* of kabbalah to which Pico refers in his *Conclusiones* and to place it instead on the *word*. It is all merely a misunderstanding arising from insufficiently defined terms. When, at the end of the *Apologia*, he rewrote the offending conclusions in a manner so as to remove the ambiguity which, so he thought, had led to their censure, the reference to kabbalah in the ninth of the *Conclusiones*

Quod adiuvat nos in cognitione divinitatis Christi ad modum iam declaratum, et licet istis duabus scientiis nomen Cabalae, ex primaria et propria impositione non conveniat, transumptive tamen potuit eis applicari."

[152] *Conclusions*, 206 (Conc. cabalisticae ... sec. opinionem propriam, 2): "Quicquid dicant alii Cabalistae, ego partem speculativam Cabalae quadruplicem dividerem, correspondentes quadruplici partitioni philosophiae, quam ego solitus sum affere. Prima est scientia, quam ego voco Alphabetariae revolutionis, correspondentem parti philosophiae, quam ego philosophiam catholicam voco."

[153] *Opera omnia*, 181: "Verum sicut, cum olim Magi tantum dicerentur Sapientes Necromantes, deinde et diabolici viri, Sapientis sibi falso nomen vendicantes, Magos se vocaverunt, ita et quidam apud Hebraeos, res divinas falsis et vanis superstitionibus polluentes, imo in rei veritate, quasi nihil a Necromantibus differentes, dixerunt se habere secreta Dei nomina, et virtutes quibus daemones ligarent, et miracula facerent, et Christum non alia via fecisse miracula. Et isti falso sibi Cabalistarum nomen vendicaverunt, dicentes, artem suam esse illam veram Cabalam quam revelavit Deus Moysi. Sicut etiam dicunt Necromantes, quod illas suas incantationes et bestialitates habuerunt a Salomone et ab Adam et ab Henoch, et a similibus. Hanc autem falso vocatam Cabalam, non solum ego non approbavi in conclusionibus meis aut sequutus sum, sed expresse reprobavi, ponens conclusionem specialem de directo contra istam, quae dicit quod miracula Christi non potuerunt fieri per viam Cabalae." See *Conclusions*, 192 (Conc. magicae ... sec. opinionem propriam, 7): "Non potuerunt opera Christi vel per viam Magiae, vel per viam Cabalae fieri."

[154] *Opera omnia*, 181: "Haec sufficiant de praesenti conclusione, quae specialem librum exigeret, si quid sit naturalis Magia, quid Cabala exacte vellemus declarare. Hic sufficit ostendisse, nihil contineri in eis, quod Catholicae et orthodoxae fidei repugnet."

magicae was redrafted as follows: "There is no science, extending the name of science to those which are revealed and non-revealed, which confirms for us the divinity of Christ, in another way than by the doctrine of the Gospels, and the science of Christian theology."[155] This is precisely what he had maintained the "true kabbalah" was; the offending word has been removed, however.

Having considered this defence as the background to the *Heptaplus*, the following points arise:

1. Given that Pico identifies the problem as deriving from the *word* 'kabbalah', it is no surprise that this word never occurs in the *Heptaplus*.
2. What Pico is discussing in the first proem is actually the *phenomenon* of kabbalah as he sees it, that is, the spiritual interpretation of the Bible, embodying a secret tradition going back ultimately to Moses.
3. His discussion is based on two previous redactions of the same argument, with all references to the word 'kabbalah' systematically excised, but with the remainder preserved, in many cases word for word.

We are faced with a deliberate rhetorical strategy. It seems likely that when Pico produced this final revision of his account of esoteric transmission, he consciously deleted the passages referring to kabbalah for reasons of prudence. The bull, which Innocent VIII had issued on 15 December 1487 condemning the *Conclusiones*, was still in force at the time he was writing the *Heptaplus*—indeed, it remained in force until 18 June 1493.[156] It might seem that this prudence is inconsistent with the obviously kabbalistic content of the final chapter of the *Heptaplus*. But this is a false perspective. Although Pico had mentioned the *ars combinandi* in the *Conclusiones* and the *Apologia*, he had not actually produced any examples of it prior to the *Heptaplus*. The *ars combinandi*, as he noted, was not without precedent in the Christian sphere, given its similarities to the *ars Raymundi*. Perhaps, therefore, he thought that it was enough to avoid the term 'kabbalah'. As noted in Chapter 1, the pope was not pleased at the appearance of the *Heptaplus*, and regarded it as a continuation of the same errors that had marked the *Conclusiones*. Nonetheless, it was not

---

[155] Ibid., 239: "Nulla est scientia, extendendo nomen scientiae, ad revelatas et non revelatas, quae nos certificet de divinitate Christi, alia ab Evangelica doctrina, et scientia Christianae theologiae."

[156] Roulier, *Pic de la Mirandole*, 42–46; Crouzel, *Une controverse sur Origène*, 25–27.

received with the same process of scrutiny which had engulfed the
earlier work. To this extent, Pico's calculation proved correct. He
had not lost interest in kabbalah. Rather, it appears, he had decided
not to emphasize it explicitly.

To reiterate: Pico (unlike most of his Christian contemporaries)
was well-informed about kabbalistic ideas of esoteric transmission,
which had obvious parallels with Greek and Christian examples.
Furthermore, although he viewed these ideas as of great antiquity,
it is also the case that (unlike the doctrine of esotericism in the
Christian tradition), they had a contemporary resonance. The sharp
dichotomy of the masses and the elite, coupled with that of literal
and non-literal reading, was a constant and emphatic feature of the
medieval Jewish tradition; and, as such, was the subject of theoretical
discussions in Italy at around the time that Pico was writing the
Heptaplus.

Notably, Johanan Alemanno devoted considerable space to a
sustained and subtle account of the double dichotomy of the elite and
the masses and of non-literal and literal reading in the introduction
to his *Ḥay ha-olamim*.[157] In discussing this work, we must remain
mindful of the caveats noted above regarding Alemanno.[158] The
treatise was not written for Pico, unlike the works produced by Elijah
Delmedigo and Flavius Mithridates. It is in Hebrew and was never
available to Pico in its entirety, since it was not finished until 1503.
On the other hand, Alemanno had been working on it since 1470
and, considering his role as colleague or in some respects teacher
of Pico, dissemination (whether written or oral) of some parts of it
cannot be discounted.[159]

The *Ḥay ha-olamim* comprises an encyclopaedic narrative of
individual ascent, through the various different sciences, to the
highest attainable level of human perfection.[160] The opening section
concentrates on, among other things, the reading of Scripture.
Alemanno distinguishes between three types of people, who derive
their knowledge of God from demonstration, from dialectic and

---

[157] The title is not easily rendered into English. *Ḥay* means 'life' or 'living'; *Olam*
can mean either 'world' or 'eternity', but is here in the plural (*Olamim*). Lelli, in his
edition, puts "The Immortal". See below, Ch. 5, n. 42.

[158] See Ch. 1, section 2.3.

[159] Alemanno, *Ḥay ha-'olamim*, ed. Lelli, 6–7, 9.

[160] For discussion and summary, see ibid., 24–27. It can be connected to a shorter
account of ascent through study by the same author: see M. Idel, "The Study Program
of R. Jochanan Alemanno", *Tarbiẓ*, 48 (1979–1980), 303–331.

from rhetoric respectively.[161] He believes that the Torah speaks to all people, but in different ways; the three types are generally conflated into a dichotomy of reading, which he works out at some length. Pythagoras, he says, when he taught "the subject of science" to his disciples, did not give them the power to interpret the causes of these things in the first stages of their speculations. He taught them the science first, then the causes.[162] Likewise, the master does not trouble to give definitions of nouns and verbs which define the essence of a thing in its two essential parts, because this is vain in the eyes of those who do not understand the substances of things which are concealed from the senses.[163] These "large and strong" conceptions were not given in order to be made clear and to be understood by the masses but only by the elite.[164] The distinction between the masses and the elite corresponds to the two parts of a text: the narrative part and the speculative part. Hence, the two parts are to be kept separate. "Therefore it is inappropriate for the author to mix the speculative part with the narrative part for the masses."[165] Alemanno follows this conceptual distinction with an exegesis of Genesis 1.[166]

The same idea is found in the introduction to Elijah Delmedigo's *Beḥinat ha-dat*, or "Examination of Religion":

> Adherents of religion who are correct in their views do not doubt the purpose of the Torah, which is to guide us in human affairs and in good deeds, and to help (insofar as is possible) the people at large acquire true opinions. The Torah also takes cognizance of the elite regarding the appropriate manner for them to acquire true opinions. For that reason the Torah and the prophets set down fundamental principles by way of tradition, principles which are accepted rhetorically and dialectically in accordance with the method of verification appropriate for the

---

[161] *Ḥay ha-ʿolamim*, ed. Lelli, 67 (Hebrew), 94 (Italian):

אם במופת או נצוח או הלצה.

[162] Ibid., 70 (Hebrew), 102–103 (Italian):

כאשר העידו על פיתגוריש אשר היה בימי הנביאים כי כשהיה מלמד את דבר החכמה לתלמידיו' לא נתן להם רשות לדרוש ממנו סבות הדברי' בתחלת עיונם: אך היה מלמד אותם החכמות בלא סבה ואחר היה מודיע להם הסבות.

[163] Ibid., 70, 103:

אך לא יחוש המורה לגדור להם גדר השמות והפעלים לגדרים מורים מהות הדבר בשני חלקיו העצמיים: כי גם זה הבל בעיני העמים אשר לא ישיגו עצמיות הדברים הנעלמים מהחושים ודי להם ידיעת המקרים הנראים לעינים.

[164] Ibid.:

הלא המה השגות גדולות ועצומות לא נתנו להבין ולהשכיל להמונים כי אם לשרידים.

[165] Ibid.:

לא ידיעת ההמון הרחוקה מהם. ולכן הוא בלתי ראוי למחבר לערב החלק העיוני עם החלק הספור להמוני.

[166] Ibid., 106–108 (Italian translation).

masses. The Torah also stimulates the elite to search for the methods of verification suitable for them. ... The Torah requires both methods of study, for the Torah aims at the perfection of every adherent of religion in accordance with his capabilities, and the demonstrative method is impossible for the masses but possible for the elite. Verily it is clear that the employment of the demonstrative method is beneficial to the elite in proving some of the fundamental principles. The demonstrative method brings us to the knowledge of the things which are caused and from the knowledge of the latter we can proceed to the knowledge of the Creator. The Torah stimulates the elite in the pursuit of this knowledge of the Creator, as we have said. It is apparent that the demonstrative method is obligatory for the wise man but not for the ordinary Jew.[167]

Even more than in the case of Alemanno, we cannot argue direct textual influence on the *Heptaplus,* since Delmedigo did not write the *Beḥinat ha-dat* until he had returned to Crete in 1490. What these two passages from two of Pico's Jewish contemporaries show, however, is the centrality of this idea to the Jewish tradition: two different writers, with different interests and (arguably) not otherwise in agreement, placed it in a prominent position in the introductions to their two major works.[168] We may therefore suspect a mutual source or series of sources.

The terms of Alemanno's and Delmedigo's discussions derive from Averroes's *Kitab faṣl al-maqal* ("Book of the Decisive Treatise"), which distinguishes between three types of interpreter: those who understand demonstration; those who understand dialectic; and the multitude, who only understand rhetoric. According to Averroes, the multitude should not be introduced to interpretations, but should merely be reminded that their knowledge is limited.[169]

The general emphasis on the exclusivity of certain elements of Scripture, however, is also a part of medieval Jewish tradition and finds classic expression in the *Guide of the Perplexed.* The compar-

---

[167] Translated by Geffen, "Faith and Reason", 392–394.

[168] On Delmedigo's opposition to Neoplatonic trends in kabbalah, see Bland, "Elijah del Medigo's Averroist Response", 35–37. On the influence of Platonism in Alemanno's kabbalah, see M. Idel, "The Magical and Neoplatonic Interpretation of the Kabbalah in the Renaissance", in *Jewish Thought in the Sixteenth Century,* ed. B.D. Cooperman, 186–242 (Cambridge, Massachusetts: Harvard University Centre for Jewish Studies, 1983).

[169] Averroes, *Decisive Treatise,* 44–46, in *The Book of the Decisive Treatise Determining the Connection between the Law and Wisdom, and Epistle Dedicatory,* ed. and tr. C.E. Butterworth (Provo, Utah: Brigham Young University Press, 2001), 26–27. On Alemanno's reception of the *Decisive Treatise,* see *Ḥay ha-ʿolamim,* ed. Lelli, 94 and n. 113. For its influence on Delmedigo, see Geffen, "Faith and Reason", 43–63.

ison between the ignorant and the learned forms the underlying framework of Maimonides's introduction and then recurs at various points throughout the work. In the first place, Maimonides does not intend to make his treatise readily comprehensible to those who have only a basic education.[170] His case rests on his identification of the two most hidden parts of Scripture, the 'Work of the Beginning' (i.e., Genesis 1) and the 'Work of the Chariot' (i.e., Ezekiel 1), with physics and metaphysics respectively, and on the rabbinic injunction that the audience for these two parts should be severely restricted: the Work of the Chariot ought not to be taught even to one man, unless he is already wise, and able to understand by himself, in which case only the chapter headings may be transmitted to him; the Work of the Beginning ought not to be taught in the presence of two men.[171] For this reason, these matters are taught in parables and allegories ("in parabolis et similitudinibus"). The truth can, and should, appear like a flash of light; the highest achievement of man is that it should flash so regularly that "it appears to his eyes that night is day", which is the level of prophecy. On the other hand, there are those who, no matter how clear their instruction in the

---

[170] Maimonides, *Dux*, f. 2ʳ (*Guide*, tr. Pines, 5): "Et non est intentio mea in hoc libro docere communia ipsarum gentes: nec illos qui incipiunt in speculatione sapientiae, nec illos qui non sunt speculati nisi in doctrina legis solummodo: quoniam intentio huius libri totius est, ut intelligatur lex per viam veritatis."

[171] Maimonides, *Dux*, f. 2ᵛ (*Guide*, tr. Pines, 6–7): "opus de Beresith est scientia naturalis, et opus de Mercana [=Mercava, i.e., 'The Work of the Chariot'] est sapientia specialis [=spiritualis]. Et exposuimus quid dixerunt, quod non debent instruere in Mercana nec unum solum nisi sit sapiens, et intelligens ex sensu suo. Et tunc dabit ei initia rationum: et ideo non quaerat a me nisi initia rationum: et tamen illa initia non sunt ordinata in libro isto, nec unum post aliud: sed sunt dispersa, et immutata modis aliis ab eo quid est nostrae voluntatis exponere. ... Scias etiam quod naturalia similiter non possunt exponi ab homine expositione perfecta, nec potest homo facere, ut sciatur pars principiorum suorum sicut sunt. Et tu scis quod dixerunt sapientes, et non in opere de Beresith in duobus." Here, as elsewhere in this edition, the printer has tended to confuse the words 'specialis' and 'spiritualis', presumably on account of misunderstanding a manuscript abbreviation; in the British Library copy, BL 519 i. 5, these instances have been corrected by a reader with reference to the Arabic text. The injunctions against teaching to more than one person are found in the Babylonian Talmud, *Hagigah*, 11b. Another prohibition against study of the 'Work of the Beginning', that it should only be attempted by someone "already of mature age", was noted by Pico in the *Heptaplus* (H. P1; Garin, 176): "Propterea fuit decretum veterum Hebraeorum, cuius etiam meminit Hieronymus, ne hanc mundi creationem quisquam nisi matura iam aetate attingeret". Jerome actually wrote that "apud Hebraeos istae partes cum exordio Geneseos ante annos triginta non legantur" (*Epistola* 53, in *Patrologiae latinae cursus completus*, ed. Migne, XXII, 547). Pico himself was about 26 at the time of writing the *Heptaplus*; this fact presumably accounts for his deliberately vague rephrasing of the injunction as repeated by Jerome.

truth, are never able to perceive it and always remain in the dark.
These, says Maimonides, are the masses of the earth, and there is
no mention of them in this book.[172] The *Guide* is intended as an
aid to the intelligent man wishing to further his understanding, one
who has already gone through a rigorous programme of training in
various disciplines.[173]

These ideas are developed throughout the work. The special
status of the 'Work of Creation' is reiterated on the next page: it is
a prerequisite to understanding metaphysics, which, because of the
depth of the knowledge contained in it, it was necessary to express in
parables.[174] This is reiterated in chapter 17, entitled, in the Latin, "De

---

[172] Maimonides, *Dux*, f. 2ᵛ (*Guide*, tr. Pines, 7–8): "Et si poneret homo omnes illas
rationes, esset expositor. Et ideo fuerunt dictae illae rationes in libris prophetiae
in parabolis, et loquuti sunt in eis sapientes in parabolis et similitudinibus, ut
ambulent in eis per viam librorum sanctitatis: quoniam est inter illas, et sapientiam
specialem [=spiritualem] coniunctio firma, et colligatio fortis, et etiam sunt secreta
secretorum sapientiae specialis [=spiritualis]. Nec ascendat in cor tuum quod illa
magna secreta sint a nobis scita usque ad finem suum, sed aliquando apparet veritas
donec credimus quod sit dies, et postea abscondunt ipsam potentiae nostrae et
consuetudines quousque revertimur in obscuritatem et tenebram, iuxta quod fuimus
in ipsa prius. Et idcirco sumus nos sicut ille cui apparet coruscatio una post aliam
interpolate dum ipse est in obscura nocte, et est aliquis cui apparet coruscatio una
post aliam: ita quod credit quod est continue in clara luce quae non recedit, et
apparet oculis eius quod nox sit dies. Et iste fuit gradus eximii prophetarum cui
dictum fuit: Et tu sta hic mecum. ... sed de illis qui nunquam viderunt lucem, et
qui semper in tenebris ambulant, dictum est: nescierunt neque intellexerunt, qui in
tenebris ambulant. Et abscondetur ab oculis eorum veritas universaliter quamvis sit
multum clara sicut dictum est: quomodo non viderunt: lux clara est in caelis. Et isti
sunt gens populorum terrae: et non est rememoratio illis in hoc libro." See further,
C. Sirat, *A History of Jewish Philosophy in the Middle Ages*, tr. M. Reich (Cambridge: CUP,
1996), 159–166.

[173] See Maimonides, *Dux*, f. 2ʳ (*Guide*, tr. Pines, 3–4).

[174] Ibid., f. 3ʳ (*Guide*, tr. Pines, 8–9): "Nonne vides quando creator benedictus voluit
perficere mores nostros et ornare modos conscientiae nostrae praeceptis suis quae
sunt mandata ad faciendum, et non firmantur: nisi post opiniones intelligibiles:
initium suum est, ut intelligatur praeceptum dei secundum possibilitatem suam.
Et etiam non firmantur nisi cum scientia spirituali: quae scientia spiritualis non
appraehenditur nisi post scientiam naturalem, quoniam scientia naturalis posterior
est sapientia spirituali: sed est prior ea, ordine doctrinae, sicut patet studentibus in
hoc. Et ideo creator posuit apertionem legis nostrae in ratione operis de Beresit
quid est scientia naturalis sicut praeexposuimus: propter hoc difficultatem etiam
magnitudinis rationis: et propter brevitatem potentiae nostrae in comprehendendo
magnitudinem rationum secundum quod sunt vel fuerunt verba creatoris nobiscum
in ipsis rationibus occultis que fecit, necessaria sapientia spiritualis de necessitate
ad loquendum nobiscum in illis parabolis: et verbis multis occultis sicut dixerunt
sapientes ad annunciandum fortitudinem operis de Beresit carni et sanguini non
potest esse. Iccirco conclusit scriptura dicens: in principio creavit deus caelum et
terram."

occultatione doctrinae". If philosophers such as Plato felt it necessary to conceal their teachings on form, matter and privation, *a fortiori* so too must have Moses.[175] The idea of the intellectual difference between humans, meanwhile, is the subject of chapters 30–32.[176] Those who attempt to fathom the secrets of Scripture without proper preparation will be destroyed.[177] The harmfulness of metaphysical wisdom requires its transmission in allegories.[178] It is said that the Torah speaks the language of men.[179] This is so that it can be taught to infants and the uneducated, that is, to those who are unable to understand its words *secundum veritatem suam*. The *homo perfectus*, on the other hand, "arrives at a level on which he believes true opinions

---

[175] Ibid., f. 8ᵛ (*Guide*, tr. Pines, 42–43): "Non putes quod necessarium est ut sapientia spiritualis tantummodo occultetur gentibus: quia necesse est etiam ut maior pars scientiae naturalis occultetur eisdem. Et iam praedixi tibi quod dixerunt sapientes, Non propalandum opus de beresit in duobus: nec istud solummodo accidit sapientibus nostrae legis: sed etiam prophetis et sapientibus aliarum gentium qui credunt antiquitatem mundi. Ipsi enim occultabant verba sua cum loquebantur de antiquitate mundi et loquebantur in parabolis. Unde Plato et qui praecesserant eum vocabant materiam feminam, et formam masculum. ... Cum igitur praedicti Philosophi quos non consequebatur inconveniens vel damnum si palam loquerentur, verbis transsumptivis utebantur: et multiplicabant similitudines in doctrina sua ne fieret manifesta: quanto magis nos receptores legis quibus necesse est ne propalemus verbum quod gentes non intelligant diversum ab eo quid fuit in intentione?"

[176] Ibid., f. 11ʳ (*Guide*, tr. Pines, 65). The difference is great but not infinite: "unus homo ductu propriae investigationis inveniet aliquid novum quid alius homo nunquam poterit intelligere .... Et huiusmodi differentia non tendit in infinitum: sed intellectus humanus terminum habet usque ad quem poterit sine dubio pervenire et in eo stare."

[177] Ibid., f. 11ᵛ (*Guide*, tr. Pines, 68–69): "tunc acquires intellectum humanum. Et eris in gradu de Rabi Aqiba: cuius ingressus et egressus fuit in pace in speculatione rerum spiritualium. Quod si perseveraveris appraehendere amplius quam est in potentia tua ... eris de societate Telixa [i.e. Elisha]: et non solum deerit tibi perfectio, sed eris imperfectior omnibus imperfectis." Maimonides refers obliquely to the account of the entry of the four rabbis into Pardes. This account is in the Babylonian Talmud, *Hagigah*, 15a. The four rabbis were Ben Azzai, Ben Zoma, Elisha Aḥer and Akiva. All of them except for Akiva were destroyed. 'Pardes', literally meaning garden or paradise, came to represent (via an acronym of its consonants PRDS) the fourfold interpretation of Scripture: *Peshat* (plain meaning), *Remez* (allegorical meaning), *Derash* (Talmudic-style exposition) and *Sod* ('secret' meaning): see Scholem, *On the Kabbalah and its Symbolism*, 57.

[178] Maimonides, *Dux*, f. 12ʳ (*Guide*, tr. Pines, 70): "Scias quod incipere in ista sapientia scilicet spirituali multum nocet: et similiter expositio similitudinum quae inveniuntur in libris prophetarum."

[179] Ibid. (*Guide*, tr. Pines, 71): "hoc est causa propter quam lex loquitur lingua hominis." This is another quotation from the Babylonian Talmud: see *Yebamoth*, 71a and *Baba Mesi'a*, 31b. It is repeated and discussed by Alemanno: see *Ḥay ha-'olamim*, ed. Lelli, 70 (Hebrew text), 104 (Italian translation).

in true ways".[180] Maimonides goes on to explain, in the next chapter, five reasons why it is impossible to teach this ability to the multitude.[181]

I have already commented on Pico's relationship to the *Guide*.[182] The esotericism which, as we see here, was already characteristic of Maimonides, is multiplied in the commentary on the *Guide* by Abulafia, entitled (in the version translated for Pico by Mithridates) *De secretis legis*. In the first book of this work Abulafia cites two ways of reading the first words of Genesis, depending on the word breaks: a method which, he says, is taken from Nahmanides. According to this view, in Nahmanides's words, repeated by Abulafia, "the whole of the Torah is full of the names of God".[183] Abulafia's next comment has one of Pico's marginal markers beside it:

---

[180] Maimonides, *Dux*, f. 12ʳ (*Guide*, tr. Pines, 71–72): "Similiter istas veras opiniones occultaverunt sapientes: et locuti sunt de eis in parabolis: et docuerunt eas ingeniose sine expositione in omni genere morum: non quia in ipsis aliquid mali lateat, vel quod destruant fundamenta legis: sicut putant stulti in quorum corda ascendit, quod attingit gradum speculationis: sed celaverunt eas sapientes propter bonitatem [marginal correction: brevitatem] potentiae intellectus in initio recipiendi illas, et posuerunt ex eis summas per quas sciat illa homo perfectus: et ideo vocata sunt secreta legis, sicut explanabimus: et hoc est causa propter quam lex loquitur lingua hominis. Hoc est quia praesto sunt ut incipiatur ab eis: et addiscant ea pueri, et populus, et mulieres. Et non est in potentia eorum ut intelligant verba secundum veritatem suam: et idcirco abundat in eis receptio in omni opinione vera et cogitatione et arbitrio, secundum quod ostendit cogitatio assimilatoria super essentia creatoris: non in appraehendendo veritatem substantiae ipsius. Cum vero fuerit homo perfectus: et data fuerint ei secreta legis: et per se vel per alium perceperit partem ipsorum: tunc perveniet ad gradum in quo credet opiniones veras in viis veris: vel per viam demonstrationis in quibus oportet eam inducere: vel cum rationibus fortibus in quibus conveniat illas inducere. Similiter ascendent in cor eius verba quae dicta fuerunt ei similitudinarie, et cognoscet ea secundum veritatem suam."

[181] Ibid., ff. 12ʳ⁻ᵛ (*Guide*, tr. Pines, 72): "Adhuc etiam explanabimus causam quae impedit ne doceatur populus in via considerationis verae. Et quod non propalantur eis verba secundum quod sunt: et quod hoc expedit et necessarium sit quod ita sit, dicemus in capitulo sequenti." Ibid., 13ᵛ (*Guide*, tr. Pines, 79): "Igitur secundum has omnes opiniones fuerunt secreta ista necessaria solis et singularibus qui sunt paucissimi non universitati gentium. Et ideo celant illa incipientem addiscere, et prohibent ipsum attingere illa: sicut prohibetur puer parvulus ne comedat cibos duros, et ne portet onus grave."

[182] See Ch. 3, section 2.5.

[183] Vat. Ebr. 190, f. 345ʳ (transcribed in Wirszubski, *Pico's Encounter*, 128): "Similiter dicam de magno doctore rabi Moise filio Nahaman Gerundinensi qui dixit in principio legis expositionis quam ipse commentatus est in hec verba: habemus in manibus nostris traditum a sapientibus cabale ipsius veritatis quod tota lex est plena nominibus dei sancti et benedicti *et angelorum ordinis sacri celestis*, et ut dixit ipse idem in dictionibus brexith bara elohim quod ibi sint quatuor nomina que sunt אלהים רא יתב בראש barox iathab ra elohim". The italicized phrase was identified by Wirszubski as an interpolation. See Nahmanides, *The Commentary of Nahmanides on*

Our law is called holy, and our language holy, because in it all the aforementioned names are hidden, and these make it so that divine comprehensions are understood and are in the heart and mind of the intelligent; and especially because things are profound, and the more profound they are, the more they should be hidden from the multitude of the people and the ignorant. ... Because Moses our master was at the height of perfection and was the chief father in the law and chief and father in prophecy, a higher power flowed into him, in which he was joined to receive the law from God (holy and blessed) similarly in two ways. One is the way of knowing the law according to the understanding of it in the literal sense, according to its mysteries and its precepts received and handed down together with the exposition composed from these things; and this is what we call Talmud, completely according to itself and whatever imitates its modes of proceeding, which are said to be of its kind. The second is the way of knowing the law according to the understandings of it together with its secrets and the things hidden in the mystery, that is, of the secrets of the divine names contained in it and in the reasons of its precept which is handed down from mouth to mouth. These are called the secrets of the law.[184]

Abulafia goes on to say that there are two types of people to whom these two types of reading correspond; the two dichotomies are inseparable.[185] His argument here is essentially an expansion of the

---

Genesis, Chapters 1–6: Introduction, Critical Text, Translation and Notes, ed. J. Newman (Leiden: E.J. Brill, 1960), 27–28.

[184] Vat. Ebr. 190, f. 345ᵛ (transcribed in Wirszubski, *Pico's Encounter*, 128–129): "lex nostra dicitur sancta et lingua sancta quia in ea omnia praedicta nomina in lingua hac oculta sunt et que faciunt comprehendere et esse in corde et animo intelligentium comprehensiones divinas; et precipue quod res sunt profunde et quanto magis profunde sunt tanto magis ocultande sunt a vulgari populo et ab ignaris ... . Quia Moises magister noster erat in summa perfectione perfectus et erat princeps pater in lege et princeps et pater in sapientia et princeps et pater in prophetia induxit eum influentia superior in qua coniunctus est ad recipiendum legem a deo sancto et benedicto similiter per duos modos quorum unus est modus sciendi legem secundum intellectum suum ad sensum literalem secundum misteria sua et praecepta sua cum expositione recepta et tradita que est de ea composita et est quam dicimus Talmud secundum se totum et quicquid imitatur modos eius procedendi quod dici possunt specie sue; secundus vero modus est sciendi legem secundum intelligentias suas cum suis secretis et ocultamentis in misterio scilicet secretorum nominum divinorum contentorum in ea et in rationibus precepti sui quod ore ad os traditur quod vocantur secreta legis."

[185] Vat. Ebr. 190, ff. 345ᵛ–346ʳ: "et hoc quidem ut proficantur in ea et per eam due species hominum que in pronuntiacione non differunt sed bene in orthographia scilicet per sin et samech ... et his quidem datur secundum opinionem suam quantum sufficit eis secundum imaginationem eorum, velut eis cibus lactis infantulis, his vero aliis datur secundum opinionem eorum quantum sufficit eis secundum intellectum eorum, ut est potus vini ad senes." The distinction between the two sorts of people according to the letters 'sin' and 'samech' is explained by Mithridates in parentheses:

passage from Nahmanides noted above, distinguishing between the text read according to its normal rules of grammar and syntax and the text read as a succession of divine names (ignoring these rules).

The exegetical works of the kabbalists, as presented to Pico through Mithridates's translations, offered several such radical methods of reading, which undermine the biblical text's grammar and syntax in the search for the non-literal sense.[186] Three of these should be noted here.

5.1. *Sefirotic Exegesis*

The metaphysical structure of the *sefirot* is one of the most central (and controversial) features of kabbalah in general, although some schools of thought emphasized it, while others neglected it. The Hebrew word *sefirot* (singular: *sefirah*) literally means "numbers"; in Mithridates's translations, they are referred to by the term *numerationes*. Essentially, the *sefirot* are ten hierarchical emanations of divine power which connect the inmost aspect of God to the created universe. They were frequently, for this reason, considered heretical, as they appeared to contradict the strict monotheism of Judaism. Each of the *sefirot* was named after a certain attribute of God. Although alternative terminologies exist, a typical list of names is *Keter* (Crown), *Ḥokhmah* (Wisdom), *Binah* (Understanding), *Ḥesed* (Love), *Gevurah*

---

the Hebrew word for the learned is שכלים, which begins with a 'sin'; the word for ignorant is סכלים with a 'samech'; hence Abulafia's comment that the words differ in spelling but not pronunciation. For Abulafia's division between the elite and the masses in general, see M. Idel, *Language, Torah and Hermeneutics in Abraham Abulafia*, tr. M. Kallus (Albany, New York: State University of New York Press, 1989), xii–xiii.

[186] Kabbalah is not a single strand of Jewish mysticism; there are opposing, and contradictory, currents in kabbalah, just as there are in philosophy in general. This was as true among practitioners of kabbalah in Pico's day, some of whom he knew personally, as it was in the period when most of the kabbalistic texts he studied were written (13th century): see Geffen, "Faith and Reason", 433–435, discussed in Bland, "Elijah del Medigo's Averroist Response", 42–44. To some extent, these different forms of exegesis reflect philosophical differences between groups of kabbalists. In the translations of Mithridates the differences become less clear on account of his habit of interpolation: see, e.g., the superimposition of sefirotic imagery typical of the Geronese school on the combinatory kabbalah of Abulafia, discussed by Wirszubski, *Pico's Encounter*, 100–105. It is not clear to what extent Pico was aware of distinctions between kabbalistic schools. Equally, exegetical techniques involving the manipulation of letters were not an invention of the medieval kabbalists, but also occurred in earlier Judaism; see A. Green, *A Guide to the Zohar* (Stanford, California: Stanford University Press, 2004), 10, and J. Dan, *Jewish Mysticism: The Modern Period* (Northvale, New Jersey: Jason Aronson, 1999), 231–232.

(Power), *Tiferet* (Beauty or Compassion), *Neẓaḥ* (Endurance), *Hod* (Splendour), *Yesod* (Foundation) and *Malkhut* (Kingdom). As the system was elaborated, particularly in the Zohar, each of the *sefirot* took on a series of metaphorical identifications and became associated with various other words and images.[187] It was therefore possible to interpret biblical passages as containing references to the *sefirot*. As the *sefirot* were in themselves the vessels through which the universe was drawn from non-being to being, it was particularly appropriate to link the creation narrative to them. For a concise example of how sefirotic symbolism could be applied to the creation narrative, we can turn to the *Mysterium operis Geneseos*, translated for Pico by Mithridates:

> In this way, the work of Genesis is both universal and particular. It shows the being of the world, and the procession of the *sefirot* and the drawing of them from potentiality to actuality. They indicate everything in both a universal and a particular way. "In the beginning" = wisdom; "created" = the ancient of days; "God" = understanding, as it is written "and a stream went out from Eden", and Eden is wisdom, and the stream is understanding, the stream that does not lack waters. "Eth" [את] contains right and left, piety and power; "hascamaim" [heavens] = clemency; "vieth" [ואת] contains right and left, eternity and beauty; and the foundation of the ages is designated by the letter "w" [ואו, "and"]; "ha-ares" [the earth] is the assembly of Israel. Thus, you have everything in the universal way.[188]

This can be put in tabular form as follows:

Gen. 1.1 (Heb.)	Gen. 1.1 (Lat.)	*Sefirah* (Heb.)	*Sefirah* (Lat.)
Bereshit	in principio	Ḥokhmah	Sapientia
Bara	creavit	Keter	Antiquus Dierum
Elohim	dii	Binah	Intelligentia

---

[187] See, e.g., *The Zohar*, tr. D.C. Matt, I, (Stanford, California: Stanford University Press, 2004), xi; *Bahir*, ed. and tr. Gottfarstein, 168–169. A treatise explaining the different identifications was translated for Pico by Mithridates: *Expositio decem numerationum*, in Vat. Ebr. 191, ff. 60ᵛ–107ʳ.

[188] *Mysterium operis geneseos*, in Vat. Ebr. 191, ff. 125ᵛ–126ʳ: "Et secundum hanc viam opus geneseos est universale et particulare monens esse mundi et processionem numerationum et eductionem earum de potentia in actum, indicantes omnes via universali et particulari. In principio sapientia; creavit antiquus dierum; dii [*Dii* because *Elohim* is plural in Hebrew] intelligentia ut scribitur et fons exibat de heden [Gen. 2.10] de eden id est sapientia; fluvius est intelligentia, que est fluvius cuius non deficiunt aque; eth continet dextram et sinistram, pietatem et potentiam; hascamaim clementiam; vieth continet dextram et sinistram eternitatem et decorem et fundamentum seculi quod designatur in littera ואו; ha.ares est cheneseth israel et sic habes omnia via universali."

Eth	[particle]	Ḥesed, Gevurah	Pietas, Potentia
Ha-scamaim	caelum	Tiferet	Clementia
Eth	[particle]	Neẓaḥ, Hod	Eternitas, Decor
ואו i.e. w	et	Yesod	Fundamentum
Ha-ares	terram	Malkhut	Cheneseth Israel

Of the ten attributes, nine—*sapientia, intelligentia, pietas, potentia, clementia, eternitas, decor, fundamentum* and *cheneseth israel*—are the Latin terms for nine of the ten *sefirot* in one of the translation systems known to Pico.[189] The remaining phrase, *antiquus dierum*, is identifiable through other sources with the first *sefirah, Keter*, usually called *corona* in Latin, although I have not come across Pico's direct source for this wording.[190] The opening phrase of Genesis is thus interpreted as expressing the entire coming into being, in general terms, of the divine attributes: the basis for creation, as this kabbalist perceived it.

This is a classic instance of sefirotic exegesis.[191] A more extended treatment of the same idea can be found in Recanati's commentary on the Pentateuch, and I shall have occasion, in Chapter 7, to make some comments regarding this. Many of the *Conclusiones* exhibit precisely this form of sefirotic kabbalah.[192] Though prominent in the texts available to Pico, and also in the *Conclusiones*, it is striking that this type of exegesis has no place in the *Heptaplus*. The *sefirot*, as a metaphysical system, are entirely absent. The exegesis relating to them correspondingly fails to appear.[193]

5.2. *Isopsephic Equivalence (Gematria)*

As each letter of the Hebrew alphabet is also a number, every word has a numerical sum. Some exegetes made use of this to link apparently unconnected concepts or scriptural passages. Instances are scattered throughout the corpus of texts translated for Pico

---

[189] For these terms in Latin, see the *Expositio decem numerationum* cited in n. 187 above.

[190] See C.F. Knorr von Rosenroth, *Kabbala denudata*, 2 vols (Sulzbach 1677–1684, repr. Hildesheim and New York: G. Olms, 1974), I, 635–636.

[191] For a similar interpretation, with Pico's marginal markings, see *Liber de radicibus vel terminis cabale*, Vat. Ebr. 190, f. 231ʳ.

[192] Wirszubski, *Pico's Encounter*, esp. 19–52.

[193] Some commentators have attempted to relate the cosmic structure proposed by Pico to the *sefirot*. I shall discuss this in Ch. 5, section 1.2. My own opinion is that, although such links can be inferred from the *Conclusiones*, they are not explicitly present in the *Heptaplus*, and do not contribute to its comprehension.

by Mithridates, but particularly noteworthy in this regard are the works of Abraham Abulafia. For a simple example, we may turn to the "secretum de opere geneseos" in part three of the *Sitrei Torah*. Abulafia demonstrates the ancient saying that the world was created with ten utterances by pointing to the numerical equivalence between the phrases "the work of creation" and "in ten words".[194] The letters of each are added up and found to equal the same total:

מעשה בראשית = 40+70+300+5+2+200+1+300+10+400 = 1328.

בעשרה השמות = 2+70+300+200+5+5+300+40+6+400 = 1328.

In the same way, he proves that the heavens were created with God's name, since the numerical sums of "heavens" (שמים), "from where were they created?" (ומהיכן נבראו) and "from my name" (משמי) all equal the same figure: 390.[195] Most pages of the *Sitrei Torah* have at least one instance of this exegetical technique.[196] Again, it is entirely absent from the *Heptaplus*.

5.3. *Ars combinandi*

As noted above, in his discussion in the *Apologia*, Pico distinguished between various different meanings of the word 'kabbalah'. One of these distinctions refers to a "way of proceeding in sciences" similar to the Art of Raymond Lull, which is called "ars combinandi". This is what Pico in the *Conclusiones* calls "alphabetaria revolutio".[197] By this term, Pico refers to the *ḥokhmat ha-ẓeruf* (חכמת הצירוף), or letter-combinatory method of exegesis.

---

[194] Vat. Ebr. 190, f. 462ʳ: "Et postquam res sunt ita quid potero ego narare tibi de misterio operis geneseos quod dicitur mahase brexith מעשה בראשית nisi que universaliter licet scribere. Et est quidem quod indicat opus geneseos per decem nomina que hebraice dicuntur baasara axemoth בעשרה השמות probatur quia opera geneseos habent hos numeros scilicet 40, 70, 300, 5, 2, 200, 1, 300, 10, 400 et per decem nomina hos eosdem numeros 2, 70, 300, 200, 5, 5, 300, 40, 6, 400." On the tradition of the ten utterances, see Ch. 7, n. 18.

[195] Vat. Ebr. 190, f. 464ʳ.

[196] See, for a more complex example and discussion, Wirszubski, *Pico's Encounter*, 70–72.

[197] *Opera omnia*, 180–181: "In universali autem duas scientias, hoc etiam nomine honorificarunt, unam quae dicitur ars combinandi, et est modus quidam procedendi in scientiis, et est simile quid, sicut apud nostros dicitur ars Raymundi, licet forte diverso modo procedant. ... Illa enim ars combinandi, est quam ego in conclusionibus meis voco, Alphabetariam revolutionem ..." On this statement, see Wirszubski, *Pico's Encounter*, 258–261.

There is a clear instance of this in the *Heptaplus*. It is outside the main body of the text, in the final, untitled chapter, where Pico recombines the letters of the first word of the Bible, *bereshit*, to form a series of new words. I shall discuss this in Chapter 7. Pico made only one reference to this method in the *Conclusiones*; but it is clear from this, and from his discussion in the *Apologia*, that he regarded it as quintessentially kabbalistic.[198] When he uses it in the *Heptaplus*, however, he avoids explicit reference to kabbalah, describing it simply as "another method of interpretation".[199]

The other kabbalistic forms of reading—whether involving the *sefirot*, numeric sums, or altered word breaks—do not occur at any point in the *Heptaplus*. The hermeneutic concept which stands behind these methods, however—the idea that the literal and non-literal senses are appropriate for two distinct bodies of people—is, as we have seen, fundamental to it.

6. Conclusion: Pico and the Traditions of Esotericism

The historical outline sketched above forms the basis for contextualization of the *Heptaplus*. In its aims and methods, the hermeneutic stance developed by Pico in the *Commento* and *Apologia* and refined in the *Heptaplus* has more affinity with early Greek Christian interpreters than with the later Latin ones. We find in this early phase of the Christian tradition the same general frame of reference, the same appeal to historical authority, the same programme of aligning Christianity with Greek philosophy, and in some cases the same examples. The limitations imposed on the subsequent circulation of this material, however, make it likely that Pico's direct sources for his approach are to be found in later authors. Not all of the elements of Pico's justification of esotericism can be traced to a particular source, and given the breadth of his reading any assignment of sources has to be approached with some caution. The following list makes some suggestions based on textual proximity and availability.

1. The Book *Sapientia*, attributed to Solomon. No precise source located.[200]

---

[198] See n. 152 above.

[199] H. 50; Garin, 374. See Ch. 2, n. 136.

[200] Reference to such a work is found in Nahmanides's commentary on the Pentateuch, a Hebrew copy of which appears in Pico's library inventory. *Commentary*

2. Moses's knowledge of Egyptian things, attributed by Pico to Luke and Philo. Acts, 7.22: "Moses was instructed in all the wisdom of the Egyptians"; Philo, *De vita Mosis*, 1.21–24.[201]

3. The Greeks who learnt from the Egyptians: Pythagoras, Plato, Empedocles, Democritus. A similar list appears in Iamblichus, *De mysteriis Aegyptiorum, Chaldeorum, atque Assyriorum*, which was translated by Ficino.[202]

4. Numenius, Plato as Attic Moses. Transmitted in Eusebius, *Preparatio evangelica*, IX, 6 and XI, 10.[203]

5. Hermippus: Pythagoras transferred things from Mosaic law. Hermippus's *Life of Pythagoras* was an important source for Diogenes Laertius. This idea does not appear in the fragments of Hermippus, however.[204]

6. Indians: possibly Eusebius, *Preparatio evangelica*, IX, 6 and 7.[205]

7. Ethiopians: no source located.

8. The Sphinxes: Plutarch, *De Iside et Osiride*, 9: "A king chosen from among the warriors instantly became a priest and shared in the philosophy that is hidden for the most part in myths and stories which show dim reflections and insights of the truth, just as they of course suggest themselves when they place sphinxes appositely before the shrines, intimating that their teaching about the gods holds a mysterious wisdom."[206]

---

of Nahmanides on Genesis, ed. Newman, 25–27; see Wirszubski, *Pico's Encounter*, 219. Nahmanides, however, says that the "Book of Wisdom" attributed to Solomon is written in Aramaic (המתורגם), whereas Pico writes that it is in a secret language called "hierosolyma". On whether Pico read Nahmanides's commentary, see further Ch. 7, section 3.

[201] Philo, *De vita Mosis*, in *Oeuvres*, XXII, ed. and tr. R. Arnaldez et al. (Paris: Editions du Cerf, 1967), 34–36.

[202] Ficino, *Opera omnia*, 2 vols (Basel, 1576, repr. Turin: Bottega d'Erasmo, 1962), II, 1873: "Pythagoras, Plato, Democritus, Eudoxus, et multi ad sacerdotes Aegyptios accesserunt."

[203] Eusebius, *La préparation évangélique*, ed. E. des Places et al., 9 vols (Paris: Editions du Cerf, 1974–1991), VI (Sources Chrétiennes 369), tr. G. Schroeder and E. des Places, 210 (693C); VII (Sources Chrétiennes 292), tr. G. Favrelle, 106 (873B).

[204] See J. Bollansée, *Hermippos of Smyrna and his Biographical Writings: A Reappraisal* (Leuven: Peeters, 1999).

[205] Eusebius, *La préparation évangélique*, ed. des Places et al., VI, 208–210 (693B) and 212 (696A).

[206] Plutarch, *De Iside et Osiride*, ed. and tr. J.G. Griffiths (Cardiff: University of Wales Press, 1970), 9 (354B): "ὁ δ' ἐκ μαχίμων ἀποδεδειγμένος εὐθὺς ἐγίνετο τῶν ἱερέων καὶ μετεῖχε τῆς φιλοσοφίας ἐπικεκρυμμένης τὰ πολλὰ μύθοις καὶ λόγοις ἀμυδρὰς ἐμφάσεις τῆς ἀληθείας καὶ διαφάσεις ἐχούσιν, ὥσπερ ἀμέλει καὶ παραδηλοῦσιν αὐτοὶ πρὸ τῶν ἱερῶν τὰς σφίγγας ἐπιεικῶς ἱστάντες, ὡς αἰνιγματώδη σοφίαν τῆς θεολογίας αὐτῶν ἐχούσης."

9. Pythagoras wrote nothing, except for a few small things which he entrusted to his daughter Dama. Letter from Lysis to Hipparchus: "Many people say that you philosophize in public, which Pythagoras disclaimed as unworthy: he, entrusting his written notes to his daughter Dama, made an injunction that she should not hand them down to anyone outside his associates."[207]

10. Philolaus, rather than Pythagoras, wrote the Golden Verses: Diogenes Laertius, on the life of Pythagoras: "Until Philolaus, it was not possible to acquire knowledge of Pythagorean doctrine; he alone reproduced the widely-known three books, which Plato sent to buy for 10,000 drachmas."[208]

11. Lysis complained that Hipparchus had broken the rule against written transmission. See point 9 above. Another version of this letter is quoted in Iamblichus, *De vita Pythagorica*, 75.[209]

12. The pact of the disciples of Ammonius. Porphyry, *Life of Plotinus*, 3: "A pact was made by Herennius, Origen and Plotinus not to reveal the doctrines of Ammonius, which he had taught them in lectures."[210]

13. Plato's letter: The partially parallel citation in the *Apologia* is from *Epistle* II 312D–E.

14. Jesus preached in parables, and passed on deeper mysteries only to his disciples. Mark, 4.33.[211] This idea became fairly common-

---

[207] *Epistolographi Graeci*, ed. R. Hercher (Paris: Ambrosio Firmin Didot, 1873), 603: "λέγοντι δὲ πολλοί τυ καὶ δαμοσίᾳ φιλοσοφέν, τόπερ ἀπαξίωσε Πυθαγόρας, ὅς γε Δαμοῖ τᾷ ἑαυτοῦ θυγατρὶ τὰ ὑπομνάματα παρακαταθέμενος ἐπέσκαψε μηδενὶ τῶν ἐκτὸς τᾶς οἰκίας παραδιδόμεν."

[208] Diogenes Laertius, *Vitae philosophorum*, ed. M. Marcovich, 3 vols (Stuttgart: B.G. Teubner and Leipzig: K.G. Saur, 1999–2002), I, 581 (8.15): "μέχρι τε Φιλολάου οὐκ ἦν τι γνῶναι Πυθαγόρειον δόγμα· οὗτος δὲ μόνος ἐξήνεγκε τὰ διαβόητα τρία βιβλία, ἃ Πλάτων ἐπέστειλεν ἑκατὸν μνῶν ὠνηθῆναι."

[209] Iamblichus, *De vita Pythagorica liber*, ed. A. Nauck (St Petersburg: Eggers and S. and I. Glasunof, 1884), 54 (17): "φαντὶ δέ τυ καὶ δαμοσίᾳ φιλοσοφὲν τοῖς ἐντυγχάνουσι, τόπερ ἀπαξίωσε Πυθαγόρας, ὡς ἔμαθες μέν, Ἵππαρχε, μετὰ σπωδᾶς, οὐκ ἐφύλαξας δὲ, γευσάμενος, ὦ γενναῖε, Σικελικᾶς πολυτελείας, ἃς οὐκ ἐχρῆν τυ γενέσθαι δεύτερον. εἰ μὲν ὦν μεταβάλοιο, χαρησοῦμαι· εἰ δὲ μή γε, τέθνακας." For Clement's role in the transmission of the text of this letter, see Clement, *Stromata*, V, ed. Le Boulluec, II, 208–211, and M. Tardieu, "La lettre à Hipparque et les réminiscences pythagoriciennes de Clement d'Alexandrie", *Vigiliae Christianae*, 28.4 (1974), 241–247.

[210] Porphyry, *La vie de Plotin*, II, ed. Brisson et al., 136 (3): "Ἑρεννίῳ δὲ καὶ Ὠριγένει καὶ Πλωτίνῳ συνθηκῶν γεγονυιῶν μηδὲν ἐκκαλύπτειν τῶν Ἀμμωνίου δογμάτων ἃ δὴ ἐν ταῖς ἀκροάσεσιν αὐτοῖς ἀνεκεκάθαρτο".

[211] Mark 4.33–34: "καὶ τοιαύταις παραβολαῖς πολλαῖς ἐλάλει αὐτοῖς τὸν λόγον καθὼς ἠδύναντο ἀκούειν· χωρὶς δὲ παραβολῆς οὐκ ἐλάλει αὐτοῖς, κατ' ἰδίαν δὲ τοῖς ἰδίοις μαθηταῖς ἐπέλυεν πάντα."

place: see, e.g., Clement, *Stromata* I.13.1–2.[212] Pico attributes it to Origen in the *Commento* and *Apologia*. Note, however, that Pico introduces a further level of esotericism: not even all the disciples are granted all the knowledge.

15. Matthew's Gospel as limited to the acts of Christ: no source located.
16. John only revealed the mystery of the *logos* to combat Ebionites: see Jerome, *De viris illustribus*, 9: "John ... asked by the bishops of Asia, rising up against Cerinthus, and other heretics, and then especially against the beliefs of Ebionites, who maintained that Christ did not exist before Mary. Whence he was compelled to teach his divine nativity."[213]
17. Paul denied the Corinthians solid food: 1 Corinthians 5.11.
18. Dionysius the Areopagite: Pico summarizes the direct quotation from *Ecclesiastical Hierarchy*, I.4 which was previously included in the *Apologia*.[214]

This analysis points to a series of sources, not from the earliest Christian exegetes, but (excepting those deriving from the Bible itself) from later compilers—Eusebius, Diogenes Laertius, Plutarch—and Neoplatonic sources to which Pico had ready access—Porphyry, Iamblichus and Pseudo-Dionysius. As we have seen, the Neoplatonic tradition—especially Macrobius and Pseudo-Dionysius—kept the esoteric approach in circulation after it had faded from mainstream Christian biblical exegesis.

The same general hermeneutic stance also flourished in the Jewish tradition and Pico was acquainted with several of its manifestations there. In this tradition various methods of reading had been developed specifically to undermine the exoteric grammatical and syntactical structure of the biblical text and to reveal an esoteric stratum of meaning. Pico was aware of these methods but made no use of most of them throughout the *Heptaplus*. Instead he developed his own theory of allegory, which is the subject of the next chapter.

---

[212] See n. 50 above.

[213] Jerome, *Gli uomini illustri*, ed. A. Ceresa-Gastaldo (Florence: Nardini, 1988), 92 (654C): "Iohannes ... rogatus ab Asiae episcopis, adversus Cerinthum aliosque haereticos et maxime tunc Ebionitarum dogma consurgens, qui asserunt Christum ante Mariam non fuisse. Unde etiam compulsus est divinam eius nativitatem edicere."

[214] Pseudo-Dionysius, *Corpus Dionysiacum*, II, ed. Heil and Ritter, 67 (*De ecclesiastica hierarchia*, 376C).

CHAPTER FIVE

THE SECOND PROEM: PICO'S COSMIC
MODEL AND EXEGESIS AS ANAGOGY

Whereas the first proem provides a justification, in general terms, for the esoteric interpretation of the Genesis narrative, the second proem looks in detail at how this reading is to be carried out. In the previous chapter I argued that although Pico's argument for esotericism has affinities with the tradition of early Christian apologetics, his direct textual sources were more likely to have been the later Neoplatonists. This chapter will deepen the grounding of the *Heptaplus* in late Neoplatonism, specifically the works of Proclus and (in a Christian context) Pseudo-Dionysius.

The second proem has three main subjects: the structure of the cosmos, the theory of allegory and the arrangement of the *Heptaplus*. These subjects are intimately linked and Pico argues that both the theory of allegory and the total arrangement of the whole book grow out of the cosmic structure. I shall, however, defer comment on the arrangement of the work as a whole until Chapter 7.

1. *Cosmic Structure*

Pico devotes about a third of the second proem to the structure of the cosmos. Two aspects of this structure emerge as central. The first is the distribution of worlds, that is, the division of the cosmos into three parts. The second is the relationship between these worlds. Although these aspects are connected, it will aid this inquiry to try to approach them separately.

The three worlds are arranged hierarchically.[1] Topmost is the "angelic" or "intellectual" world, in the terminology of theologians and philosophers respectively. Second is the "celestial" world, in

---

[1] H. P2; Garin, 184–186: "Tres mundos figurat antiquitas. Supremum omnium ultramundanum, quem theologi angelicum, philosophi autem intellectualem vocant, quem a nemine satis pro dignitate decantatum Plato inquit in Phaedro [247 C]. Proximum huic caelestem; postremum omnium sublunarem hunc, quem nos incolimus. Hic tenebrarum mundus; ille autem lucis; caelum ex luce et tenebris temperatur. Hic per aquas notatur, fluxa instabilique substantia; ille per ignem, lucis candore et loci sublimitate; caelum natura media idcirco ab Hebraeis asciamaim, quasi ex es

which the heavenly spheres turn. Bottommost is the sublunar and elemental world. These three worlds are inter-related primarily by comparison. The highest world is characterized by light, fire, perpetual life and stability. The lowest world is its opposite in every respect, a place of darkness, watery instability, and the vicissitude of life and death. The middle world is composed of a mixture of fire and water, of light and shadow, and is unchanging in its "operation" but changing via motion. The third world is moved by the second, and the second by the first. The individual characteristics of the three worlds are the subjects of the first three expositions; the fifth and sixth expositions examine the interconnections between them.

1.1. *Ten spheres: Sources*

This threefold division is essentially a 'philosophical' rearticulation of a fairly typical 'physical' model of the cosmos. Pico espouses a geocentric universe composed of ten concentric spheres: the empyrean, the *primum mobile*, the sphere of the fixed stars and the seven planets.

Some minor but not insignificant points must be made concerning this structure. It follows one of the various versions of contemporary astronomical orthodoxy. This arrangement of the spheres, to give just one example, echoes that of an influential medieval text, *De sphaera* of Johannes de Sacrobosco:

> The cosmos can be divided in two ways, that is to say, according to substance or according to accident. According to substance, it is divided into: the ninth sphere, which is called the "first moved" or "first moving"; the eighth sphere, of the fixed stars, which is known as the firmament; and the seven planetary spheres.[2]

---

et maim, idest ex igne et aqua quam diximus, compositum nuncupatur. Hic vitae et mortis vicissitudo; illic vita perpetua et stabilis operatio; in caelo vitae stabilitas, operationum locorumque vicissitudo. Hic ex caduca corporum substantia; ille ex divina mentis natura; caelum ex corpore, sed incorrupto, ex mente, sed mancipata corpori constituitur. Movetur tertius a secundo; secundus a primo regitur, et sunt praeterea inter eos differentiae plurimae quas hic enarrare non est consilium, ubi haec praeterfluimus potius quam inundamus."

[2] L. Thorndike, *The Sphere of Sacrobosco and Its Commentators* (Chicago, Illinois: University of Chicago Press, 1949), 77: "Spera autem dupliciter dividitur, scilicet secundum substantiam et secundum accidens. Secundum substantiam enim in speram nonam, que primus motus sive primum mobile dicitur, et in speram stellarum fixarum, que firmamentum nuncupatur, et in septem speras septem planetarum".

The ten-sphere model was also used by Thomas Aquinas.[3] On the other hand, many writers proposed an additional, 'crystalline', sphere between the firmament and the *primum mobile*, making a total of eleven spheres.[4] In Pico's time, and indeed subsequently, there was no consensus.[5]

De sphaera itself does not discuss the empyrean sphere, but the subject does appear in a commentary on it, attributed to Michael Scot (d. 1235 or before). Here, it is characterized in terms similar to Pico's: it is immobile, the source of light to the lower spheres, simple rather than composite and the first term in the genus of spheres.[6] Like Pico, the commentator refers to the *Glossa ordinaria* in his discussion of the empyrean, which is above all a theological concept, the abode of the angels.[7] As Pico says, it is only "believed to exist"; it does not arise as a logical necessity from the Aristotelian model of the universe which he and his contemporaries had adopted.[8]

At this point we should note an inconsistency in Pico's scheme. Given that his 'philosophical' taxonomy of the universe breaks down into angelic, celestial and terrestrial, we would naturally expect the empyrean to be equated with the first of these worlds. But Pico, like the commentator on *De sphaera*, regards it as the foremost of the celestial spheres: the first term in the genus, or, as he puts it, the ruler of the other nine, "like the leader of an army", the monad which fills the denary.[9] It is likely that the overall numerological significance of

---

[3] Thomas Aquinas, *Summa theologiae*, I.68.4. For evidence of the fifteenth-century reception of Thomas's description of the cosmos, see A. Cattaneo, "La mappamunda di Fra Mauro Camaldolese, Venezia, 1450" (PhD Dissertation, European University Institute, Florence, 2005), 130–134.

[4] See, to give just two prominent examples, Hartmann Schedel, *Liber chronicarum* (Nuremberg, 1493), f. 5ᵛ; Apianus, *Cosmographicus liber* (Landshut, 1524), f. 6ᵛ.

[5] See Grant, *Planets, Stars and Orbs*, 315–323.

[6] Thorndike, *Sphere of Sacrobosco*, 283: "Primum celum a theologis dicitur empyreum non ab ardore sed a splendore et est uniformiter plenum lumine et immobile, non uniformiter tamen influit lumen suum in inferioribus celis eo quod actio agentis non recipitur in passum per modum ipsius agentis sed etiam per modum patientis, ut dicitur in libro De substantia orbis [by Averroes]. Sicut autem est unum ante multa, sic uniforme ante difforme vel multiforme, quia in genere celorum erit primum celum habens uniformitatem et simplicitatem. Nam simplex ante compositum est diuturnius."

[7] *Biblia latina cum glossa*, I, sig. a5ʳ, on Genesis 1.1: "caelum non visibile firmamentum sed empyreum idest igneum vel intellectuale, quod non ab ardore, sed a splendore dicitur, quod statim repletum est angelis". Cf. H. 2.1; Garin, 224.

[8] H. 2.1; Garin, 224: "creditum esse decimum caelum"; see also Grant, *Planets, Stars and Orbs*, 371: "Its existence was derived from faith, not rational argument."

[9] H. 2.1; Garin, 226: "Praeest hic igitur novem sibi serie consequenti succeden-

the structure led him to overlook this inconsistency; for by adopting it, he could generate a symmetrical correspondence between the arrangements of all three worlds: God and nine ranks of angels in the first; the empyrean and nine heavenly spheres in the second; and "prime matter" and nine categories of corruptible forms in the third.[10] The nature of the *Heptaplus* as a whole suggests that it was this consideration, rather than any particular astronomical school of thought, that led Pico to articulate the cosmic structure in the way that he did.[11] Other instances in the *Heptaplus* argue that Pico was not overly concerned when writing it with the minutiae of contemporary astronomical problems.[12]

1.2. *Three worlds: Sources*

More important than the matter of the ten spheres is the question of what I have called the 'philosophical' structure of the cosmos— the three worlds. This is deeply embedded in the fabric, not only of the *Heptaplus*, but of several of Pico's works.[13] Two parallel examples suggest themselves. The nearer, chronologically and thematically, comes from the description of God's creation of the universe in the *Oratio*:

> He had decorated the super-celestial region with minds; he had animated the heavenly spheres with eternal souls; he had filled the degraded and filthy parts of the lowest world with a crowd of all sorts of animals.[14]

---

tibus caelis, quasi dux exercitui, quasi forma materiae, et monados typum gerens denarium implet."

[10] H. P2; Garin, 190: "In primo mundo Deus, unitas prima, novem angelorum ordinibus quasi sphaeris totidem praeest, immobilisque ipse omnes movet ad se. In mundo medio, idest caelesti, caelum empyreum novem itidem sphaeris caelestibus quasi dux exercitui praeest, quae cum singulae motu incessabili volvantur, illud tamen, Deum imaginans, immotum est. Sunt et in mundo elementari post materiam primam ipsius fundamentum novem sphaerae formarum corruptibilium."

[11] On the relationship between this structure and the kabbalistic concept of *sefirot*, see below, n. 39.

[12] See, e.g., the end of H. 2.4 (Garin, 238), where Pico explicitly refuses to adjudicate between the views of Aristotle, Averroes and Avicenna (among others) over the relationship of light and heat coming from the sun, arguing that support for all three views can be found in the biblical text.

[13] For a general overview of the three worlds as presented in Pico's writings, see Roulier, *Pic de la Mirandole*, 227–285.

[14] Garin, 104: "Supercaelestem regionem mentibus decorarat; aetheros globos aeternis animis vegetarat; excrementarias ac feculentas inferioris mundi partes omnigena animalium turba complerat."

The other is from the *Commento,* where Pico's focus is less on the constituents of the three worlds than on the extent to which they are or are not visible and corporeal:

> The Platonists divide all created things into three levels, of which there are two extremes. Under one are included all corporeal and visible things, such as the heavens, the elements, plants, animals and everything composed of the elements. Under the other is understood everything which is invisible, and not only incorporeal, but entirely free and separate from any body. This is properly called intellectual nature, and by our theologians is called angelic nature. In between the two extremes is a median nature which, although incorporeal, and invisible and immortal, is nonetheless a mover of bodies and is tied to this function. This is called the rational soul, which comes after the angelic and before the corporeal, and is subject to the former and in charge of the latter.[15]

Pico offers no more explicit source for this structure than these unnamed "Platonists". In the *Heptaplus,* he is even more vague, ascribing it simply to "antiquity".[16] Correspondingly, the Neoplatonic nature of the model—emphatic in the *Commento* and still visible in the *Oratio*—is less evident in the *Heptaplus.* The *Commento* passage involves a fairly orthodox Plotinian conception of Soul as a hypostasis: and, of course, the *Commento* is largely concerned with human psychology, not with cosmology. It is in the *Oratio* that the crucial shift is made: Pico retains the terminology of the Plotinian hypostases Mind and Soul, but by linking the latter to the celestial spheres adds a different dimension to the model. Contextually, we are now closer to the *Heptaplus*: the matter under discussion is cosmology (or, more precisely, cosmogony) rather than psychology. In the *Heptaplus,* the Neoplatonic terminology has been abandoned, but the threefold schema remains. Given this gradual transformation, we may legitimately inquire to what extent we should think of this cosmic structure as 'Platonic'.

---

[15] Garin, 463 (*Commento,* I.2): "Distinguono e' Platonici ogni creatura in tre gradi, de' quali sono dua estremi. Sotto l'uno si comprende ogni creatura corporale e visibile, come è el cielo, gli elementi, le pianti, gli animali ed ogni cosa degli elementi composta. Sotto l'altro s'intende ogni creatura invisibile e non solo incorporea, ma etiam da ogni corpo in tutto libera e separata, la quale si chiama proprie natura intellettuale e da' nostri teologi è detta natura angelica. Nel mezzo di questi dua estremi v' è una natura mezza la quale benchè sia incorporea e invisibile e immortale, nondimeno è motrice de' corpi ed alligata a questo ministerio; e questa si chiama anima razionale, la quale alla angelica è sottoposta e preposta alla corporale, subietta a quella e padrona di questa."

[16] H. P2; Garin, 184: "Tres mundos figurat antiquitas."

Generally, the role of Platonism and Neoplatonism in Pico's cosmic model requires some clarification. It is, I shall argue, of the greatest significance as a context for his ideas of correspondence and hierarchy. It does not, however, sit happily with the threefold cosmic division. The hypostases of Plotinus—One, Mind, Soul—do not correspond well with the three worlds. On the one hand, Pico must correlate Mind with the angelic or intellectual world; but he has placed God, or the One, here as well.[17] The distinction between the first two hypostases is therefore blurred. On the other hand, the third hypostasis, Soul, clearly correlates with the celestial spheres; but there is no term to apply to sublunar life. Later Neoplatonism introduced more terms into the series, but did not come significantly closer to solving this initial problem.[18] For an overview of typical Neoplatonic cosmology, it is instructive to look at one of the most popular syntheses of Platonic thought available to medieval and Renaissance Europe, the *Somnium Scipionis* of Macrobius.[19] Macrobius discusses three contrasting distributions of the universe. None of these agrees with Pico's cosmic model. Two are twofold: a division between active and passive, separated at the boundary of the moon and the sphere directly above it; and a division between the firmament, on the one hand, and the other heavenly spheres, on the other. One is threefold: the first group comprising earth, air, fire and water, the second group including the four spheres from the moon to the sun, and the third group the four spheres from Mars to the firmament.[20] We have seen

---

[17] See n. 10 above.

[18] See, e.g., Proclus's seven levels of being: *soma, physis, psyche, nous, zoe, on/ousia, henas,* discussed in L. Siorvanes, *Proclus: Neo-Platonic Philosophy and Science* (Edinburgh: Edinburgh University Press, 1996), 121–126.

[19] In the early Middle Ages, Macrobius was almost the sole transmitter of Platonic thought in Latin: see, for a general discussion with references, *Commentary on the Dream of Scipio by Macrobius,* tr. W.H. Stahl (New York: Columbia University Press, 1952, repr. 1990), 39–46.

[20] Macrobius, *Commentarii in Somnium Scipionis,* ed. Scarpa, 150–154 (I.11). Apart from the summary of theoretical divisions of the universe, this passage contains two pieces of information which occur side by side in the *Heptaplus:* the identification of the moon as the *aetheria terra* and the twofold mapping of the elements onto the planetary spheres: Macrobius, *Commentarii in Somnium Scipionis,* ed. Scarpa, 152–154; H. 2.2, Garin 228. Both these ideas are to be found in Proclus's commentary on the *Timaeus:* see *In Platonis Timaeum commentaria,* ed. Diehl, I, 147 (45D) and II, 48 (154A–B). The latter had already appeared in the *Conclusiones* under the name of Iamblichus: *Conclusions,* 74 (Conc. sec. Iamblichum, 4). Although Pico could have found both these ideas in Proclus, the close juxtaposition of the two, which do not occur in the same place in the commentary on the *Timaeus,* remains suggestive of a reading of Macrobius.

that Pico owned a copy of the *Somnium Scipionis*.[21] He also owned a copy of Proclus's commentary on the *Timaeus* in which this set of distinctions is repeated.[22] Despite the connection between Platonism and the threefold model of the universe set out in the *Commento*, there is little evidence that Platonists tended to structure the cosmos in the way Pico proposes.[23] Proclus himself, in the *Elements of Theology*, proposed another threefold cosmic model; but this one is still not consonant with that of Pico.[24]

The recognition of the evolution which the threefold model underwent in Pico's thought between 1486 and 1489 is part of a broader issue. What was important about the model for Pico was not that it could be traced back to a particular author, but that it was in agreement with, or at least not directly contradicted by, a spectrum of cosmological systems. Considering the evidence assembled above, it seems likely that Pico abandoned the specifically Platonizing terminology of his earlier work to assist this syncretistic

---

[21] Kibre, *Library*, item 244.

[22] Ibid., item 967.

[23] The peculiarities of Pico's cosmic scheme were addressed by O. Kristeller, in a comment which bears repeating here. Kristeller's conclusion that this model is derived from Jewish sources is in agreement with my discussion below. See "Pico and his Sources", 73–74: "Surely the general notion that the angels, stars and elementary spheres form a hierarchical order is quite common, but the special presentation of the scheme as a sequence of three worlds is quite unusual, at least within the Greek and Latin traditions. A Neoplatonist would treat the angels or ideas and the corporeal things as two worlds after the model of Plato, and he would take over from Aristotle the distinction between celestial and sublunar things, but within the corporeal world. In other words, the scheme of the three worlds is really a combination of two dualistic schemes, and it makes quite a difference that the stars and elements, instead of being mere subdivisions of the corporeal world, now come to form each a separate world of their own, equal in status, if not in rank, to that of the ideas or angels. Since this scheme was repeated by several thinkers in the sixteenth century, it is of some interest to know whether Pico invented it, or took it over from his cabalistic or other Hebrew sources. Blau considers Menahem of Recanati as Pico's direct source in this matter [J.L. Blau, *The Christian Interpretation of the Cabala in the Renaissance* (New York: Columbia University Press, 1944), 9, 28–29]. Scholem informs me that the scheme is quite common in medieval Hebrew philosophy, but not specifically cabalistic. We may hence conclude that Pico did take it over from Hebrew sources, and probably from cabalistic sources."

[24] Proclus, *Elements of Theology*, ed. and tr. Dodds, 16–17 (Proposition 14): "All that exists is either moved or unmoved; and if the former, either by itself or by another, that is, either intrinsically or extrinsically: so that everything is unmoved, intrinsically moved, or extrinsically moved." This ontological breakdown does not fit Pico's three worlds, as it extends only to the heavenly spheres: the unmoved mover or tenth sphere in the first category, the *primum mobile* in the second, and the other eight spheres in the third.

effort. Although the shift from the psychological model of the *Commento* to the ontological model of the *Heptaplus* creates problems for a Platonist reading, it has other advantages. First among these is that the model of the *Heptaplus* is in accordance with the ontology proposed by Aristotle at the beginning of *Metaphysics* XII:

> There are three kinds of substance—one that is sensible (of which one subdivision is eternal and another is perishable, and which all recognize, as comprising e.g. plants and animals) ... and another that is immovable ... . The former two kinds of substance are the subject of natural science (for they imply movement); but the third kind belongs to another science, if there is no principle common to it and the other kinds.[25]

This ontological division, certainly, is not specifically presented in terms of a cosmic hierarchy. On the other hand, the distinction Aristotle makes between perishable things having motion (the sublunar world), eternal things having motion (the celestial bodies) and eternal things not having motion (the "intellectual" world) is consonant with Pico's model. It would be implausible to connect Pico's very precise formulation with this rather general statement of Aristotle's were it not for various subsequent developments in the Aristotelian tradition.

These developments occur predominantly in a Jewish context. The closest formulation to Pico's which I have found, in any intellectual tradition, is in Maimonides's *Guide of the Perplexed*. Maimonides noted that the reconciliation of Ptolemaic astronomy, which required epicycles and eccentric orbits, with Aristotelian physics, which demanded fixed orbits, was problematic.[26] But this problem (which in any case was to remain throughout the Middle Ages and well into the Renaissance) was not, he decided, relevant to his work, the nature of which was philosophical and exegetical:

> Our whole intention is that all entities except for the creator are divided into three parts. The first part is of the separate intellect. The second part is the heavenly bodies, the forms of which are eternal: they are not moved from one place to another, and they are not varied

---

[25] Aristotle, *Metaphysics*, 1069 a. 30; translation by W.D. Ross, in Aristotle, *Complete Works*, ed. J. Barnes, 2 vols (Princeton, New Jersey: Princeton University Press, 1984), II, 1689. The idea that there are three kinds of substance is reiterated in *Metaphysics*, 1071 b. 2.

[26] See S. Pines, "The Philosophic Sources of the Guide of the Perplexed" in *Guide*, tr. Pines, lxxi; T. Langermann, "The True Perplexity: The *Guide of the Perplexed*, Part II, Ch. 24", in *Perspectives on Maimonides*, ed. J.L. Kraemer, 159–174 (Oxford: OUP, 1991).

with regard to the basis of their substances. The third part is bodies subject to generation and corruption, because they have common matter.[27]

This idea was also diffused by Maimonides's translator Samuel ibn Tibbon.[28] Ibn Tibbon translated into Hebrew two treatises by Averroes and one by 'Averroes Iunior' on the nature and operation of the intellect. He inserted these treatises into his commentary on Ecclesiastes, prefacing them with the following introductory section:

> Inasmuch as I recognized from the words of this noble book [i.e., Ecclesiastes] that its primary purpose is to set forth the opinion of thinkers regarding the ascension of the human soul; and the meaning of the soul's ascension is that it should be perfected ... until it conjoins with the incorporeal intellect and unites therewith—now, the incorporeal intelligence is undoubtedly at the highest level of existence. For existent beings are known to fall into three species: lowest matter and what is generated from it ... ; above it ... the celestial bodies ... ; and above them ... the incorporeal intelligences.[29]

Around the first quarter of the fourteenth century, two of the three treatises, together with this introductory note, were translated into Latin in a composite form, originally under the title *De perfectione naturalis intellectus*. This work did not become widely known until the sixteenth century, when it was printed twice: firstly in Bologna in 1501, as *De beatitudine animae*, and secondly in the Giuntine Aristotle edition of 1550, as *Tractatus de animae beatitudine*. There are some indications of earlier diffusion, however. An Italian fifteenth-century manuscript of it is extant in Venice, and a copy made by an Englishman in the middle of the fourteenth century appears also to have originated in Italy. A commentary on the work was

---

[27] Maimonides, *Dux*, f. 45ᵛ (*Guide*, tr. Pines, 274–275): "Sed tota intentio est quod omnia entia praeter creatorem tripartite dividuntur. Prima pars, intellectus separati. Secunda pars, corpora caelorum, quorum formae sunt sempiternae: nec mutantur de loco in locum, nec variantur hoc fundamentum in substantiis ipsorum. Terta vero pars, corpora generabilia et corruptibilia, quoniam communem habent materiam."

[28] For a brief account of his life and works, see Sirat, *History of Jewish Philosophy*, 217–222.

[29] Samuel ibn Tibbon, commentary on Ecclesiastes, from an unpublished Hebrew manuscript, translated in H.A. Davidson, "Averrois tractatus De animae beatitudine", in *A Straight Path: Studies in Medieval Philosophy and Culture. Essays in Honour of Arthur Hyman*, ed. R. Link-Salinger, 66 (Washington DC: Catholic University of America Press, 1988).

composed by Agostino Nifo in 1492, and references were made to it in *De universalibus* of Alessandro Achillini, which was published in 1501; the same year as the *editio princeps* of *De beatitudine animae*.[30]

Whether or not Pico had access to this text is unclear.[31] Two other facts emerge, however. First, Ibn Tibbon's manner of introducing this threefold cosmic division in the introduction to a work about intellectual ascent (itself residing in a biblical commentary) implies that the idea was, in his tradition at least, a commonplace. Secondly, Ibn Tibbon's work, containing this reference to the three worlds, circulated widely in Hebrew.[32] This data, together with the passage already quoted from Maimonides, suggests not only that the threefold cosmic division was unexceptional, but also that it was frequently encountered in the Jewish tradition in a predominantly Aristotelian, rather than Platonic, context.

Evidence that Pico himself considered the doctrine of the three worlds as relating to Jewish tradition appears in the *Conclusiones*, where we read that "the three parts of particular philosophy, that is, those concerning divine, intermediate and sensible natures" are to be identified with the "triple Merkavah" or Chariot.[33] Then, in the *Heptaplus*, two further metaphorical identifications of the threefold world division occur: one linking it to the tabernacle, the other to man.[34] After the death of Maimonides, several kabbalist writers made use of the idea of a threefold cosmos.[35] Given that Pico viewed Maimonides himself as a kabbalist, we may assume that he regarded the triple world division as related to kabbalah.[36] In the

---

[30] On the relationships between Pico, Nifo and Achillini, see Mahoney, "Pico and Del Medigo, Vernia and Nifo", 143–154.

[31] See Ch. 6, n. 81.

[32] It circulated in the commentary on Ecclesiastes and also independently: see Averroes, *La béatitude de l'âme*, ed. and tr. M. Geoffroy and C. Steel (Paris: Vrin, 2001), 9–31.

[33] *Conclusions*, 206 (Conc. cabalisticae ... sec. opinionem propriam, 2): "Secunda, tertia et quarta pars est triplex Merchiava, correspondentes triplici philosophiae particulari de divinis, de mediis, et sensibilibus naturis."

[34] H. P2; Garin, 186–188; H. 50; Garin, 380.

[35] Wirszubski, *Pico's Encounter*, 245–251, discusses not the threefold division of worlds itself but the two metaphorical identifications of it which appear in the *Heptaplus*: the tabernacle and man. He suggests sources for these images in the commentary on the Pentateuch of Baḥya ben Asher (13th century) and the *Me'irat Einayim* of Isaac of Acre (late 13th or early 14th century). The question of the transmission of these texts to Pico remains problematic.

[36] See Ch. 3, section 2.5.

same way, in the *Conclusiones* he drew a correspondence between
the ten spheres and the ten *sefirot*.[37] It seems likely that these ideas
remained in his mind during the writing of the *Heptaplus*, just as I
have argued, in Chapter 4, that the aspect of kabbalah as an example
of esoteric tradition remained in his mind while writing the first
proem, although he did not mention it. But the connection between
the *sefirot* and the spheres is one of shared structure. The particular
complex of names and attributes which accrued around the *sefirot*
and allowed them (as we saw earlier) to be used as an exegetical tool
is entirely absent from the *Heptaplus*. All that remains is the residue:
the number ten.[38] The threefold structure itself, as presented in the
Heptaplus, does not require a kabbalistic reading to make sense of it;
in fact, the application of sefirotic metaphysics to it would probably
achieve the opposite.[39]

Although the threefold structure may have kabbalistic *analogies*, we must distinguish between these and the argument that
it has a kabbalistic *source*. This has been proposed, for example,
as a hypothesis connecting the *Heptaplus* to the *Einei ha-edah* of
Joḥanan Alemanno.[40] In the introduction to his own Genesis commentary, Alemanno raises various questions concerning the creation narrative, one of which appears to entail a threefold division
of the cosmos: do the words of the Torah refer to the "world of
change", the "world of motion" or the "world of *sefirot*"?[41] It may
well be that Alemanno helped Pico to develop more fully his frame
of reference for the triple cosmic division. But we have already
noted that Pico was working with the idea of a threefold division,
and refining it, since 1486 if not earlier, whereas he does not

---

[37] *Conclusions*, 218 (Conc. cabalisticae ... sec. opinionem propriam, 48).

[38] See also my argument in Ch. 7 concerning Pico's reading of Recanati and his
disposal of the sefirotic contents of his source.

[39] Wirszubski, *Pico's Encounter*, 136–138, argues that the three worlds, said in
Conclusiones cabalisticae ... secundum opinionem propriam, 2, to be equivalent to the
triple *merkavah*, are (on evidence drawn from the fiftieth Conclusion) therefore
equivalent to a triadic grouping of the *sefirot*. While this is entirely possible as regards
the kabbalistic symbolism at work in the *Conclusiones*, I cannot detect any use of this
symbolism in the *Heptaplus*.

[40] Novak, "Pico and Alemanno", 133.

[41] Paris, Bibliothèque Nationale, Ms. Ebr. 270, f. 2ʳ. The question is part of the
ninth point (התשיעית):

ואם תורה על אשר ... עולם התמורה או עולם התנועה או עולם הספירה...

See also J. Perles, "Les savants juifs à Florence à l'époque de Laurent de Médicis",
Revue des études juives, 12 (1886), 248. For another reference by Alemanno to the
"world of the *sefirot*", see *Song of Solomon's Ascents*, ed. Lesley, 130.

appear to have met Alemanno until 1488. Taking this into account, along with the Latin dissemination of such authors as Maimonides, we cannot infer that this passage, in an untranslated work, is his source.[42]

This survey is obviously not exhaustive. Further analysis would no doubt uncover other examples of a threefold cosmic division and also demonstrate the important role of the number three in medieval approaches to the cosmos in general.[43] My aim is simply to redress the balance towards a broadly Judeo-Aristotelian perspective on the threefold cosmos, not overly beholden either to Platonism or kabbalah. I do not think identification of a single source is possible, or even desirable: this is a fine example of Pico's celebrated syncretism at work, choosing a model which could be linked to Aristotelian, Platonic or Jewish ideas according to context. The structure of the *Heptaplus* is intimately reliant on the fact that there are three worlds; in analysing Pico's allegorical method, however, it is the sympathetic affinities between the worlds that are important, not their actual number.

1.3. *"Mutual Containment"*

Pico regards the three worlds as exhibiting what he calls "mutual containment".[44] They are arranged hierarchically—angelic world at the top, sublunar world at the bottom—but they are actually deeply intertwined. Each world contains the same things (relatively and by analogy) as the other two. This forms the basis of Pico's programme ("nostra fere tota pendet intentio"). It has three aspects:

1. "All things are drawn from one beginning and to one and the same end."

---

[42] The Hebrew word *olam* (עולם), translated above as "world", actually has a broad semantic range (see, e.g., Jastrow, *Dictionary*, 1052); in Mithridates's translations, it is rendered not as *mundus* but as *seculum*.

[43] A prolonged discussion of the importance of the number three, seen as the controlling number of the universe, occurs at the beginning of Nicole Oresme's *Livre du ciel et du monde*, ed. A.D. Menut and A.J. Denomy (Madison, Wisconsin: University of Wisconsin Press, 1968), 48–53. For a brief account of various cosmic divisions, see L. Spruit, *Il problema della conoscenza in Giordano Bruno* (Naples: Bibliopolis, 1988), 101–105. The reader of Spruit's account will note that those who wrote after Pico (e.g., Henricus Cornelius Agrippa and Giordano Bruno) adhered more closely to Pico's model than Pico did to the models which antedated him, which, again, are of largely Platonic inspiration.

[44] See n. 52 below.

2. "All things are arranged by necessary numbers so that they are bound together by a certain harmonic kinship of nature and by a graduated series of steps."

3. "Whatever is in all of the worlds is also in each of them, and there is not one of the worlds in which there is not everything that is in each world."[45]

The first proposition is expanded on in the proem to the seventh exposition, where Pico argues that God is the beginning and end of everything, and that this can be read into the Pythagorean doctrines of the One and the Good.[46] The second proposition introduces the relationship of hierarchy and number, which dictates the division of each of the three worlds into ten subsections, as already noted.[47] It is the third proposition which is fundamental to the idea of the work as a whole. Things occur correspondingly at different points in the hierarchy, but with a successive degradation of condition. The things which are in the lower world are in the upper worlds in a better condition, and the same things that are in the upper worlds are also in the lower, but in a worse condition.[48] The interplay of correspondence and difference created by this structure is drawn out by the example of heat or fire.[49] In the lowest world, which we inhabit, "heat" exists as a quality of an element ("apud nos calor qualitas elementaris"). In the celestial world, there is a "heating power" ("virtus excalfactoria"). In the angelic world, there is the "idea of heat" ("idea caloris"). The particular manifestations of each of these is that "in our world there is fire, which is an element; the sun

---

[45] H. P2; Garin, 188: "Haec satis de tribus mundis in quibus illud in primis magnopere observandum, unde et nostra fere tota pendet intentio, esse hos tres mundos mundum unum, non solum propterea quod ab uno principio et ad eumdem finem omnes referantur, aut quoniam debitis numeris temperati et armonica quadam naturae cognatione atque ordinaria graduum serie colligentur, sed quoniam quicquid in omnibus simul est mundis, id et in singulis continetur, neque est aliquis unus ex eis in quo non omnia sint quae sunt in singulis."

[46] H. 7.P; Garin, 326: "Idem igitur finis omnium quod omnium principium: Deus unus omnipotens et benedictus, optimum omnium quae aut esse aut cogitari possunt; hinc duae illae appellationes apud Pythagoricos, unum scilicet et bonum. Unum enim cognominatur, qua omnium est principium, quemadmodum unitas principium est totius numeri; bonum autem, qua omnium finis, omnium quies et absoluta felicitas est."

[47] See above, n. 10.

[48] H. P2; Garin, 188: "Verum quae in mundo sunt inferiori, in superioribus sunt, sed meliore nota; quae itidem sunt in superioribus in postremis etiam visuntur, sed degeneri conditione et adulterata, ut sic dixerim, natura."

[49] Ibid.: "Est apud nos calor qualitas elementaris, est in caelestibus virtus excalfactoria, est in angelicis mentibus idea caloris."

is a fire in heaven; in the ultramundane region fire is the seraphic intellect". These are the correspondences; as for the differences, "the elemental fire burns; the celestial fire nourishes; the supercelestial fire loves".[50] The case of water is analogous: three different forms of it exist correspondingly but with different operations.[51] We shall return to this idea, and a probable source for it, at the end of this chapter. This cosmic scheme, Pico argues, is a physical reality; it precedes and defines the rest of the book.

2. *Allegorical Theory*

The cosmic scheme is the basis for Pico's theory of allegory. This argument is initially expressed in rather compressed and obscure terms in the middle of the second proem:

> I shall add only this: the mutual containment of the worlds is also indicated in the Scriptures, as, for example, it is written in the Psalms "... who created the heavens in intellect", and as we read that God's angels are "spirits" and his messengers are "a flame of burning fire". Often, in this way, names properly belonging to celestial things are applied to divine things, and often also [names properly belonging to] terrestrial things [are applied to divine things]: [these divine things] are figured now by stars, now by wheels and animals, now by elements. Also, in this way, names properly belonging to celestial things [are applied to] terrestrial things. As if bound by chains of concord, all these worlds exchange not only natures, but likewise names, with mutual liberality. This, if anyone has perhaps not yet grasped it, is the principle from which the teaching of the whole allegorical sense has flowed.[52]

---

[50] Ibid.: "Dicam aliquid expressius: est apud nos ignis quod est elementum; sol ignis in caelo est; est in regione ultramundana ignis saraphicus intellectus. Sed vide quid differant. Elementaris urit, caelestis vivificat, supercaelestis amat."

[51] Ibid., 188–190: "Est aqua apud nos; est aqua in caelis, huius motrix et domina, vestibulum scilicet caelorum luna; sunt aquae et super caelum mentes cherubicae. Sed vide quae in eadem natura disparilitas conditionis: humor elementaris vitae calorem obruit; caelestis eumdem pascit; supercaelestis intelligit."

[52] Ibid., 190–192: "Hoc tantum addiderimus: mundorum mutuam continentiam sacris etiam literis indicari, cum et scriptum in Psalmis [135.5] sit: Qui creat caelos in intellectu, et angelos Dei legimus spiritus esse et ministros eius flammam ignis urentis; hinc saepe divinis caelestia cognomenta, saepe etiam terrena: dum nunc per stellas, nunc per rotas et animalia, nunc per elementa figurantur: hinc et terrenis saepe caelestia nomina. Quoniam scilicet astricti vinculis concordiae uti naturas ita etiam appellationes hi omnes mundi mutua sibi liberalitate condonant. Ab hoc principio (si quis fortasse hoc nondum advertit) totius sensus allegorici disciplina manavit."

The ancient fathers, he continues, were able to represent certain things with other images because they were trained in the "bonds and affinities" of all things. Otherwise, there would be no explanation for why they represented a certain thing with one particular image rather than its opposite. Because (1) they knew all things and (2) they were inspired by the Spirit which both knew and made all things, they fittingly represented the things of one world by means of those things which they knew corresponded to them in the other worlds. Therefore, would-be interpreters of their books who wish properly to understand their "figures and allegorical senses" require either the same inspiration or the same knowledge.[53]

The initial discussion of the allegorical method concludes here. What follows in the remainder of the second proem is, firstly, a discussion of the role of man as microcosm; secondly, the rationale behind the distribution of the seven expositions that make up the *Heptaplus*; and thirdly, some subsidiary interpretative criteria geared towards ensuring that the *Heptaplus* does not resemble those commentaries which heap up eclectic information without consideration of relevance.[54] Pico returns to his allegorical theory in the introduction to the second exposition. Before this, in the first exposition, which is concerned with the sublunar world, he had identified the efficient and material causes with heaven and earth, the qualities with the waters, and form with light.[55] At the start of the second exposition, therefore, he asks why this process of interpretation has been necessary:

> Why, for example, when Moses was about to discuss the efficient and material causes, did he not call the former efficient, the latter material, in these express words, but instead "heaven" and "earth"? Why did he call the dispositions of matter, not qualities, as philosophers say, but instead "waters"? Why did he call form "light" rather than "form"? Why, similarly, did he call comets and thunderbolts and other things of that sort, not by their proper names, but instead "stars" and "planets"?[56]

---

[53] Ibid., 192: "Nec potuerunt antiqui patres aliis alia figuris decenter repraesentare, nisi occultas, ut ita dixerim, totius naturae et amicitias et affinitates edocti. Alioquin nulla esset ratio cur hoc potius hac imagine, aliud alia quam contra repraesentassent. Sed gnari omnium rerum et acti Spiritu illo … naturas unius mundi, per ea quae illis in reliquis mundis noverant respondere, aptissime figurabant. Quare eadem opus cognitione (nisi idem adsit et Spiritus), his qui illorum figuras et allegoricos sensus interpretari recte voluerint."

[54] Ibid., 196.

[55] See Ch. 2, section 1.

[56] H. 2.P; Garin, 220–222: "Cur gratia exempli dicturus Moses de agente causa et de materia, non illam agentem expressis verbis, hanc materiam, vocavit, sed caelum

He notes that there are several possible answers to this question. The first two reiterate the general argument of the first proem: the concealment of knowledge in texts was sanctioned by tradition, and in antiquity it was commonplace for "great natural and divine truths" to be hidden or veiled by the very words in which they were expressed, if for no other reason than that the ignorance of the audience required this.[57] But there is another reason for it as well. Moses uses a "wondrous and unknown art" and chooses the words of his text in such a way that "the same words, the same context and the same series of the entire Scripture appropriately correspond by representing the secrets of all the worlds and of all things". In other words, the same words are able to express the account of not just one of the three worlds, but of all of them. Pico goes on to explain that this "art" has three notable aspects:

1. Through it, Moses's book may claim to be pre-eminent with regard to the writings and doctrines of the gentiles.
2. Its exposition constitutes the novelty of Pico's book.
3. It makes Moses the archetype of all writers, in two ways. Firstly, his use of words is based on the correspondences which (as Pico has already argued) constitute the cosmos; therefore, Moses imitates nature itself. Secondly, his text is able to comprehend all things with very few words. This quality, says Pico, makes it supreme among texts, just as, according to Dionysius and Thomas, the ability of angelic minds to comprehend with the fewest number of forms makes them superior to lower minds, which require a multiplicity of forms.[58] This final point was summed up by

---

et terram; et materiae dispositiones non qualitates, ut dicunt philosophi, sed aquas, et formam lucem potius quam formam appellavit; cometas item et fulmina et cetera id genus, non propriis cognominibus, sed astra et stellas nominavit ..."

[57] Ibid., 222: "cum veterum consuetudo scribendi res grandes physicas et divinas occulte et figurate, tum ruditas auditorum ... oportuit velata facie verba facere illis".

[58] Ibid., 222–224: "Quare illud est incogitatum et mirum Moseos artificium, divinaque vere non humana industria, eis uti dictionibus itaque orationem disponere ut eadem verba, idem contextus, eadem series totius scripturae figurandis mundorum omnium et totius naturae secretis apte conveniat. Hoc illud est in quo Moseos liber omnem gentem et doctrinam et eloquentiam et ingenium superat, hoc novum illud et intactum adhuc quod nos afferre temptavimus, ut scilicet factum a Mose id nostris hominibus re ipsa comprobaremus. Haec est idea, hoc est exemplar absolutissimi scriptoris, non ob id solum quia huiuscemodi scribendi genus, ut supra demonstravimus, naturam effigiat et aemuletur, quam quod, sicut inter mentes angelicas, auctore Dionysio et divo Thoma, splendore nostrae theologiae, illa est suprema quae paucissimis ea notionibus et formis per intelligentiam comprehendit, quae inferiores variis et multiplicibus, ita inter scripturas illa est summa, illa apicem

a marginal comment in the *editio princeps*: "the Mosaic text emulates the angelic intelligence".[59]

In approaching an understanding of these ideas, I shall begin by exploring the notion of the "mutual containment of the worlds", which Pico identifies as the foundation of his allegorical theory. I shall then look at the assertion that the Mosaic text has a parallel with angelic intelligence and that its *words* are somehow analogous to *forms*. I hope to make it clear that these two strands of investigation are actually very closely connected. By looking at the points where they connect, I shall suggest a model for Pico's allegorical theory, which in turn will help us to locate the *Heptaplus* more precisely within the context of biblical exegesis.

2.1. *Proclus (412–485)*

Pico's observation that things which occur in the lower worlds mirror those in the upper but in a worse condition, and that things in the upper worlds mirror those in the lower but in a better condition, is based on a Neoplatonic commonplace. The mechanics of emanation and causation, as envisaged by the Neoplatonists, render this idea of mirror imaging necessary. Pico uses this model not simply to make a point about the increasing imperfection of created things, from the intellectual world downwards; his emphasis is on the fact that it is the *same* things which occur, somehow, in each world. The crucial sentence, already quoted, is: "Whatever is in all of the worlds is also in each of them, and there is not one of the worlds in which there is not everything that is in each world."[60]

Although Pico claims that this idea originates with the Pre-socratic philosopher Anaxagoras, it is in later Neoplatonism that this particular expression of the cosmic structure is to be found.[61] The most important text for our purposes here is the *Elements of Theology* by the fifth-century pagan Neoplatonist Proclus. In this treatise, Proclus

---

tenet omnis perfectionis, quae paucissimis verbis omnia veluti singula et congrue et profunde complectitur." I discuss the origin of the citations of Pseudo-Dionysius and Thomas in section 2.4 below.

[59] *Heptaplus* (Florence, 1489), sig. b8ᵛ: "scriptura mosaica intelligentiae angelicae emulatrix".

[60] See n. 45 above.

[61] H. P2; Garin, 188: "Quam Anaxagorae credo fuisse opinionem, si recte eum sensisse putamus, explicatam deinde a Pythagoricis et Platonicis." For the source of Pico's mention of Anaxagoras, Garin refers the reader to Simplicius's commentary on Aristotle's *Physics*, where the saying that "there is a part of everything in everything"

systematized the thought of Plotinus, with particular reference to the mechanics of causation and emanation. Proclus's system passed into Arabic in the ninth century. From there, it was translated into Latin in the second half of the twelfth century, in a version commonly entitled *Liber de causis*. In its Arabic version it had acquired an attribution to Aristotle and this was perpetuated in the Latin tradition until the thirteenth century.[62] When William of Moerbeke translated the *Elements of Theology* itself in 1268, it was read by Thomas Aquinas, who realized that the *Liber de causis* was actually based on Proclus's work.[63]

In the Renaissance, both the *Liber de causis* and the Latin version of Proclus's *Elements of Theology* continued to circulate.[64] By this time, the *Elements of Theology* was also widely available in Greek, and a Greek manuscript of it, dated 1358 and previously in Pico's possession, is to be found in the Bodleian library, Oxford.[65] For this reason, I quote this work from the Greek edition with English translation by E.R. Dodds, cross-referring to the Latin of William of Moerbeke.

In mapping the lines of thought which led to Pico's position in the *Heptaplus*, we should start with Proposition 103 of Proclus's *Elements of Theology*:

> All things are in all things, but properly in each: for in being there is life and intellect, in life there is being and intellect, and in intellect there is

---

is attributed to Anaxagoras: Simplicius, *In Aristotelis Physicorum libros quattuor priores commentaria*, ed. H. Diels, Commentaria in Aristotelem Graeca, IX (Berlin: Reimer, 1882), 27.

[62] Thomas Aquinas, *Super Librum de causis expositio*, ed. H.D. Saffrey (Fribourg: Société Philosophique and Leuven: E. Nauwelaerts, 1954), xv–xxv; C. D'Ancona Costa, *Recherches sur le Liber de causis* (Paris: J. Vrin, 1995), 195–197.

[63] Thomas Aquinas, *Super Librum de causis expositio*, ed. Saffrey, 3 (prooemium): "Inveniuntur igitur quaedam de primis principiis conscripta, per diversas propositiones distincta, quasi per modum sigillatim considerantium aliquas veritates. Et in graeco quidem invenitur sic traditus liber Procli Platonici, continens ccxi propositiones, qui intitulatur Elementatio theologica; in arabico vero invenitur hic liber qui apud Latinos De causis dicitur, quem constat de arabico esse translatum et in graeco penitus non haberi: unde videtur ab aliquo philosophorum arabum ex praedicto libro Procli excerptus, praesertim quia omnia quae in hoc libro continentur, multo plenius et diffusius continentur in illo."

[64] C.B. Schmitt and D. Knox, *Pseudo-Aristoteles Latinus: A Guide to Latin Works Falsely Attributed to Aristotle Before 1500* (London: Warburg Institute, 1985), 18–20; Proclus, *Elementatio theologica*, tr. William of Moerbeke, ed. H. Boese (Leuven: University Press, 1987), x–xviii.

[65] Bodleianus Laud. graec. 18, ff. 242–288^v: see Proclus, *Elements of Theology*, ed. and tr. Dodds, xxxvii. Dodds (ibid., xxxii) notes that over forty 15th- and 16th-century manuscripts of the *Elements of Theology* are extant.

being and life; but all things are on one level intellectually, on another level vitally, and on another existentially.[66]

The same idea recurs in the *Liber de causis*.[67] Before including it in the *Heptaplus*, Pico included it in his *Conclusiones*, in the section on Proclus: "Although, according to Theology, the divine hierarchies are distinct, it must nevertheless be understood that *everything is in all things in its own mode*" (my italics).[68]

How did this idea reach Pico? Proclus was not the first to explore it. It occurs in Syrianus's *In Metaphysica*, which Pico probably owned.[69] It was also used by Iamblichus's student, the emperor Julian, in his *Hymn to King Helios*, which was a popular work in the Renaissance and was certainly read by Pico.[70] We could regard any of these as Pico's direct source. But none of these works articulates this idea in an exegetical context; and, for this reason, it is worth pursuing the reception of this idea a little further.

---

[66] Proclus, *Elements of Theology*, ed. and tr. Dodds, 92: "πάντα ἐν πᾶσιν, οἰκείως δὲ ἐν ἑκάστῳ· καὶ γὰρ ἐν τῷ ὄντι καὶ ἡ ζωὴ καὶ ὁ νοῦς, καὶ ἐν τῇ ζωῇ τὸ εἶναι καὶ τὸ νοεῖν, καὶ ἐν τῷ νῷ τὸ εἶναι καὶ τὸ ζῆν, ἀλλ' ὅπου μὲν νοερῶς, ὅπου δὲ ζωτικῶς, ὅπου δὲ ὄντως ὄντα πάντα". Cf. *Elementatio theologica*, ed. Boese, 52. The relation between this proposition and the *Heptaplus* was noted by Wirszubski, *Pico's Encounter*, 250–251. For a useful comment on this idea, see Proclus, *Elements of Theology*, ed. and tr. Dodds, 254: "Are Being, Life and Intelligence to be regarded as three aspects of a single reality or as three successive stages in the unfolding of the cosmos from the One? Proclus characteristically answers that both are true: they are aspects, for each of them implies the other as cause or as consequent; they are successive, not co-ordinate, for each is predominant (though not to the exclusion of the others) at a certain stage of the πρόοδος. This may be expressed by saying that the triad is mirrored within each of its terms, so that while e.g. the first term has Being as its predominant character, it is at the same time Life and Intelligence *sub specie aeternitatis*. The scheme is elaborately worked out in Th. Pl. IV i–iii; its purpose, as we there learn, is to reconcile distinctness with continuity."

[67] *Liber de causis*, ed. A. Pattin, *Tijdschrift voor Filosofie*, 28 (1966), 161 (Propositions 103–104): "Primorum omnium quaedam sunt in quibusdam per modum quo licet ut sit unum eorum in alio. Quod est quia in esse sunt vita et intelligentia, et in vita sunt esse et intelligentia, et in intelligentia sunt esse et vita."

[68] *Conclusions*, 78 (Conc. sec. Proclum, 17): "Licet, ut tradit Theologia, distinctae sint divinae hierarchiae, intelligendum est tamen omnia in omnibus esse modo suo."

[69] Syrianus, *Commentaria in Metaphysica*, ed. G. Kroll, Commentaria in Aristotelem Graeca, VI (Berlin: Reimer, 1892), 81–82 (879B): "τὰς δ' οὖν ὡς ἐν πλάτει τρεῖς ἔλεγον τάξεις τῶν ὄντων, νοητὴν διανοητὴν αἰσθητήν, εἶναι δὲ καθ' ἑκάστην τὰ εἴδη πάντα μέν, οἰκείως δὲ ἀπανταχοῦ τῇ τῆς ὑπάρξεως ἰδιότητι." See Kibre, *Library*, item 1029.

[70] Julian the Apostate, *De sole*, ed. Lacombrade, 104–105 (133B–D). Pico quotes Julian in H. 2.2 (Garin, 226). For his copy of this text, see Kibre, *Library*, item 440. The *Hymn to King Helios* was the only one of Julian's works to retain its popularity into the Renaissance: see *De sole*, ed. Lacombrade, 97–99.

2.2. Dionysius

Soon after their formulation by Proclus these ideas entered the Christian tradition via the works of Pseudo-Dionysius the Areopagite, whom we encountered briefly in the previous chapter. This corpus circulated widely in a number of Latin translations;[71] it was used by (among others) Thomas Aquinas, who produced a commentary on Dionysius's *On the Divine Names*.[72] Both the original work and the commentary develop the idea of "mutual containment" which I discussed above. Dionysius writes in the fourth chapter:

> This—the One, the Good and the Beautiful—is uniquely the cause of all good and beautiful things. From it come all the essential substances of things: those which are common and those which are distinct; those which are the same and those which are different; those which are similar and those which are dissimilar; those which have congruence in opposites and those which maintain common things as discrete; the foreknowings of things of higher rank, the inter-relationships of those of the same rank, the return upwards of those of lower rank; the protecting and immutable abidings and stabilities of all things among themselves; and, on the other hand, *the communions of all things in all things according to the property of each, and the harmonious and unconfused friendships and harmonies of everything* (my italics).[73]

Thomas, commenting on this passage, discusses the "habitation" (*mansio*) of one thing in another thing, and concludes that there are

> communions of all things in all things according to the property of each. All things are in all things, not just in one way: but the higher things are in the lower by participation, and the lower in the higher in an outstanding manner, and nevertheless all things have something in common with all things.[74]

---

[71] See Ch. 4, n. 124.

[72] Thomas Aquinas, *In librum beati Dionysii De divinis nominibus expositio*, ed. C. Pera (Rome: Marietti, 1950).

[73] *De divinis nominibus*, 4.7, in *Corpus Dionysiacum*, I, ed. Schula, 152: "τοῦτο τὸ ἓν ἀγαθὸν καὶ καλὸν ἑνικῶς ἐστι πάντων τῶν πολλῶν καλῶν καὶ ἀγαθῶν αἴτιον. ἐκ τούτου πᾶσαι τῶν ὄντων αἱ οὐσιώδεις ὑπάρξεις, αἱ ἑνώσεις, αἱ διακρίσεις, αἱ ταὐτότητες, αἱ ἑτερότητες, αἱ ὁμοιότητες, αἱ ἀναμοιότητες, αἱ κοινωνίαι τῶν ἐναντίων, αἱ ἀσυμμιξίαι τῶν ἡνωμένων, αἱ πρόνοιαι τῶν ὑπερτέρων, αἱ ἀλληλουχίαι τῶν ὁμοστοίχων, αἱ ἐπιστροφαὶ τῶν καταδεεστέρων, αἱ πάντων ἑαυτῶν φρουρητικαὶ καὶ ἀμετακίνητοι μοναὶ καὶ ἱδρύσεις, καὶ αὖθις αἱ πάντων ἐν πᾶσιν οἰκείως ἑκάστῳ κοινωνίαι καὶ ἐφαρμογαὶ καὶ ἀσύγχυτοι φιλίαι καὶ ἁρμονίαι τοῦ παντός …"; cf. *Dionysiaca*, ed. Chevallier, I, 186–188.

[74] Thomas Aquinas, *In librum Beati Dionysii de divinis nominibus expositio*, ed. Pera, 118 (lectio 6): "Tertio ponit ea quae pertinent ad mansionem unius rei in alia. Unde

These two passages point us simultaneously back to Proclus and forward to the *Heptaplus*.

This idea of cosmic inter-relation, although Neoplatonic and pagan in origin, was received into Christian thought via Pseudo-Dionysius and subsequently Thomas Aquinas. Although Pico was able to read the original Neoplatonic sources in Greek, he was no doubt aware of their scholastic reception. The significance of the chain of reception outlined here is that, in the progress of this doctrine from its Eastern Greek roots to the Latin West, we have encountered the same two names which Pico bracketed together at the end of his second discussion of his allegorical method: "auctore Dionysio et divo Thoma".[75] I shall therefore turn to an examination of the second idea mentioned above—the connection of Pseudo-Dionysius and Thomas Aquinas and the subject of angelic cognition, which, according to Pico, Moses's text emulates.

2.3. *Human and Angelic Cognition*

The notions which I have just been discussing are concerned with the *similarity* between the different cosmic levels: "whatever is in all of the worlds is also in each of them". I shall now present Pico's articulation of *difference* within the cosmos. The Neoplatonic hierarchical cosmos, which is the foundation of the *Heptaplus*, has as a central tenet the idea that the condition of all things degenerates progressively as one moves down the hierarchy. This degeneration in condition is directly related to *number*: things become progressively further removed from unity and participate more in multiplicity. Equally importantly, this order is reversible. This is the bearing of Proposition 21 of the *Elements of Theology*:

> Every order, beginning from unity, proceeds to a multiplicity in respect to that unity, and the multiplicity of any order is led back to a single unity.[76]

---

sciendum est quod, cum ex aliquibus aliquid constitui oportet, primo quidem requiritur quod partes conveniant: sicut multi lapides conveniunt ad invicem ex quibus constituitur domus et similiter omnes partes universi conveniunt in ratione existendi; et hoc ideo dicit, quia non solum ex pulchro sunt mansiones rerum in seipsis, sed etiam *communiones omnium in omnibus secundum proprietatem uniuscuiusque; non enim uno modo omnia sunt in omnibus, sed superiora quidem in inferioribus participatione, inferiora vero in superioribus excellenter et tamen omnia cum omnibus aliquid commune habent*" (my italics). The word *mansio* renders for Thomas the Greek word ἀμετακίνητοι (see above, n. 73).

[75] See n. 58 above.

[76] Proclus, *Elements of Theology*, ed. and tr. Dodds, 24; cf. *Elementatio theologica*,

My concern in the remainder of this chapter is to explain: (1) the effect which this progression from unity to multiplicity has on the operation of the intellect; and (2) the relationship of this effect to Pico's concept of allegory.

According to Pico, Dionysius and Thomas Aquinas both argue that the intelligence of angels is superior to that of humans because it comprehends with fewer forms, whereas human intelligence, situated lower down the hierarchy (and therefore more subject to multiplicity and further removed from unity), requires more forms. Similarly, elsewhere in the *Heptaplus* Pico notes that although "intelligible forms" are accidental to an angel's intellect and not part of its essence, nonetheless the bond between them and the angel is "indivisible" and "perpetual" whereas between them and the human intellect it is "vague and ordinary".[77] The precise nature and operation of intelligible forms or species (Pico uses the terms interchangably) was a matter of controversy in the Middle Ages and Renaissance, and Pico has little else to say about them.[78] We need not be overly concerned with this question, however, since what is crucial to the argument is not what exactly the forms are, but merely the relative paucity or plenitude of them according to the type of mind—angelic or human—which is doing the receiving.

In Dionysius we find this argument in *On the Divine Names*, VII.[79] Angels have "simple and blessed conceptions" (τὰς ἁπλᾶς καὶ μακαρίας ἔχουσι νοήσεις). They gather knowledge of God neither from divisible things, nor from sense perceptions, nor from discursive reasoning (οὐκ ἐν μεριστοῖς ἢ ἀπὸ μεριστῶν ἢ αἰσθήσεων ἢ λόγων διεξοδικῶν συνάγουσαι τὴν θείαν γνῶσιν). In their process of understanding they are free from all matter and multiplicity (παντὸς δὲ ὑλικοῦ καὶ πλήθους καθαρεύουσαι). They "think the intelligible things of God spiritually, without matter and in a single form" (νοερῶς, ἀΰλως, ἐνοειδῶς

---

ed. Boese, 14. Note the comment of Dodds, 208: "The formula is based on the Pythagorean conception of the arithmetical series ... . Each member of the series evolves from, or is generated by, the preceding members, and the series as a whole is thus generated by the unit or 'monad' which is its first member. We may either start from this monad and trace the emergence of the series from it, or follow the series in the reverse direction until it ends in the monad: in the former case we move from cause to effect, in the latter from effect to cause."

[77] See Ch. 2, n. 62.

[78] For details of the controversy see L. Spruit, *Species intelligibilis: From Perception to Knowledge*, 2 vols (Leiden: E.J. Brill, 1994–1995).

[79] Garin, 222, refers rather to *De caelesti hierarchia*, 7, but the specific subject of the perception of simple forms by the angelic intellect is not present in that chapter.

τὰ νοητὰ τῶν θείων νοοῦσιν). Human souls are also endowed with a rational ability (τὸ λογικόν), but "they travel discursively and in a circle around the truth of things" (διεξοδικῶς μὲν καὶ κύκλῳ περὶ τὴν τῶν ὄντων ἀλήθειαν περιπορευόμεναι). They fall short of angelic minds on account of their divided and manifold variety (καὶ τῷ μεριστῷ καὶ παντοδαπῷ τῆς ποικιλίας ἀπολειπόμεναι); but, insofar as they have the ability to "roll up the many things into the one" (τῇ δὲ τῶν πολλῶν εἰς τὸ ἓν συνελίξει), they too are worthy of conceptions equal to those of the angels (καὶ τῶν ἰσαγγέλων νοήσεων ... ἀξιούμεναι). In conclusion, it is fair to say that all perceptions are "an echo of the object of wisdom" (σκοποῦ τῆς σοφίας ἀπήχημα).[80]

Thomas Aquinas, meanwhile, in his *Summa theologiae*, summarized the matter as follows:

> In all intellectual substances one finds an intellective power through the influence of divine light. Whatever is in the first principle is one and simple; the more distant intellectual beings are from the first principle, the more this light is divided and differentiated, as happens in lines departing from a point. So it is that God understands everything through his single essence; the higher intellectual beings, although they understand through many forms, nonetheless understand through fewer, more universal and more powerful forms for the comprehension of things, on account of the efficacy of the intellective power which is in them. The lower intellectual beings, however, insofar as they lack the intellective power of the higher, require more numerous and less universal forms, which are less effective for the comprehension of things.[81]

It is clear, Thomas concludes, that the human intellect is at the lowest end of this scale.[82] Thomas's more detailed theory bears the imprint of a reading of the *Liber de causis*;[83] and, as he himself pointed out in

---

[80] Pseudo-Dionysius, *Corpus Dionysiacum*, I, ed. Suchla, 195 (*De divinis nominibus*, 868B); cf. *Dionysiaca*, ed. Chevallier, I, 387–392.

[81] Thomas Aquinas, *Summa theologiae*, I.89.1: "In omnibus enim substantiis intellectualibus invenitur virtus intellectiva per influentiam divini luminis. Quod quidem in primo principio est unum et simplex; et quanto magis creaturae intellectuales distant a primo principio, tanto magis dividitur illud lumen et diversificatur, sicut accidit in lineis a centro egredientibus. Et inde est quod Deus per unam suam essentiam omnia intelligit; superiores autem intellectualium substantiarum, etsi per plures formas intelligant, tamen intelligunt per pauciores, et magis universales, et virtuosiores ad comprehensionem rerum, propter efficaciam virtutis intellectivae quae est in eis; in inferioribus autem sunt formae plures, et minus universales, et minus efficaces ad comprehensionem rerum, inquantum deficiunt a virtute intellectiva superiorum."

[82] Ibid.: "Manifestum est autem inter substantias intellectuales, secundum naturae ordinem, infimas esse animas humanas."

[83] *Liber de causis*, ed. Pattin, 158–160 (Propositions 92–95): "Omnis intelligentia plena est formis; verumtamen ex intelligentiis sunt quae continent formas minus

his commentary on the *Liber de causis*, the common root of all these speculations is Proposition 177 of the *Elements of Theology*.[84]

This account of knowledge is part of the more general theory of the hierarchy of being, originally Neoplatonic, and subsequently received by the scholastics, from whom it passed in an unbroken chain to Pico. Pico's reference in the fifth exposition of the *Heptaplus* to the "golden chain of Homer" alludes to one image by which this hierarchy was commonly known in the Middle Ages.[85] Prominent exponents of this system included Albertus Magnus, Henry of Ghent, Aegidius Romanus, Cardinal Bessarion and Marsilio Ficino. According to this ontology, which originates with Plotinus, the universe has a twofold dynamic: the procession of all things from God or the One, called the *proodos*; and a complementary reversion of things back to the One or God, known as the *epistrophe*.[86] The influence of this model on Pico's theory of allegory is the subject of the final section of this chapter.

2.4. *Names and Things*

The preceding two lines of enquiry have intersected in the discussion of the hierarchy of being: we have established an aspect of correspondence within this hierarchy (the co-existence of all things at

---

universales et ex eis sunt quae continent formas plus universales. Quod est quoniam formae quae sunt in intelligentiis secundis inferioribus per modum particularem, sunt in intelligentiis primis per modum universalem; et formae quae sunt in intelligentiis primis per modum universalem sunt in intelligentiis secundis per modum particularem. Et in primis intelligentiis est virtus magna, quoniam sunt vehementioris unitatis quam intelligentiae secundae inferiores; et in intelligentiis secundis inferioribus sunt virtutes debiles, quoniam sunt minoris unitatis et pluris multiplicitatis. Quod est quia intelligentiae quae sunt propinquae uni, puro vero sunt minoris quantitatis et maioris virtutis, et intelligentiae quae sunt longinquiores ab uno, puro vero sunt pluris quantitatis et debilioris virtutis."

[84] Proclus, *Elements of Theology*, ed. and tr. Dodds, 156; cf. *Elementatio theologica*, ed. Boese, 87.

[85] H. 5.P; Garin, 286–288. The image occurs in Macrobius, *Commentarii in Somnium Scipionis*, ed. Scarpa, 176 (I.14.15): "Haec est Homeri catena aurea, quam pendere de caelo in terras deum iussisse commemorat." On its reception in late antiquity, see P. Lévêque, *Aurea catena Homeri: une étude sur l'allégorie grecque* (Paris: Les Belles Lettres, 1959).

[86] For the history of this concept and associated problems, see the discussion and bibliography in E.P. Mahoney, "Metaphysical Foundations of the Hierarchy of Being According to Some Late-Medieval and Renaissance Philosophers", in *Philosophies of Existence*, ed. P. Morewedge, 165–257 (New York: Fordham University Press, 1982). On the Neoplatonic concepts of procession and reversion, see also A.C. Lloyd, *The Anatomy of Neoplatonism* (Oxford: Clarendon Press, 1990), 123–139.

different levels) and an aspect of difference (in particular, between angelic and human understanding). I have pointed to prominent sources for both these aspects in the works of the same two writers, Pseudo-Dionysius and Thomas Aquinas, both of whom were building on the foundations laid by Proclus. It is now time to explore the relationship between these two aspects, which is at the centre of Pico's model of allegorical writing and reading.

As we have seen, Pico claimed that the three worlds (which reflect different levels of the hierarchy of being) "exchange not only natures but also names". In other words, he believed that language mirrors the cosmic structure. As an example, he says that "divine things" can be represented by things from either of the two lower worlds: "now by stars, now by wheels and animals, now by elements".[87]

An extended discussion of the way the Bible depicts angels by reference to elements (specifically fire), animals and wheels takes up much of the final chapter of Pseudo-Dionysius's *On the Celestial Hierarchy*. After several examples of the use of fire to indicate divine matters, he notes that parts of the human body, clothes, implements, weather phenomena, lions, oxen, eagles, horses, rivers, wheels and chariots are all used in the Bible to signify divine things.[88] The majority of these references are to the prophecy of Ezekiel. We should not, therefore, lay too much emphasis on the fact that there is a consonance between some of these images and Pico's own, rather succinct, account: both authors could simply have been reading Ezekiel. I think, however, that the connection is stronger than this. The clue lies in the opening sentences of the same chapter of *On the Celestial Hierarchy*:

> Come, now, let us rest, if we may, the intellectual eye from the exertion which concerns the contemplation of simple and lofty things, fit for angels. Let us descend to the divisible and manifold plane of the many and various forms of the shapes which angels take. Then, let us return from them, as from images, by retracing, to the simplicity of heavenly minds.[89]

---

[87] See n. 52 above.

[88] Pseudo-Dionysius, *Corpus Dionysiacum*, II, ed. Heil and Ritter, 50–59 (*De caelesti hierarchia*, 328A–340B); cf. *Dionysiaca*, ed. Chevallier, II, 983–1039.

[89] Pseudo-Dionysius, *Corpus Dionysiacum*, II, ed. Heil and Ritter, 50–51 (*De caelesti hierarchia*, 328A): "φέρε δὴ λοιπὸν ἀναπαύοντες ἡμῶν εἰ δοκεῖ τὸ νοερὸν ὄμμα τῆς περὶ τὰς ἑνικὰς καὶ ὑψηλὰς θεωρίας ἀγγελοπρεποῦς συντονίας ἐπὶ τὸ διαιρετὸν καὶ πολυμερὲς πλάτος τῆς πολυειδοῦς τῶν ἀγγελικῶν μορφοποιῶν ποικιλίας καταβάντες πάλιν ἀπ' αὐτῶν ὡς ἀπ' εἰκόνων ἐπὶ τὴν ἁπλότητα τῶν οὐρανίων νοῶν ἀναλυτικῶς ἀνακάμπτωμεν." Cf. *Dionysiaca*, ed. Chevallier, II, 985–986.

I have already discussed the dynamic of the hierarchy of being and its connection to cognition. The importance of this passage is that it rearticulates this doctrine from the standpoint of the exegete.[90] Exegesis of the Bible—and in particular of the various epithets attached to angels—is Dionysius's subject in this section of *On the Celestial Hierarchy*. Whether the action of understanding is simple or complex, as we have seen in *On the Divine Names*, depends on the location in the cosmic hierarchy of the being who seeks to understand. The passage quoted above represents an important addition to this idea: the exegete is not tied to his human plane, but, through the biblical symbols, is able to rise to a higher cognitive level. By using the multiple images in the biblical narrative as a launching pad, he can rise up to a comprehension of the true simplicity which underlies these images.

This proposition, placed at the end of *On the Celestial Hierarchy*, is Dionysius's solution to the problem with which he began that work: the scriptural representation of divine things. At the start of chapter 2, he warns against the literal interpretation of biblical passages which suggest that angels are actually shaped like lions, oxen, birds or wheels:

> The word of God used poetic imagery to represent the formless intelligences [i.e. angels], not according to the rules of art, but rather, as I have already said, having considered our own mind and having provided a method of uplifting (ἀναγωγῆς) which is suitable for and of congruent quality to it, and having modelled uplifting sacred symbols for it (πρὸς αὐτὸν ἀναπλάσασα τὰς ἀναγωγικὰς ἱερογραφίας).[91]

What is this "method of uplifting" and how does it work? The remainder of chapter 2 of *On the Celestial Hierarchy* proposes an answer to these questions. The author emphasizes the sharp distinction between material and immaterial things. He concludes, however, that language from the domain of the former can appropriately be used to refer to the latter:

> It is possible to model forms which are not inappropriate for celestial things from the least honourable parts of matter, since this [i.e. matter],

---

[90] See Pseudo-Dionysius, *Complete Works*, tr. and ed. Luibheid et al., 182 n. 126.

[91] Pseudo-Dionysius, *Corpus Dionysiacum*, II, ed. Heil and Ritter, 10 (*De caelesti hierarchia*, 137B): "καὶ γὰρ ἀτεχνῶς ἡ θεολογία ταῖς ποιητικαῖς ἱεροπλαστίαις ἐπὶ τῶν ἀσχηματίστων νοῶν ἐχρήσατο τὸν καθ᾽ ἡμᾶς ὡς εἴρηται νοῦν ἀνασκεψαμένη καὶ τῆς οἰκείας αὐτῷ καὶ συμφυοῦς ἀναγωγῆς προνοήσασα καὶ πρὸς αὐτὸν ἀναπλάσασα τὰς ἀναγωγικὰς ἱερογραφίας." Cf. *Dionysiaca*, ed. Chevallier, II, 743–744.

too, owes its existence to the Beautiful and retains certain echoes of intellectual dignity throughout its entire material structure. It is possible to be lifted up from it to immaterial archetypes: understanding similar things dissimilarly, as we have said, and the same things not in the same way, but harmoniously and fittingly as regards intellectual and perceptible beings.[92]

The correspondence between the levels of the hierarchy, and the fact that everything flows from one simple and archetypal Good— in Neoplatonic terminology, the *proodos*—means that there is a route back up the hierarchy—the *epistrophe*. This is a basic tenet of Neoplatonic ontology. What we see here is the articulation of this 'route back' from the standpoint of the exegete. It is accomplished through analogy—"understanding similar things dissimilarly ... and the same things not in the same way". Dionysius gives the examples of "anger" and "desire". Anger is irrational among lower beings, but represents something rational among higher ones; desire is sensory among lower beings, conceptual among higher. Words with bad connotations when applied to lower beings have good connotations when applied to higher ones.[93]

It should by now be clear that there is a connection between this group of ideas in the Dionysian corpus and Pico's theory in the *Heptaplus*. Both authors advocate a model of reading based on an understanding of the correspondences inherent in the universe, and both link this model to the distinction between angelic and human cognition. I believe that the connection between Pico and Dionysius is sealed by a final passage from the Dionysian corpus, in which the author exemplifies this method in a way strikingly similar to Pico's example of fire and water quoted above.[94] The passage in question comes from Dionysius's *Ninth Letter*. After quoting Paul's statement in Romans 1.20 that the invisible things of God are to be known through the visible things of creation, he demonstrates how

---

[92] Pseudo-Dionysius, *Corpus Dionysiacum*, II, ed. Heil and Ritter, 15 (*De caelesti hierarchia*, 144B–C): "ἔστι τοιγαροῦν οὐκ ἀπᾳδούσας ἀναπλάσαι τοῖς οὐρανίοις μορφὰς κἀκ τῶν ἀτιμωτάτων τῆς ὕλης μερῶν, ἐπεὶ καὶ αὐτὴ πρὸς τοῦ ὄντως καλοῦ τὴν ὕπαρξιν ἐσχηκυῖα κατὰ πᾶσαν αὐτῆς τὴν ὑλαίαν διακόσμησιν ἀπηχήματά τινα τῆς νοερᾶς εὐπρεπείας ἔχει καὶ δυνατόν ἐστι δι᾽ αὐτῶν ἀνάγεσθαι πρὸς τὰς ἀΰλους ἀρχετυπίας, ἀνομοίως ὡς εἴρηται τῶν ὁμοιοτήτων ἐκλαμβανομένων καὶ τῶν αὐτῶν οὐ ταὐτῶς, ἐναρμονίως δὲ καὶ οἰκείως ἐπὶ τῶν νοερῶν τε καὶ αἰσθητῶν ἰδιοτήτων ὁριζομένων"; cf. *Dionysiaca*, ed. Chevallier, II, 771–773.
[93] Pseudo-Dionysius, *Corpus Dionysiacum*, II, ed. Heil and Ritter, 14 (*De caelesti hierarchia*, 141D–144A); cf. *Dionysiaca*, ed. Chevallier, II, 765–769.
[94] See above, nn. 49 and 50.

one word—in this case "fire"—can be interpreted at differing levels on the hierarchy of being:

> It is not only transcendent lights, intellectual things and absolutely divine things which are variously adorned with symbolic forms—as the word "fire" (πῦρ) means the transcendent God and the word "enflamed" (πεπυρωμένα) refers to the intellectual scriptures of God. It is also the case that the Godlike forms and ranks of angels, intelligible and intelligent beings, are represented by diverse shapes, including formations of fire (ἐμπυρίοις σχηματισμοῖς). It is necessary to understand the same image of fire in different ways when it refers to God who is above conception, or to his intelligible providence, or to angels. It is one thing as a cause (κατ᾽ αἰτίαν), another thing as a substance (καθ᾽ ὕπαρξιν), another thing as participation (κατὰ μέθεξιν), and other things in other ways (ἄλλα ἄλλως), as the contemplation and wise arrangement of these things requires.[95]

In other words, *different* non-literal interpretations of the *same* word, within the context of the hierarchy of being, and for reasons of epistemology derived from this hierarchy, provide the key to interpreting the Bible.

3. *Conclusion*

The comparison of Dionysius's *On the Divine Names* and *On the Celestial Hierarchy*, on the one hand, and the *Heptaplus*, on the other, illuminates similarities and differences. All three works are engaged in interpreting the words of the Bible—they are all works of exegesis. Formally, they are not very similar: while the *Heptaplus* follows a comprehensive and sequential trajectory through one chapter of Genesis, the Dionysian corpus plucks words from various places throughout the Bible, resulting in a scattered commentary, arranged thematically rather than sequentially. Despite their mutual reliance on the framework of the hierarchy of being, the two exegetes have a

---

[95] Pseudo-Dionysius, *Corpus Dionysiacum*, II, ed. Heil and Ritter, 199–200 (*Epistola IX*, 1108C–D): "καὶ γὰρ οὐ μόνα τὰ ὑπερούσια φῶτα καὶ τὰ νοητὰ καὶ ἁπλῶς τὰ θεῖα τοῖς τυπωτικοῖς διαποικίλλεται συμβόλοις, ὡς πῦρ ὁ ὑπερούσιος θεὸς λεγόμενος καὶ τὰ νοητὰ τοῦ θεοῦ λόγια πεπυρωμένα. προσέτι δὲ καὶ τῶν νοητῶν ἅμα καὶ νοερῶν ἀγγέλων οἱ θεοειδεῖς διάκοσμοι ποικίλαις μορφαῖς διαγράφονται καὶ πολυειδέσι καὶ ἐμπυρίοις σχηματισμοῖς. καὶ ἄλλως χρὴ τὴν αὐτὴν τοῦ πυρὸς εἰκόνα κατὰ τοῦ ὑπὲρ νόησιν θεοῦ λεγομένην ἐκλαβεῖν, ἄλλως δὲ κατὰ τῶν νοητῶν αὐτοῦ προνοιῶν ἢ λόγων καὶ ἄλλως ἐπὶ τῶν ἀγγέλων, καὶ τὴν μὲν κατ᾽ αἰτίαν, τὴν δὲ καθ᾽ ὕπαρξιν, τὴν δὲ κατὰ μέθεξιν καὶ ἄλλα ἄλλως, ὡς ἡ κατ᾽ αὐτὰ θεωρία καὶ ἐπιστημονικὴ διάταξις ὁροθετεῖ." Not included in *Dionysiaca*, ed. Chevallier.

different scope: Dionysius concentrates on the representation of the upper levels of the hierarchy—the ranks of angels and, above them, God himself—whereas Pico is concerned with the entire cosmic taxonomy below God.

Pico claimed that his mode of reading was new and had not previously been attempted.[96] I have tried to show here that its seeds can be found in Neoplatonic metaphysics, especially Proclus and the *Liber de causis*;[97] but that the clear expression of this idea as a means of *exegesis* originates in the Dionysian corpus.[98] Pico used the writings of Pseudo-Dionysius to develop a theory of scriptural exegesis which was anagogical in the Dionysian sense—which led the reader upwards towards God. As we saw in Chapter 3, the idea of 'anagogical' exegesis also made its way into the standard Christian framework of the four senses of Scripture. Here, however, it was defined as a property of the signification of a word (for example, the idea of Jerusalem as the heavenly city), not as an intellectual action undergone by the reader.

The result of this chapter's investigation, therefore, is to propose that Pico's theory of allegory should be viewed as an expression of this type of 'anagogy' and that it must be understood in the context of intellectual ascent. The next two chapters will examine this context: as an issue in medieval philosophy, as a theme in Pico's works and as a structural principle in the *Heptaplus*.

---

[96] H. 2.P; Garin, 222: "novum illud et intactum adhuc".

[97] For earlier Neoplatonic sources, see Lloyd, *Anatomy of Neoplatonism*, 30, and R. Lamberton, *Homer the Theologian* (Berkeley, Los Angeles: University of California Press, 1986), 166–167.

[98] See P. Rorem, *Biblical and Liturgical Symbols within the Pseudo-Dionysian Synthesis* (Toronto: Pontifical Institute of Medieval Studies, 1984), 58–65.

CHAPTER SIX

KNOWLEDGE, *FELICITAS* AND HERMENEUTICS

Medieval philosophers, Pico among them, generally held that there was such a thing as *felicitas*: the proper end or ultimate attainment of human life. This concept was assimilated with religious teaching on immortality and concerned the nature of the soul. A substantial proportion of philosophers viewed it as being specifically a function of the part of the soul which engaged in cognition—that is, the intellect. The period from the mid-thirteenth to the mid-sixteenth centuries saw the development of a long-running debate concerning the nature of the soul and the operation of its intellectual part; the attainment of *felicitas* therefore fell within the compass of this debate. In this chapter, I propose that the ongoing controversy over the intellect provides a context for Pico's thought in general and for the *Heptaplus* in particular. In several of his works, Pico argued that *felicitas* was the culmination of an intellectual ascent. His 'anagogical' hermeneutics, discussed in the previous chapter, should be seen as an expression of this idea. Sources for such an idea were known to him from the Jewish tradition as well as the Christian and Neoplatonic.

1. Felicitas *and the Intellect in Medieval Philosophy*

At the heart of the controversy surrounding the intellect were a number of competing interpretations of Aristotle. Prior to the late twelfth century, a relatively unproblematic philosophical conception of the soul was current in the Latin west. It was derived principally from Augustine, and held that souls were individual, immortal, had innate knowledge and could think by themselves.[1] In the late twelfth and thirteenth centuries the growing knowledge of Aristotle's *De anima* and its commentaries generated a reassessment of this conception and introduced a group of problems which remained

---

[1] *The Cambridge History of Later Medieval Philosophy*, ed. N. Kretzmann et al. (Cambridge: CUP, 1982), 596; R.C. Dales, *The Problem of the Rational Soul in the Thirteenth Century* (Leiden and New York: E.J. Brill, 1995), 4–5; J. Obi Oguejiofor, *The Arguments for the Immortality of the Soul in the First Half of the Thirteenth Century* (Leuven: Peeters, 1995), 67–105.

insoluble well into the sixteenth century.[2] These problems gave rise to controversies which were not only philosophical but also (in a broad sense) political.

The fundamental source of disagreement was the need to correlate Aristotle's statements about the soul with the Christian doctrine of an individual afterlife for eternity. Aristotle himself had been unclear as to whether the soul was subject to generation and corruption, but allowed for the possibility that its rational or intellectual part was eternal.[3] In an enigmatic chapter of *De anima*, he argued that "in every class of things, as in nature as a whole, we find two factors involved" and that these two factors are related "as an art to its material".[4] He therefore determined that some such "two factors" must also be present in the intellective soul, and that their interaction accounted for its operation, namely, thought.

The Peripatetic tradition devoted considerable attention to this division of the intellective soul into two aspects, which were commonly referred to as the agent or active intellect and the material or potential intellect. Unfortunately, however, Aristotle's lack of clarity prevented any subsequent agreement as to quite how he envisaged the operation of these "two factors". Specifically, no consensus was reached on whether the potential intellect was mortal or immortal, or on whether the active intellect was God himself, or a transcendent entity between God and man, or an aspect of the individual human soul. The numerous and divergent interpretations of Greek and Arab commentators all had one common strand, however, which was that the question of *felicitas* tended to be viewed as an *epistemological* question. The immortality of the soul, in other words, was—for

---

[2] On the medieval reception of *De anima*, see L. Minio-Paluello, "Le texte du 'De anima' d'Aristote: La tradition latine avant 1500", in *Autour d'Aristote: Recueil d'études ... offert à Monseigneur A. Mansion*, 217–243 (Leuven: Publications Universitaires de Louvain, 1955).

[3] Aristotle, *Metaphysics*, 12.3 (1070a); *De anima*, I.4 (408b), II.1 (413a); the question is discussed by H.A. Davidson, *Alfarabi, Avicenna, and Averroes, on Intellect: Their Cosmologies, Theories of the Active Intellect, and Theories of Human Intellect* (Oxford: OUP, 1992), 35.

[4] Aristotle, *De anima*, III.5, tr. J.A. Smith, in *Complete Works*, ed. Barnes, I, 684. For the relevant passage as received in the Latin tradition, see Averroes, *Commentarium magnum in Aristotelis De anima libros*, ed. F.S. Crawford (Cambridge, Massachusetts: The Mediaeval Academy of America, 1953), 436: "Et quia, quemadmodum in Natura, est aliquid in unoquoque genere quod est materia (et est illud quod est illa omnia in potentia), et aliud quod est causa et agens (et hoc est illud propter quod agit quidlibet, sicut dispositio artificii apud materiam), necesse est ut in anima existant hee differentie."

these thinkers, and hence for the tradition which developed from them—bound up with the question of its acquisition of knowledge.

The reason for this is that each of these commentators, in some form or other, subscribed to a model of progression or ascent in intellectual ability and capacity which culminated in the potential intellect becoming somehow united or conjoined with the active intellect. The parameters of this ascent, the stages the human intellect needed to pass through and the nature of the final state achieved were all subject to discussion. In outline, however, Aristotelians held that the human intellect was tied to matter and therefore dependent on it for its thought. All the differing models attempted to provide a mechanism by which its connection to sense and matter could eventually be overcome. Conjunction with the active intellect represented a state in which immaterial substances or intelligibles could be directly comprehended by the human intellect; at that point the action of thinking could take place without any recourse to sense or matter.

The idea of two sorts of cognition—one based on matter, discursive and essentially inaccurate, the other based on the direct apprehension of immaterial things, intuitive and accurate—was present in the Neoplatonic tradition, as we have seen.[5] But in charting the development of this idea and its effect on the Latin Middle Ages the most significant works are commentaries on Aristotle: in particular, those by Alexander of Aphrodisias (fl. c. 200), Themistius (c. 317—c. 388), Al-Farabi (872–950), Avicenna (980–1037) and Averroes (1126–1198).[6]

Alexander of Aphrodisias, who interpreted Aristotle as saying that the human soul was mortal, proposed that the potential intellect could nonetheless attain a state in which it perceived the active intellect and somehow became identical with it. This state constituted a form of immortality.[7] Themistius, on the other hand, in his

---

[5] For Pseudo-Dionysius, see above, Ch. 5, n. 80. See also Siorvanes, *Proclus*, 156. The root of the Neoplatonic model may be traced to Plato, *Phaedo*, 79C–D.

[6] Others such as Plotinus, Simplicius, Al-Kindi and Ibn Bajja contributed to the discussion; the commentators I dwell on here were most significant for the development of the tradition as it was received by the scholastics. On the transmission of ideas from Alexander to Al-Farabi, see M. Geoffroy, "La tradition arabe du Περὶ νοῦ d'Alexandre d'Aphrodise et les origines de la théorie farabienne des quatre degrés de l'intellect", in *Aristotele e Alessandro di Aphrodisia nella tradizione araba*, ed. C. D'Ancona and G. Serra, 191–231 (Padua: Il Poligrafo, 2002). On Ibn Bajja, see A. Altmann, "Ibn Bajja on Man's Ultimate Felicity", in his *Studies in Religious Philosophy and Mysticism*, 73–107 (Ithaca, New York: Cornell University Press, 1969).

[7] Davidson, *Alfarabi, Avicenna, and Averroes, on Intellect*, 37–38, argues that "the

paraphrase of *De anima*, interpreted Aristotle as meaning that both
the potential and the active intellects were immaterial and immortal;[8]
he, too, viewed human cognition as resulting from their conjunction
with each other, however.[9]

Al-Farabi, in his *Al-madina al-faḍila*, proposed that the human
intellect has a hierarchy of states, the highest of which—"acquired
intellect"—is attained when it "has been perfected" by having appre-
hended "all intelligibles".[10] One who attains this state "holds the most
perfect rank of humanity and has reached the highest degree of felicity (*saʿada*)".[11] In it, the human soul is united—in some sense—with
the active intellect, is gifted with prophecy, has no further need for
matter and is therefore immortal.[12] He also discussed this in his *Risala
fi al-ʿaql*, which circulated in a medieval Latin translation. According

---

Greek text of Alexander's *De anima* ... makes clear that only a detached human
thought of an incorporeal being, and no part of the human intellectual faculty,
attains immortality. Readers of the Arabic translation could, however, have been
misled into supposing that Alexander recognized the survival of something more." A
slightly different account is given in *De intellectu* (attributed also to Alexander). The
disparities between *De anima* and *De intellectu* are discussed by Averroes, *Commentarium
magnum in Aristotelis De anima libros*, ed. Crawford, 481–485. See B. Nardi, "La mistica
averroistica e Pico della Mirandola", in his *Saggi sull'aristotelismo padovano dal secolo
XIV al XVI*, 128–129 (Florence: G.C. Sansoni, 1958).

[8] Themistius, *Commentaire sur le traité de l'âme d'Aristote: traduction de Guillaume
de Moerbeke*, ed. G. Verbeke (Leiden, E.J. Brill, 1973), 237–239: "Quare manifestus
est ... intellectum [here referring to the potential intellect] autem tanquam non
utentem organo corporali ad actum et immixtum corpori omnino et impassibilem et
separatum. Sed si talis est qui potentia, quem utique iam dicet activum intellectum et
incorruptibilem? ... Quare manifestus est existimans quidem ambos separatos, magis
autem separatum activum et magis impassibilem et magis immixtum". Cf. Themistius,
On Aristotle's On the Soul, tr. R.B. Todd (Ithaca, New York: Cornell University Press,
1996), 130–131.

[9] Themistius, *Commentaire sur le traité de l'âme d'Aristote*, ed. Verbeke, 226: "Sic
enim et qui secundum actum intellectus intellectui potentia superveniens unus fit
cum ipso; unum enim quod ex materia et forma". Cf. Themistius, *On Aristotle's On
the Soul*, tr. Todd, 123.

[10] Al-Farabi, *On the Perfect State*, ed. and tr. R. Walzer (Oxford: Clarendon Press,
1985), 243. See Davidson, *Alfarabi, Avicenna, and Averroes, on Intellect*, 49.

[11] Al-Farabi, *On the Perfect State*, ed. and tr. Walzer, 245. On Al-Farabi's views on
conjunction with the active intellect, see Davidson, *Alfarabi, Avicenna, and Averroes,
on Intellect*, 53–56, 70–73.

[12] Al-Farabi, *On the Perfect State*, ed. and tr. Walzer, 243–247; see Davidson, *Alfarabi,
Avicenna, and Averroes, on Intellect*, 53–58, and Nardi, "Mistica averroistica", 130. In
his lost commentary on the *Nicomachean Ethics*, however, Al-Farabi is reported (by Ibn
Bajja, Ibn Ṭufayl and Averroes) to have decided against the possibility of immortality
arising from conjunction with the active intellect, and to have disdainfully referred to
it as an "old wives' tale": Davidson, *Alfarabi, Avicenna, and Averroes, on Intellect*, 70–73.
Averroes's remark on this matter is quoted in n. 87 below.

to this account man needs the body when in his lowest grade of existence but can rise to a higher grade where the body is no longer necessary. This point, at which he is in proximity to the active intellect, is the *finis ultimus.*[13]

Avicenna differs from Al-Farabi in that his hierarchy of intellectual states—from material intellect, through intellect *in habitu* and intellect *in effectu* to acquired intellect—is a necessary condition of any act of thought; every thought entails a fleeting conjunction between the potential and active intellects.[14] Nonetheless, he, too, envisages a state in which the potential intellect is in such close proximity to the active intellect that it is able to receive all information from the active intellect either immediately, or almost immediately; this is the highest level of attainment possible, and is equated with prophecy.[15]

Common to all these philosophers, therefore, is a model in which intellectual achievement and the acquisition of knowledge eventually lead to the overcoming of the innate human cognitive limitations and the attainment of some form of perfection, immortality and *felicitas.* Several of their texts discussing these ideas circulated in Latin in the Middle Ages.[16] Whatever reception they had in their own right

---

[13] Al-Farabi, *De intellectu et intellecto*, in E. Gilson, "Les sources gréco-arabes de l'augustinisme avicennisant", *Archives d'histoire doctrinale et littéraire du Moyen Age*, IV (1929), 123–124: "Et sic substantia anime hominis vel homo cum eo per quod substantiatur, fit propinquius ad intelligentiam agentem et hic est finis ultimus, et vita alia. ... Igitur sua essentia et sua actio et suum agere est unum et idem et tunc ad suam existentiam non indigebit ut corpus sit sibi materia, nec ad aliquam suarum actionum indigebit adiuvari virtute animali que est in eius corpore, nec indigebit in ea instrumento corporali omnino. Minimus enim ex gradibus suis est ut ad existentiam sui necessarium sit corpus sibi esse materiam ut ipsa sit forma in corpore. Supra hunc autem gradum est ut ad sui existentiam non sit necesse corpus sibi esse materiam, quamvis ad plures ex suis actionibus egeat uti instrumento corporali et adiuvari virtute eius, scilicet sensu et imaginatione".

[14] D.N. Hasse, *Avicenna's De anima in the Latin West: The Formation of a Peripatetic Philosophy of the Soul, 1160–1300* (London: Warburg Institute, 2000), 178–179; Davidson, *Alfarabi, Avicenna, and Averroes, on Intellect*, 103. Avicenna, *Liber De anima*, ed. S. Van Riet, introd. G. Verbeke, 2 vols (Leuven: Editions orientalistes and Leiden: E.J. Brill, 1968–1972), I (containing books IV–V), intro., 59*–72*.

[15] Avicenna, *Liber De anima*, ed. Van Riet, 153: "Possibile est ergo ut alicuius hominis anima eo quod est clara et cohaerens principiis intellectibilibus, ita sit inspirata ut accendatur ingenio ad recipiendum omnes quaestiones ab intelligentia agente, aut subito, aut paene subito ... . Et hic est unus modus prophetiae qui omnibus virtutibus prophetiae altior est. Unde congrue vocatur virtus sancta, quia est altior gradus inter omnes virtutes humanas." See also Davidson, *Alfarabi, Avicenna, and Averroes, on Intellect*, 84–86, 103–105, 322; Hasse, *Avicenna's De anima in the Latin West*, 154–155.

[16] *De intellectu* (attributed to Alexander of Aphrodisias) was translated into Latin

was overshadowed by the use made of them by Averroes, however. Averroes engaged with the problem of the intellect in seven different works.[17] Despite differences in opinion from one work to the next he generally maintained that conjunction of the potential and active intellects was possible, and that this conjunction constituted man's ultimate *felicitas*.[18] Of his works, the one which was read by the Christian scholastics—and which provided the impetus for the series of quarrels which followed—was his long commentary on *De anima*, which was translated into Latin around 1230.[19] In this, Averroes reassessed the theories of previous commentators and concluded that they were all mistaken in various respects. On the matter of conjunction with the active intellect, he decided that, contrary to the proposal of Alexander, this would be impossible if one assumed that the potential intellect was mortal.[20] He therefore argued (like

---

in the second half of the 12th century: see F.E. Cranz, "Alexander Aphrodisiensis", in *Catalogus translationum et commentariorum: Medieval and Renaissance Latin Translations and Commentaries*, ed. P.O. Kristeller et al., 8 vols (Washington DC: Catholic University of America Press, 1960–2003), I, 79–81, 84–88, 111–113. Themistius's paraphrase of *De anima* was translated into Latin by William of Moerbeke in 1267: see Themistius, *Commentaire sur le traité de l'âme d'Aristote*, ed. Verbeke, lxiii–iv; R.B. Todd, "Themistius", in *Catalogus translationum et commentariorum*, ed. Kristeller et al., VIII, 59–67, 78–79. It was retranslated by Ermolao Barbaro and published in 1481. For the medieval Latin translation of Al-Farabi's *De intellectu* see n. 13 above. Avicenna's commentary on *De anima* was translated in Toledo by Dominicus Gundissalinus and Abraham ibn Daud in the second half of the 12th century: see Avicenna, *Liber De anima*, ed. Van Riet, 1*; Hasse, *Avicenna's De anima in the Latin West*, 5–8, 189–191. It was printed at Pavia in 1485. See also, in general, Davidson, *Alfarabi, Avicenna, and Averroes, on Intellect*, 209–217.

[17] Averroes wrote three commentaries on *De anima* (epitome, middle and long); the *Epistle on the Possibility of Conjunction*; two short treatises on conjunction, which were translated into Hebrew by Samuel ibn Tibbon and inserted into his commentary on Ecclesiastes; and a commentary on parts of the *De intellectu* attributed to Alexander of Aphrodisias. See Davidson, *Alfarabi, Avicenna, and Averroes, on Intellect*, 262–265; A.L. Ivry, "Averroes's Three Commentaries on *De anima*", in *Averroes and the Aristotelian Tradition: Sources, Constitution and Reception of the Philosophy of Ibn Rushd (1126–1198): Proceedings of the Fourth Symposium Averroicum (Cologne, 1996)*, ed. G. Endress and J.A. Aertsen, 199–216 (Leiden and Boston, Massachusetts: Brill, 1999); Averroes, *The Epistle on the Possibility of Conjunction with the Active Intellect by Ibn Rushd with the Commentary of Moses Narboni*, ed. and tr. K.P. Bland (New York: The Jewish Theological Seminary of America, 1982); Averroes, *La béatitude de l'âme*, ed. Geoffroy and Steel.

[18] Davidson, *Alfarabi, Avicenna, and Averroes, on Intellect*, 321–340.

[19] Ibid., 300.

[20] Averroes, *Commentarium magnum in Aristotelis De anima libros*, ed. Crawford, 481: "Dicamus igitur: qui autem ponit intellectum materialem esse generabilem et corruptibilem nullum modum, ut michi videtur, potest invenire naturalem quo possumus continuari cum intellectibus abstractis."

Themistius) that it must be immortal—and also that it must be one in number.[21]

This doctrine, generally known as the unicity of the potential intellect, became a central issue in the ensuing controversy. The framework of the debate was set by Thomas Aquinas in his attack on Averroes composed in 1270 and entitled *De unitate intellectus.* Averroes, according to Thomas, had maintained not only that there was one potential intellect for all mankind but also that it was a separate substance which did not unite with the body as its form.[22] Such a conception, Thomas continued, was "repugnant" to the Christian faith because after death there would be no individuality and therefore no possibility of reward or punishment.[23] It was also— he maintained—"contrary to the principles of philosophy" and the words of Aristotle.[24]

More generally, in his two *Summae*, Thomas criticized the episte-mological models of *felicitas* and their idea that there could be a state of conjunction in which intelligibles could be perceived without the need for matter. He summarized his position in the *Summa theologiae*: "according to the state of the present life, we cannot—either through the potential intellect or the active intellect—cognize immaterial substances in their own mode", nor can we "attain a perfect cogni-tion of immaterial substances by means of material substances".[25] In

---

[21] See, for a summary, Davidson, *Alfarabi, Avicenna, and Averroes, on Intellect,* 295–297.

[22] Thomas Aquinas, *Tractatus de unitate intellectus contra Averroistas,* ed. L.W. Keeler (Rome: apud aedes Pont. universitatis gregoriannae, 1957), 1–2: "intellectum quem Aristoteles possibilem vocat, ipse autem inconvenienti nomine materialem, esse quandam substantiam secundum esse a corpore separatam, nec aliquo modo uniri ei ut formam; et ulterius quod iste intellectus possibilis sit unus omnium hominum."

[23] Ibid., 2: "Nec id nunc agendum est ut positionem praedictam in hoc osten-damus esse erroneam quia repugnat veritati fidei Christianae. ... Subtracta enim ab hominibus diversitate intellectus, qui solus inter animae partes incorruptibilis et immortalis apparet, sequitur post mortem nihil de animabus hominum remanere nisi unicam intellectus substantiam; et sic tollitur retributio praemiorum et paenarum et diversitates eorundem."

[24] Ibid., 2–3: "Intendimus autem ostendere positionem praedictam non minus contra philosophiae principia esse, quam contra fidei documenta. Et quia quibusdam (ut dicunt) in hac materia verba Latinorum non sapiunt, sed Peripateticorum verba sectari se dicunt, quorum libros nunquam in hac materia viderunt, nisi Aristotelis qui fuit sectae peripateticae institutor; ostendemus primo positionem praedictam eius verbis et sententiae repugnare omnino."

[25] Thomas Aquinas, *Summa theologiae,* I.88.1–2: "secundum statum praesentis vitae, neque per intellectum possibilem, neque per intellectum agentem, possumus intel-ligere substantias immateriales secundum seipsas", and "per substantias materiales non possumus perfecte substantias immateriales intelligere".

the *Summa contra Gentiles* he pursued the debate in more detail. He began by asking "whether in this life man can comprehend separate [i.e., immaterial and intelligible] substances through study and investigation of the speculative sciences", concluding that he could not.[26] He then specifically attacked the arguments in favour of comprehending intelligible substances which had been put forward by Alexander and Averroes.[27] Finally, he argued that man's *ultima felicitas* does not reside in such knowledge and that "we cannot in this life comprehend separate substances".[28]

The Latin reception of Averroes's long commentary on *De anima*, therefore, stimulated philosophers to look again at Aristotle's description of the soul and the later interpretations of it. The ensuing war between adherents and detractors of 'Averroism' continued for over two centuries, the former arguing that although the Averroist position was incorrect because it was contrary to Christian revelation, it was nonetheless the only correct interpretation of Aristotle. At sporadic intervals during the conflict the Averroist tenets described above were legislated against by the Church, and their adherents (or even, in some cases, those who merely discussed the matter) threatened with excommunication. Several 'Averroist' doctrines on the intellect were included among the miscellaneous collection of 219 propositions condemned by Etienne Tempier, Bishop of Paris, in 1277.[29] At the Council of Vienne in 1311 the idea that the intellective soul was not the form of the body was declared heretical.[30] Despite these events, Averroist philosophy continued to be taught and debated: its centres of popularity included Paris, Bologna and, at the end of the fifteenth century, Padua.[31] On 4 May 1489 (just as

---

[26] Thomas Aquinas, *Summa contra Gentiles*, III.41: "utrum in hac vita homo possit intelligere substantias separatas per studium et inquisitionem scientiarum speculativarum".

[27] Ibid., III.42–43.

[28] Ibid., III.44: "Quod ultima felicitas hominis non consistit in cognitione substantiarum separatarum qualem praedictae opiniones fingunt"; III.45: "Quod non possumus in hac vita intelligere substantias separatas".

[29] See *La condemnation parisienne de 1277*, ed. D. Piché (Paris: Vrin, 1999).

[30] Decree 1, *Conciliorum oecumenicorum decreta*, ed. Alberigo et al., 336–337: "Porro doctrinam omnem seu positionem, temere asserentem aut vertentem in dubium, quod substantia animae rationalis seu intellectivae vere ac per se humani corporis non sit forma, velut erroneam ac veritati catholicae fidei inimicam praedicto sacro approbante concilio reprobamus, diffinientes ... quod quisquis deinceps asserere, defendere seu tenere pertinaciter praesumpserit, quod anima rationalis seu intellectiva non sit forma corporis humani per se et essentialiter, tanquam haereticus sit censendus."

[31] See Davidson, *Alfarabi, Avicenna, and Averroes, on Intellect*, 310–313, and his com-

Pico was writing the *Heptaplus*) the Bishop of Padua, Pietro Barozzi, published a decree forbidding all discussion of the doctrine of unicity of the potential intellect.[32]

Pico had been in Padua between 1480 and 1482. He came into contact there with several prominent exponents of Averroist thinking, including Elijah Delmedigo and Nicoletto Vernia.[33] Delmedigo is notable as a transmitter of Averroes's thought. He was the first philosopher in the Jewish tradition to base his interpretation of Aver-

---

ment at 309 that "the tradition [of Averroism] survived so long and so stubbornly in the face of repeated attempts to suppress it that its perdurability is no less a sociological than a philosophic phenomenon." For a specific analysis of Christian responses to Averroes in the thirteenth century, see Dales, *Problem of the Rational Soul*, 138–191. The attempts at suppression continued into the sixteenth century: the Fifth Lateran Council, on 19 Dec. 1513, reiterated the conclusion of the Council of Vienne regarding the soul being the form of the body, and officially condemned the doctrine of the unicity of the potential intellect, along with the doctrine of Alexander of Aphrodisias that the potential intellect was material and therefore mortal. See Session 8 (19 Dec. 1513), *Conciliorum oecumenicorum decreta*, ed. Alberigo et al., 581: "Cum itaque diebus nostris (quod dolenter ferimus) zizaniae seminator, antiquus humani generis hostis, nonnullos perniciosissimos errores a fidelibus semper explosos in agro Domini superseminare et augere sit ausus, de natura praesertim animae rationalis, quod videlicet mortalis sit, aut unica in cunctis hominibus; et nonnulli temere philosophantes, secundum saltem philosophiam verum id esse asseverant; contra huiusmodi pestem opportuna remedia adhibere cupientes, hoc sacro approbante concilio damnamus et reprobamus omnes asserentes animam intellectivam mortalem esse, aut unicam in cunctis hominibus et haec in dubium vertentes: cum illa non solum vere per se et essentialiter humani corporis forma existat [as established by Council of Vienne] ... verum et immortalis, et pro corporum quibus infunditur multitudine singulariter multiplicabilis, et multiplicata, et multiplicanda sit." See also E. Gilson, "L'affaire de l'immortalité de l'âme à Venise au debut de XVIe siècle", in *Umanesimo europeo e umanesimo veneziano*, ed. V. Branca, 31–61 (Florence: Sansoni, 1964).

[32] See F.S. Dondi dall'Orologio, *Dissertazione nona sopra l'istoria ecclesiastica padovana* (Padua, 1817), second section (renumbered from 1), entitled "Documenta nonae dissertationis", 130–131: "Et postremo existimantes eos qui de unitate intellectus disputant ob eam potissimum causam disputare quod sublatis ita tum premiis virtutum, tum vero suppliciis vitiorum existimant se liberius maxima quaeque flagitia posse committere. Mandamus ut nullus vestrum sub pena excommunicationis ... audeat vel presumat de unitate intellectus quovis quesito colore publice disputare. Et si hoc ex Aristotelis sententia fuisse secundum Averoin hominem doctum quidem sed scelestum." The effect of the decree was only local, however; see B. Nardi, "I *Quolibeta de intelligentiis* di Alessandro Achillini", in his *Saggi sull'aristotelismo padovano dal secolo XIV al XVI*, 179–180 (Florence: G.C. Sansoni, 1958).

[33] Vernia, after Bishop Barozzi's decree of 1489, shifted his position on the interpretation of Aristotle away from Averroes and towards such Greek commentators as Themistius and Simplicius. See Mahoney, "Pico and Del Medigo, Vernia and Nifo", 127–156; id., "Nicoletto Vernia on the Soul and Immortality", in *Philosophy and Humanism: Renaissance Essays in Honor of Paul Oskar Kristeller*, ed. E.P. Mahoney, 144–163 (Leiden: E.J. Brill, 1976).

roes's ideas of intellect on the long commentary on *De anima*;[34] and, as we saw in Chapter 1, he composed two works on Averroes's ideas of the intellect and conjunction specifically for Pico.[35] This fact alone goes some way to attesting Pico's interest in the matter.

Regarding the reception of Averroes's writings in the Jewish tradition, I have already noted that his two short treatises on the intellect (along with the third attributed to 'Averroes Iunior') circulated widely in Hebrew in the translation by Maimonides's translator, Samuel ibn Tibbon. As we saw, Ibn Tibbon placed these treatises in his commentary on Ecclesiastes, and prefaced them with the remark that "the meaning of the soul's ascension is that it should be perfected ... until it conjoins with the incorporeal [i.e. active] intellect and unites therewith".[36]

Prior to the reception of Averroes's thought, however, the idea of a progression to *felicitas*, epistemologically articulated, was already a prominent feature of Jewish philosophy. Its *locus classicus* is Maimonides's parable of the king's palace, at the end of the *Guide of the Perplexed*, which can be summarized as follows. The king is in his palace.[37] Some of his people are inside his city and some outside. Some of those in the city have their backs to his palace; others have their faces to it, and wish to enter it, but cannot see its wall. Some have found the wall, but not yet the gate; others have entered the gate and are in the hall. Some have progressed further and are near to the king but cannot see him; if they investigate further still they will find him, and either see him, hear him or talk with him.

Maimonides explains the parable in the following terms.[38] Those who are outside the city are the unbelievers, whose judgement is like

---

[34] Davidson, *Alfarabi, Avicenna, and Averroes, on Intellect*, 298–300; Bland, "Elijah Del Medigo, Unicity of the Intellect, and Immortality of the Soul", 7, 10–13.

[35] See Ch. 1, section 2.1.

[36] See Ch. 5, n. 29.

[37] Maimonides, *Dux*, f. 109ᵛ–110ʳ (*Guide*, tr. Pines, 618): "Rex quidam sedet in munitione sua: servorum autem illius quidam sunt in eadem civitate, alii vero extra. Illorum autem qui sunt in civitate, quidam converterunt dorsum ad palatium regis: faciem vero suam versus aliam partem. Quidam vero faciem habent versus palatium regis: et tenderunt ad ipsum: et vellent ipsi appropinquare et stare coram ipso: sed tamen nunquam viderunt murum palatii regis. Sunt et alii qui appropinquant domui: et circuierunt eam quaerentes portam: alii vero intraverunt ianuam et ambulant per atrium. Alii vero intraverunt domum et propinqui sunt regi, sed non vident eum neque loquuntur cum eo. Sed postquam intraverunt domum necesse habent quaerere et investigare qualiter possint interius intrare: et tunc videbunt faciem regis: vel longe, vel prope, vel audient verba regis, vel loquentur cum eo."

[38] Ibid., f. 110ʳ (*Guide*, tr. Pines, 618–619): "Exponam tibi similitudinem istam quam induxi. Scito igitur quod qui sunt extra civitatem, sunt omnes illi qui non

that of animals. Those who are inside with their backs to the palace are those whose speculation is based on false principles, so that the further they go, the further they are removed from the king. Those who are in the city with their faces turned to the palace, unable to see it, are the multitude who simply follow the commandments. Those who have found the palace and are looking for the door are the ones who have received correct beliefs but have not plumbed the depths of the principles of those beliefs. Those who devote themselves to these principles have entered the door of the palace. The one, however, who is able to prove what can be proved, and has ascertained the truth as far as is possible, has entered into the palace and is with the king.

Maimonides comments further: those who are studying "scientific disciplines and dialectic" are going around the wall looking for the door; those who have understood "natural things" (i.e., physics) have entered the hall; and those who have understood "spiritual things" (i.e., metaphysics) are with the king.[39] In the final chapter of the *Guide* he summarizes the aim of this process, which is the attainment of "true perfection" through the acquisition of intelligibles, leading to immortal life.[40]

---

credunt deum ... . Iudicium vero istorum est sicut animalium irrationalium. ... Qui vero sunt in civitate, sed dorsum vertunt ad domum regis, sunt illi qui in opinionibus et speculatione sua credulitates habent vanas, vel per errorem qui accidit in speculatione sua, vel per receptionem quam perceperunt ab aliquo erroneo, et semper permanent in illis credulitatibus, et quanto magis vadunt tanto magis elongantur a domo regis. ... Illi vero quorum facies est versus domum regis et volunt intrare, sed nunquam viderunt eam: isti sunt universitas tenentium legem scilicet laici qui exercent se in praeceptis. Qui autem appropinquaverunt domui regis et circuierunt eam, isti sunt qui legunt et tenent credulitates rectas ex parte receptionis: et cavent sibi et custodiunt se a prohibitionibus, neque laborant in consideratione intellectus radicis credulitatis: nec inquirunt veritatem credulitatis. Qui autem separaverunt se ab aliis principalibus credulitatis, illi sunt qui intraverunt, quilibet autem secundum gradum suum, et secundum comprehensionem suam. Qui vero scit probare quicquid est probabile, et credit de rebus spiritualibus quicquid credit per probationem, et est prope veritatem in omni re in qua non potest apprehendi veritas: iste talis est qui intravit cum rege in domum suam."

[39] Ibid. (*Guide*, tr. Pines, 619): "Scito fili mi quod dum studueris in scientiis disciplinalibus et in arte dialectica, eris de illis qui circueunt domum regis quaerentes portam ipsius ... . Cum vero intellexeris naturalia: tunc iam intrasti munitionem regis et ambulas per atrium. Cum vero perfectus fueris in naturalibus: et intellexeris spiritualia, tunc iam intrasti in domum regis: et eris cum ipso in eadem domo: sed nondum vidisti eum. Hic autem est gradus sapientum: diversi tamen sunt in suis perfectionibus." On Maimonides's dichotomy between *naturalia* and *spiritualia* see Ch. 4, n. 171 above.

[40] Maimonides, *Dux*, f. 113ʳ (*Guide*, tr. Pines, 635): "Quarta species [of human perfection] est hominis perfectio vera, et consistit in acquisitione moralium, scilicet

The idea of a hierarchical progression through philosophical disciplines circulated widely among Jewish philosophers. We shall encounter its use by Gersonides below. In Pico's time it was still current, as can be seen (to take the example most proximate to Pico) in the works of Johanan Alemanno. Alemanno extrapolated from it an entire curriculum, beginning with the Torah and moving through the Midrash, language and rhetoric, logic, mathematics, physics and astronomy, politics and medicine and metaphysics, finally to encompass what he took to be the highest reaches of divine science: kabbalah and magic.[41] A similar theme, expressed at greater length, is to be found in his *Ḥay ha-olamim.*

In summary, there was a considerable body of material in the medieval Peripatetic tradition concerned with the epistemological basis of *felicitas* and the stages of progression towards it. Much of this material was caught up in the controversy over Averroism and as such occupied hotly disputed territory. In essence, therefore, there was a choice available to a philosopher who wished to assert that human *felicitas* was a function of intellectual attainment. On the one hand he could adopt some version of one of the Peripatetic models of conjunction outlined above. In so doing he would specifically be disagreeing with Thomas Aquinas and his followers. More generally, he would be running the risk of being indirectly associated with the heresies of Alexander and Averroes concerning the nature of the potential intellect. On the other hand there was the route of Platonism. This was the option chosen by (to give the most prominent example) Marsilio Ficino. Ficino considered Platonism to be the only

---

intelligibilia per quae acquiruntur credulitates rectae in rebus spiritualibus. Hic autem est ultimus finis qui perficit hominem perfectione vera, et sunt sui solummodo: et dant ei vitam et permanentiam sempiternam, et propter hoc homo vocatur homo." There appears to be an error in the 1520 edition here. Maimonides formulates the fourth species of perfection in opposition to the third. In a fourteenth-century manuscript copy of the Latin version of the *Guide* which I consulted (Oxford, Bodleian Library, Ms. Bodl. 437, f. 114ᵛ), the third species is described as "perfectio morum corporalium" and the fourth, if I interpret the abbreviation correctly, as "acquisitione morum rationalium". The printed edition, *Dux*, f. 113ʳ, likewise refers to the third as "perfectio morum corporalium" but apparently misconstrues "morum rationalium" as "moralium". As I have noted, this edition is not free of printing errors (see Ch. 4, nn. 171, 180). Pines's translation supports my reading: the third species is "the perfection of the moral virtues" whereas the fourth is "the acquisition of the rational virtues—I refer to the conception of intelligibles, which teach true opinions concerning the divine things". The rest of this phrase tallies with the Latin edition ("scilicet intelligibilia per quae acquiruntur credulitates rectae in rebus spiritualibus"). See also Sirat, *History of Jewish Philosophy*, 169–170.

[41] Idel, "Study Programme".

way to revitalise the philosophy of his era, which he perceived as being mired in these very problems concerning the nature and operation of the soul and in the heresies with which they were associated. He, too, considered Alexander and Averroes to be especially representative of the parlous state of contemporary thinking; and he was keen to co-opt Pico into his pro-Platonist, anti-scholastic movement, as the introduction to his commentary on Plotinus (published in 1492) demonstrates:

> For almost the whole of the world is occupied by Peripatetics, who are mostly divided into two sects, the Alexandrian and the Averroist. The former think that our intellect is mortal and the latter think it is unique. Both of them utterly ruin all religion, especially since they seem to deny divine providence concerning men. And in both cases [they seem] to have abandoned their Aristotle, whose mind few today— with the exception of the sublime Pico, my co-Platonist—interpret with that piety with which previously Theophrastus, Themistius, Porphyry, Simplicius and Avicenna, and recently Pletho, interpreted him.[42]

Pico's own position regarding these matters, however, was more nuanced than this remark might suggest, and represented (in the *Heptaplus*, at least) a concerted effort to maintain the idea of intellectual ascent without committing himself exclusively to any one camp.

2. *The Ascent to Perfection in Pico's Works*

Pico's works—up to and including the *Heptaplus*—are marked by a strong interest in the idea of progression to *felicitas*. Differences in how this idea is expressed exist from one work to the next. Despite these differences a fundamentally consistent conception underlies the various expressions.

The *Conclusiones* (in their disorderly and fragmentary way) present something approaching an overview of the variety of philosophi-

---

[42] Ficino, preface to *Plotini Epitomae seu argumenta, commentaria et annotationes*, in his *Opera omnia*, II, 1537: "Totus enim ferme terrarum orbis a Peripateticis occupatus in duas plurimum sectas divisus est, Alexandrinam et Averoicam, illi quidem intellectum nostrum esse mortalem existimant, hi vero unicum esse contendunt, utrique religionem omnem funditus aeque tollunt: praesertim, quia divinam circa homines providentiam negare videntur, et utrobique a suo etiam Aristotele defecisse, cuius mentem hodie pauci, praeter sublimem Picum complatonicum nostrum ea pietate, qua Theophrastus olim et Themistius, Porphyrius, Simplicius, Avicenna et nuper Plethon interpretantur." See J. Hankins, *Plato in the Italian Renaissance*, 2 vols (Leiden and New York: E.J. Brill, 1990), I, 274–275.

cal positions which existed concerning *felicitas* and the intellect. The
third conclusion according to Averroes states that the ultimate *felicitas*
of man is when the active intellect unites with the potential intellect as
its form; it goes on to castigate the Latins, especially John of Jandun,
for "totally corrupting and depraving" the doctrine of Averroes.[43] The
seventh conclusion according to Plotinus, meanwhile, states that the
ultimate *felicitas* of man is when his particular intellect is fully joined
to the first intellect.[44] In one theological conclusion Pico calls it the
"common opinion" that God is to be reached via the intellect;[45] in
another in the same section, he says that common opinion is divided
over whether *felicitas* is attained via the intellect or the will.[46] In yet
another conclusion, it is asserted that *felicitas* may lie in "speculative
perfection".[47] Other related issues, too, appear: Averroes on the unicity of the intellect and "Abumaron Babylonius" on the identity of the
active intellect with God.[48] Frequent further references to the operation of the intellect occur in the conclusions derived from ancient
commentators on *De anima*: Alexander, Themistius and Simplicius.

Quite where Pico himself stood on these matters cannot always
be determined. Since none of these conclusions was censured by the

---

[43] *Conclusions*, 40 (Conc. sec. Avenroen, 3): "Felicitas ultima hominis est, cum
continuatur intellectus agens possibili, ut forma, quam continuationem et Latini
alii quos legi, et maxime Iohannes de Gandauo, perverse et erronee intellexit, qui
non solum in hoc, sed ferme in omnibus quaesitis philosophiae, doctrinam Avenrois
corrupit omnino et depravavit."

[44] Ibid., 66 (Conc. sec. Plotinum, 7): "Felicitas hominis ultima est, cum particularis
intellectus noster totali primoque intellectui plene coniungitur."

[45] Ibid., 150 (Conc. in Theologia ... sec. opinionem propriam, 11): "Si teneatur
communis via, quod actu intellectus attingatur Deus, dico duas sequentes conclusiones ..."

[46] Ibid., 152–154 (Conc. in Theologia ... sec. opinionem propriam, 24–25):
"Tenendo communem viam theologorum, quod felicitas sit in intellectu vel in
voluntate, dico duas conclusiones, quarum prima est haec: Quod intellectus ad
felicitatem non perveniret nisi esset actus voluntatis, qui in hoc est ipso actu
intellectus potior. Secunda conclusio est haec: Licet actus intellectus formaliter
felicitantis attingat obiecti essentiam, tamen quod actus suus circa illum actus sit
felicitatis, formaliter habet ab actu voluntatis." See also ibid., 184 (Quaestiones
ad quas pollicetur se per numeros responsurum, 51): "Utrum felicitas consistat in
intellectu, an in voluntate."

[47] Ibid., 174 (Conc. de mathematicis, 2): "Si felicitas sit in speculativa perfectione,
mathematicae non faciunt ad felicitatem"; see also ibid., 164 (Conc. sec. propriam
opinionem ... in doctrinam Platonis, 33).

[48] Ibid., 40 (Conc. sec. Avenroen, 4): "Possibile est tenendo unitatem intellectus,
animam meam ita particulariter meam, ut non sit mihi communis cum omnibus,
remanere post mortem"; ibid., 54 (Conc. sec. Abumaron Babylonium, 2): "Intellectus
agens nihil aliud est quam Deus."

papal commission, they are not defended in the *Apologia*, and consequently we do not know how he would have argued them. Given the provocative and sometimes paradoxical nature of the *Conclusiones*, it is not clear to what extent it is possible to synthesize a coherent position from them.[49] Pico's other works are more forthcoming, however.

The general notion of man's *felicitas* is the subject of the *Oratio*. At the beginning of this work, Pico announces that he thinks he has finally understood why man has the greatest *felicitas* of any animal and is to be envied by all, "not only by beasts, but by the stars and the ultramundane minds".[50] The unique ingredient of man's *felicitas*, compared to that of other entities, is that he has a choice in what he becomes.[51] His soul is multifaceted and he can behave in accordance with any one of its aspects:

> The Father imparted to man at the moment of his birth seeds of all sorts and the buds of all kinds of life. The ones he cultivates will grow and bear their fruits in him. If [he cultivates] vegetable seeds, he will become a plant; if sensual ones, he will become brutish. If [he cultivates] rational ones, he will turn into a heavenly animal. If he cultivates intellectual ones, he will be an angel and a son of God. If, not content with the lot of any creature, he withdraws into the centre of his unity, having become one spirit with God, he will stand before all things, in the solitary darkness of the Father who is above all things.[52]

---

[49] A pertinent example of the difficulty in interpreting the *Conclusiones* can be seen in the case of the first of the *Conclusiones secundum Alexandrum Aphrodiseum* (ed. Schefer, p. 62) which states "Anima rationalis est immortalis." The contention that according to Alexander the rational soul is immortal is contrary to common understanding of Alexander's position and we have no information as to how Pico would have presented his case; see B. Nardi, "Il commento di Simplicio al *De anima* nelle controversie della fine del secolo XV e del secolo XVI", in his *Saggi sull'aristotelismo padovano*, 369–370. Various attempts have been made, however, to interpret the *Conclusiones* as a coherent whole: e.g. Roulier, *Pic de la Mirandole*, 376–420; Farmer, *Syncretism in the West*, 102–114.

[50] Garin, 102: "Tandem intellexisse mihi sum visus, cur felicissimum proindeque dignum omni admiratione animal sit homo, et quae sit demum illa conditio quam in universi serie sortitus sit, non brutis modo, sed astris, sed ultramundanis mentibus invidiosam."

[51] Ibid., 106: "O summam Dei patris liberalitatem, summam et admirandam hominis felicitatem! cui datum id habere quod optat, id esse quod velit."

[52] Ibid.: "Nascenti homini omnifaria semina et omnigenae vitae germina indidit Pater; quae quisque excoluerit illa adolescent, et fructus suos ferent in illo. Si vegetalia, planta fiet. Si sensualia, obrutescet. Si rationalia, caeleste evadet animal. Si intellectualia, angelus erit et Dei filius, et si nulla creaturarum sorte contentus in unitatis centrum suae se receperit, unus cum Deo spiritus factus, in solitaria Patris caligine qui est super omnia constitutus omnibus antestabit."

Pico then discusses the relationship of man with angels. The three highest orders are Seraphim, Cherubim and Thrones, each of which has its own function. The function of the Cherubim is contemplation.[53] Pico urges his audience to approach the Cherubim first, since they will provide the path to the others.[54] They are the "exemplar" on which human life should be formed.[55] The example they provide is the method of intellectual ascent, which Pico interprets allegorically from a phrase of Pseudo-Dionysius: "they are cleansed, then illuminated, finally perfected".[56] The initial stage of cleansing he interprets as twofold: it involves the control of the passions through morality and the removal of ignorance through dialectic.[57] Illumination then corresponds to knowledge of natural philosophy, and perfection to knowledge of "divine things".[58]

Other analogies follow, all of which Pico interprets in the same way, as illustrating a hierarchical progression via morality, to knowledge and ending in religion: the ascent of Jacob's ladder;[59] Empe-

---

[53] Ibid., 110: "Videamus quid illi agant ... . fulget Cherub intelligentiae splendore ... . Si ab actionibus feriati ... in contemplandi ocio negociabimur, luce cherubica undique corruscabimus."

[54] Ibid., 112: "Ergo medius Cherub sua luce et saraphico igni nos praeparat et ad Thronorum iudicium pariter illuminat; hic est nodus primarum mentium, ordo palladicus, philosophiae contemplativae praeses; hic nobis et aemulandus primo et ambiendus, atque adeo comprehendendus est, unde et ad amoris rapiamur fastigia et ad munera actionum bene instructi paratique descendamus."

[55] Ibid.: "At vero operae precium, si ad exemplar vitae cherubicae vita nostra formanda est, quae illa et qualis sit, quae actiones, quae illorum opera, prae oculis et in numerato habere."

[56] Ibid.: "... Dionysio interprete: purgari illos, tum illuminari, postremo perfici". See Pseudo-Dionysius, *Corpus Dionysiacum*, II, ed. Heil and Ritter, 30 (*De caelesti hierarchia*, 209C).

[57] Garin, 112–114: "ergo et nos cherubicam in terris vitam aemulantes, per moralem scientiam affectuum impetus coercentes, per dialecticam rationis caliginem discutientes, quasi ignorantiae et vitiorum eluentes sordes animam purgemus, ne aut affectus temere debacchentur aut ratio imprudens quandoque deliret."

[58] Ibid., 114: "Tum bene compositam ac expiatam animam naturalis philosophiae lumine perfundamus, ut postremo divinarum rerum eam cognitione perficiamus."

[59] Ibid., 114–116: "Quod si hoc idem nobis angelicam affectantibus vitam facitandum est, quaeso, quis Domini scalas vel sordidato pede, vel male mundis manibus attinget? ... Sed qui hi pedes? quae manus? Profecto pes animae illa est portio despicatissima, qua ipsa materiae tamquam terrae solo innititur, altrix inquam potestas et cibaria, fomes libidinis et voluptuariae mollitudinis magistra. Manus animae cur irascentiam non dixerimus ... ? Has manus, hos pedes, idest totam sensualem partem ... morali philosophia quasi vivo flumine abluamus. At nec satis hoc erit, si per Iacob scalam discursantibus angelis comites esse volumus, nisi et a gradu in gradum rite promoveri ... . Quod cum per artem sermocinalem sive rationariam erimus consequuti, iam cherubico spiritu animati, per scalarum, idest naturae gradus philosophantes ..."

docles's concept of peace;[60] Moses's tabernacle;[61] the Greek mysteries;[62] the precepts of Apollo and Pythagoras;[63] the four rivers of the Chaldeans.[64] This constitutes the framework within which the next part of the *Oratio*—the defence of philosophy, and hence of the *Conclusiones*—is elaborated.[65]

The *Commento*, on the other hand, expresses Pico's vision of the function of the intellect and the ascent to *felicitas* in more particular terms. Benivieni's *canzone* relates the progress of the heart in search of love.[66] Pico interprets this allegorically as signifying the progress of the intellect from knowledge of particulars to knowledge of the intelligible essence, which is arrived at through conjunction with the first mind. In so doing, he sketches a taxonomy of the soul contradicting common scholastic opinion. The human soul is generally divided into parts—vegetative, sensitive and rational—and the Latin Aristotelians think that the rational soul is "the ultimate and noblest part". Pico, however, holds that above it there is a higher part, "the intellectual and angelic part, through which man is linked to angels in the same way that through the sensitive part he is linked

nunc ... descendemus, nunc ... ascendemus, donec in sinu Patris qui super scalas est tandem quiescentes, theologica felicitate consummabimur."

[60] Ibid., 116–120.

[61] Ibid., 120: "qui polluti adhuc morali indigent, cum plebe habitent extra tabernaculum sub divo, quasi Thessali sacerdotes interim se expiantes. Qui mores iam composuerunt, in sanctuarium recepti, nondum quidem sacra attractent, sed prius dialectico famulatu seduli levitae philosophiae sacris ministrent. Tum ad ea et ipsi admissi, nunc superioris Dei regiae multicolorem, idest sidereum aulicum ornatum, nunc caelestem candelabrum septem luminibus distinctum, nunc pellicea elementa, in philosophiae sacerdotio contemplentur, ut postremo per theologicae sublimitatis merita in templi adita recepti, nullo imaginis intercedente velo, divinitatis gloria perfruantur."

[62] Ibid., 122: "Quid enim aliud sibi volunt in Graecorum arcanis observati initiatorum gradus, quibus primum per illas quas diximus quasi februales artes, moralem et dialecticam, purificatis, contingebat mysteriorum susceptio? Quae quid aliud esse potest quam secretioris per philosophiam naturae interpretatio? Tum demum ita dispositis illa adveniebat ἐποπτεία, idest rerum divinarum per theologiae lumen inspectio."

[63] Ibid., 124–126.

[64] Ibid., 128.

[65] Ibid., 130: "Haec sunt, Patres colendissimi, quae me ad philosophiae studium non animarunt modo sed compulerunt. Quae dicturus certe non eram, nisi his responderem qui philosophiae studium in principibus praesertim viris, aut his omnino qui mediocri fortuna vivunt, damnare solent. Est enim iam hoc totum philosophari (quae est nostrae aetatis infelicitas) in contemptum potius et contumeliam, quam in honorem et gloriam."

[66] The text of the *canzone* is in Garin, 453–458; the relevant section runs from the middle of the seventh stanza to the end of the poem.

to animals".[67] Man therefore has a twofold intellectual potential. On the one hand he can think with his rational part, which is dependent on sense data and therefore subject to error; on the other hand he can think with his "intellectual part", which receives true intellectual forms directly, through illumination.[68]

Pico reads the last stanzas of Benivieni's poem as dramatizing the ascent from the former to the latter, from knowledge of a particular beautiful person to knowledge of the complete essence of beauty. This ascent is demarcated in six stages. The process of cognition begins with the reception of a particular thing by the sense organs (stage 1).[69] This particular and material object of sense passes into the rational soul; here it is subjected to a process of abstraction, occuring in the imagination, which rids it of some of its material and individual context (stage 2).[70] Eventually, there comes a point when consideration of "various and numerous beauties" leads to a 'concept' of the beautiful, a notion of universal beauty without a material dimension (stage 3).[71] Even this advanced stage of

---

[67] Garin, 479 (*Commento*, I.12): "Similmente nello uomo sono dua corpi, come nel concilio nostro proveremo, secondo la mente di Aristotele e di Platone, uno eterno, chiamato da' Platonici veiculo celeste, il quale da l'anima razionale è immediatamente vivificato; l'altro corruttibile, quali noi veggiamo con gli occhi corporali composto de' quattro elementi. Poi è in lui la vegetativa, per la quale questo corruttibile corpo si genera, si nutrisce e cresce, e quello eterno vive di perpetua vita. Tertio, è la parte sensitiva e motiva, per la quale ha convenienzia con gli animali irrazionali. Quarto, è la parte razionale, la quale è propria de gli uomini e de gli animali razionali, e da' Peripatetici latini è creduta essere l'ultima e la più nobile parte dell'anima nostra, cum nondimeno sopra essa sia la parte intellettuale ed angelica, per la quale l'uomo così conviene con gli Angeli, come per la parte sensitiva conviene con le bestie." Cf. the distinction between rational and intellectual in the *Oratio*, n. 52 above.

[68] Garin, 481 (*Commento*, I.13): "Però l'anima nostra quando si volge alla parte sua intellettuale e angelica è da quella illuminata participando le vere forme delle cose le quali così come nello intelletto si chiamano idee, così poichè nell'anima sono, si chiamano ragione e non idee, e in questo sono differente l'anime de' corpi corruttibili, come le nostre ... secondo e' Platonici, dall'anime celeste, però che le celeste ... non si partono dalla parte intellettuale ... . L'altre, addite alla cura de' corpi caduchi e terreni, occupate in questo, si privano della contemplazione intellettuale e mendicano la scienza delle cose da' sensi, a' quali in tutto sono inclinate e però sempre di molti errori e opinione false sono piene".

[69] Garin, 567: "All'anima a' sensi conversa prima per li occhi se gli presenta la particulare beltà di Alcibiade, di Fedro, o di qualche altro corpo spezioso".

[70] Ibid.: "l'anima quella immagine per gli occhi ricevuta con la virtù sua interiore, ma pure ancora materiale e fantastica, in sè riforma e tanto più perfetta la fa quanto la fa più spirituale, e dalla materia più separandola, alla ideale beltà, benchè ancora assai lontana, più l'appropinqua."

[71] Ibid., 567–568: "quando col lume dello intelletto agente l'anima, quella forma

conceptualization is still ultimately derived from sense impressions, however, and so the universal concept is veiled "like a sunbeam under water".[72] Pico here remarks that many Aristotelians, especially the Latin scholastics, think that this is the highest state of knowledge attainable by the human soul while still attached to the body. He disagrees, however,[73] and believes that a further three stages of higher knowledge are attainable. This higher knowledge, in keeping with the disagreement with the scholastics noted earlier in the work,[74] comes from the use of the "intellectual part" rather than the "rational part". When the soul turns away from the contemplation of things derived from sense and looks into itself, it sees "a more perfect beauty" which is "not a mere shadow" but "a truer image of the true sun" (stage 4).[75] This "truer image" is still partial, however, because what the soul sees is universal beauty as *participated* within the soul; an individual soul cannot receive the complete *essence* of universal beauty.[76] In order to rise to the comprehension of the complete essence, the soul has to rise from contemplation of itself to conjunction with the first mind (stages 5 and 6): this, in the

---

ricevuta da ogni particularità separando, la natura propria della corporale bellezza in sè considera, nè più alla propria immagine di uno solo corpo ma alla universale bellezza di tutti e' corpi insieme intende."

[72] Benivieni, *Canzone*, stanza VIII; Garin, 457. For Pico's commentary, see Garin, 568: "quantunque in questo ultimo grado la beltà in sè riguardi ... nondimeno da' sensi e da' fantasmi particulari tale cognizione riceve, onde nasce che chi per questa via sola alla cognizione della natura delle cose perviene non può perspicuamente e sanza velo di grandissima ambiguità vederle"; ibid., 579: "In questa universal cognizione l'anima come in cosa da lei fabricata si diletta ... e in lei el lume della vera beltà, come lume di sole sotto acqua, vede."

[73] Ibid., 568: "hanno creduto e credono molti Peripatetici, e massimi e' Latini, non potere l'anima nostra unita al corpo a più perfetta cognizione ascendere, il che nel nostro concilio dimonstreremo dalla mente di Aristotile e quasi di tutti e' Peripatetici arabi e greci essere grandemente alieno".

[74] See n. 67 above.

[75] Benivieni, *Canzone*, stanza VIII; Garin, 458. For Pico's commentary, see Garin, 568–569: "l'anima ... vede sè cognoscere la natura della bellezza universalmente come non ristretta ad alcuna particularità, e cognosce che ogni cosa, che nella materia è fundata, è particulare, di che conclude questa tale universalità non dallo obbietto esteriore sensibile, ma dallo intrinseco suo lume e sua virtù procedere; ... E così in sè conversa vede la immagine della beltà ideale a sè dall' intelletto participata ... e questo è il quarto grado, perfetta immagine dello amore celeste"; ibid., 579: "Questo è lo ascenso dal terzo grado al quarto, cioè alle idee all'anima participate, nella quale non è più ombra di bellezza, ma si vede la beltà vera".

[76] Ibid. 569: "Di poi da sè all'intelletto proprio ascendendo ... ove la celeste Venere in propria forma e non immaginaria, ma non però con totale plenitudine della sua beltà, che in intelletto particulare non cape, se gli dimostra"; ibid., 579: "si vede la beltà vera, quantunque non essenziale ma participata".

poem, is the light which is "suspended near that sun", the sun itself
representing God.[77]

Pico also notes the existence of an even higher state. This
state does not form a legitimate part of the soul's progress towards
knowledge, however:

> When the soul has arrived at this point, in the sixth grade, its path is
> completed, and it is not licit for it to move still further to the seventh
> grade, as if to the sabbath of celestial love. Instead it must rest there
> happily, as if in its end, beside the first Father, source of beauty.[78]

These sections of the *Commento* constitute Pico's most detailed expression of his ideas about intellect.[79] All these ideas recur in the
Heptaplus, sometimes literally repeated. On the other hand, there is
also a significant change of emphasis.

Firstly, Pico's belief that there is a higher "intellectual part" above
the rational soul "through which man in linked to angels" reappears
in the second chapter of the fourth exposition; it is called *intelligentia*
and is signified by the supercelestial waters.[80] The explicit refutation
of scholastic psychology which this occasioned in the *Commento* is
absent from the *Heptaplus*, however. Instead of launching into the
controversy surrounding the taxonomy of the human intellect, as

---

[77] Benivieni, *Canzone*, stanza VIII; Garin, 458. For Pico's commentary, see Garin,
569: "l'anima cerca el proprio e particulare intelletto alla universale e prima mente
coniungere, prima delle creature, albergo ultimo e universale della ideale bellezza";
ibid., 579–580: "Ed è l'ascenso dal quinto grado al sesto, nel quale el proprio
particulare intelletto con la universale e prima mente, assai più della nostra aperta e
chiara, coniunge, la quale mente è immediata e prossima a Dio, primo e intelligibile
sole".

[78] Ibid., 569: "Al quale pervenendo, grado in ordine sesto, termina el suo cam-
mino, nè gli è licito nel settimo, quasi sabbato del celeste amore, muoversi più oltre,
ma quivi debbe come in un suo fine a lato al primo Padre, fonte della bellezza,
felicemente riposarsi."

[79] In his commentary on Psalm 10 Pico sketches a roughly parallel model of seven
levels of intellectual ascent linked to seven "gradus beatorum". *Expositiones in Psalmos*,
ed. Raspanti, 86: "Quod si Platonice distinguere hos gradus vellemus, sic forte dici
posset: primi esse in imaginatione, secundi in anima rationali, quae est Dei domus,
tertii a ratione ascendunt ad intellectum, quarti sunt in ideis intellectualibus, quinti
in intelligibili, sexti in unitate mentis suae, septimi in virtute prima, sed haec sunt
alterius negocii."

[80] Garin, 274: "quoniam non minor nobis cum angelis quam cum brutis communicatio, quemadmodum infra rationem est sensus unde commercium cum animalibus,
ita supra rationem intelligentia est, per quam dicere illud Ioannis possumus 'societas
nostra cum angelis est'." For the parallel passage in the *Commento*, see n. 67 above; on
the citation from John, see Ch. 2, n. 72. See also the *Oratio*, Garin, 110–112: "Super
Cherub, idest contemplatore, volat [i.e., Deus] atque eum quasi incubando fovet.
Spiritus enim Domini fertur super aquas, has, inquam quae super caelos sunt".

he did in the earlier work, Pico discusses the divergence of opinion among philosophers regarding the higher intellect which illuminates the human intellect:

> For the intellect which is in us is illuminated by a greater and truly divine intellect, whether it is God (as some wish) or a mind which is nearer to and cognate with man (as almost all the Greeks, and many of the Arabs and Jews wish). Jewish philosophers, as well as Al-Farabi in the work he wrote *On Principles*, explicitly called this substance "Spirit of the Lord". Not without reason did he [i.e., Moses] mention this (that is, the Spirit "being borne" over the waters) before the composition of man from soul and body with a bond of light. He did this so that we should not believe that this spirit is only present in our intellect when it is joined to the body, as Maimonides, Abubacher the Arab and some others falsely believed.[81]

---

[81] H. 4.2; Garin, 274–276: "Cum igitur primo die Spirius Domini incubantem legimus aquis, sintque aquae bifariam discretae, utique de his aquis quae sunt sub caelo dictum non accipiemus, quoniam super has non Spiritus Domini, sed caelum potius defertur. Reliquum ut de his dictum sit, quae sunt super caelum. Unde nobis maximum dogma de anima reseratur. Intellectum enim, qui est in nobis, illustrat maior atque adeo divinus intellectus sive sit Deus (ut quidem volunt), sive proxima homini et cognata mens, ut fere omnes Graeci, ut Arabes, ut Hebraeorum plurimi volunt. Quam substantiam et Judaei philosophi et Abunasar Alpharabius, in libro quem scribit de principiis, expressis verbis Spiritum Domini appellavit. Nec factum sine causa ut, priusquam hominem ex animo et corpore vinculo lucis constituisset, huius rei meminerit, idest delationis spiritus super aquas, sed ob id factum, ne forte crederemus non adesse spiritum hunc nostro intellectui, nisi cum esset corpori copulatus. Quod et Moses Aegyptius et Abubacher Arabs et quidam alii falso crediderunt." The citation of Al-Farabi deserves some comment. The correlation of transcendent active intellect and Holy Spirit is found in Al-Farabi's *Kitab al-siyasa al-madaniyya*: see Al-Farabi, *Obras filosófico-políticas*, ed. R.R. Guerrero (Madrid: Debate, 1992), 7. It is also mentioned in the "Appendix to the Summary" of Al-Farabi's *Al-madina al-fadila* (*On the Perfect State*, ed. and tr. Walzer, 53; see Walzer's note, ibid., 364). These texts did not exist in Latin in direct transmission. On the other hand, extracts from Al-Farabi's work, including the idea to which Pico refers here, formed part of the composite text, attributed to Averroes, which circulated under the title *De perfectione naturalis intellectus* (see Ch. 5, section 1.2). The section from Al-Farabi, at the end of the text, is introduced as follows: "Et nunc autem volumus claudere sermonem nostrum et cum hoc non stantes tibi in brevibus referre verbis ut in ultimum ordinem principiorum velut ponit Avennasar" (*La béatitude de l'âme*, ed. Geoffroy and Steel, 181). The reference to "ultimum ordinem principiorum" relates to Pico's comment that the idea is found "in libro quem scribit de principiis". The reference to 'spiritus' runs: "Et substantia quidem intellectus agentis est una, quamvis gradus suus contineat istud quod dependet ab omnibus animalibus rationalibus receptivis beatitudinis, et hoc est quod vocatur spiritus sanctus" (ibid., 183–185). We know that versions of this text were in the hands of Achillini and Nifo by the last decade of the fifteenth century. Nifo was apparently working on this text in 1492; the Al-Farabi section of the composite version was found by him in the library of San Giovanni di Verdara in Padua. Equally, we know that the composite version circulated

Although Pico does not explicitly refute those who think that
the higher intellect is identical with God, his sympathies seem to lie
with the majority verdict that it is "nearer to and cognate with man";
and this, as we shall see, is consonant with his position regarding
felicitas, which I shall discuss below. He does, however, take the
opportunity to reject the idea that the illuminating action of the
"greater intellect" only takes place when the human intellect is
attached to the body.[82]

Secondly, the notion that the human intellect can conjoin with
the first mind is reaffirmed in the sixth chapter of the sixth exposition, and the first mind itself is described in terms strikingly similar
to those of the *Commento*:

---

in Italy before this date, as other extant manuscripts seem to originate from there. See
ibid., 83–129, for a summary of the Latin tradition of this text. Steel, ibid., 126 writes
that "malgré de nombreuses recherches, nous n'avons pas trouvé une seule citation
ou utilisation du *Traité sur la béatitude de l'âme* chez des auteurs latins avant Achillini
et Nifo." It is at least possible that this is one such instance. Garin's reference, 276
n. 1, to Al-Farabi's *De intellectu et intellecto* does not correspond to Pico's text here.

[82] This is the idea which Pico attributes to "Moses Aegyptius [Maimonides] et
Abubacher Arabs [Ibn Bajja] et quidam alii". I have not found the direct source for
Pico's citation of these authors. The idea itself, however, seems to have been fairly
commonplace. See, for example, the letter of Pier Candido Decembrio (1399–1477)
to Ugolino Pisano, criticizing the "freneticas opiniones" of "Aristotle" that "mundum
ab aeterno, animam nisi in corpore non intelligi, et multa satis profecto scholastica
et non minus ridenda" (quoted by Hankins, *Plato in the Italian Renaissance*, I, 144–
145, who comments that the notion of "animam nisi in corpore non intelligi" is "a
garbled account of the Averroistic interpretation of Aristotelian psychology"). The
idea is specifically attributed to Maimonides and Ibn Bajja by Isaac Abrabanel (1437–
1508), quoted by A.J. Reines, *Maimonides and Abrabanel on Prophecy* (Cincinnati, Ohio:
Hebrew Union College Press, 1970), 84: "Maimonides associates the imagination
with all the prophets in accordance with the opinion of Abu Bekr al-Zaig [i.e. Ibn
Bajja], who writes that there is no conceptualization by an incorporeal intellect until
the content of a corporeal faculty is united with it." Abrabanel himself did not arrive
in Italy until after 1492 and therefore could not have been Pico's direct source,
but his citation at least shows that the idea was current. Roulier, *Pic de la Mirandole*,
402 n. 217, misinterprets this passage: "Dans l'*Heptaplus* Pic se contente d'accepter
la distinction entre intellect actif et intellect passif et d'admettre l'existence d'un
'intellect supérieur à l'intellect humain et qui l'éclaire' et qui, contrairement à ce
qu'ont cru Maïmonide, Ibn Bajja et quelques autres, n'est présent à notre esprit
qu'après l'union de l'âme à son corps." Apart from going against the grammar of
the passage, this is contrary to Pico's argument, the point of which is to explain why
Moses mentioned the movement of the greater intellect over the 'waters' before he
mentioned the composition of man from body and soul ("Spiritus Domini ferebatur
super aquas [= action of greater intellect on human *intelligentia*]. Et dixit Deus: fiat
lux. Et facta est lux. ... Et factum est vespere et mane dies unus [= formation of
man]"). It is this order of events which demonstrates that the greater intellect acts
on the *intelligentia* regardless of the presence of the body.

Just as it is the *felicitas* of drops of water that they arrive at the ocean, where there is a plenitude of water, so, it is our *felicitas* that, whatever portion of intellectual light is in us, should one day be joined to the very first of all intellectual things and first mind, where there is a plenitude and totality of all knowledge.[83]

Thirdly, the general dependence of the human intellect on its "rational part", operating through the senses, and the comparatively limited use it makes of its higher "intellectual part" can be found in the fourth chapter of the fourth exposition:

In the meantime we will explain it [i.e., the creation of the sun and moon in Gen. 1.14–19] thus: that the soul, in its part which turns to the higher waters, to the Spirit of the Lord, shall be called "sun", because all of it shines; and in its part which looks at the lower waters, that is, the sensual powers from which it contracts some stain of imperfection, it shall have the name of "moon". The Greek Platonists would call the sun (understood in this way) *dianoia*, and the moon *doxa*, in accordance with the tenets of their doctrine.[84] Since, while we wander away from our native land and live in the night and shadows of this present life, we use that part most which is turned downwards to the senses, we think we know more things than we know. But when the day of the life to come dawns, becoming removed from the senses and turned towards divine things, we shall understand with the other higher part. Therefore this dictum of ours is correct, that the sun rules the day and the moon the night. In the same way, after stripping off this moribund clothing, we will gaze by the light of the sun alone on that which, in this most miserable night of the body, we try to see (with many powers and forces) rather than do see. Therefore the day shines by the sun alone. On the other hand, the night brings together and unites the stars as helpers to the moon, as less powerful; these are the power of combining and of dividing, that of reasoning and defining, and whatever others there are.[85]

---

[83] H. 6.6; Garin, 322: "Continetur autem et hic altius mysterium: quemadmodum scilicet guttis aquae ea est felicitas ut ad oceanum, ubi aquarum plenitudo, accedant, ita esse nostram felicitatem ut, quae in nobis intellectualis luminis portio est, ipsi primo omnium intellectui primaeque menti, ubi plenitudo, ubi universitas omnis intelligentiae, aliquando coniungatur." Cf. the description of the first mind in the *Commento*, n. 77 above.

[84] This comparison is incorrect. In Neoplatonic terminology *dianoia* represents discursive thought, i.e. the type of cognition symbolized for Pico by the moon, not the sun, and *doxa* represents a still lower level. See Siorvanes, *Proclus*, 194; R. Sorabji, *Time, Creation and the Continuum* (London: Duckworth, 1983, repr. 2002), 137.

[85] H. 4.4; Garin, 278–280: "nos interim sic exponamus ut qua parte ad aquas superiores, ad Domini Spiritum animus vergit, propterea quod totus lucet, sol nuncupetur; qua vero aquas inferiores, idest sensuales potentias respicit, unde infectionis aliquam contrahit maculam, lunae habeat appellationem. Solem hoc modo acceptum Graeci Platonici dianoiam, lunam vero doxam pro suae doctrinae

Here, Pico equates the typical human mode of discursive rational thought—"the power of combining and of dividing, of reasoning and defining"—with the night, and contrasts it with a direct form of intellectual operation which is characteristic of man when "removed from the senses and turned towards divine things". Man will use this latter mode of thought "when the day of the life to come dawns". Pico does not deny its use during the present life, however: he merely states that while alive we use the "night" mode of cognition "most" and in the life to come we use the "day" mode "alone". The *Heptaplus* therefore represents a more cautious formulation of his ideas than the *Commento*: it emphasizes 'normal' sense-based cognition while leaving a loophole so as not to rule out the action of *intelligentia* during the present life.

Fourthly, both the *Commento* and the *Heptaplus* maintain a distinction between two different levels of *felicitas*. We have seen in the *Commento* that intellectual attainment—or, allegorically, the love of beauty—culminates in uniting with the first mind, but that there is also a mysterious higher state, a "sabbath of celestial love".[86] The

---

dogmatis appellarent. Quoniam autem, dum a patria peregrinamur et in hac vitae praesentis nocte et tenebris vivimus, ea parte plurimum utimur quae ad sensus deflectitur, unde et plura opinamur quam scimus, cum vero dies futurae vitae illuxerit, alieni a sensibus ad divina conversi, superiori alia parte intelligemus, recte est dictum hunc nostrum solem praeesse diei, lunam autem praeesse nocti. Itidem quia exuti nos moribundam hanc vestem, unico solis lumine id contuebimur quod in hac corporis miserrima nocte plurimis viribus atque potentiis videre potius conamur quam videamur, idcirco unico sole dies lucescit; nox contra plurimas stellas, componendi scilicet vim et dividendi, ratiocinandi item definiendi, et quae sunt reliquae, lunae, quasi minus potenti, auxiliares corrogat et counit."

[86] See above, n. 78. The distinction between the two seems to correlate with that described in the *Commento particulare*, stanza IV (Garin, 557). There is a state in which the soul is separated from the body but the body is not separated from the soul, and man thinks only with his intellectual part; this is the first death. There is then a second death, in which body and soul are both separated from each other; this is the death of the kiss: "qualche volta si dice l'anima essere separata dal corpo, ma non el corpo da lei; e questo è quando ciascuna delle potenzie dell'anima, eccetto quella che'l corpo nutrisce, chiamata vegetativa, è ligata e non opera niente come se in tutto non fusse; il che, come è detto, accade quando la parte intellettuale, regina dell'anima, è in atto e opera ... . Ma se molto si fortifica e si prolunga l'operazione intellettuale, bisogna che eziandio con questa parte ultima vegetativa l'anima si separi talmente che e lei dal corpo e il corpo da lei sia separato. Può dunque per la prima morte, che è separazione solo dell'anima dal corpo, e non per l'opposito, vedere lo amante l'amata Venere celeste e a faccia a faccia con lei, ragionando della divina immagine sua, e' suoi purificati occhi felicemente pascere; ma chi più intrinsecamente ancora la vuole possedere e, non contento del vederla e udirla, essere degnato de' suoi intimi amplessi e anelanti baci, bisogna che per la seconda morte dal corpo per totale separazione si separi, e allora non solo vede e ode la celeste Venere, ma con

distinction between these two states recurs in the *Heptaplus*, where it is considered in depth in the proem to the seventh exposition. There are, Pico says, two forms of *felicitas*, "natural" and "supernatural". The first is the sort of *felicitas* debated by philosophers and can be actively sought and attained by man; the second is the gift of Christ and can only be passively accepted. Exactly what constitutes natural *felicitas*, however, is something which philosophers have not been able to agree on:

> Concerning man, although different [philosophers] have thought different things, all of them nonetheless have restricted themselves within the narrow bounds of the human faculty. They limit the *felicitas* of man either (as do the Academics) solely to the search for truth, or (as Al-Farabi said) to its attainment through the study of philosophy.[87] Avicenna, Averroes, Abubacher, Alexander and the Platonists seemed to offer something more, strengthening our reason in the intellect which is active, or in something higher but still joined to us, as if in its end. … I do not reject or despise their arguments and opinions, if they are seen to be discussing only natural *felicitas*.[88]

This brief overview is a compressed sketch of some of the ideas of intellectual *felicitas* and conjunction discussed in section 1 of this chapter. Rather than designating one of these models as correct,

---

nodo indissolubile a lei s'abbraccia, e con baci l'uno in l'altro la propria anima trasfundendo, non tanto cambiano quelle, quanto che sì perfettamente insieme si uniscono, che ciascheduna di loro dua anime e ambedue una sola anima chiamare si possono." On the death of the kiss, see also n. 120 below.

[87] In other words, Pico does not number Al-Farabi among those who allow some form of conjunction (see n. 12 above). A common source for this understanding of Al-Farabi's position was the remark of Averroes, *Commentarium magnum in Aristotelis De anima libros*, ed. Crawford, 433: "In libro enim de Nicomachia videtur negare continuationem esse cum intelligentiis abstractis, et dicit hoc esse opinionem Alexandri, et quod non est opiniandum quod finis humanus sit aliud quam perfectio speculativa. Avempeche autem exposuit sermonem eius, et dixit quod opinio eius est opinio omnium Peripateticorum, scilicet quod continuatio est possibilis, et quod est finis." See, generally, S. Pines, "Les limites de la métaphysique selon Al-Farabi, Ibn Bajja et Maïmonide; sources et antithèses de ces doctrines chez Alexandre d'Aphrodise et chez Themistius", in Miscellanea Mediaevalia, 13, 2 vols, I: *Sprache und Erkenntnis im Mittelalter*, 211–225 (Berlin: De Gruyter, 1981).

[88] H. 7.P; Garin, 330: "De homine autem, etsi diversi diversa senserint, omnes tamen intra humanae facultatis angustias se tenuerunt, vel in ipsa tantum veri vestigatione, quod Academici, vel in adeptione potius per studia philosophiae, quod Alpharabius dixit, felicitatem hominis determinantes. Dare aliquid plus visi Avicenna, Averrois, Abubacher, Alexander et Platonici, nostram rationem in intellectu, qui actu est, aut aliquo superiore, nobis tamen cognato, quasi in suo fine firmantes … . Quas ego eorum disputationes atque sententias nec reprobo nec aspernor, si de naturali se tantum felicitate dicere videantur."

Pico prefers to state that they all have a certain validity, as long as it is recognized that they deal with natural and not supernatural *felicitas*. Despite the differences between these two types of *felicitas*, however, he ends the proem by affirming not their separation but their mutual dependence:

> Religion pushes, directs and drives us to this [supernatural] *felicitas*, just as we use philosophy as a guide to natural *felicitas*. If nature is the beginning of grace, undoubtedly also philosophy is the basis of religion, and there is no philosophy which removes man from religion. Therefore it is right that we, since we have philosophized with Moses about nature for six days, being able to devote ourselves on the seventh day to divine things, should talk about supernatural *felicitas*.[89]

In so doing, he provides another comment on the structure of the *Heptaplus*. The first six expositions are concerned with natural *felicitas*, that is, philosophy; as we have seen, the sixth exposition refers near its end to the uniting of the human mind with the first mind. The seventh exposition is concerned with supernatural *felicitas*, that is, religion; as such, it concentrates on the progress of sacred history, from the Fall to the coming of the Messiah and, finally, redemption.

The repetitions of the *Commento* in the *Heptaplus* therefore inform us both by their similarities and their differences. In both works Pico proposes a distinction between two levels of *felicitas*; in the *Commento* he leaves the higher level unexplored, whereas in the *Heptaplus* he devotes an exposition to it. In both works he maintains a psychological model at odds with common scholastic practice and makes polemical use of his allegorical readings. In the *Commento* he explicitly charges his scholastic opponents with having misunderstood Aristotle.[90] Given the nature of the dispute surrounding Aristotelian psychology and epistemology it can be seen that this was a controversial claim in a sensitive area. In the *Heptaplus*, however, he redirects his overt polemic away from Christian scholastic philosophers towards well-known heterodox positions: the idea, which he attributes to Maimonides, "Abubacher the Arab" and "some others", that the "greater intellect" only operates on the human intellect

---

[89] Ibid., 338: "Ad hanc felicitatem religio nos promovet, dirigit et impellit, quemadmodum ad naturalem duce utimur philosophia. Quod si natura rudimentum est gratiae, utique et philosophia inchoatio est religionis, neque est philosophia quae a religione hominem semovet, recte igitur et nos, cum a Mose postquam sex dies de natura sumus philosophati, septimo die divinis vacantes de supernaturali felicitate dicemus."

[90] See n. 73 above.

when the human intellect is attached to the body;[91] and the Averroist doctrine of the unicity of the potential intellect.[92] In the *Commento* he gives details of three stages of cognition by which man can attain a direct knowledge of intelligibles; in the *Heptaplus*, although he maintains the psychological structure which makes this attainment possible, he emphasizes that it is not the normal human mode of thought during this life.

Beyond the detailed comparisons between the *Commento* and the *Heptaplus*, we should also note the links with the general hierarchical progression described in the *Oratio*. I have already referred to these parts of the *Oratio*.[93] Here I shall return to just one of them: the interpretation of Job in terms derived from Empedocles.[94] The soul, Pico says, is a battleground.[95] Peace can only be achieved by the application of moral philosophy, followed by dialectic, followed by natural philosophy and finally by theology.[96] The distinction between the peace brought by natural philosophy and that attained through theology relates to the discussion of the two forms of *felicitas* in the *Heptaplus*.

> [We should remember that] in [natural philosophy] true quiet and solid peace cannot stand before us; this is the function and privilege of [philosophy's] mistress, most holy theology. ... Let us fully enjoy the longed-for peace; the most holy peace, the indivisible bond, the friendship which is one soul, in which all souls do not only come together in one mind which is above every mind, but become absolutely one thing in some ineffable way.[97]

---

[91] See n. 82 above.

[92] This is the most likely interpretation of the veiled reference in H.4.4 (Garin, 278–280): "philosophi iuniores solem intellectum qui actu est, lunam eum qui est potentia forte interpretarentur; sed quoniam nobis magna de hac re cum illis controversia, nos interim sic exponamus ..." (for remainder, see n. 85 above). The point is presumably that there is one sun and one moon, hence (in the interpretation of the "philosophi iuniores") *one* active and *one* potential intellect. See also Roulier, *Pic de la Mirandole*, 403.

[93] See nn. 56–64 above.

[94] Garin, 116: "interpretetur nobis Iob theologi verba Empedocles philosophus".

[95] Ibid.: "Multiplex profecto, patres, in nobis discordia; gravia et intestina domi habemus et plus quam civilia bella."

[96] Ibid., 116–118.

[97] Ibid., 118: "in ea veram quietem et solidam pacem se nobis praestare non posse, esse hoc dominae suae, idest sanctissimae theologiae, munus et privilegium. ... optata pace perfruemur; pace sanctissima, individua copula, unanimi amicitia, qua omnes animi in una mente, quae est super omnem mentem, non concordent adeo, sed ineffabili quodam modo unum penitus evadant."

Pico envisages a level of intellectual attainment in which "all souls come together in one mind which is above every mind". As we have seen, this mind is the "first of all intellectual things" but it is not, according to most philosophers, God.[98] The union with the first mind is an intellectual union, accomplished when someone has mastered the forms of knowing available to mankind, not merely through knowledge obtained discursively via the rational soul, but also through knowledge obtained directly via *intelligentia*. This union constitutes man's natural *felicitas*. Above it, a higher, "ineffable" union also exists. This state in which "souls ... become absolutely one thing" (as Pico says in the *Oratio*) is the supernatural *felicitas* of the *Heptaplus* and the "sabbath of celestial love" of the *Commento*.[99] It is also discussed at the beginning of the *Oratio*, in a passage already quoted.[100] If man cultivates the rational seeds of his nature—the capacity to obtain knowledge discursively—he will become a "heavenly animal". If he cultivates the higher intellectual seeds—the capacity to obtain knowledge of intelligibles directly—"he will be an angel and a son of God". Beyond even this, however, is a state in which "he withdraws into the centre of his unity" and becomes "one spirit with God". This is the state which Pico later calls supernatural *felicitas*. He is clear throughout all the works under discussion that this higher *felicitas* transcends intellectual achievement; that is why it is not the subject of the *Commento*, and equally that is why it is not the subject of the first six expositions of the *Heptaplus*. Nonetheless, as the proem to the seventh exposition shows, he regarded it as a development towards which natural *felicitas*—that is, intellectual achievement—constituted the necessary preliminary step.

These examples should suffice to demonstrate that Pico maintained throughout this series of works a coherent theme of the progression to *felicitas*, in which intellectual ascent played a partial but vital role. This ascent is not merely the accumulation of knowledge: it entails a shift in the mode of cognition by which knowledge is attained. Not all philosophers subscribed to this view—Thomas Aquinas being a notable dissenter—but a large proportion of influential Peripatetics did. Those who did were not necessarily in mutual agreement as to precisely how the cognitive shift took place, but they generally affirmed that, as Pico put it, it involved "strengthening our reason in the intellect which is active, or in something higher but

---

[98] See above, nn. 81, 83.
[99] See above, n. 78.
[100] See above, n. 52.

still joined to us".[101] The result of this shift is that the mind leaves behind its characteristic inaccurate mode of discursive sense-based cognition and attains an accurate ability to comprehend intelligibles or 'separate substances' directly. It thereby arrives at the "fullness and entirety of all understanding".[102]

Although he adopted the broad outline of this model, Pico modified it with his own personal contribution to the debate, which was the division of *felicitas* into two. This did not 'solve' the controversy, nor did it align him with one or other of the disputing factions. Instead, it deprived the controversy of some of its force, in the sense that if all sides accepted the existence of the higher, supernatural *felicitas*, their differences of opinion concerning the lower, natural sort were no longer of such grave consequence. This approach is characteristic of his syncretism. As a Christian, he was keen to insist that whatever active role the philosopher played in reaching his natural *felicitas* was overshadowed by the passive acceptance of the supernatural *felicitas* which transcended it. In other words, he circumscribed the limits of intellectual achievement rather more tightly than many (such as Avicenna, Maimonides and Averroes) but rather less tightly than some (such as Thomas Aquinas). Likewise, although (as I have argued) he maintained his stance that the intellect could reach a state in which it cognizes intelligibles directly while still attached to the body, his affirmation of this was more discrete than before. As a corollary to this, it should be pointed out that, for many of the commentators mentioned, this state was equated with the human capacity for prophecy.[103] Pico, however, never mentions this (except, obviously, in the case of Moses himself).

The theme of intellectual ascent therefore provides us with a perspective in which to view all of Pico's philosophical works up to 1489. It is the thread which connects the *Commento*, the *Conclusiones*, the *Oratio* and *Apologia* and the *Heptaplus*. Pico tried expressing this theme in different ways: firstly in an allegorical reading of Benivieni's poem, secondly as a justification for his treatment of differing philosophies in the *Conclusiones*, and thirdly in a biblical commentary. It is the link between this theme and biblical commentary which most concerns me here. Among those who advocated the general idea that intellectual progress leads to *felicitas* I have already

---

[101] See n. 88 above.

[102] H. 6.6; Garin, 322: "ubi plenitudo, ubi universitas omnis intelligentiae".

[103] E.g. Al-Farabi (n. 12 above), Avicenna (n. 15). Maimonides, too, discusses this at length: see Maimonides, *Dux*, ff. 61^v–71^r (Guide, tr. Pines, 360–412).

noted the presence of Gersonides. I now wish to consider the example of Gersonides's commentary on the Song of Songs. This, it will be seen, has strong affinities with all of Pico's works discussed in this chapter; and, notably for my investigation, it frames its ideas in the context of biblical interpretation.

3. Felicitas, *Knowledge and Biblical Exegesis: The Example of Gersonides*

The epistemological basis of *felicitas*, and the ascent of the human intellect to its attainment, is the subject of Gersonides's commentary on the Song of Songs.[104] This was among the texts translated for Pico by Mithridates; the translation is extant in Ms. Vat. Lat. 4273.[105] It is clear simply from this manuscript that Pico read this text with interest: there are copious highlighting marks and marginal comments in his hand.[106]

I shall concentrate here on Gersonides's introduction, in which he summarizes the framework of intellectual ascent and sketches the broad outline of its application to the Song of Songs. The text begins with a definition of *felicitas*:

> It is clear, according to our theologians who study theology in the law and in *derash* or kabbalah, as well as according to speculative philosophers, that the highest good and perfection of the *felicitas* of man consists in this, that he may know and understand God insofar as is possible for him and that he will arrive at this end when he has understood the things which are, and the order and right principle of beings, and the way of the wisdom of God himself, which arranged these things in the way in which they are and are thought to be; and this is because these intelligible things direct [us] to the knowledge of God himself in a certain manner.[107]

---

[104] Gersonides, *Commentary on the Song of Songs*, tr. M. Kellner (New Haven, Connecticutt: Yale University Press, 1998). On Gersonides generally, see C. Touati, *La pensée philosophique et théologique de Gersonide* (Paris: Editions de Minuit, 1973); *Les méthodes de travail de Gersonide et le maniement du savoir chez les scolastiques*, ed. C. Sirat, S. Klein-Braslavy and O. Weijers (Paris: J. Vrin, 2003).

[105] See Ch. 3, n. 113.

[106] Pico's hand is identified by Mercati, *Codici Latini Pico Grimani Pio*, 22–23. The first page of this text (Vat. Lat. 4273, f. 5ʳ) contains the annotation of the equivalence of the four senses of Scripture, in the Christian and Jewish traditions, reported in the *Apologia*, which I partially quoted in Ch. 3, n. 31.

[107] Vat. Lat. 4273, ff. 5ᵛ–6ʳ: "Manifestum per se est secundum theologos nostros theologizantes in lege et prophetis dras [i.e., derash] *aut cabala* [an interpolation], nec non et secundum philosophos speculativos, quod summum bonum, **et perfecta**

For this reason, as wise men in general (and especially Aristotle) have said, whoever has knowledge of God himself, who is "the law of beings, their steward, their right principle and their order", has necessarily made an approach to God.[108] Ultimate *felicitas*, which depends on the achievement of this knowledge, is extremely difficult for humans to attain, and scarcely any manage it.[109] In the first place, this is because it is difficult to reach an understanding of things which are in a state of perfection. In the second place, there are a variety of specific impediments which prevent such an understanding: the desires of the body can prevent the mind from following the right path; and the mind itself can make errors, confounding the substantial with the accidental, so that it is unable to approach the true nature of things, "thinking about that which is not, that it is, and vice versa".[110] In effect, these two specific impediments stem from moral ("fervor nature") and speculative ("error imaginative et cogitative") behaviour, respectively. Gersonides emphasizes the primacy of the Torah for overcoming these difficulties. Prophets and wise men have never ceased from helping men to achieve *summa felicitas*; but of all the guides, the Torah ("Moisi lex") is the best. It works "not only for the multitude and the *vulgares* in general, but also for the *particulares*."[111]

---

felicitatis hominis est in eo quod cognoscat et sciat deum quo ad eius possibilitatem et ad hunc finem perveniet cum intellexerit ea que sunt et ordinem entium et rectitudinem, et modum sapientie ipsius dei que disposuit ea in eo modo in quo sunt et esse habentur, et / hoc quia ista intelligibilia dirigent ad cognitionem ipsius dei quodammodo." Here and below, the text in bold indicates a section highlighted in the manuscript.

[108] Ibid., f. 6^r: "de deo ipso, qui sit lex entium, et eorum iconomos, rectitudo et ordo".

[109] Ibid., f. 7^v: "Itaque difficile est alicui individuo humano posse pervenire ad eius finem, quanto minus ad aliquam partem eius, ad quam vix perveniunt homines pauci numero."

[110] Ibid.: "**Prima est propter difficultatem comprehensionis rerum que sunt in perfectione; secunda ob multitudinem prohibentium, neque possis se exerrere ad comprehensionem. Verum prima istarum prohibitionum est fervor nature in principio rei, ut attrahatur post voluptates corporeas. Secunda est error imaginative, et cogitative que ducunt nos ad miscendas res accidentales cum substantialibus, ad putandum de eo quod non est, quod sit, et contra.**"

[111] Ibid., f. 8^r: "**universaliter igitur pervenire ad felicitatem, non solum difficile est, sed difficillimum, non solum propter causas predictas, sed propter alias eis similes, et propterea non removerunt se prophete, nec sapientes viri quin direxissent homines ad medium ducens ad felicitatem, quoad eorum posse, et fuit lex data ad dirigendum ad summam felicitatem preter cetera directoria cuius moisi lex, nostra est que inter alias summe ad summam felicitatem dirigit, non solum ad vulgares et multitudinem in universali, verum etiam ad particulares.**" Mithridates uses *vulgares et multitudinem*

This distinction between the masses and the elite, linked to the twin problems of moral turpitude and speculative confusion, is fundamental to Gersonides's account. The commandments of Scripture direct the reader—all readers—to moral perfection, that is, to overcoming the first impediment of *fervor nature*. On the other hand, Scripture also contains a concealed 'speculative' knowledge which is not known to the masses. The difficulty of this speculation is matched by the damage that is caused by getting it wrong. The masses are incapable of this type of speculation because they do not know what the end of human life is and are consequently unable to deduce a final cause towards which they can direct their actions. This end is for man to be united with God ("coniungi hominem in deo benedicto"), and it is referred to in various parts of Scripture (such as the image of the Tabernacle) which provide guidance to the *particulares*, that is, the intellectual elite.[112] As for the masses, they must be contented with knowing that whoever follows the commandments will have a long life "and many imaginary happinesses". In this way, they are spurred on by utilitarian considerations towards a good whose true nature they cannot understand.[113] There are, therefore, two perfec-

---

to translate המון ('masses') and *particulares* to translate יחידים ('individuals', in this context meaning the elite); see Gersonides, *Commentary on Five Scrolls* (Königsberg 1860), f. 3ʳ.

[112] Pico, too, made use of the image of the tabernacle (in the *Oratio*) as a symbol of intellectual progression: see n. 61 above.

[113] Vat. Lat. 4273, ff. 8ʳ–9ʳ: "Dicimus igitur quod primo et principaliter id ad quod / dirigimur, est perfectio morum ad quod lex dirigit tamquam ad perfectionem in preceptis servandis, et eorum declaratione, ut vero id quod est in ipsis preceptis positum ad anime ordinationem seu dispositionem occultum est, cum ignoretur a vulgaribus, et maior pars eorum ad que lex nos dirigit speculatione⟨m⟩, est in articulis speculativis in quorum comprehensione est sapienti maxima difficultas. et quanto magis in articulis maioribus, in quibus error distare facit hominem nimis a summa perfectione que ad hominem pertinet; et quia omnis actio dirigitur ad finem quendam, oportet considerare finem a principio suo ut dirigatur operatio tota in virtute finis quod est impossibile hoc vulgaribus in eo quod iussit lex de perfectione morum quia ipsi non cognoscunt finem humanum quid sit e[ad]e[m] causa vafre usa est lex, et congregavit illam vafritatem inter [hec] duo primum quod ipsa innuit finem, et iussit ratione finis, et [sic] ad finem coniungi hominem in deo benedicto, et excitavit de multis rebus speculativis mirabilibus in parte narrationum, et preceptorum, et in qualitate tabernaculi, et vasorum eius perque direxit particulares homines ad hoc scilicet quod reliqua precepta legalia sint ad hunc finem et propter hunc finem et addidit propter vulgares in multis preceptis, quod qui servaverit ea, habebit longitudinem vite, et multas felicitates imaginarias, et contra, qui non servantur cum tamen finis preceptorum legalium non sit iste, neque ipsa propter hunc finem et hoc quia vulgares apud quos non potest imaginari hic finis propter quem legalia precepta sunt, nec esset homo avidus facere aliquod opus nisi imaginaretur in eo

tions: moral perfection for the masses, and intellectual perfection for the elite. The Song of Songs can be understood only by the latter group.[114]

According to Gersonides, the Song of Songs is to be interpreted as a guide for philosophers through various levels which are necessary to achieve intellectual perfection. These levels correspond to the training of the mind in certain disciplines. Having separated speculation from moral behaviour, Gersonides divides it into four elements: it starts with the fundamental necessity of distinguishing truth from falsehood and moves on to a hierarchical arrangement of knowledge comprising mathematics, natural science (i.e., physics) and divine science (i.e., metaphysics). Mathematics forms the basis and is necessary for advancement in both the subsequent sciences; likewise, physics must precede metaphysics.[115] The study of metaphysics, the divine science, is to be forbidden except to those whose intellect is "firm, settled and strong in true opinions, with respect both to Scripture and to speculation".[116]

---

aliqua utilitas, ideo direxit lex eos ad hoc, ut observent hec precepta legalia ad hanc utilitatem / et postquam servaverint hunc cultum et religionem primo non ad finem predictum dirigentur postea observare eum ad finem, quamvis eis ignotum ..." The paper is damaged at one point near the left margin, and I am grateful to Charles Burnett for his help with the conjectures which I have given in square brackets.

[114] Ibid., f. 9ʳ: "**Verum hic liber que dicitur canticum canticorum dirigit particulares solum ad viam perveniendi ad felicitatem, et hac de causa non intelligitur a vulgaribus, nec secundum sensum literalem prodest ut sciatur ab ipsis vulgaribus.**"

[115] Ibid., ff. 10ʳ⁻ᵛ: "coegit natura rerum per se, ut sint gradus speculationis in entibus secundum hunc ordinem. Et hoc quod quicquid designant scientie disciplinabiles sunt ad corpus in quantum est corpus absolute, non inquantum est corpus quoddam, utputa grave vel leve, aut nec grave nec leve quod est mathematici. Et quicquid inquirit scientia naturalis est ad corpus in quantum est hoc corpus utputa corpus mobile seu transmutabile, aut grave vel leve, aut nec grave nec leve. Et inquisitio comprehendentium corpus absolute, precedat inquisitionem comprehendentium corpus quoddam, quia res universales sunt notiores nobis, sicut in primo de Physico auditu patet [189a]. ... / Et rursus quod in sapientia mathematica est directio quedam ad sapientiam naturalem, et sapientiam divinam sicut probatum est in primo almagesti [I.1]. Et sapientia naturalis est necessario prior sapientia que est post physica quia scientia metaphysica sequitur eam via perfectionis et finis."

[116] Ibid., f. 11ʳ: "**ideo prohibetur hec sapientia, ne quis studeat in ea, nisi haberit intellectum firmum et quietum ac roboratum in opinionibus veris tam legalibus quam speculativis.**"

This completes the framework for establishing what Gersonides calls the "final intention" of the Song of Songs.[117] He now outlines his actual reading, which breaks the text up into sections and allots to each one a corresponding element in the hierarchy of intellectual perfection. So, after an introduction, the Song of Songs deals, first, with the problem of morality; then, the problem of distinguishing truth from falsehood; then, the knowledge of mathematics; then, the knowledge of natural science; and, finally, the knowledge of divine science. He further comments that the opening words of the Song of Songs—"Let him kiss me with the kisses of his mouth, for thy love is better than wine"—are placed there to demonstrate that attainment of *felicitas* is possible.[118] His actual exegesis of these words, a few pages later, is one which evidently struck a chord with Pico: the "kiss" referred to is the "death of the kiss", from which Moses, Aaron and Mary died, and it signifies "conjunction with God himself".[119] Pico, too, used the image of the "death of the kiss" to signify the attainment of *felicitas*. It appears as such in the *Commento*, where, just like in Gersonides's commentary, it is interpreted as referring to the "total intention of the book [i.e. the Song of Songs] and the ultimate end of [Solomon's] love".[120]

By my reckoning, therefore, the following themes, which I have discussed in this and the previous two chapters with reference to the *Heptaplus*, are also to be found in Gersonides's commentary:

---

[117] Ibid., f. 5^r: "quamobrem qui vult istas materias, et eis similes comentari, non debet eas trahere ad dras seu allegoriam; sed conetur ea comentari secundum finalem intentionem, ad quam tendunt."

[118] Ibid., f. 15^v: "Propterea quod in perventione ad hanc felicitatem, est aliquid distantie, ita ut putetur multas esse causas prohibentes ad illam pervenire. Praemittit hic sapiens probare possibilitatem perventionis ad eam, ut sit intentum huius libri id est quomodo posset esse quod perveniatur ad hanc perfectionem". See Wirszubski, *Pico's Encounter*, 157.

[119] Vat. Lat. 4273, f. 19^r: "Dicit de hoc appetitu: utinam oscularetur me deus benedictus de obsculis oris sui, scilicet quod coniungeretur cum eo secundum posse, obsculum enim significat coniunctionem et applicationem, et hoc est dictum *cabalistarum* de Moyse Aarone et Maria, quod mortui sunt per osculum id est quod quando mortui sunt, coniuncti erant cum ipso deo." The word 'cabalistarum' in italics is an interpolation.

[120] Garin, 558 (*Commento particulare*, stanza IV): "Questo è quello che il divino nostro Salomone nella sua Cantica desiderando esclama: 'Baciami co' baci della bocca tua'. Monstra nel primo verso Salomone la intenzione totale del libro e l'ultimo fine del suo amore". See further, n. 86 above. Other features in Pico's account derive from his reading of Recanati: see Wirszubski, *Pico's Encounter*, 153–160. Maimonides, too, mentions the death of the kiss in the context of the Song of Songs in *Dux*, f. 112^r (*Guide*, tr. Pines, 628).

1. The dichotomy of the masses and the elect.
2. The distinction between literal and non-literal reading.
3. Man's goal as *felicitas* resulting from the soul's capacity for comprehending intelligibles.
4. The progress to this goal by moving from moral to speculative knowledge, with the latter divided into a hierarchy of sciences.
5. The ultimate attainment of this goal as 'union' with God.
6. The role of Scripture as the ideal guide to the attainment of this goal, incorporating not only moral instruction but also speculative knowledge.

I have already devoted a certain amount of attention to points 1 to 5. In conclusion I shall comment briefly on point 6, that is, on the role of Scripture in intellectual ascent.

4. *Genesis and Knowledge*

Gersonides, like Maimonides before him and Alemanno after him, argues that the ascent to *felicitas* is composed of a number of stages, which represent a structured programme of study. In his interpretation, the Song of Songs instructs the reader (assuming he is one of the *particulares* who can interpret it correctly) as to the order and nature of these stages. Pico takes this idea a step further. The Genesis narrative, for him, does not merely instruct the reader to achieve knowledge; it actually contains this knowledge—described as "the emanation of all things from God, the grade, number and order of the parts of the worlds"—hidden within it, like buried treasure.[121] The first six expositions of the *Heptaplus* are dedicated to "the orders of things proceeding from God, their distribution, the explanation of their union and their difference, their bonds and their conditions":[122] in other words, to the three worlds, man, and their inter-relation. They therefore indicate the knowledge which is necessary for the ascent to natural *felicitas*.

---

[121] H. P1; Garin, 176: "Quod si satis est confutatum, iam illud creditu facile, sicubi de natura, de totius opificio mundi tractatum ab eo, idest, si qua in parte operis sui velut agri cuiuspiam sint ab eo thesauri defossi omnis verae philosophiae, factum in primis hoc in hac parte, ubi vel ex professo de rerum omnium emanatione a Deo, de gradu, de numero, de ordine partium mundanarum altissime philosophatur."

[122] H. P2; Garin, 196: "procedentium a Deo rerum ordines distributos et explicatam eorum unionem et differentiam foederaque et habitudines".

The concealment of this information in the Genesis narrative is made possible by the "union and difference" of created entities: that is, by the nature of the hierarchy of being which structures them and its principle of mutual containment. The constituent parts of the cosmos, apparently distinct, are in reality related to each other in such a way that they can be said to contain each other. The "ancient fathers", Pico says, were aware of this: not only through their own knowledge, but also through the inspiration of the Holy Spirit "which not only knew all these things, but made them".[123] This double knowledge reflects the two cognitive levels discussed earlier in this chapter: the normal human level of discursive rational thought and the higher level of "inspiration" or direct illumination, characteristic of angels and prophets.[124] Pico contrasts the human mind's requirement for many 'forms' with the angelic mind's requirement for only a few.[125] He connects this concept of 'forms' with words, and uses it to express the uniqueness of Moses's text. Moses, he says, was the foremost of all the ancient fathers.[126] His special ability, as author of the Pentateuch, was to apply the principle of mutual containment to his words. A normal text needs many words to express the material which Moses was able to express in only a few words. It needs, for instance, different words for 'material cause' and 'moon'; but for Moses, the single term *terra* is sufficient. As a result, the complex body of knowledge which represents all that there is to know about man, the three worlds and their mutual connections— and which, furthermore, must be mastered if the philosopher is to be successful in his intellectual ascent—can be encoded in a short text of merely a few sentences. This, Pico argues, is what Moses did in the Genesis narrative. The aim of the *Heptaplus* is to decode this same body of knowledge from Moses's simple words.

---

[123] Ibid., 192: "Nec potuerunt antiqui patres aliis alia figuris decenter repraesentare, nisi occultas, ut ita dixerim, totius naturae et amicitias et affinitates edocti. Alioquin nulla esset ratio cur hoc potius hac imagine, aliud alia quam contra repraesentassent. Sed gnari omnium rerum et acti Spiritu illo, qui haec omnia non solum novit sed fecit, naturas unius mundi, per ea quae illis in reliquis mundis noverant respondere, aptissime figurabant."

[124] See the description of the Holy Spirit as the "greater and truly divine intellect" which illuminates the human intellect, in n. 81 above.

[125] See Ch. 5, nn. 58–59.

[126] H. Pı, Garin 170: "Nam, ut illud omittam quod haec omnia Propheta noster, deo plenus ac caelesti dictante spiritu totius magistro veritatis, excepit, nonne eumdem nobis cum nostrorum, tum suorum, tum gentium denique testimonia prorsus humanae sapientiae doctrinarumque omnium et litterarum consultissimum prodiderunt?"

At the very end of the *Heptaplus* Pico argues that there also exists a yet more extreme level of encoding, where the plan of the whole Genesis narrative is concealed in one single word. I shall discuss this in the following chapter. I shall also look at the structure of the *Heptaplus* as a whole and its connection to the theme of intellectual ascent.

CHAPTER SEVEN

THE BEGINNING AND THE END:
BERESHIT AND THE SABBATH

1. Bereshit: *"Expositio primae dictionis, idest in principio"*

The main body of the *Heptaplus* is complete in itself. Numerically, it fulfils its seven by seven structure; thematically, it completes Pico's exegetical programme and ends with a glance towards the Christian's future possession of the "celestial Jerusalem".[1] The final chapter is not a continuation of what has gone before. It is a new beginning, "something which it seemed should have been expounded in the first place".[2] Pico turns his attention to the first word of the Bible—*bereshit*—translated in the Vulgate as "in principio".

This word had already, by Pico's time, been the subject of considerable commentary in the Jewish and Christian traditions. It was especially brought into the debate over *creatio ex nihilo*.[3] Pico chose a different approach.[4] He also chose "another method".[5] While allegory operates on the plane of the word, the other method adopted here by Pico investigates "the letters themselves, from which the words of the law are made up".[6] Reading on the level of words reveals "nothing but the common and trivial"; but words operate like

---

[1] H. 7.7; Garin, 372: "Qui igitur Spiritu vivunt, ii sunt filii Dei, ii Christi fratres, ii destinati aeternae hereditati, quam mercedem et fidei et bene actae vitae in caelesti Hierusalem feliciter possidebunt."

[2] H. 50; Garin, 374: "Iam ad calcem ventum est operis, septiformi universi contextus expositione decursa. Sed superesse aliquid adhuc cognosco intactum a nobis et indiscussum, quod etiam primo loco exponendum videbatur, idest quid sibi velit prima dictio legis, quae est in principio."

[3] See M. Alexandre, *Le commencement du Livre Genèse I–V: la version grecque de la Septante et sa réception* (Paris: Beauchesne, 1988), 65–71; *In Principio: interprétations des premiers versets de la Genèse* (Paris: Etudes Augustiniennes, 1973).

[4] A frequent Christian interpretation of the opening word of Genesis correlated the *principium* with Christ: see, e.g., Alexandre, *Le commencement du Livre Genèse*, 69–70. Hence Pico's comment, H. 50; Garin, 374, "Nec ... de Dei filio hic sum disputaturus, quod est principium per quod facta sunt omnia (est enim sapientia Patris)".

[5] H. 50; Garin, 374: "per aliam interpretandi rationem". On the veiling of explicit references to kabbalah in the *Heptaplus*, see Ch. 4, section 5.

[6] H. 50; Garin, 374: "[cognitionem] dissimulatam autem et occultatam in litteris ipsis quibus dictiones legis contextae sunt; quo modo, nunc declarabimus".

a "shell" (*cortex*) and can be opened up to reveal a "concealed kernel" (*medulla abdita*) of hidden mysteries.[7] This method—when rightly applied to the entire text of the Pentateuch—reveals "all learning and the secrets of all liberal disciplines".[8] And even when applied merely to the first word of the Bible it reveals "the complete plan of the creation of the world and of all things, uncovered and explained in this one word."[9] In other words, the correct interpretation of the word *bereshit* reveals (schematically) the knowledge which, I argued in the previous chapter, is necessary for man's intellectual ascent.

By selecting and combining letters from the word *bereshit*, Pico derives the following words. (The transliterations are Pico's.)

בראשית	*bereshit*	in principio
אב	*ab*	pater
בבר	*bebar*	in filio / per filium
ראשית	*resith*	principium
שבת	*sciabat*	quies et finis
ברא	*bara*	creavit
ראש	*rosc*	caput
אש	*es*	ignis
שת	*seth*	fundamentum
רב	*rab*	magni
איש	*hisc*	hominis
ברית	*berith*	foedere
תב	*thob*	bono

Placing them in series, and reading them as a single sentence, Pico gives us: "The *father, in / through* the *son*, who is the *beginning* and the *end / rest, created* the *head*, the *fire* and the *foundation* of the *great man*

---

[7] Ibid.: "Sumamus, gratia exempli, primam particulam libri Geneseos, videlicet ab exordio usque ad locum ubi est scriptum 'Et vidit Deus lucem quod esset bonum'. Est tota illa scriptura tribus et centum elementis coagmentata, quae, eo modo disposita quo ibi sunt, dictiones constituunt quas legimus, nihil nisi commune et triviale prae se ferentes. Corticem scilicet conflat hic litterarum ordo, hoc textum, medullae interius abditae latentium mysteriorum."

[8] Ibid., 374–376: "At, vocabulis resolutis, elementa eadem divulsa si capiamus et iuxta regulas, quas ipsi tradunt, quae de eis conflari dictiones possunt rite coagmentemus, futurum dicunt ut elucescant nobis, si simus capaces occlusae sapientiae, mira de rebus multis sapientissima dogmata, et si in tota hoc fiat lege, tum demum ex elementorum hac quae rite statuatur et positione et nexu erui in lucem omnem doctrinam secretaque omnium liberalium disciplinarum."

[9] Ibid., 376: "Igitur praeter spem meam ... inveni ... universam de mundi rerumque omnium creatione rationem in una ea dictione apertam et explicatam."

with a *good pact.*" This single sentence, derived from a single word, summarizes the *Heptaplus* as a whole, with references to the universe (the macrocosm or "great man"), the three worlds (the "head, fire and foundation") and their inter-relationship (the "pact") which is "good" because it unites them all with God.[10]

In itself, the letter combinatory method is not difficult to master, particularly in a language such as Hebrew where vocalization remains implicit. It is worth pointing out that in one instance Pico strayed beyond the letters he was allowed to use and excused himself with a reference to Hebrew grammar which is not entirely accurate.[11] Of the remaining eleven words, seven appear in a passage in the *Liber combinationum,* a Hebrew work on letter combinations translated for Pico by Mithridates. These seven are: *pater, ignis, filius, creavit, foedus, magnus* and *fundamentum.*[12] The question of *how* Pico made this discovery might therefore seem banal: a simple idea, coupled with a fairly small amount of Hebrew, is enough to process the data in the appropriate manner and achieve the desired results. Under these circumstances, finding a direct source for the remaining words might not seem necessary. Pico appears, however, to give the impression that he is not simply jumbling letters, but rather obeying undisclosed "rules".[13] Any instance of textual authority for the words he derives is therefore of interest; and in one particular case it can lead us further into the heart of his hermeneutics.

The derivation of one of the remaining words—*shabbat* (שבת), meaning "sabbath" and translated here by Pico as "quies et finis"— from *bereshit* occurs in another source, previously identified as playing an influential role in Pico's kabbalistic studies: the commentary on the Pentateuch by Menaḥem Recanati. The passage in which Recanati comments upon the word *bereshit* deserves to be quoted

---

[10] Ibid., 378–382.

[11] Pico spells the word *tov* (טב, 'good') wrongly, with a ת rather than a ט, and argues that the change of consonant is "frequentissimum apud Hebraeos" (Garin, 378). It is not: see Wirszubski, *Pico's Encounter,* 258 n. 1. He may, however, have been extrapolating from a remark by Gersonides about the letters *sin* and *samech,* and *alef* and *he* being interchangeable: see Wirszubski, "Pico's Book of Job", 174.

[12] *Liber combinationum,* Vat. Ebr. 190, ff. 60ᵛ–62ᵛ; see Wirszubski, *Pico's Encounter,* 220–221, 258. Wirszubski notes that the author of this book was "a disciple or latter-day follower of Abraham Abulafia (unless he was Abulafia himself)".

[13] H. 50; Garin, 374: "si capiamus et *iuxta regulas, quas ipsi tradunt*"; ibid., 376: "Libuit periclitari in prima operis dictione, quae apud Hebraeos 'Beresit', apud nos 'in principio' legitur, an ego quoque, *usus regulis antiquorum,* eruere in lucem inde cognitu dignum aliquid possem" (my italics).

THE BEGINNING AND THE END: BERESHIT AND THE SABBATH 217

at length. As it is somewhat obscure in places, I shall follow this quotation with a thematic outline. I have therefore labelled the sentences with letters in square brackets for ease of reference.

[A] *Sefer ha-zohar*: Rabbi Yiẓhak said this word *bereshit* is an utterance which contains all the rest of the utterances, and it points to *Hokhmah*, which contains everything. [B] And according to this opinion, the first *sefirah* [i.e., *Keter*] is not signified in this verse at all, for the reason that we pointed at. [C] However, there are those who explain that the tail of the *beth* [ב] in *bereshit* points to it [i.e., to *Keter*]; it appears that this is the opinion of Ramban [i.e., Nahmanides], of blessed memory, who says "and the word is crowned with a crown of *beth* because the *beth* with its tail is an indication of it". [D] And it is the case that in the letters *resh* [ר], *alef* [א], *shin* [ש], *yod* [י] and *tav* [ת] the first three *sefirot* are signified, when you count the letters of the alphabet from ten to ten, and you will get hold of the tens by finding [the letters] *alef, yod* and *resh*, which refer to them, because the *alef* points to the first and the *yod* to the second, and in its end, which belongs to the *yod*, it points to the *alef*. [E] Therefore, it is bent over, this is its attribute of humility, and it has an opening under it to cause the emanation which is emanated from it to pour out. [F] And the *resh* points to [the third *sefirah*] *Bina*, which through its fifty gates causes things to go from potentiality to actuality. [G] And understand its form because it is the essence of the letter *he* and the small dot which is in the middle of it points to the Community of Israel, and this is signified in the verse "Come, let us ascend to the mountain of the Lord" [Isaiah 2.3].

[H] It is also signified in the letter *gimel*, as our rabbis of blessed memory have said in *Sefer ha-bahir*: why does *gimel* have a tail below? He said to them, *gimel* has a head on top and it resembles a canal; just as the canal draws from above and empties out into its lower part, so too *gimel* draws by means of its top and empties by means of its tail, and this is [the explanation of the form of the] *gimel*.[14]

[I] It acts thus: it is emanated from the second [*sefirah*] and its tail underneath points to the fact that it empties into [the fourth *sefirah*] *Ḥesed* and the whole of the structure, and therefore they are called gates, because they are a door which is opened to receive the superabundance of *Hokhmah* and to bring everything out from potentiality to actuality, as it says "counsel is deep waters in the heart of men; a man of understanding [only has] to draw it" [Proverbs 20.5]. The paths, however, are covered, as it is said, "a path birds of prey do not know" [Job 28.7]. Seek the paths of the world.

[J] The remainder of the word *bereshit*, the letters *shin, beth* and *tav*, point to the foundation of the world, which is called *shabbat*.

---

14 See *Bahir*, section 20; ed. and tr. Gottfarstein, 27.

[K] *Sefer ha-zohar*: Rabbi Abba said, everything was completed in twenty-two letters, and they are all contained in that word *bereshit*. [L] *Alef* contains all the letters up to *yod*, which is tenth; *yod* contains all up to *resh*, which is tenth; there remain *shin* and *tav* to be unfolded. That is what is meant by: "This is the book of the generations of man". [M] *Alef* is the secret of the upper crown, which contains all the rest of the crowns, holy of holies, concerning which no one knows its place and no one knows it. [N] *Yod* is the secret of the holy crown which is called *Ḥokhmah*, from whose paths issue forth thirty-two paths to complete everything. [O] *Resh* is the holy crown which points to *Bina* from which the well-springs issue to the fifty gates and this is the completion of all: *alef, yod, resh*. [P] From here onwards Rabbi Eleazar said, Sabbath of God, Holiness of God, everything is contained in this word *bereshit* and through this the upper and lower are completed.[15]

Using a variety of methods, the passage illustrates the process of creation (viewed as emanations through the structure of the *sefirot*) and its relationship to the first word of the Bible, *bereshit*. As an exegesis of this word, it clearly has parallels to the contents of Pico's last chapter, and it illuminates his work with regard to what he does and does not do in his own exegesis. Thematically, it can be summarized as follows:[16]

1. *Bereshit* is an utterance which contains all the rest of the utterances [A, K, P].
2. It points to the second highest of the *sefirot*, *Ḥokhmah*, not to the topmost *sefirah* which is *Keter* [A, B], although some believe that a part (the "tail") of the written letter does point to *Keter* [C].
3. Three of the remaining letters in *bereshit—alef* [א], *yod* [י] and *resh* [ר]—can be taken as signifying the first three *sefirot*, because they represent the first, tenth and twentieth letters of the alphabet respectively [D, L, N, O]. The *alef* signifies *Keter*, which is topmost and most hidden of all the *sefirot* [M].
4. The *yod* refers to the second highest *sefirah*, *Ḥokhmah*, and its shape represents both its humility and its function as a channel for emanation [E]. Thirty-two paths exit from it, representing the ten *sefirot* and the twenty-two letters of the Hebrew alphabet [N].
5. The *resh* refers to the third *sefirah*, *Bina*, which in turn refers to the doctrine of the fifty gates of creation. These fifty gates are

---

[15] See Appendix to Ch. 7 for the Hebrew text.

[16] I shall not endeavour to plumb all the depths of this difficult passage. Its symbolism derives from the *Bahir* and the Zohar; see, apart from these two fundamental texts, the discussions in *The Wisdom of the Zohar*, ed. Lachower and Tishby, II, 549–586; Green, *Guide to the Zohar*, 101–108.

regarded as causing a movement from potentiality to actuality [F, O].

6. The shapes of the letters *he* and *gimel* indicate other aspects of the sefirotic structure. *He* has a dot in it which points to the tenth *sefirah* (*Knesset Israel,* "The Community of Israel") [G]. *Gimel* indicates emanation and acts as an intermediary between the second *sefirah* (*Ḥokhmah*) and the fourth (*Ḥesed*) [H, I].

7. Once the three letters in *bereshit* that signify the three highest *sefirot* are discounted, the remainder of the letters spell שבת (*shabbat,* "sabbath") [J].

This summary can help us to see that there are three interpretative methods at work in this passage:

– Connections between the *sefirot* and the letters of the Hebrew alphabet made with reference to the position of the letters in the alphabet: see point 3.
– Connections between the *sefirot* and the letters of the alphabet made with reference to a letter's shape as reflecting an aspect of the structural configuration of the *sefirot*: see points 2, 4, 6.
– A letter-combinatory reading of the word *shabbat*: see point 7.

In the first two cases, letters are considered outside the context of the words which they make up: they, along with numbers, represent parts of the sefirotic structure. I have previously argued that Pico ignores this structure in the *Heptaplus*.[17] As further evidence of this, we should now note that he also ignores the possibilities for interpretation which this structure offers. Only the following sections of the Recanati passage are relevant to the *Heptaplus*:

> [A] *Sefer ha-zohar*: Rabbi Yiẓhak said this word *bereshit* is an utterance which contains all the rest of the utterances … [J] The remainder of the word *bereshit*, the letters *shin, beth* and *tav,* point to the foundation of the world which is called *shabbat.* [K] *Sefer ha-zohar*: Rabbi Abba said, everything was completed in twenty-two letters and they are all contained in that word *bereshit.* … [P] … Rabbi Eleazar said, Sabbath of God, Holiness of God, everything is contained in this word *bereshit* and through this the upper and lower are completed.

It is unfortunate that the manuscript in which Pico read this text is no longer extant. We cannot, therefore, know precisely the form in which he read it. We can, however, make certain deductions based on the remainder of the translated corpus. Notable in the

---

[17] See Ch. 4, section 5.1; Ch. 5, section 1.2.

first sentence [A] is the word "utterance", representing the Hebrew
ma'amar (מאמר). This is to be distinguished from the common
Hebrew terms for "word" (דבר, שם) in that it refers not to words
or utterances in general but to the ten particular utterances with
which the world was created. This exegesis is ancient. We find it, for
example, in the Mishnah *Avot*, V.1: "The world was created with ten
utterances."[18] Given that there were ten utterances, it was probably
inevitable that later kabbalist interpreters should go on to correlate
them with the ten *sefirot*, insofar as they represent the ten stages of
creation and the movement from potentiality to actuality.

The word *ma'amar* also occurs in the *Bahir*, which was translated
for Pico by Mithridates and is still extant in Ms. Vat. Ebr. 191. Here,
however, we find that Mithridates merely translates it as *verbum*,
thus losing its particular numerical and structural connotations.[19] If
Mithridates was consistent throughout the corpus, then Pico would
merely have read this sentence as "this word *bereshit* is a word which
contains all the rest of the words". The sefirotic implications are
diminished while the verbal implication, of words containing other
words, is strengthened.

The reason behind Pico's decision to abandon the sefirotic
framework (of which he had made effective use in the *Conclusiones*)
must remain a matter for speculation. For our present purpose,
the most important aspect of Recanati's text is that the derivation
of *shabbat* from the letters of *bereshit* occurs in the middle of an
argument stating that *bereshit contains everything*. It is this idea—
not the mere fact of the combinatory technique, which is easily
learned and readily utilized—which underlies the last chapter of
the *Heptaplus*.

One could simply argue that Pico wished to extract the maximum
amount of exegesis from the Genesis narrative as a *tour de force* of
his own ingenuity. No doubt there is some truth in this argument:

---

[18] *Die Mischna: Text, Übersetzung und ausführliche Erklärung*, IV.9, *Avot*, ed. K. Marti
and G. Beer (Giessen: Alfred Töpelmann, 1927), 116: בעשרה מאמרות נברא העולם;
Bereshit Rabbah, 17.1, in *Midrach Rabba: tome I: Genèse Rabba*, tr. Maruani and Cohen-
Arazi, 197; Babylonian Talmud, *Hagigah*, 12a. See also Urbach, *The Sages*, 196–197.

[19] See, e.g., *Bahir*, section 49; ed. and tr. Gottfarstein, 44; Vat. Ebr. 191, f. 293ᵛ.
In a slightly later translation of Recanati's Genesis commentary, by Giles of Viterbo
or an associate, we find that מאמר is again translated as *verbum*: see Paris, Bibliothèque Nationale, Lat. 598. This manuscript is briefly discussed by Wirszubski, *Pico's
Encounter*, 204–208. The parallel passage is ff. 165ʳ⁻ᵛ, beginning "Liber haZohar:
dixit Robi Izhac ut dicitur: brescit [i.e., *bereshit*]: verbum id quod collegit omnia alia
verba ..."

he took a certain delight in ostentatious cleverness. But on the basis of the evidence presented here, I believe that this would be an incomplete explanation. The radical exegetical method which he adopted is the most likely interpretation available to him of the opening pages of Menaḥem Recanati's Genesis commentary, a text which, it has been demonstrated, he read with care and attention.

The second notable feature of this passage is that it has led us to an examination of the symbolism of the sabbath. Recanati quotes the Zohar, in which the sabbath is identified as "the foundation of the world". What is the meaning of the sabbath in the *Heptaplus*?

2. *Structural Role of the Sabbath*

The *Heptaplus* has a definite and determined structure, based on the number seven. Near the end of the first proem, Pico remarks that the reason for this sevenfold structure will be explained in the second proem:

> Why seven expositions have been put forward by us, with what reason they are undertaken, what our plan was, and what necessity has driven us to them, what this altogether new thing might be which we struggle to put forward, we shall make clear in the following chapter. In it, producing an ideal image of the author who wrote most absolutely about this material, that is, the creation of the world, in imitation of nature itself, we shall then try to prove, in reality, in what follows, that our prophet in no way fell short of it, as though it were an archetype.[20]

The second proem offers two such explanations. The first is based on the cosmic structure of the three worlds. There is one exposition for each of the worlds; one exposition for man, who is "a fourth world, in which are also found all the things that are in the other worlds";[21] two further expositions concerning various aspects of the links between

---

[20] H. P1; Garin, 182: "Cur autem septem a nobis allatae expositiones, qua ratione susceptae, quod nostrum consilium et quae necessitas nos ad eas impulerit, quid omnino sit novum hoc quod afferre molimur, sequenti capite palam faciemus. In quo illius, qui de hac materia, idest de mundi creatione, absolutissime ad naturae ipsius aemulationem sit scripturus, ideam pingentes, conabimur tum in sequentibus re comprobare Prophetam nostrum ab illa nihil quasi archetypo decidisse."

[21] H. P2; Garin, 192: "Est autem, praeter tres quos narravimus, quartus alius mundus in quo et ea omnia inveniantur quae sunt in reliquis. Hic ipse est homo ..."

man and the three worlds;[22] and a final exposition corresponding to the sabbath. This last is described in the following terms:

> Just as, after the six days of creation, there followed the sabbath, that is, rest, so, after the orders of things proceeding from God, their distribution, the explanation of their union and their difference, their bonds and their conditions, it is appropriate that as a seventh and (so to speak) sabbatical narration, we should now briefly touch on the *felicitas* of created beings, and of their return to God, … unlocking what Moses, in the present Scripture, very openly hid concerning these matters, so that it may happen that this very explicit prophecy of the advent of Christ, the advancement of the Church and the conversion of the Gentiles is plainly read. So that truly this book, if there is any such, is a book sealed with seven seals, full of all learning and all mysteries.[23]

The second explanation, at the end of the second proem, gives the following justification for the work's structure:

> I have divided the entire discourse into seven books or treatises, so that I might imitate Basil and Augustine, rather than so that the attention of the reader may be refreshed by this frequent division, as if resting. Also, since the expositions are distributed into seven books, and each book is divided into seven chapters, everything corresponds to the seven days of creation. It has likewise been done by us, with very fitting reason, that just as the seventh day in Moses's account is the day of rest, so each of our expositions in its seventh chapter always turns aside towards Christ, who is both the end of the law and our sabbath, our rest, our *felicitas*.[24]

---

[22] Ibid., 194: "Rursus sicut naturae quamquam in se ipsis promiscuae invicem contineantur, discretas tamen proprias sedes et peculiaria quaedam iura sortitae sunt, ita etsi singulis in partibus praesentis operis de quadruplici natura eadem serie litterae disseratur, credendum tamen prima in parte de prima agi natura peculiarius, atque eodem ordine deinceps in reliquis, unde et quintae exoritur expositionis necessitas. Accedit quod, qua ratione haec sunt distincta, quia tamen nulla est multitudo quae non sit una, discordi quadam concordia ligantur et multiformibus nexuum quasi catenis devinciuntur. Quod cum toto etiam opere agere Mosem sit verisimile, ad sextam iam nos interpretationem vel invitos vocat."

[23] Ibid., 196: "quemadmodum sex dierum geneseos sabbatum succedit, idest quies, congruum ut et nos, post procedentium a Deo rerum ordines distributos et explicatam eorum unionem et differentiam foederaque et habitudines, septima iam et sabbataria (ut sic dixerim) enarratione de creaturarum felicitate deque reditu ad Deum, qui per Mosaicam et Christianam legem elongato inde ob peccatum primi parentis homini contigit, aliqua perstringamus, reserantes quae de his in praesenti scriptura Moses apertissime occultavit, ut fiat palam de Christi adventu, de Ecclesiae profectu, de gentium vocatione, expressissimum hic vaticinium legi. Ut sit vere hic liber, si quis alius talis, liber septem signaculis obsignatus, plenus omni doctrina, omnibus mysteriis."

[24] Ibid., 202: "Totam autem expositionem in septem libros sive tractatus partitus sum, potius ut imitarer Basilium et Augustinum quam propterea quod hac crebra distinctione quasi interiungens legentis intentio recreatur. Accedit quod, cum septem

These two explanations overlap without being entirely identical. The crucial element, common to both, is the sabbath. The first explanation, grounded in man, the three worlds and their relationship, appears to be dependent on the idea of the sabbath—as if Pico selected his material so as to attain a sevenfold structure, which was dictated not by the material itself but by his desire to correlate the final exposition with the sabbath. This is not to say that the fifth and sixth expositions are weaker in content than the others; the sixth, in particular, is ingenious. My point is rather that their justification is less fully argued. Pico essentially relies on the numerical structure to perform the task of justification for him: he is drawn to include the sixth exposition, as he says, almost unwillingly.[25] As we have seen, the sixth exposition is a combination of two separate readings of the Genesis narrative, but the numerical structure conceals this. It is, therefore, the requirement of the sevenfold structure which appears to be the formative element, not the matter contained within this structure.

Given the importance of the sabbath as the defining feature of this numerical structure, Pico's alternative explanation that he divided his work into seven books "in imitation of Basil and Augustine" is somewhat unsatisfactory, and especially so, given that neither the hexaemeron of Basil nor the various Genesis commentaries of Augustine are divided into seven sections.

In his own text, meanwhile, the manner in which Pico goes about dealing with the sabbath is unusual and prompts a reflection on the nature of allegorical commentary, namely, that it is composed of two elements: the source text and the allegorical projection of this source into a different frame of reference. For simplicity I shall refer to these as the subject and object of the allegory, respectively. Regarding the *Heptaplus*, in each of the seven expositions, the subject (that is, the biblical account of the six days of creation) remains constant, while the object (the philosophical framework of the exposition) changes. To use an Aristotelian analogy, one could call the former the 'material cause' of the work and the latter the 'final cause'.[26] The subject has a

---

sint expositiones septem libris digestae singulique libri septem capitibus dividantur, septem creationis diebus omnia respondent. Factum item a nobis ratione congruentissima ut quemadmodum septima dies apud Mosem sabbatum est et dies quietis, ita expositio quaelibet nostra septimo semper capite in Christum derivetur, qui et finis est legis et nostrum est sabbatum, nostra quies, nostra felicitas."

[25] Ibid., 194: "Quod cum toto etiam opere agere Mosem sit verisimile, ad sextam iam nos interpretationem *vel invitos* vocat" (my italics).

[26] In Mithridates's translation of Gersonides's commentary on the Song of Songs

sixfold pattern: the biblical text, which Pico expounds and which he quotes at the end of the second proem, finishes with the creation of man on the *sixth* day (Genesis 1.27), stopping short of the sabbath, which occurs in Genesis 2. The object is sevenfold: Pico travels over the same ground seven times, in seven separate expositions. In this aspect, as Pico says, the *Heptaplus* deals with *seven* days of creation. But he never comments directly on the text which introduces the seventh day. The sabbath is the object, not the subject, of the allegory.

This tension is immediately evident on the title-page of the work, where it is announced as "*Hepta*plus, de *septi*formi *sex* dierum geneseos enarratione"—a *seven*fold *hexa*emeron. It is a characteristic feature of the *Heptaplus* that, from the title-page to the final chapter, the reader is persistently presented with the question of form, and this form is equated with the sabbath.

To understand the structure of the *Heptaplus*, therefore, we should try to understand what the sabbath meant to Pico. As we have already seen, he made some of its connotations explicit in the second proem. It represents *quies* and *felicitas*. Associated with these is the "return of created things to God". In this respect it is the antithesis of the beginning of human history, which starts with the Fall and separation from God. Exegetically, it has various other affinities: prophecies of the coming of Christ, the advancement of the Church and the conversion of the Gentiles.

Among the features which distinguish the *Heptaplus* from other Genesis commentaries, one of the most notable is its temporal dimension. Genesis 1, of course, tells the narrative of the beginning of the cosmos, over a period of six days. Pico believed in the literal truth of this event, which he located in the year 3508 BC.[27] Genesis commentaries, when they comment 'literally', engage with questions relating to these original six days. Was there any matter before creation? How was it that light was created on the first day, but the source of light, the sun, not until the fourth day? And so on. In other words, the literal dimension involves comprehending the biblical narrative with reference to *things as they occurred at the time of creation*. But those events of 3508 BC, the "drama of creation", to use Gershom Scholem's phrase,[28] are not *literally* discussed at any point in the *Heptaplus*. There is no reference, for example, to that most

---

we find the term "intentio finalis" used to designate the allegorical purpose of the work: see Ch. 6, n. 117.

[27] H. 7.4; Garin, 350.

[28] Scholem, *Major Trends*, 73.

controversial of Genesis problems, *creatio ex nihilo*. Instead, Pico's allegory projects the creation events out of their literal past time: firstly, into a static, timeless conception of the cosmos *as it is*; and secondly, to the final destiny of man in the future. It is this destiny which Pico envisages when he contemplates the sabbath: not so much God's rest after the act of creation as man's rest after the successful completion of his worldly journey. As such, the sabbath comes to signify redemption, the end of man's existence, and an anticipated final quietus to take place at an unspecified future time. This is the "supernatural" *felicitas* discussed in the previous chapter. The point is made explicit at the beginning of the proem to the seventh exposition:

> If, with the completion of the sixth exposition, we have treated the grade, order and nature of the whole world, it remains that in the seventh treatise—the sabbath, as it were, of our commentary—we should discuss the sabbath of the world and the repose—that is, the *felicitas*—of those created things, the nature of which we drew up in the previous sections. Or, to speak more accurately, it remains that we should listen to Moses, discussing as a true prophet all the things to come.[29]

This reading expands the creation narrative and projects it outside the framework of the literally conceived seven days. It is characteristic of Pico's approach to the cosmos and man as macrocosm and microcosm that he emphasizes this point: the literal sabbath is a microcosm of the allegorical sabbath. This microcosmic approach is also evident in the subdivisions of the work, as we can see from Pico's comment, quoted above, that in the seventh and final chapter of each exposition, he will discuss Christ, "who is the end of the law and our sabbath, our rest and our *felicitas*".[30]

3. *Sabbath, Jubilee and the Gates of Understanding*

The idea that the sabbath represents an eschatological end of time as well as the end of the creation narrative is not absent from the Christian tradition. To mention just one example, it is on this note

---

[29] H. 7.P; Garin, 324: "Si totius mundi gradus ordinem et naturam sexta absoluta expositione quasi sex diebus exagimus, reliquum ut septimo hoc tractatu quasi sabbato nostrae commentationis de sabbato mundi et quiete creaturarum, quarum naturam in superioribus instituimus, idest de earum felicitate tractemus, aut (ut dicam rectius) tractantem Mosem ut verum vatem futurorum omnium audiamus."

[30] See above, n. 24.

that Augustine finishes his *Confessions*.[31] The specific conglomeration of ideas surrounding the sabbath in the *Heptaplus*, however—as macrocosm, ultimate goal of man, redemption and rest—has strong links with the Jewish tradition, particularly in its esoteric form as made available to Pico by Mithridates; and in turn, via these links, it is connected to the ideas of knowledge and hermeneutics discussed in the previous chapter.

The biblical root of all subsequent variations on this theme is to be found in Leviticus 25, where we encounter the institution of the jubilee:

> And thou shalt number seven sabbaths of years unto thee, seven times seven years; and the space of the seven sabbaths of years shall be unto thee forty and nine years. ... And ye shall hallow the fiftieth year, and proclaim liberty throughout all the land unto all the inhabitants thereof: it shall be a jubilee unto you; and ye shall return every man unto his possession, and ye shall return every man unto his family. A jubilee shall that fiftieth year be unto you: ye shall not sow, neither reap that which groweth of itself in it, nor gather the grapes in it of thy vine undressed.[32]

The jubilee is a macrocosm of the sabbath. In the accretion of interpretations which build up around it, just as the sabbath signifies temporary rest, so the jubilee comes to signify ultimate rest, or redemption.

Pico refers to the jubilee in the *Conclusiones*: "He who knows in kabbalah the mystery of the gates of understanding will know the mystery of the great jubilee."[33] There are a number of sources for this comment in the manuscript corpus, of which I shall cite three:

---

[31] Augustine, *Confessions*, ed. J.J. O'Donnell, 3 vols (Oxford: Clarendon Press, 1992), I, 204–205 (867–868): "Domine deus, pacem da nobis (omnia enim praestitisti nobis), pacem quietis, pacem sabbati, pacem sine vespera. Omnis quippe iste ordo pulcherrimus rerum valde bonarum modis suis peractis transiturus est. Et mane quippe in eis factum est et vespera. Dies autem septimus sine vespera est nec habet occasum, quia sanctificasti eum ad permansionem sempiternam, ut id, quod tu post opera tua bona valde, quamvis ea quietus feceris, requievisti septimo die, hoc praeloquatur nobis vox libri tui, quod et nos post opera nostra ideo bona valde, quia tu nobis ea donasti, sabbato vitae aeternae requiescamus in te. Etiam tunc enim sic requiesces in nobis, quemadmodum nunc operaris in nobis, et ita erit illa requies tua per nos, quemadmodum sunt ista opera tua per nos. Tu autem, domine, semper operaris et semper requiescis, nec vides ad tempus nec moveris ad tempus nec quiescis ad tempus, et tamen facis et visiones temporales et ipsa tempora et quietem ex tempore." See O'Donnell's notes on this passage, ibid., III, 418. Cf. Augustine, *De doctrina Christiana*, ed. Green, 140 (III 5.9), discussed by Markus, *Signs and Meanings*, 23.

[32] Leviticus 25.8–11.

[33] *Conclusions*, 96 (Conc. cabalisticae ... sec. secretam doctrinam sapientum He-

1. From the work entitled *Expositio decem numerationum*: "The great sabbath is the great jubilee. It is called great because it is made up of seven lots of seven years; and it is called the fiftieth year. This *numeratio* has fifty gates, which are called gates of understanding, all of which God (holy and blessed) handed down to our learned Moses, except one.[34] Therefore, this *numeratio* is called the jubilee; and it is the great sabbath, because it indicates the law handed down orally, which explains the written law, which is called the mountain of the Lord. This is the secret of the text which says, 'when they have observed the jubilee, then they will climb on the mountain ... '."[35]

2. Joseph Gikatilla, *Portae iustitiae*: "There are forty-nine gates; and forty-nine days of Pentecost up to the act of giving of the law; and forty-nine years up to jubilee, and then to redemption ... as is written in that text, 'redemption will be to him and he will go out in the jubilee', and note well these secrets because they are the principal mysteries and articles of law and of faith."[36] This text is highlighted in the margin.

3. Gikatilla, *Portae iustitiae*: "The letter *nun* is the number fifty, and it is the secret of the fifty gates of understanding, and this place is called *Geulla*, that is, redemption .... If you understand the secret of the jubilee and the secret of the fifty gates of understanding, you will understand this mystery with perfect understanding.

---

braeorum Cabalistarum, 13): "Qui noverit in cabala mysterium portarum intelligentiae, cognoscet mysterium magni Iobelei."

[34] *Numeratio* commonly means 'counting'. I have left it untranslated here because Mithridates uses it to translate the Hebrew term *sefirah*: see Ch. 4, section 5.1.

[35] Vat. Ebr. 191, f. 73^r: "Sabatum magnum est magnus Iobeleus et dicitur magnum quia constat ex septem ebdomadibus annorum; et dicitur annus quinquagesimus; et hec numeratio habet quinquaginta portas que dicuntur porte inteligentie quas omnes deus sanctus et benedictus tradidit moisi doctori nostro preter unam et ideo hec numeratio dicitur iobel et est sabatum magnum quia indicat legem de ore natam, que exponit legem scriptam que vocatur mons domini et hoc est secretum textus dicentis cum secuti fuerint Iubeleum tunc ipsi ascendent in monte".

[36] Chigi A VI 190, f. 15^r: "sunt 49 porte; ⟨et 49 dies⟩ et 49 dies pentecostes ad legis dationem; et 49 anni ad iobeleum et tunc redemptionem dabitis terre; prout scribitur in illo textu redemptio erit ei in iobeleo exibit, et nota bene hec secreta quia sunt misteria principalia et articuli legis et fidei." On the connection of jubilee and Pentecost, see also Pico's commentary on Psalm 50 (*Expositiones in Psalmos*, ed. Raspanti, 236): "Mysterium quinquagesimi numeri celebrari solet in iubileo et in pentecoste satis expresso; ibi enim revertebantur in pristinas facultates et cessabat servitus, in hoc sancti Spiritus copia fundebatur. Magna certe hoc in psalmo nobis exempla praestat David."

... He who understands these secrets understands the text, 'redemption will be to him and in jubilee he will go out'; and you should know that this *numeratio* is called jubilee, and so the text says 'a jubilee is the year of the fiftieth year, indeed it will be the fiftieth to you', which is the secret of the fifty gates of understanding."[37]

I have already argued that the jubilee, as Pico understood it, signifies supernatural *felicitas*, "the repose of created things".[38] In the remainder of this chapter I shall investigate the gates of understanding and their connection with the theme of intellectual ascent.

The doctrine of the gates of understanding appears as early as the Babylonian Talmud (third to fifth century). Here, it is stated that fifty gates of understanding were created in the world, of which forty-nine were revealed to Moses, "because God made him just a little lower than the angels".[39] The gates go on to become a common feature of kabbalistic symbolism; I have already noted an occurrence in the extract from Recanati, discussed above.

So far we have only encountered allusions to these "gates of understanding". A fuller and more detailed discussion of them occurs in another text which was owned by Pico: the commentary on the Pentateuch by Moses ben Naḥman (Nahmanides). The following extract is from the introduction to that work:

Everything that has been said in prophecy about the *Ma'aseh Merkavah* [i.e., Work of the Chariot] and *Ma'aseh Bereshit* [i.e. Work of the Beginning] and what has been transmitted about them to the sages, with the origin of the four forces in the earthly things, the force of the minerals, the force of the plants of the ground, the vital force which gives motion and rational soul, concerning all these Moses, our teacher, was told of their creation, their essence, their powers and their functions, and the disintegration of those among them that perish. Everything is written in the Torah explicitly or by a hint. Our Rabbis long ago said: "Fifty gates of understanding were created in the world, and all of them were opened to Moses save one, as it says: yet thou hast

---

[37] Ibid., ff. 127ᵛ–8ʳ: "nun numero est quinquaginta et est secretum quinquaginta portarum intelligentie et locus hic vocatur Geulla idest redemptio ... ; si vero intellexeris secretum iobelei et secretum quinquaginta portarum intelligentie intelliges hoc misterium intellectu perfecto; et ... / ... qui intelliget hec secreta intelliget illud quod dicit textus redemptio erit ei et in iobeleo exibit; et scias quod haec numeratio vocatur iobeleus et sic textus dicit iobeleus est anus quinquagesimi ani erit vobis equidem quinquagesima quod est secretum quinquaginta portarum intelligentie." This passage is partly transcribed by Wirszubski, *Pico's Encounter*, 32.

[38] See above, n. 29.

[39] Babylonian Talmud, *Rosh Hashana*, 21b; quoting Psalm 8.6.

made him but a little lower than angels."[40] What they mean by saying
that in the creation of the world there are fifty gates of understanding
is that there is, for instance, in regard to the creation of minerals one
gate of understanding revealing their force and origin; and in regard
to the creation of that which springs up from the earth one gate of
understanding; in the creation of the trees one gate; in the creation of
beasts one gate; in the creation of fowl one gate, and so also in regard to
the creation of creeping things and the creation of fish. This series leads
up to the creation of possessors of a speech-giving soul, enabling him to
contemplate the secret of the soul and know her essence and her force
in her palace … . From there Moses rose to the [contemplation of] the
spheres and to the heavens and their hosts. For in every one of these
there is one gate of wisdom which is not like the wisdom of the other.
Their number was traditionally known to them, peace be unto them,
to be fifty less one. It is possible that this gate concerns the knowledge
of the Creator, blessed shall He be, which has not been transmitted to
any created being. Take no regard of their statement that they were
"created" in the world, for this refers to the majority, but one gate was
not created. This number [is] hinted at in the Torah in the counting
of Omer and the counting of the jubilee year, the secret of which I will
disclose when I reach that point, by the grace of the Holy One, blessed
be He.[41]

This passage reiterates what was certainly known to Pico from other
sources: the doctrine of the gates and their connection to the jubilee.
But at the same time it provides a deepening of this doctrine, in
its explicit identification of the gates with a complete taxonomy of
creation, from the lowest entities (minerals) to the highest ("the
heavens and their hosts"). In effect, Nahmanides claims that there
are forty-nine different categories of created thing ("For in every one
of these there is one gate of wisdom which is not like the wisdom of
the other. Their number was traditionally known to them, peace be
unto them, to be fifty less one") and that Moses acquired knowledge
of each of them.

Nahmanides's work was well known in the Jewish tradition. At
least one if not two editions had already been printed before Pico
wrote the *Heptaplus*, and, as I pointed out above, one of these was
in his library.[42] Whether or not we can be confident that Pico read
this text is a problematic question, however. He cites Nahmanides
in the *Heptaplus*, in the passage in the seventh exposition where he

---

[40] Ibid.

[41] Translation from *Commentary of Nahmanides on Genesis*, ed. and tr. Newman,
23–24.

[42] See Ch. 3, nn. 105–106.

compares each of the days of creation to a span of a thousand years.[43]
This idea is indeed to be found in Nahmanides's Pentateuch commentary, in the exegesis of Genesis 2.3.[44] But it is equally possible
(and more demonstrable) that Pico used an intermediate source:
Recanati's own commentary on the Pentateuch.[45] Likewise, the parallel between Nahmanides's Pentateuch commentary and Pico's reference in the first proem to the "Book of Wisdom" attributed to
Solomon does not fully account for Pico's text.[46] Further instances
of Pico's apparent use of Nahmanides have also been shown to have
other sources in authors whom we know he definitely read: Recanati
and Abulafia.[47] There is no evidence that Nahmanides's commentary
was available to Pico in Latin, although a few years later a translation
of it belonged to Giles of Viterbo.[48]

On the other hand, Pico did own this text (although we do not
know when he obtained it), so the possibility that it fell within his
compass of study remains; and if he did read any of it, he is likely
to have read the introduction, from which the extract quoted above
comes. Furthermore, it is precisely in such circumstances as these
that we must bear in mind the possibility of oral transmission via the
Jewish scholars with whom he was in contact.

The status of this extract as an influence on Pico must remain a
matter of speculation. It is useful, however, as an explicit unwrapping
of the various ideas with which we are concerned here. According
to tradition, forty-nine gates of understanding were revealed to
Moses on Mount Sinai. They comprised the knowledge of all created

---

[43] H. 7.4; Garin, 348–350: "Est inter decreta veteris hebraicae disciplinae per
sex dies geneseos sex mille annos mundi sic designari, ut sint quae hic dicuntur
opera primi diei vaticinium eorum quae primo mundi millenario futura erant ut
contingerent; opera item secundi, eorum quae in secundo, et sic deinceps eodem
semper utrobique successionis ordine servato; cui sententiae etiam attestatur, inter
iuniores, Moses Gerundinensis, theologus primae celebritatis apud Hebraeos."

[44] *Commentary of Nahmanides on Genesis*, ed. and tr. Newman, 61–63.

[45] Bacchelli, *Giovanni Pico e Pier Leone da Spoleto*, 93, quoting Biblioteca Universitaria di Genova, A IX 29, ff. 119^v, 120^v: "Indicat dictum sapientum nostrorum dicen-
tium sex milium annorum est mundi terminus ... et sic dicunt quod sic invenies quod
secundum opus cuiuslibet diei particularis huius evenit in singulo millenario mundi
et hoc diffusius exposuit magnus doctor Rabi Moyses filius Naman"; "'Sex diebus
fecit dominus' et non dicit 'in sex'. Docet quod singula dies habet virtutem suam et
dictio ad faciendum indicat adhuc secretum temporis durationis mundi ut exposuit
magnus doctor Rabi Moises Naamanides."

[46] See Ch. 4, n. 200.

[47] Wirszubski, *Pico's Encounter*, 213–215.

[48] F. Secret, "Notes sur les hebraïsants chrétiens de la Renaissance", *Sefarad*, 22
(1962), 107–117.

things—the same knowledge that Pico argued was to be found in the Genesis account. A previously-cited passage from Abulafia, which we can more confidently state that Pico read, also comments on Moses's experience on Mount Sinai and the writing of the Pentateuch:

> Because Moses our master was at the height of perfection and was the chief father in the law and chief and father in prophecy, a higher power flowed into him, in which he was joined to receive the law from God (holy and blessed) similarly in two ways. One is the way of knowing the law according to the understanding of it in the literal sense ... . The second is the way of knowing the law according to the understandings of it together with its secrets and the things hidden ... . These are called the secrets of the law.[49]

This second "way of knowing" is the non-literal way, by which the contents of Moses's prophetic vision—the forty-nine gates, in other words—were incorporated into the Pentateuch. This provides the key to understanding a crucial statement in the second proem where Pico connects Moses's experience on Mount Sinai with the contents of the *Heptaplus*:

> Therefore, if we establish these four worlds [i.e., the three worlds plus man] it is probable that Moses, intending to speak sufficiently of the world, discussed all of them; and given that a writer is portraying nature, if he is knowledgeable about nature (which I believe our writer, if anyone, was), it is probable that his doctrine about these things has been arranged in the same way that God the almighty craftsman arranged them in themselves. Therefore, this writing of Moses has truly portrayed an image of the world, just as we read that he was also commanded on the mountain where he learnt these things to make everything according to the exemplar which he had seen on the mountain.[50]

The "writing of Moses" which "truly" portrays an "image of the world" is the Pentateuch, and especially, in Pico's account, the Genesis narrative. The "exemplar which [Moses] had seen on the mountain" is the forty-nine gates of understanding which comprise knowledge of the entire taxonomy of created things. This knowledge, as we saw in Chapter 6, is the necessary condition for natural (and therefore also

---

[49] See Ch. 4, n. 184.

[50] H. P2; Garin, 192–194: "Quattuor igitur hos mundos si statuamus, credibile est Mosem, dicturum de mundo sufficienter, de his omnibus disseruisse, et cum naturam scriptor effiget, si sit naturae consultus, qualem hunc nostrum si quem alium credimus, credibile doctrinam de illis non aliter dispositam, quam in se ipsis illos omnipotens Deus opifex disposuit, ut sit vere scriptura haec Moseos imago mundi expressa, quemadmodum legimus etiam ei praeceptum in monte ubi haec didicit, ut omnia faceret secundum exemplar quod in monte viderat."

supernatural) *felicitas*. The *Heptaplus* is a guide to how this knowledge is contained in the biblical text. As such it reflects the forty-nine gates in content. It also reflects them in structure, through its seven expositions of seven chapters.

APPENDIX TO CHAPTER 7

I am indebted to Joanna Weinberg for help with the translation and interpretation of this extract. I have followed the text of Menaḥem Recanati, *Commentary on the Torah* (Venice, 1545), ff. 3^{r–v}.

[A] ספר הזוהר אמר רבי יצחק האי דאמר בראשית מאמר הוא מאמר דכליל כל שאר מאמרות חרמז לחכמה שכוללת הכל. [B] והנה לפי זה הדעת הספירה הראשונה לא נרמזה בזה הפסוק כלל מן הטעם שרמזנו. [C] אמנם יש מפרש כי עוקק בי״ת בראשית רומז אליה וכן נראה שהיה דעת הר״מבן ז״ל שאמר והמלה מוכתרת בכתר ב׳ כי הב׳ בעקצה מורה עליה.
[D] ותמצא כי באותיות ראשית נרמזו השלש ספירות הראשונות כשתמנה אותיות ה״א בי״ת מי׳ לי׳ ותאחז העשיריות תמצא א׳ י׳ ר׳ הרומזים להם כי האלף רומזת לראשונה והיו״ד לשנייה ובקצו של יו״ד רומז לאלף [E] ועל כן היא כפופה והיא מדת ענוה ויש לה פתח תחתיה להשפיע השפע הנאצל ממנה [F] והרי״ש רומזת לבינה שבחמשים שעריה מוציאה הדברים מן הכח אל הפועל [G] והתבונן בצורתה כי היא עיקר אות הה״א והנקודה הקטנה שבתוכה רומזת לכנסת ישראל וזה רמוז בפסוק לכו ונעלה אל־הר־יהוה. [H] גם נרמזה באות ג׳ כמו שאמרו רבותינו ז״ל בס״פר הב״היר מפני מה יש לה זנב למטה לגימ״ל אמר להם ראש יש לה לג׳ למעלה ודומה לצנור מה צנור זה שואב מלמעלה ומריק מלמטה אף ג׳ שואבת דרך הראש ומריקה דרך הזנב וזהו גימ״ל. [I] הענין הוא כי היא נאצלת מן השנייה ועוקצה למטה רמז כי היא מריקה אל החסד ולכל הבנין ועל כן נקראו שערים כי הם פתח פתוח לקבל שפע החכמה להוציא כל דבר מן הכח אל הפועל כענין שנאמר מים עמוקים עצה בלב איש ואיש תבונה ידלונה. אמנם הנתיבות הם מכוסים שנאמר: נתיב לא ידעו עיט. ושאלו לנתיבות עולם. [J] נשארו ממלת בראשית אותיות שב״ת הרומזו ליסד עולם הנקראת שבת. [K] ספר הזוהר רבי אבא אמר בשנים ועשרים אתוון אשתלים כולא וכולהו סתימין בהאי מלה דבראשית. [L] א כליל כל אתוון עד יו״ד דאיהי עשיראה יו״ד כליל כל אתוון עד רי״ש דאיהי עשירא׳ אשתארו ש״ת לאתגלגלה בינייהו והיינו דכתיב זה ספר תולדות אדם [M] א׳ רזא דכתרא עילאה דכליל כל שאר כתרין קדש קדישי׳ דלית דידהו אתריה ולית דידע ליה. [N] י׳ רזא דכתרא קדישה דאיקרי חכמה די שבילוהי נפקין תלתין ותרין שבילין לאשלמא כולא. [O] רי״ש כתרא קדישא דרמיזה בבינה דנפקן מייהא דמבועוי דנפקין לחמש׳ תרעין ורא הוא אשלמות דכולא אי״ר. [P] מכאן ולהלא אמר רבי אלעזר שבת ליי׳ קדש ליי׳ וכולא כליל בהאי מלה דבראשית ובהאי אשתכללו עלאין ותתאין.

CONCLUSION

I have concentrated throughout this study on Pico's theory of allegory, on the grounds that it is his theory which allows us to contextualize and interpret the *Heptaplus* in relation to his other works,
the works he read and the ideas circulating at the time. The core of
my argument is that his theory derives from the connection between
epistemology and ontology encountered in the writings of Proclus
and Pseudo-Dionysius. This connection means that the process of
creation—the procession from God of a hierarchical chain of entities, from simplicity to multiplicity, by way of emanation—is matched
by a process of intellection—the reversion along the same chain by
way of knowledge, culminating in union with God.

Given the constraints imposed on the human intellect, its general dependence on sense impressions and matter, and the difficulty
it has in comprehending intelligibles, knowledge of the 'simple' conceptions at the top of this chain is extremely difficult for mankind
to attain; it is, in fact, the type of knowledge associated with angels.
Although this idea has its basis in Neoplatonic texts, it nonetheless resonates in a number of ways with the Aristotelian tradition.
Commentators on Aristotle in late antiquity and the Middle Ages,
while generally affirming the dependence of the rational soul on
sense data and therefore on matter, grappled with ways in which the
human intellect could rise to a comprehension of immaterial, 'separate' substances—and thus to *felicitas*. If it succeeds, they argued, it
becomes equivalent to the angelic intellect, and (in some accounts)
is gifted with prophecy.

In the Jewish tradition—as exemplified not only by such kabbalists as Gikatilla and Nahmanides but also by the philosophical
writings of Maimonides—Moses, author of the Pentateuch, was considered to have attained the highest intellectual level possible for
mankind; hence the efficacy of his books. He had, in other words,
ascended from the level of knowledge of manifold material substances (which make up the lowest strata of creation) to the highest
level of angels, separate intelligences and pure intelligibles. Pico's
project was to find and interpret the ways in which this knowledge
was encoded in Moses's text. As we have seen, he did this by proposing
that whereas average human understanding requires a large number
of forms with which to understand concepts 'discursively', Moses's

text shows how the same concepts can be expressed with very few 'forms', that is, words. As such, it represents the 'simplicity' of forms by which angels (and, by extension, prophets) can understand things normally out of human reach.

Pico's exegesis in the *Heptaplus* is therefore *anagogical*, in the sense of this term as it occurs in the works of Pseudo-Dionysius: that is, it leads the exegete upwards along the hierarchy of being. Although medieval Christian exegetes continued to use this term in the framework of the four senses of Scripture they did not emphasize its relationship with epistemology and the hierarchy of being in the way that the Dionysian corpus did. In Chapter 3 I argued that hermeneutic theory and practice in the fifteenth century was characterized by the continuing dominance of the medieval fourfold scheme. The latter part of the century also witnessed the preliminary steps in the new direction of humanistic philology. As his *Expositiones in Psalmos* show, Pico was able to make effective use of both these methods. Their absence from the *Heptaplus* indicates that it is a fundamentally different type of work, with different goals.

As we saw in Chapter 4, Pico insisted on the social and semiotic separateness of the two levels of meaning in the biblical text. This 'esotericism', as I have called it, was a constant feature of his career, as comparisons with the *Commento, Apologia* and *Oratio* demonstrate. The extent to which the *Heptaplus* is divorced from the literal sense is clearly visible from the fact that, in it, Pico never discusses the events of the Genesis narrative in relation to their own time. His subject is cosmology (the taxonomy of the cosmos) and not cosmogony (the process by which the cosmos came into being). As we have seen, until the last chapter he does not even comment on the words "in principio"; and when he does, he projects them out of their literal temporal frame. In this respect his hermeneutic stance owes more to Neoplatonism and Judaism than to the Christian scholastic and monastic traditions. Although the separation of the literal and non-literal senses was characteristic of Christianity at an early stage of its development, the exegetical trend of the late Middle Ages and Renaissance was towards their closer alignment.

In the light of this historical development the esotericism of the *Heptaplus* appears anachronistic. Equally, the commonplace of some modern scholarship—that Pico's vision of philosophy, emerging from its scholastic cocoon and taking flight on the wings of man's newly fledged dignity, is a potent symbol for the transition from Middle Ages to Renaissance—is not supported by the *Heptaplus*. Pico's only nod to humanism is in the elegant Latin style in which the treatise is written; he neglects the developing tools of textual criticism and appraisal of sources. As an example of biblical commentary, the *Heptaplus* was already outdated before it was composed; and Pico's reliance on the structure of the ontological and epistemological hierarchy anchors the work firmly in pre-Renaissance thinking. On the other hand, his engagement with the problem of *felicitas* and the intellect gives the *Heptaplus* a distinct contemporary resonance.

In choosing to derive a theory of allegory from ideas of epistemological and ontological hierarchy, Pico was pursuing one of his principal interests: intellectual ascent. This is the thread which binds the *Heptaplus* to his previous works. I have tried to show that despite various differences in expression there is a coherent conception of the intellect and its operation underlying his works from the *Commento* to the *Heptaplus*. In outline, this conception is of a soul with two different intellectual faculties: a rational faculty for sense-based discursive reasoning and a faculty of *intelligentia* for direct and non-discursive comprehension of intelligibles. Although the former is the typical mode of thought for the human soul while attached to the body, the latter represents a possible goal and as such leads man to his natural *felicitas*, that is, union with the first mind. Above this there is a higher and essentially inexpressible level of *felicitas* which is union with God. The specific contribution of the *Heptaplus* to this overall theme is to reformulate it in relation to biblical interpretation. I have suggested that a precedent for this, which Pico was aware of, can be found in Gersonides's commentary on the Song of Songs. Gersonides argues that the Song of Songs instructs the reader to approach God via a programme of study and knowledge, culminating in intellectual perfection and *felicitas*. Pico applied this idea to the Genesis narrative, to which, in his view, it was especially appropriate.

He deliberately gave the *Heptaplus* a numerical structure based on the number seven, reflecting the sabbath. His concept of the sabbath was, I argued in Chapter 7, influenced by his readings of kabbalistic texts. These texts give the sabbath a polyvalent significance. As a microcosm, it is related to the beginning of time, representing God's rest after creation and the completion of the procession of entities downwards along the hierarchy of being. As a macrocosm, it represents the jubilee, redemption, the end of time and the reversion of all things back to God: in other words, it represents supernatural *felicitas*. This idea is, in turn, related to the fifty gates of understanding. Moses passed through forty-nine of these in his intellectual ascent on Mount Sinai: that is to say, he acquired knowledge of all created entities. The *Heptaplus*, I have proposed, is a guide to how the knowledge of the forty-nine gates was concealed by Moses in the Genesis narrative. It reflects them not only in content but also in structure.

The theme of intellectual ascent does not only unite the *Heptaplus* with Pico's previous works, but also locates it within an important contemporary philosophical controversy. Responses to this controversy are contained in both the *Commento* and the *Heptaplus*. The earlier work's outspoken attack on the Christian scholastics is replaced with a more discrete and ambiguous formulation in the later work, however. It is possible that this discretion was due to the recent memory of the affair of 1487 and to the papal condemnation which was still hanging over Pico as he wrote the *Heptaplus*. The Barozzi enactment of 1489, which banned discussion of Averroes's idea of the unicity of the intellect, although limited to Padua, provides evidence that epistemology remained a fraught area at this time. It is also possible, however, that Pico's desire was to find the common ground in competing epistemological models rather than to decide between them. In Chapter 5 I argued that he progressively broadened his model of the cosmos in such a way that it could coexist with a variety of schools of thought. Similarly, in Chapter 6 I proposed that, although he took the opportunity to criticize some well-known heterodox positions regarding the intellect, he did not otherwise attempt to arbitrate or resolve the internal disputes which existed on this matter within the Christian tradition or between the Christian Peripatetics and their Muslim and Jewish counterparts. Instead, he sought to defuse the issue by focusing on the higher, 'supernatural', *felicitas* which he saw as transcending philosophies and their differences. This strategy of dividing *felicitas* into two, which was already present (although less fully theorized) in the *Commento* and *Oratio*, is another example of his syncretism.

The links between the *Heptaplus* and the earlier works cast doubt on Gianfrancesco Pico's claim that his uncle underwent a 'conversion'. On the contrary, there is a clear continuity in Pico's writings between the period before his imprisonment and the period after it. The *Commento* and the *Oratio* both make use of allegory as an exegetical tool. The *Heptaplus* takes this interest further, in that it offers a specific *theory* of allegory. This theory provides a structure within which the themes of the other works can be redeveloped.

The reader of the *Heptaplus* may feel that its fecund allegorical landscape has more to do with Pico's verbal dexterity than with his actual 'theory'; or, to put it another way, that the allegorical readings arise naturally from the juxtaposition of the Genesis text and its series of philosophical contexts without requiring or justifying the conceptual framework that Pico wishes to impose on them. There is some truth in this argument and in the final analysis Pico's allegory, and perhaps all allegory, is of so transformable a nature as to elude theoretical imprisonment; the theorist, whether of the fifteenth century or the twenty-first, wrestles with its Protean forms in vain. Whatever its relevance to the actual instances of allegorical reading occurring in the text, however, I have tried to show that Pico's allegorical theory is situated at the centre of his ideas about man, the cosmos, the intellect and the ascent to *felicitas*.

BIBLIOGRAPHY

Works by Giovanni Pico della Mirandola

Heptaplus. Florence, 1489

Le sette sposizioni del S. Giovanni Pico della Mirandola intitolate Heptaplo, sopra i sei giorni del Genesi. Tradotte in lingua toscana da M. Antonio Buonagrazia Canonico di Pescia ... . Pescia, 1555

Opera omnia, I. Basel, 1557, repr. Hildesheim: Olm, 1969

L'Heptaple ... translaté par N. Le Fèvre de la Boderie, in F. Giorgio, *L'harmonie du monde,* tr. Guy Le Fèvre de la Boderie, 829–878. Paris, 1578

De hominis dignitate, Heptaplus, De ente et uno e scritti vari, ed. E. Garin. Florence: Vallecchi, 1942

On the Dignity of Man, On Being and the One, Heptaplus, tr. C.G. Wallis, P.J.W. Miller and D. Carmichael. Indianapolis: Bobbs-Merrill, 1965

Commentary on a Canzone of Benivieni, tr. S. Jayne. New York: Peter Lang, 1984

Expositiones in Psalmos, ed. A. Raspanti. Florence: L.S. Olschki, 1997

900 conclusions philosophiques, cabalistiques et théologiques, ed. B. Schefer. Paris: Allia, 1999

Manuscript Sources

Oxford, Bodleian Library:
    Bodl. 437

Paris, Bibliothèque Nationale:
    Ebr. 270
    Lat. 598
    Lat. 6508

Vatican City, Biblioteca Apostolica Vaticana:
    Chigi A. VI 190
    Ebr. 189
    Ebr. 190
    Ebr. 191
    Lat. 4273

Primary Sources

Alemanno, Joḥanan, *Ḥay ha-'olamim: parte I: la retorica*, ed. F. Lelli. Florence: L.S. Olschki, 1995

Al-Farabi, *De intellectu et intellecto*, in E. Gilson, "Les sources gréco-arabes de l'augustinisme avicennisant", *Archives d'histoire doctrinale et littéraire du Moyen Age*, IV (1929), 108–141

——, *On the Perfect State*, ed. and tr. R. Walzer. Oxford: Clarendon Press, 1985

——, *Obras filosófico-políticas*, ed. R.R. Guerrero. Madrid: Debate, 1992

Ambrose, *Exameron*, in *Opera*, I, Corpus Scriptorum Ecclesiasticorum Latinorum 32, ed. C. Schenkl. Vienna: F. Tempsky, 1897

Apianus, Petrus, *Cosmographicus liber*. Landshut, 1524

Aristotle, *Aristotelis qui ferebantur librorum fragmenta*, ed. V. Rose. Leipzig: B.G. Teubner, 1886

——, *Complete Works*, ed. J. Barnes, 2 vols. Princeton, New Jersey: Princeton University Press, 1984

Augustine, *Confessions*, ed. J.J. O'Donnell, 3 vols. Oxford: Clarendon Press, 1992

——, *De doctrina Christiana*, ed. R.P.H. Green. Oxford: Clarendon Press, 1995

Averroes, *Commentarium magnum in Aristotelis De anima libros*, ed. F.S. Crawford. Cambridge, Massachusetts: The Mediaeval Academy of America, 1953

——, *The Epistle on the Possibility of Conjunction with the Active Intellect by Ibn Rushd with the Commentary of Moses Narboni*, ed. and tr. K.P. Bland. New York: Jewish Theological Seminary of America, 1982

——, *The Book of the Decisive Treatise Determining the Connection between the Law and Wisdom, and Epistle Dedicatory*, ed. and tr. C.E. Butterworth. Provo, Utah: Brigham Young University Press, 2001

——, *La béatitude de l'âme*, ed. and tr. M. Geoffroy and C. Steel. Paris: Vrin, 2001

——, *Commentaria magna in Aristotelem De celo et mundo*, ed. F.J. Carmody and R. Arnzen, 2 vols. Leuven: Peeters, 2003

Avicenna, *Liber De anima*, ed. S. Van Riet, introd. G. Verbeke, 2 vols. Leuven: Editions orientalistes and Leiden: E.J. Brill, 1968–1972

Le Bahir: livre de la clarté, ed. and tr. J. Gottfarstein. Lagrasse: Verdier, 1983

——, *The Book of Bahir: Flavius Mithridates's Latin Translation, the Hebrew Text, and an English Version*, ed. S. Campanini. Turin: Nino Aragno, 2005

Baḥya ben Asher, *Perush ha-Torah*. Naples, 1492

Barbaro, Ermolao, *Epistolae, orationes et carmina*, ed. V. Branca, 2 vols. Florence: Bibliopolis, 1943

Barbaro, Ermolao and Pico della Mirandola, Giovanni, *Filosofia o eloquenza?*, ed. F. Bausi. Naples: Liguori, 1998

Basil, *Homélies sur l'Hexaéméron*, ed. S. Giet. Paris: Editions du Cerf, 1949

Bede, *Libri quatuor in principium Genesis*, in *Opera*, II.1, Corpus Christianorum Series Latina 118A, ed. C.W. Jones. Turnhout: Brepols, 1967

Bellarmine, Robert, *Opera omnia: editio nova iuxta Venetam anni 1721*, 8 vols. Naples, 1872

Biblia latina cum glossa ordinaria, 4 vols. Strasbourg 1480–1481, facsimile repr. Turnhout: Brepols, 1992, introd. K. Froehlich and M.T. Gibson

Biblia sacra iuxta vulgatam versionem, ed. R. Weber, 2 vols. Stuttgart: Württembergische Bibelanstalt, 1969

Calvin, Jean, *Commentarii in secundam Pauli epistolam ad Corinthios*, in his *Opera exegetica*, XV, ed. H. Feld. Geneva: Droz, 1994

Canones et decreta Concilii Tridentini, ed. F. Schulte and A.L. Richter. Leipzig: Typis et sumptibus Bernhardi Tauchnitii, 1853

Clement of Alexandria, *Les stromates*, V, ed. A. Le Boulluec, 2 vols. Paris: Editions du Cerf, 1981

——, *Stromata I–VI*, ed. O. Stählin, L. Früchtel and U. Treu. Berlin: Akademie-Verlag, 1985

——, *Les stromates*, VII, ed. A. Le Boulluec. Paris: Editions du Cerf, 1997

——, *Les stromates*, VI, ed. P. Descourtieux. Paris: Editions du Cerf, 1999

Conciliorum oecumenicorum decreta, ed. J. Alberigo et al. Basel: Herder, 1962

Didymus the Blind, *Sur la Genèse*, ed. P. Nautin, 2 vols. Paris: Editions du Cerf, 1976

Diogenes Laertius, *Vitae philosophorum*, ed. M. Marcovich, 3 vols. Stuttgart: B.G. Teubner and Leipzig: K.G. Saur, 1999–2002

Epistolographi Graeci, ed. R. Hercher. Paris: Ambrosio Firmin Didot, 1873

Erasmus, Desiderius, *Annotationes in Novum Testamentum*. Basel, 1535

——, *Moriae encomium*, in *Opera omnia*, IV.3, ed. C.H. Miller. Amsterdam and Oxford: North-Holland, 1979

——, *Erasmus's Annotations on the New Testament: Acts, Romans, I and II Corinthians*, ed. A. Reeve and M.A. Screech. Leiden: Brill, 1990

——, *Collected Works*, LXIII, ed. D. Baker-Smith. Toronto: University of Toronto Press, 1997

Eusebius, *Histoire ecclésiastique*, ed. G. Bardy, 4 vols. Paris: Editions du Cerf, 1952–1960

——, *La préparation évangélique*, ed. E. des Places et al., 9 vols. Paris: Editions du Cerf, 1974–1987

Ficino, Marsilio, *Opera omnia*, 2 vols. Basel 1576, repr. Turin: Bottega d'Erasmo, 1962

Gaffarel, Jacques, *Codicum cabbalisticorum manuscriptorum quibus est usus Joannes Picus Comes Mirandulus, index*. Paris, 1651

Gersonides, *Commentary on Five Scrolls* (פירוש חמש מגלות). Königsberg, 1860

——, *Commentary on the Song of Songs*, tr. M. Kellner. New Haven, Connecticutt: Yale University Press, 1998

The Great Parchment: Flavius Mithridates's Latin Translation, the Hebrew Text, and an English Version, ed. G. Busi, S.M. Bondoni and S. Campanini. Turin: Nino Aragno, 2004

Gregory the Great, *Morales sur Job: Livres 1+2*, ed. R. Gillet and A. de Gaudemaris. Paris: Editions du Cerf, 1950

——, *Homélies sur Ezéchiel*, ed. C. Morel, 2 vols. Paris: Editions du Cerf, 1986–1990

——, *Commentaire sur le premier livre des Rois*, ed. A. de Vogüé, 5 vols. Paris: Editions du Cerf, 1989–2003

Honorius Augustodunensis, *Expositio in librum Salomonis qui dicitur Cantica Canticorum*. Cologne, c. 1490

Hugh of St Cher, *Postilla super Psalterium*. Venice, 1496

Hugh of St Victor, *Didascalion: De studio legendi*, ed. C.H. Buttimer. Washington DC: Catholic University of America Press, 1939

Iamblichus, *De vita Pythagorica liber*, ed. A. Nauck. St Petersburg: Eggers and S. and I. Glasunof, 1884

Jerome, *Epistolae*, in *Patrologiae latinae cursus completus*, ed. J.-P. Migne, 221 vols, XXII, cols 325–1224. Paris 1844–1864

——, *Tractatus de Psalmo LXXXVI*, in *Opera pars II*, Corpus Christianorum Series Latina 78, ed. G. Morin. Turnhout: Brepols, 1958

——, *Gli uomini illustri*, ed. A. Ceresa-Gastaldo. Florence: Nardini, 1988

Julian the Apostate, *De sole*, in *Oeuvres complètes*, II.2, ed. C. Lacombrade. Paris: Les Belles Lettres, 1964

Kimḥi, David, *Sefer ha-shorashim*. Naples, 1490

——, *The Commentary of Rabbi David Kimhi on the Psalms (42–72)*, ed. S.I. Esterson. Cincinnati, Ohio, 1935

Knorr von Rosenroth, Christian Freiherr, *Kabbala denudata*, 2 vols. Sulzbach 1677–1684, repr. Hildesheim and New York: G. Olms, 1974

Lefèvre d'Etaples, Jacques, *The Prefatory Epistles of Jacques Lefèvre d'Etaples and Related Texts*, ed. E.F. Rice. New York: Columbia University Press, 1972

Liber de causis, ed. A. Pattin, *Tijdschrift voor Filosofie*, 28 (1966), 90–203

Ludolphus de Saxonia, *Expositio in Psalterium*. Speyer, 1491

Luther, Martin, *Werke*, Abt. 2, *Tischreden*, 6 vols. Weimar: H. Böhlau, 1912–1920

Macrobius, *Commentary on the Dream of Scipio by Macrobius*, tr. W.H. Stahl. New York: Columbia University Press, 1952, repr. 1990

——, *Commentarii in Somnium Scipionis*, ed. L. Scarpa. Padua: Liviana 1981

Maimonides, Moses, *Dux seu Director dubitantium aut perplexorum …* . Paris, 1520

——, *The Guide of the Perplexed*, tr. S. Pines. Chicago, Illinois: University of Chicago Press, 1963

Manetti, Gianozzo, *Apologeticus*, ed. A. de Petris. Rome: Edizioni di Storia e Letteratura, 1981

Melanchthon, Philipp, *Elementa rhetorices*, in *Opera omnia*, ed. C. Bretchschneider, XIII. Berlin: C.A. Schwetschke et Filium, 1846

Midrach Rabba: tome I: Genèse Rabba, tr. B. Maruani and A. Cohen-Arazi, introd. and notes B. Maruani. Lagrasse: Verdier, 1987

Die Mischna: Text, Übersetzung und ausführliche Erklärung, IV.9, *Avot*, ed. K. Marti and G. Beer. Giessen: Alfred Töpelmann, 1927

Mithridates, Flavius, *Sermo de passione Domini*, ed. C. Wirszubski. Jerusalem: Israel Academy of Sciences and Humanities, 1963

Nahmanides, *The Commentary of Nahmanides on Genesis, Chapters 1–6: Introduction, Critical Text, Translation and Notes*, ed. and tr. J. Newman. Leiden: E.J. Brill, 1960

Nicholas of Lyra, *Postilla super totam Bibliam*, 4 vols. Strasbourg, 1492, repr. Frankfurt am Main: Minerva, 1971

——, *Prologus secundus* to *Glossa ordinaria*, in *Patrologiae latinae cursus completus*, ed. J.-P. Migne, 221 vols, CXIII, cols 30–34. Paris, 1844–1864

——, *Prologus in Moralitates Bibliorum*, in *Patrologiae latinae cursus completus*, ed. J.-P. Migne, 221 vols, CXIII, cols 33–36. Paris, 1844–1864

Oracles chaldaiques avec un choix de commentaires anciens, ed. E. des Places. Paris: Les Belles Lettres, 1971

Oresme, Nicole, *Livre du ciel et du monde*, ed. A.D. Menut and A.J. Denomy. Madison, Wisconsin: University of Wisconsin Press, 1968

Origen, *Selecta in Genesim*, in *Patrologiae graecae cursus completus*, ed. J.-P. Migne, 162 vols, XII, cols 91–146. Paris 1857–1866

——, *Contra Celsum*, tr. H. Chadwick. Cambridge: CUP, 1965

——, *Contre Celse*, ed. M. Borret, 5 vols. Paris: Editions du Cerf, 1967–1976

——, *Homélies sur la Genèse*, ed. L. Doutreleau. Paris: Editions du Cerf, 1976

——, *Traité des principes*, ed. H. Crouzel and M. Simonetti, 3 vols. Paris: Editions du Cerf, 1978–1984

Philo, *De vita contemplativa*, in *Oeuvres*, XXIX, ed. F. Daumas. Paris: Editions du Cerf, 1963

——, *De vita Mosis*, in *Oeuvres*, XXII, ed. and tr. R. Arnaldez et al. Paris: Editions du Cerf, 1967

——, *On the Creation of the Cosmos according to Moses*, tr. D.T. Runia. Leiden and Boston, Massachusetts: Brill, 2001

Pico della Mirandola, Gianfrancesco, *Opera omnia*, II. Basel, 1573, repr. Hildesheim: Olm, 1969

——, tr. More, Sir Thomas, *Giovanni Pico della Mirandola: His Life by His Nephew Giovanni Francesco Pico, etc.*, ed. J.M. Rigg. London: D. Nutt, 1890

——, *Ioannis Pici Mirandulae viri omni disciplinarum genere consumatissimi vita per Ioannem Franciscum illustris principis Galeotti Pici filium conscripta*, ed. B. Andreolli. Modena: Aedes Muratoriana, 1994

Plutarch, *De Iside et Osiride*, ed. and tr. J.G. Griffiths. Cardiff: University of Wales Press, 1970

Porphyry, *Lettre à Marcella*, ed. and tr. E. des Places. Paris: Les Belles Lettres, 1982

——, *La vie de Plotin*, ed. L. Brisson et al., 2 vols, Paris: J. Vrin, 1982–1992

Proclus, *In Platonis Timaeum commentaria*, ed. E. Diehl, 3 vols. Leipzig: B.G. Teubner, 1903–1906

——, *Elements of Theology*, ed. and tr. E.R. Dodds. Oxford: Clarendon Press, 1933, repr. 1964

——, *Elementatio theologica*, tr. William of Moerbeke, ed. H. Boese, Leuven: University Press, 1987

Pseudo-Dionysius the Areopagite, *Dionysiaca*, ed. P. Chevallier, 2 vols. Paris: Desclée, de Brower et Cie., 1937–1950

——, *Complete Works*, tr. and ed. C. Luibheid et al. New York: Paulist Press, 1987

——, *Corpus Dionysiacum*, I, ed. B.R. Suchla. Berlin: De Gruyter, 1990; II, ed. G. Heil and A.M. Ritter. Berlin: De Gruyter, 1991

Rashi, *Rashi's Commentary on Psalms 1–89 (Books I–III) with English Translation and Notes*, ed. M.I. Gruber. Atlanta, Georgia: Scholars Press, 1998

Recanati, Menaḥem, *Commentary on the Torah* (פירוש על תורה). Venice, 1545

Remigius of Auxerre, *Expositio super Genesim*, ed. B. v-N. Edwards. Turnhout: Brepols, 1999

Schedel, Hartmann, *Liber chronicarum*. Nuremberg, 1493

Simplicius, *In Aristotelis Physicorum libros quattuor priores commentaria*, ed. H. Diels, Commentaria in Aristotelem Graeca, IX. Berlin: Reimer, 1882

Syrianus, *Commentaria in Metaphysica*, ed. G. Kroll, Commentaria in Aristotelem Graeca, VI. Berlin: Reimer, 1892

Tempier, Etienne, *La condemnation Parisienne de 1277*, ed. D. Piché. Paris: Vrin, 1999

Themistius, *Commentaire sur le traité de l'âme d'Aristote: traduction de Guillaume de Moerbeke*, ed. G. Verbeke. Leiden, E.J. Brill, 1973

——, *On Aristotle's On the Soul*, tr. R.B. Todd. Ithaca, New York: Cornell University Press, 1996

Thomas Aquinas, *In librum beati Dionysii De divinis nominibus expositio*, ed. C. Pera. Rome: Marietti, 1950

——, *Super Librum de causis expositio*, ed. H.D. Saffrey. Fribourg: Société Philosophique and Leuven: E. Nauwelaerts, 1954

——, *Tractatus de unitate intellectus contra Averroistas*, ed. L.W. Keeler. Rome: apud aedes Pont. universitatis gregoriannae, 1957

Tyndale, William, *The Obedience of a Christian Man*. Marlborough 1528, repr. Menston: Scolar Press, 1970

Valla, Lorenzo, *Adnotationes in Novum Testamentum*, ed. D. Erasmus. Paris, 1505

——, *Opera omnia*, 2 vols. Basel, 1540, repr. Turin, Bottega d'Erasmo, 1962

——, *Collatio Novi Testamenti*, ed. A. Perosa. Florence: Sansoni, 1970

Varro, *De lingua latina*, ed. G. Goetz and F. Schoell. Leipzig: B.G. Teubner, 1910

Vetus testamentum multiplici lingua nunc primo impressum. Et imprimis Pentateuchus Hebraico Greco atque Chaldaico idiomate. Adiuncta unicuique sua latina interpretatione, 6 vols. Alcalá de Henares, 1514–1517

The Wisdom of the Zohar: An Anthology of Texts, ed. I. Tishby, F. Lachower and tr. D. Goldstein, 3 vols. Oxford: OUP, 1989, repr. 1994

The Zohar, tr. D.C. Matt, I. Stanford, California: Stanford University Press, 2004

Zwingli, Huldreich, *Farrago annotationum in Genesim*. Zurich, 1527

Secondary Sources

Alexandre, M., *Le commencement du Livre Genèse I–V: la version grecque de la Septante et sa réception*. Paris: Beauchesne, 1988

Alcalay, R., *The Complete Hebrew-English Dictionary*. Jerusalem: Massadah, 1963

Altmann, A., "Ibn Bajja on Man's Ultimate Felicity", in his *Studies in Religious Philosophy and Mysticism*, 73–107. Ithaca, New York: Cornell University Press, 1969

Bacchelli, F., *Giovanni Pico e Pier Leone da Spoleto: tra filosofia dell'amore e tradizione cabalistica*. Florence: L.S. Olschki, 2001

Bandini, A.M., *Dei princìpi e progressi della Real Biblioteca Mediceo Laurenziana*, ed. R. Pintaudi, M. Tesi and A.R. Fantoni. Florence: Gonnelli, 1990

Bentley, J.H., *Humanists and Holy Writ: New Testament Scholarship in the Renaissance*. Princeton, New Jersey: Princeton University Press, 1983

Berlin, M., "A Curious Ibn Ezra Manuscript", *Jewish Quarterly Review*, 8 (1896), 711–714

Berti, D., "Intorno a Giovanni Pico della Mirandola: cenni e documenti inediti", *Rivista contemporanea*, 16 (1859), 7–56

Bland, K.P., "Elijah del Medigo's Averroist Response to the Kabbalahs of Fifteenth-Century Jewry and Pico della Mirandola", *The Journal of Jewish Thought and Philosophy*, 1 (1991), 23–53

——, "Elijah del Medigo, Unicity of the Intellect and Immortality", *Proceedings of the American Academy for Jewish Research*, 61 (1995), 1–22

Blau, J.L., *The Christian Interpretation of the Cabala in the Renaissance*. New York: Columbia University Press, 1944

Bollansée, J., *Hermippos of Smyrna and his Biographical Writings: A Reappraisal*. Leuven: Peeters, 1999

Botley, P.A., "Parallel Texts: Bruni, Manetti and Erasmus on the Art and Purpose of Translation". PhD Dissertation, Cambridge University, 1999

The Cambridge History of Later Medieval Philosophy, ed. N. Kretzmann et al. Cambridge: CUP, 1982

The Cambridge History of the Bible, II; *The West from the Fathers to the Reformation*, ed. G.W.H. Lampe. Cambridge: CUP, 1969, repr. 1980

Camporeale, S.I., *Lorenzo Valla: umanesimo e teologia*. Florence: Istituto Nazionale di Studi sul Rinascimento, 1972

Cassirer, E., *The Individual and the Cosmos in Renaissance Philosophy*, tr. M. Domandi. New York: Harper and Row, 1963

Cattaneo, A., "La mappamunda di Fra Mauro Camaldolese, Venezia, 1450". PhD Dissertation, European University Institute, Florence, 2005

Clark, E.A., *Clement's Use of Aristotle: The Aristotelian Contribution to Clement of Alexandria's Refutation of Gnosticism*. New York: E. Mellen Press, 1977

Copenhaver, B.P., "The Secret of Pico's Oration: Cabala and Renaissance Philosophy", *Midwest Studies in Philosophy*, 26 (2002), 56–81

Cranz, F.E., "Alexander Aphrodisiensis", in *Catalogus translationum et commentariorum: Medieval and Renaissance Latin Translations and Commentaries*, ed. P.O. Kristeller et al., 8 vols, I, 77–135. Washington DC: Catholic University of America Press, 1960–2003

Crouzel, H., *Une controverse sur Origène à la Renaisance: Jean Pic de la Mirandole et Pierre Garcia*. Paris: J. Vrin, 1977

——, *Origen*, tr. A.S. Worrall. Edinburgh: T. and T. Clark, 1989

Dales, R.C., *The Problem of the Rational Soul in the Thirteenth Century*. Leiden and New York: E.J. Brill, 1995

Dan, J., *Jewish Mysticism: The Modern Period*. Northvale, New Jersey: Jason Aronson, 1999

D'Ancona Costa, C., *Recherches sur le Liber de causis*. Paris: J. Vrin, 1995

Daniélou, J., "Les traditions secrètes des Apôtres", *Eranos Jahrbuch* 31 (1962), 199–214

Davidson, H.A., "Averrois tractatus De animae beatitudine", in *A Straight Path: Studies in Medieval Philosophy and Culture. Essays in Honour of Arthur Hyman*, ed. R. Link-Salinger, 57–73. Washington DC: Catholic University of America Press, 1988

——, *Alfarabi, Avicenna, and Averroes, on Intellect: Their Cosmologies, Theories of the Active Intellect, and Theories of Human Intellect*. Oxford: OUP, 1992

De Lubac, H., *Exégèse médiévale: les quatres sens de l'Ecriture*, 4 vols. Paris: Aubier, 1959

Devreesse, R., *Les anciens commentateurs grecs de l'octateuque et des rois (fragments tirés des chaînes)*. Vatican City, 1959

——, *Le fonds grec da la bibliothèque vaticane des origines à Paul V*. Vatican City: Biblioteca Apostolica Vaticana, 1965

Dondi dall'Orologio, F.S., *Dissertazione nona sopra l'istoria ecclesiastica padovana*. Padua, 1817

Dorez, L. and Thuasne, L., *Pic de la Mirandole en France (1485–1488)*. Paris: E. Leroux, 1897

Dorival, G., "Des commentaires de l'Ecriture aux chaînes", in *Le monde grec ancien et la Bible*, ed. C. Mondésert, 361–383. Paris: Beauchesne, 1984

Dukas, J., *Recherches sur l'histoire littéraire du quinzième siècle*, Paris: L. Techener, 1876

Encyclopaedia Judaica, ed. C. Roth, 16 vols. Jerusalem: Keter, 1972

Engen, J. van, "Studying Scripture in the Early University", in *Neue Richtungen in der hoch- und spätmittelalterlichen Bibelexegese*, ed. R.E. Lerner and E. Müller-Luckner, 17–38. Munich: Oldenbourg, 1996

Evans, G.R., *The Language and Logic of the Bible: The Road to Reformation*. Cambridge: CUP, 1985

Farmer, S.A., *Syncretism in the West: Pico's 900 Theses (1486): The Evolution of Traditional Religious and Philosophical Systems*. Tempe, Arizona: Medieval and Renaissance Texts and Studies, 1998

Fearghail, F. Ó., "Philo and the Fathers: The Letter and the Spirit", in *Scriptural Interpretation in the Fathers*, ed. T. Finan and V. Twomey, 39–59. Dublin: Four Courts Press, 1995

Foerster, W., *Gnosis: A Selection of Gnostic Texts*, ed. R. McL. Wilson, 2 vols. Oxford: Clarendon Press, 1972

Fortin, E.L., "Clement of Alexandria and the Esoteric Tradition", in *Studia Patristica IX: Papers presented to the Fourth International Conference on Patristic Studies held at Christ Church, Oxford, 1963, Part III*, ed. F.L. Cross, 41–56. Berlin: Akademie-Verlag, 1966

Froehlich, K., "Johannes Trithemius on the Fourfold Sense of Scripture: The *Tractatus de Investigatione Sacrae Scripturae* (1486)", in *Biblical Interpretation in the Era of the Reformation: Essays Presented to David C. Steinmetz in Honor of His Sixtieth Birthday*, ed. R.A. Muller and J.L. Thompson, 23–60. Grand Rapids, Michigan: W.B. Eerdmans, 1996

——, "The Fate of the *Glossa Ordinaria* in the Sixteenth Century", in *Die Patristik in der Bibelexegese des 16. Jahrhunderts*, ed. D.C. Steinmetz, 19–47. Wiesbaden: Harrassowitz, 1999

Fryde, E.B., *Greek Manuscripts in the Private Library of the Medici*, 2 vols. Aberystwyth: National Library of Wales, 1996

Garin, E., *Giovanni Pico della Mirandola: vita e dottrina*. Florence: F. Le Monier, 1937

Geffen, M.D., "Faith and Reason in Elijah del Medigo's *Behinat ha-Dat* and the Philosophic Backgrounds of the Work". PhD Dissertation, Columbia University, 1970

——, "Insights into the Life and Thought of Elijah Medigo Based on his Published and Unpublished Works", *Proceedings of the American Academy for Jewish Research*, 41–42 (1973–1974), 69–86

Geoffroy, M., "La tradition arabe du Περὶ voῦ d'Alexandre d'Aphrodise et les origines de la théorie farabienne des quatre degrés de l'intellect", in *Aristotele e Alessandro di Aphrodisia nella tradizione araba*, ed. C. D'Ancona and G. Serra, 191–231. Padua: Il Poligrafo, 2002

Gilson, E., "L'affaire de l'immortalité de l'âme à Venise au debut de XVIe siècle", in *Umanesimo europeo e umanesimo veneziano*, ed. V. Branca, 31–61. Florence: Sansoni, 1964

Grafton, A., "Giovanni Pico della Mirandola: Trials and Triumphs of an Omnivore", in his *Commerce with the Classics: Ancient Books and Renaissance Readers*, 93–134. Ann Arbor, Michigan: University of Michigan Press, 1997

Grant, E., *Planets, Stars and Orbs: The Medieval Cosmos, 1200–1687*. Cambridge: CUP 1994

Grant, R.M., *Eusebius as Church Historian*. Oxford: Clarendon Press, 1980

Green, A., *A Guide to the Zohar*. Stanford, California: Stanford University Press, 2004

Gribomont, J., "Les succès littéraires des Pères grecs et les problèmes d'histoire des textes", *Sacris Erudiri*, 22 (1974–1975), 23–49

Hailperin, H., *Rashi and the Christian Scholars*. Pittsburgh, Pennsylvania: University of Pittsburgh Press, 1963

Halivni, D.W., *Peshat and Derash: Plain and Applied Meaning in Rabbinic Exegesis*. Oxford: OUP, 1991

Hankins, J., "Cosimo de' Medici and the 'Platonic Academy'", *Journal of the Warburg and Courtauld Institutes*, 53 (1990), 144–162

——, *Plato in the Italian Renaissance*, 2 vols. Leiden and New York: E.J. Brill, 1990

——, "The Myth of the Platonic Academy of Florence", *Renaissance Quarterly*, 44 (1991), 429–475

Hardie, P.R., "Humanist Exegesis of Poetry in Fifteenth-Century Italy and the Medieval Tradition of Commentary". M.Phil Dissertation, Warburg Institute, University of London, 1976

Harr Romeny, R.B. ter, "Eusebius of Emesa's Commentary on Genesis and the Origins of the Antiochene School", in *The Book of Genesis in Jewish and Oriental Christian Interpretation: A Collection of Essays*, ed. J. Frishman and L. van Rompay, 125–142. Leuven: Peeters, 1997

Hasse, D.N., *Avicenna's De anima in the Latin West: The Formation of a Peripatetic Philosophy of the Soul, 1160–1300*. London: Warburg Institute, 2000

Heath, M.J., "Allegory, Rhetoric and Spirituality: Erasmus's Early Psalm Commentaries", in *Acta Conventus Neo-Latini Torontonensis: Proceedings of the Seventh International Congress of Neo-Latin Studies*, ed. A. Dalzell, C. Fantazzi and R.J. Schoeck, 363–370. Binghamton, New York: Medieval and Renaissance Texts and Studies, 1991

Heide, A. van der, "Midrash and Exegesis", in *The Book of Genesis in Jewish and Oriental Christian Interpretation: A Collection of Essays*, ed. J. Frishman and L. van Rompay, 43–56. Leuven: Peeters, 1997

Hoek, A. van den, *Clement of Alexandria and his Use of Philo in the Stromateis: An Early Christian Reshaping of a Jewish Model*. Leiden and New York: E.J. Brill, 1988

Idel, M., "The Study Program of R. Jochanan Alemanno", *Tarbiz*, 48 (1979–1980), 303–331 (in Hebrew)

——, "The Magical and Neoplatonic Interpretation of the Kabbalah in the Renaissance", in *Jewish Thought in the Sixteenth Century*, ed. B.D. Cooperman, 186–242. Cambridge, Massachusetts: Harvard University Centre for Jewish Studies, 1983

——, *Kabbalah: New Perspectives*. New Haven: Yale University Press, 1988

——, *Language, Torah and Hermeneutics in Abraham Abulafia*, tr. M. Kallus. Albany, New York: State University of New York Press, 1989

——, "Jewish Mystical Thought in the Florence of Lorenzo de' Medici", in *La cultura ebraica all'epoca di Lorenzo il Magnifico*, ed. D.L. Bemporad and I. Zatelli, 17–26. Florence: L.S. Olschki, 1998

In Principio: interprétations des premiers versets de la Genèse. Paris: Etudes Augustiniennes, 1973

Ivry, A.L., "Averroes's Three Commentaries on *De Anima*", in *Averroes and the Aristotelian Tradition: Sources, Constitution and Reception of the Philosophy of Ibn Rushd (1126–1198): Proceedings of the Fourth Symposium Averroicum (Cologne, 1996)*, ed. G. Endress and J.A. Aertsen, 199–216. Leiden and Boston, Massachusetts: Brill, 1999

Jastrow, M., *Dictionary of the Targumim, Talmud Babli and Yerushalmi, and the Midrashic Literature*. New York: Judaica Press, 1996

Jensen, K., "Printing the Bible in the Fifteenth Century", in *Incunabula and their Readers: Printing, Selling and Using Books in the Fifteenth Century*, ed. K. Jensen, 115–138. London: British Library, 2003

Kibre, P., *The Library of Pico della Mirandola*. New York: Columbia University Press, 1936

Klein-Braslavy, S., "The Philosophical Exegesis", in *Hebrew Bible, Old Testament: the History of its Interpretation, I: From the Beginnings to the Middle Ages (until 1300). Part 2: The Middle Ages*, ed. C. Brekelmans, M. Haran, M. Saebo, 302–320. Göttingen: Vandenhoeck and Ruprecht, 2000

Klepper, D.C., "Nicholas of Lyra and Franciscan Interest in Hebrew Scholarship", in *Nicholas of Lyra: The Senses of Scripture*, ed. P.D.W. Krey and L. Smith, 289–311. Leiden: Brill, 2000

Klibansky, R., Panofsky, E. and Saxl, F., *Saturn and Melancholy: Studies in the History of Natural Philosophy, Religion and Art*. London: Nelson, 1964

Kluxen, W., "Literargeschichtliches zum lateinischen Moses Maimonides", *Recherches de théologie ancienne et médiévale*, 21 (1954), 23–54

Kofsky, A., *Eusebius of Caesarea against Paganism*. Leiden 2000

Kristeller, P.O., "Giovanni Pico della Mirandola and his Sources", in *L'opera*

*e il pensiero di Giovanni Pico della Mirandola nella storia dell'umanesimo:
convegno internazionale, Mirandola*, 2 vols, I, 35–142. Florence: Nella Sede
dell'Istituto, 1965

Kugel, J.L., and Greer, R.A., *Early Biblical Interpretation*. Philadelphia, Pennsylvania: Westminster Press, 1986

Lamberton, R., *Homer the Theologian: Neoplatonist Allegorical Reading and the
Growth of the Epic Tradition*. Berkeley, Los Angeles: University of California
Press, 1986

Langermann, T., "The True Perplexity: The *Guide of the Perplexed*, Part II,
Ch. 24", in *Perspectives on Maimonides*, ed. J.L. Kraemer, 159–174. Oxford:
OUP, 1991

Lelli, F., "Pico tra filosofia ebraica e 'qabbala'", in *Pico, Poliziano e l'umanesimo
di fine Quattrocento*, ed. P. Viti, 193–223. Florence: L.S. Olschki, 1994

Leslie, A.M., "The Song of Solomon's Ascents by Yohanan Alemanno: Love
and Human Perfection according to a Jewish Colleague of Giovanni
Pico della Mirandola". MA Dissertation, University of California, Berkeley,
1966

Lévêque, P., *Aurea catena Homeri: une étude sur l'allégorie grecque*. Paris: Les
Belles Lettres, 1959

Lilla, S.R.C., *Clement of Alexandria: A Study in Christian Platonism and Gnosticism*. Oxford: OUP, 1971

Lloyd, A.C., *The Anatomy of Neoplatonism*. Oxford: Clarendon Press, 1990

Mahoney, E.P., "Nicoletto Vernia on the Soul and Immortality", in *Philosophy
and Humanism: Renaissance Essays in Honor of Paul Oskar Kristeller*, ed.
E.P. Mahoney, 144–163. Leiden: E.J. Brill, 1976

——, "Metaphysical Foundations of the Hierarchy of Being According to
Some Late-Medieval and Renaissance Philosophers", in *Philosophies of
Existence*, ed. P. Morewedge, 165–257. New York: Fordham University
Press, 1982

——, "Giovanni Pico della Mirandola and Elia Del Medigo, Nicoletto
Vernia and Agostino Nifo", in *Giovanni Pico della Mirandola: convegno
internazionale di studi nel cinquecentesimo anniversario della morte (1494–
1994)*, ed. G.C. Garfagnini, 2 vols, I, 127–156. Florence: L.S. Olschki,
1997

Margolin, J.-C., "Sur la conception humaniste du 'barbare': à propos de la
controverse épistolaire entre Pic de la Mirandola et Ermolao Barbaro",
in *Una famiglia veneziana nella storia: I Barbaro*, Atti del convegno di studi
in occasione del quinto centenario della morte dell'umanista Ermolao,
Venezia ... 1993, ed. M. Marangoni and M. Pastore Stocchi, 235–276.
Venice: Istituto Veneto di Scienze, 1996

Markus, R.A., *Signs and Meanings: World and Text in Ancient Christianity*.
Liverpool: Liverpool University Press, 1996

——, *Gregory the Great and his World*. Cambridge: CUP, 1997

McLaughlin, M.L., *Literary Imitation in the Italian Renaissance: The Theory and
Practice of Literary Imitation in Italy from Dante to Bembo*. Oxford: Clarendon
Press, 1995

Mercati, G., *Codici Latini Pico Grimani Pio*. Vatican City: Biblioteca Apostolica
Vaticana, 1938

Les méthodes de travail de Gersonide et le maniement du savoir chez les scolastiques, ed. C. Sirat, S. Klein-Braslavy and O. Weijers. Paris, 2003

Minio-Paluello, L., "Le texte du 'De anima' d'Aristote: La tradition latine avant 1500", in *Autour d'Aristote: Recueil d'études ... offert à Monseigneur A. Mansion*, 217–243. Leuven: Publications Universitaires de Louvain, 1955

Minnis, A.J. and Scott, A.B., with Wallace, D., *Medieval Literary Theory and Criticism c. 1100 – c. 1375*. Oxford: OUP, 1988

Monfasani, J., "Pseudo-Dionysius the Areopagite in Mid-Quatrocento Rome", in *Supplementum Festivum: Studies in Honor of Paul Oskar Kristeller*, ed. J. Hankins, J. Monfasani and F. Purnell Jr, 189–219. Binghamton, New York: Medieval and Renaissance Texts and Studies, 1987

Müntz, E. and Fabre, P., *La bibliothèque du Vatican au XVe siècle d'après des documents inédits*. Paris: E. Thorin, 1887

Nardi, B., "La mistica averroistica e Pico della Mirandola", in his *Saggi sull'aristotelismo padovano dal secolo XIV al XVI*, 127–146. Florence: G.C. Sansoni, 1958

——, "I *Quolibeta de intelligentiis* di Alessandro Achillini", in ibid., 179–223

——, "Il commento di Simplicio al *De anima* nelle controversie della fine del secolo XV e del secolo XVI", in ibid., 365–442

Nicholas of Lyra: The Senses of Scripture, ed. P.D.W. Krey and L. Smith. Leiden: Brill, 2000

Obi Oguejiofor, J., *The Arguments for the Immortality of the Soul in the First Half of the Thirteenth Century*. Leuven: Peeters, 1995

Ocker, C., *Biblical Poetics before Humanism and Reformation*. Cambridge: CUP, 2002

Panizza, L., "Ermolao Barbaro e Pico della Mirandola tra retorica e dialettica: il *De genere dicendi philosophorum* del 1485", in *Una famiglia veneziana nella storia: I Barbaro*, Atti del convegno di studi in occasione del quinto centenario della morte dell'umanista Ermolao, Venezia ... 1993, ed. M. Marangoni and M. Pastore Stocchi, 277–330. Venice: Istituto Veneto di Scienze, 1996

——, "Pico della Mirandola's 1485 Parody of Scholastic 'Barbarians'", in *Italy in Crisis 1494*, ed. J. Everson and D. Zancani, 152–174. Oxford: Legenda, 2000

Parr Greswell, W., *Memoirs of Angelus Politianus, Joannes Picus of Mirandula, etc.* London: Cadell and Davies, 1805

Pépin, J., *Mythe et allégorie: les origines grecques et les contestations judéo-chrétiennes*. Paris: Etudes Augustiniennes, 1976

——, *La tradition de l'allégorie de Philon d'Alexandrie à Dante*. Paris: Etudes Augustiniennes, 1987

Petit, F., *L'ancienne version latine des Questions sur la Genèse de Philon d'Alexandrie*. Berlin: Akademie-Verlag, 1973

——, *Catenae graecae in Genesim et in Exodum, I. Catena Sinaitica*. Turnhout: Brepols, 1977

——, *Catenae graecae in Genesim et in Exodum, II. Collectio Coisliniana in Genesim*. Turnhout: Brepols, 1986

——, *La chaîne sur la Genèse*, 4 vols. Leuven: Peeters, 1992

Piccolomini, E., "Due documenti relevati ad acquisti di codici greci, fatti da Giovanni Lascaris per conto di Lorenzo de' Medici", *Rivista di filologia e d'istruzione classica*, 2 (1874), 401–423

Pines, S., "Les limites de la métaphysique selon Al-Farabi, Ibn Bajja et Maïmonide; sources et antithèses de ces doctrines chez Alexandre d'Aphrodise et chez Themistius", in Miscellanea Mediaevalia, 13, 2 vols, I: *Sprache und Erkenntnis im Mittelalter*, 211–225. Berlin: De Gruyter, 1981

Reines, A.J., *Maimonides and Abrabanel on Prophecy*. Cincinnati, Ohio: Hebrew Union College Press, 1970

Richard, M., "La transmission des textes des Pères grecs", *Sacris Erudiri*, 22 (1974–1975), 51–60

Rompay, L. van, "Antiochene Biblical Interpretation: Greek and Syriac", in *The Book of Genesis in Jewish and Oriental Christian Interpretation: A Collection of Essays*, ed. J. Frishman and L. van Rompay, 103–123. Leuven: Peeters, 1997

Roth, C., *The Jews in the Renaissance*. Philadelphia, Pennsylvania: Jewish Publication Society of America, 1959

Roulier, F., *Jean Pic de la Mirandole (1463–1494), humaniste, philosophe et théologien*. Geneva: Slatkine, 1989

Rorem, P., *Biblical and Liturgical Symbols within the Pseudo-Dionysian Synthesis*. Toronto: Pontifical Institute of Medieval Studies, 1984

Russell, B., *History of Western Philosophy, and its connection with political and social circumstances from the earliest times to the present day*. London: George Allen and Unwin, 1946

Scafi, A., "The Notion of the Earthly Paradise from the Patristic Era to the Fifteenth Century". PhD Dissertation, Warburg Institute, University of London, 1999

Schmitt, C.B. and Knox, D., *Pseudo-Aristoteles Latinus: A Guide to Latin Works Falsely Attributed to Aristotle Before 1500*. London: Warburg Institute, 1985

Scholderer, J.V., *Catalogue of Books Printed in the XVth Century now in the British Museum*, VI. London, 1930

Scholem, G., *Major Trends in Jewish Mysticism*. New York: Schocken, 1954

——, *On the Kabbalah and its Symbolism*, tr. R. Manheim. London: Routledge and Kegan Paul, 1965

——, *Origins of the Kabbalah*, ed. R.J. Werblowsky, tr. A. Arkush. Princeton, New Jersey: Princeton University Press, 1987

Schwarz, W., *Principles and Problems of Biblical Translation: Some Reformation Controversies and their Background*. Cambridge: CUP, 1970

Secret, F., "Pico della Mirandola e gli inizi della cabala cristiana", *Convivium*, 25 (1957), 31–47

——, "Notes sur les hebraïsants chrétiens de la Renaissance", *Sefarad*, 22 (1962), 107–127

——, "Nouvelles precisions sur Flavius Mithridates maître de Pic de la Mirandole et traducteur de commentaires de kabbale", in *L'opera e il pensiero di Giovanni Pico della Mirandola nella storia dell'Umanesimo: convegno internazionale*, 2 vols, II, 169–187. Florence: Nella Sede dell'Istituto, 1965

——, "L'*Ensis Pauli* de Paulus de Heredia", *Sefarad*, 26 (1966), 79–102

——, *Les kabbalistes chrétiens de la Renaissance.* Neuilly sur Seine: Arma Artis, 1985

Seznec, J., *La survivance des dieux antiques: essai sur le rôle de la tradition mythologique dans l'humanisme et dans l'art de la Renaissance.* London: Warburg Institute, 1940

Siorvanes, L., *Proclus: Neo-Platonic Philosophy and Science.* Edinburgh: Edinburgh University Press, 1996

Sirat, C., *A History of Jewish Philosophy in the Middle Ages,* tr. M. Reich. Cambridge: CUP, 1996

Smalley, B., *The Study of the Bible in the Middle Ages.* Oxford: B. Blackwell, 1952, repr. 1984

Smith, M., *Clement of Alexandria and a Secret Gospel of Mark.* Cambridge, Massachusetts: Harvard University Press, 1973

Sorabji, R., *Time, Creation and the Continuum.* London: Duckworth, 1983, repr. 2002

Spicq, C., *Esquisse d'une histoire de l'exégèse latine au Moyen Age.* Paris: J. Vrin, 1944

Spruit, L., *Il problema della conoscenza in Giordano Bruno.* Naples: Bibliopolis, 1988

——, *Species intelligibilis: From Perception to Knowledge,* 2 vols. Leiden: E.J. Brill, 1994–1995

Swanson, J., "The *Glossa ordinaria*", in *The Medieval Theologians,* ed. G.R. Evans, 156–167. Oxford: B. Blackwell, 2001

Tamani, G., "I libri ebraici di Pico della Mirandola", in *Giovanni Pico della Mirandola: convegno internazionale di studi nel cinquecentesimo anniversario della morte (1494–1994),* ed. G.C. Garfagnini, 2 vols, II, 491–530. Florence 1997

Tardieu, M., "La lettre à Hipparque et les réminiscences pythagoriciennes de Clement d'Alexandrie", *Vigiliae Christianae,* 28 (1974), 241–247

Le temps des Réformes et la Bible, ed. G. Bedouelle and B. Roussel. Paris: Beauchesne, 1989

Thorndike, L., *The Sphere of Sacrobosco and Its Commentators.* Chicago, Illinois: University of Chicago Press, 1949

Todd, R.B., "Themistius", in *Catalogus translationum et commentariorum: Medieval and Renaissance Latin Translations and Commentaries,* ed. P.O. Kristeller et al., 8 vols, VIII, 57–102. Washington DC: Catholic University of America Press, 1960–2003

Todorov, T., *Théories du symbole.* Paris: Editions du Seuil, 1977

Touati, C., *La pensée philosophique et théologique de Gersonide.* Paris: Editions de Minuit, 1973

Trapp, J.B., "Erasmus on William Grocyn and Ps-Dionysius: A Re-examination", *Journal of the Warburg and Courtauld Institutes,* 59 (1996), 294–303

Urbach, E.E., *The Sages: Their Concepts and Beliefs,* tr. I. Abrahams. Cambridge, Massachusetts and London: Harvard University Press, 1975, repr. 2001

Valcke, L., *Pic de la Mirandole: un itinéraire philosophique.* Paris: Les Belles Lettres, 2005

Walker, D.P., *The Ancient Theology: Studies in Christian Platonism from the Fifteenth to the Eighteenth Century.* London: Duckworth, 1972

Williams, T., "Biblical Interpretation", in *The Cambridge Companion to Augustine*, ed. E. Stump and N. Kretzmann, 59–70. Cambridge: CUP, 2001

Wirszubski, C., "Giovanni Pico's Book of Job", *Journal of the Warburg and Courtauld Institutes*, 32 (1969), 171–199

——, *Pico's Encounter with Jewish Mysticism*. Cambridge, Massachusetts: Harvard University Press, 1989

Zatelli, I., Lelli, F. and Avanzinelli, M.V., "Pico: La cultura biblica e la tradizione rabbinica", in *Pico, Poliziano e l'Umanesimo di fine Quattrocento*, ed. P. Viti, 159–191. Florence: L.S. Olschki, 1994

INDEX

STUDIES IN MEDIEVAL AND REFORMATION TRADITIONS

(Formerly Studies in Medieval and Reformation Thought)

Founded by Heiko A. Oberman†
Edited by Andrew Colin Gow

1. DOUGLASS, E.J.D. *Justification in Late Medieval Preaching.* 2nd ed. 1989
2. WILLIS, E.D. *Calvin's Catholic Christology.* 1966 *out of print*
3. POST, R.R. *The Modern Devotion.* 1968 *out of print*
4. STEINMETZ, D.C. *Misericordia Dei.* The Theology of Johannes von Staupitz. 1968 *out of print*
5. O'MALLEY, J.W. *Giles of Viterbo on Church and Reform.* 1968 *out of print*
6. OZMENT, S.E. *Homo Spiritualis.* The Anthropology of Tauler, Gerson and Luther. 1969
7. PASCOE, L.B. *Jean Gerson: Principles of Church Reform.* 1973 *out of print*
8. HENDRIX, S.H. *Ecclesia in Via.* Medieval Psalms Exegesis and the *Dictata super Psalterium* (1513-1515) of Martin Luther. 1974
9. TREXLER, R.C. *The Spiritual Power.* Republican Florence under Interdict. 1974
10. TRINKAUS, Ch. with OBERMAN, H.A. (eds.). *The Pursuit of Holiness.* 1974 *out of print*
11. SIDER, R.J. *Andreas Bodenstein von Karlstadt.* 1974
12. HAGEN, K. *A Theology of Testament in the Young Luther.* 1974
13. MOORE, Jr., W.L. *Annotatiunculae D. Iohanne Eckio Praelectore.* 1976
14. OBERMAN, H.A. with BRADY, Jr., Th.A. (eds.). *Itinerarium Italicum.* Dedicated to Paul Oskar Kristeller. 1975
15. KEMPFF, D. *A Bibliography of Calviniana.* 1959-1974. 1975 *out of print*
16. WINDHORST, C. *Täuferisches Taufverständnis.* 1976
17. KITTELSON, J.M. *Wolfgang Capito.* 1975
18. DONNELLY, J.P. *Calvinism and Scholasticism in Vermigli's Doctrine of Man and Grace.* 1976
19. LAMPING, A.J. *Ulrichus Velenus (Oldřich Velenský) and his Treatise against the Papacy.* 1976
20. BAYLOR, M.G. *Action and Person.* Conscience in Late Scholasticism and the Young Luther. 1977
21. COURTENAY, W.J. *Adam Wodeham.* 1978
22. BRADY, Jr., Th.A. *Ruling Class, Regime and Reformation at Strasbourg, 1520-1555.* 1978
23. KLAASSEN, W. *Michael Gaismair.* 1978
24. BERNSTEIN, A.E. *Pierre d'Ailly and the Blanchard Affair.* 1978
25. BUCER, M. *Correspondance.* Tome I (Jusqu'en 1524). Publié par J. Rott. 1979
26. POSTHUMUS MEYJES, G.H.M. *Jean Gerson et l'Assemblée de Vincennes (1329).* 1978
27. VIVES, J.L. *In Pseudodialecticos.* Ed. by Ch. Fantazzi. 1979
28. BORNERT, R. *La Réforme Protestante du Culte à Strasbourg au XVIᵉ siècle (1523-1598).* 1981
29. CASTELLIO, S. *De Arte Dubitandi.* Ed. by E. Feist Hirsch. 1981
30. BUCER, M. *Opera Latina.* Vol I. Publié par C. Augustijn, P. Fraenkel, M. Lienhard. 1982
31. BÜSSER, F. *Wurzeln der Reformation in Zürich.* 1985 *out of print*
32. FARGE, J.K. *Orthodoxy and Reform in Early Reformation France.* 1985
33. 34. BUCER, M. *Etudes sur les relations de Bucer avec les Pays-Bas.* I. Etudes; II. Documents. Par J.V. Pollet. 1985
35. HELLER, H. *The Conquest of Poverty.* The Calvinist Revolt in Sixteenth Century France. 1986

36. MEERHOFF, K. *Rhétorique et poétique au XVIᵉ siècle en France.* 1986
37. GERRITS, G. H. *Inter timorem et spem.* Gerard Zerbolt of Zutphen. 1986
38. POLIZIANO, A. *Lamia.* Ed. by A. Wesseling. 1986
39. BRAW, C. *Bücher im Staube.* Die Theologie Johann Arndts in ihrem Verhältnis zur Mystik. 1986
40. BUCER, M. *Opera Latina.* Vol. II. Enarratio in Evangelion Iohannis (1528, 1530, 1536). Publié par I. Backus. 1988
41. BUCER, M. *Opera Latina.* Vol. III. Martin Bucer and Matthew Parker: Flori-legium Patristicum. Edition critique. Publié par P. Fraenkel. 1988
42. BUCER, M. *Opera Latina.* Vol. IV. Consilium Theologicum Privatim Conscriptum. Publié par P. Fraenkel. 1988
43. BUCER, M. *Correspondance.* Tome II (1524-1526). Publié par J. Rott. 1989
44. RASMUSSEN, T. *Inimici Ecclesiae.* Das ekklesiologische Feindbild in Luthers "Dictata super Psalterium" (1513-1515) im Horizont der theologischen Tradition. 1989
45. POLLET, J. *Julius Pflug et la crise religieuse dans l'Allemagne du XVIᵉ siècle.* Essai de synthèse biographique et théologique. 1990
46. BUBENHEIMER, U. *Thomas Müntzer.* Herkunft und Bildung. 1989
47. BAUMAN, C. *The Spiritual Legacy of Hans Denck.* Interpretation and Translation of Key Texts. 1991
48. OBERMAN, H.A. and JAMES, F.A., III (eds.). in cooperation with SAAK, E.L. *Via Augustini.* Augustine in the Later Middle Ages, Renaissance and Reformation: Essays in Honor of Damasus Trapp. 1991 *out of print*
49. SEIDEL MENCHI, S. *Erasmus als Ketzer.* Reformation und Inquisition im Italien des 16. Jahrhunderts. 1993
50. SCHILLING, H. *Religion, Political Culture, and the Emergence of Early Modern Society.* Essays in German and Dutch History. 1992
51. DYKEMA, P.A. and OBERMAN, H.A. (eds.). *Anticlericalism in Late Medieval and Early Modern Europe.* 2nd ed. 1994
52. 53. KRIEGER, Chr. and LIENHARD, M. (eds.). *Martin Bucer and Sixteenth Century Europe.* Actes du colloque de Strasbourg (28-31 août 1991). 1993
54. SCREECH, M.A. *Clément Marot: A Renaissance Poet discovers the World.* Lutheranism, Fabrism and Calvinism in the Royal Courts of France and of Navarre and in the Ducal Court of Ferrara. 1994
55. GOW, A.C. *The Red Jews: Antisemitism in an Apocalyptic Age, 1200-1600.* 1995
56. BUCER, M. *Correspondance.* Tome III (1527-1529). Publié par Chr. Krieger et J. Rott. 1989
57. SPIJKER, W. VAN 'T. *The Ecclesiastical Offices in the Thought of Martin Bucer.* Translated by J. Vriend (text) and L.D. Bierma (notes). 1996
58. GRAHAM, M.F. *The Uses of Reform.* 'Godly Discipline' and Popular Behavior in Scotland and Beyond, 1560-1610. 1996
59. AUGUSTIJN, C. *Erasmus. Der Humanist als Theologe und Kirchenreformer.* 1996
60. McCOOG SJ, T.M. *The Society of Jesus in Ireland, Scotland, and England 1541-1588.* 'Our Way of Proceeding?' 1996
61. FISCHER, N. und KOBELT-GROCH, M. (Hrsg.). *Außenseiter zwischen Mittelalter und Neuzeit.* Festschrift für Hans-Jürgen Goertz zum 60. Geburtstag. 1997
62. NIEDEN, M. *Organum Deitatis.* Die Christologie des Thomas de Vio Cajetan. 1997
63. BAST, R.J. *Honor Your Fathers.* Catechisms and the Emergence of a Patriarchal Ideology in Germany, 1400-1600. 1997
64. ROBBINS, K.C. *City on the Ocean Sea: La Rochelle, 1530-1650.* Urban Society, Religion, and Politics on the French Atlantic Frontier. 1997
65. BLICKLE, P. *From the Communal Reformation to the Revolution of the Common Man.* 1998
66. FELMBERG, B.A.R. *Die Ablaßtheorie Kardinal Cajetans (1469-1534).* 1998